The Talking Cure

THE TALKING CURE:

Literary Representations
of Psychoanalysis

JEFFREY BERMAN

New York University Press
New York *and* London
1985

Library of Congress Cataloging in Publication Data

Berman, Jeffrey, 1945–
The talking cure.

Bibliography: p.
Includes index.
1. American literature—20th century—History and
criticism.   2. Psychoanalysis in literature.
3. Psychoanalysts in literature.   4. English literature—
20th century—History and criticism.   I. Title.
PS228.P74B47   1985   810'.9'35215   85-3080
ISBN 0-8147-1075-1 (alk. paper)

*Clothbound editions of New York University Press books are Smyth-sewn
and printed on permanent and durable acid-free paper.*

For Barbara
and Arielle and Jillian

CONTENTS

ACKNOWLEDGMENTS

It is a pleasure to acknowledge the help I received while researching and writing this book. I am grateful to my former Department Chairperson, Professor John C. Gerber, whose timely support was crucial in more ways than one. A State University of New York Faculty Research Fellowship allowed me to begin work on this project. The following individuals read one or more chapters of the book: Frederick J. Beharriell, Professor of German, State University of New York at Albany; Sheldon Grebstein, Professor of English and President, State University of New York at Purchase; James W. Hamilton, M.D., Director of Psychiatry, Veteran's Administration Medical Center, Wood, Wisconsin; Richard B. Hovey, Professor of English, University of Maryland; Richard W. Noland, Professor of English, University of Massachusetts, Amherst; Charles L. Proudfit, Professor of English, University of Boulder, Colorado; Phyllis A. Roth, Associate Professor of English, Skidmore College; Mark Shechner, Professor of English, State University of New York at Buffalo; and Harry Trosman, M.D., Professor of Psychiatry, University of Chicago. I am indebted to their constructive comments; whatever errors appear in *The Talking Cure* are, of course, mine alone.

Special thanks go to Joanne Greenberg and D. M. Thomas, who graciously answered my queries about *I Never Promised You a Rose Garden* and *The White Hotel*, respectively, and supplied me with additional information about each novel.

The chapter on Fitzgerald's *Tender Is the Night* appeared in abridged form in *Literature and Psychology,* Vol. 29 (1979), pp. 34–48. "Philip Roth's Psychoanalysts" was read to the Western New York Psychoanalytic Society in June, 1984, at the Upstate Medical Center in Syracuse, New York. I wish to thank the University of Chicago Press for allowing me to quote an extended passage from *Principles of Intensive Psychotherapy,* by Frieda Fromm-Reichmann. Copyright © 1950.

I am indebted to the many bright and lively SUNY-Albany students who took "Freud and the Literary Tradition" and "The Psychiatric Case Study in Literature" with me, where I first tested out many of the psychoanalytic interpretations that appear in this book. On more than a few occasions, my students' questions and responses found their way into *The Talking Cure*.

I wish to thank the Training Institute of the National Psychological Association for Psychoanalysis (N.P.A.P.), the first non-medical psychoanalytic institute in the United States, for the opportunity to study there as a research scholar from 1980 to 1983. Anyone seriously interested in learning more about psychoanalysis would do well to study there or at the other excellent analytic institutes, many of which are now open to non-medical students. Were it not for my research and study at N.P.A.P., this book could not have been written, at least not in its present form. Special thanks to Dr. Esther Menaker, a magical and inspiring figure in the psychoanalytic movement.

I appreciate the help I received from the hard-working staff of the SUNY-Albany Interlibrary Loan. Both Sally Stevenson and Wendy Deiber were able to locate the dozens of obscure books and articles that were necessary for my research. I also wish to thank the entire staff of New York University Press, in particular, Despina Papazoglou, Managing Editor, and Kitty Moore, Senior Editor, for their enthusiasm and expertise in the production of the book.

I am grateful most of all to those colleagues, friends, and relatives who helped live this book with me: Professor Barbara B. Adams, Pace University; Professor Randall Craig, SUNY-Albany; Professor Michael Kaufman, Brandeis University; Drs. Alfred and Sybil Nadel of New York City; my parents, Isadore and Roslyn Berman; and finally, my wife Barbara and my children, Arielle and Jillian. No acknowledgment can adequately repay my appreciation for their support.

ONE

Introduction: The Talking Cure

IT WAS Bertha Pappenheim, Josef Breuer's celebrated "Fräulein Anna O." of *Studies on Hysteria* (1893–1895), who coined the term "talking cure" to describe the magical power of language to relieve mental suffering. Described by her physician as possessing unusual poetic and imaginative gifts, the 21-year old woman entered therapy in 1880 shortly after falling ill. During the following months she developed severe hysterical symptoms that today might be diagnosed as schizophrenia: frightening hallucinations of black snakes, near-total physical paralysis of arms and legs, and major disturbances of speech and sight. Breuer was mystified by her mad jumble of syntax, fusion of four or five languages, and prolonged silences. Her personality alternated between two contrasting states of consciousness, a normal but melancholy state in which she recognized her surroundings, and an hallucinatory state in which she became abusive and "naughty." Intrigued by the case, Breuer began visiting his patient regularly and spending more and more time with her. Guessing that he had somehow offended her at one point—he never tells us why or how—the physician obliged the patient to talk about her feelings toward him. Soon her verbal inhibitions inexplicably began to disappear, along with a remission of her other symptoms. The situation worsened, however, after the death of her beloved father, whom she had been nursing during his convalescence.

Around this time, Breuer noticed a curious phenomenon. While she was in an altered personality state, she would mutter a few words to herself that seemed to be related to her bizarre illness. Suspecting that her language held a clue to her disease, Breuer hypnotized her and requested the patient to relate the hallucinations she had experienced during the day. After the narration, she would wake up with a calm and cheerful disposition. Sometimes she invented sad stories the starting point of which resembled her own situation—a girl or young woman anxiously sitting by a sickbed. If for any reason she was unable to narrate these stories to Breuer during the evening hypnosis, she would fail to achieve therapeutic relief, and the next day she was compelled to tell him two stories before the talking cure took effect. This "chimney-sweeping," as she jokingly referred to the novel treatment, allowed her to use the products of her imagination—art—to sweep clean the terrifying demons of her life.

It is an intriguing accident of history that the first patient of psychoanalysis was also a storyteller. And the motive that prompted her to enter therapy, escape from imaginative terrors, was also the impulse behind her fiction. It was as if the creative and therapeutic process were inseparably joined. Yet, the relief she experienced from the talking cure lasted only a couple of days, after which she would once again grow moody and irritable. Sometimes she refused to talk at all. Breuer, who was both her physician and audience, then had to search for the right formula to unlock her stories, as if the key to her art was the only escape from a baffling illness. Like Kafka's Hunger Artist, whose performances depended upon the entertainer's starvation, Anna O. created stories from the depths of suffering. Her artistic gifts to Breuer affirmed both the destructive and creative uses of the imagination. Without a sympathetic audience, the artist could not create nor the patient improve. Unfortunately, Bertha Pappenheim never wrote about her experiences with Breuer, and so we do not have an account of therapy written from the point of view of the patient who achieved such prominence in the psychoanalytic movement. But we do have Breuer's account of the case history, supplemented by various comments Freud later made about his former collaborator's treatment of Anna O. The emerging story is filled with the ironies and contradictions that inevitably characterize most fictional and nonfictional accounts of psychological breakdown and recovery—the literature of the talking cure.

"I have suppressed a large number of quite interesting details," Breuer curiously acknowledges near the end of "Fräulein Anna O."[1] Indeed, the case study is riddled with omissions, evasions, and inaccuracies. In the beginning of the story, Breuer describes his patient's sexuality as "astonishingly undeveloped," thus rendering her into an asexual woman. He was unprepared for the intense infatuation she developed for him. When the physician saw her on a daily schedule, her health markedly improved; during his absences, she grew angry and uncontrollable, as if to punish

him for his infidelity. According to Ernest Jones, who first revealed Anna
O.'s identity in 1953, Breuer became so preoccupied with his lively, attractive patient that his wife eventually grew jealous.[2] When the proper
Victorian doctor realized this, he became nervous and abruptly terminated treatment, pronouncing his patient cured. Breuer speaks confidently of Anna O.'s complete recovery and imposes a fairy-tale ending to
the story. But the tidy resolution of the case study was far from the truth,
as Freud later disclosed. According to Freud's account, which he arrived
at many years later from isolated clues Breuer had given him, a few hours
after the physician's departure the cured patient went into hysterical
childbirth (pseudo-cyesis), believing Breuer was the father of her child.
"Now Dr. B.'s child is coming!" she cried, suggesting that, if she couldn't
give him any more stories, she would present him with a baby.[3] Breuer
was again summoned, and, after calming her down, he hastily took his
wife to Venice for a second honeymoon. He never again saw or treated
Fräulein Anna O.

Understandably reluctant to write up or publish the case history, Breuer
finally agreed to do so only after pressure from Freud, who was eager to
announce to the world his new theory of hysteria. Shortly after the publication of *Studies on Hysteria,* the coauthors parted company forever, Breuer
severing all ties to the young psychoanalytic movement. Breuer, whom
the partisan Jones portrays as the villain of the story, reportedly told Freud
a year after the case that Bertha Pappenheim was "unhinged" and that he
hoped death would release her from suffering.[4] Freud remained generally
silent about the case study, giving only a few details about the "untoward
event" that compelled Breuer to break off treatment. James Strachey, the
editor of the *Standard Edition,* reports that Freud once put his finger on
an open copy of "Fräulein Anna O." to indicate a hiatus in the text. The
implication is that Breuer's timidity was responsible for the omissions in
the story and the failure of the patient's treatment.

From Freud's point of view, Breuer failed because he was not intellectually audacious enough, not a *conquistador,* as Freud viewed himself.
Publicly, Freud criticized Breuer's inability to understand Anna O.'s
transference love toward the physician; privately, Freud condemned
Breuer's failure to maintain clinical detachment from the young woman.
When Bertha Pappenheim later confided to her friend Martha Freud the
details of her therapy, Martha immediately identified with Breuer's wife
and expressed the wish that her own husband would never allow the same
situation to arise. "For that to happen," Freud replied with more than a

little sexual disgust in his voice, "one has to be a Breuer."[5] Yet, it is unfair to vilify Breuer, for he, too, was a pioneer, albeit an ambivalent one.
Few nineteenth-century physicians tried to make sense of the bizarre
symptomatology of hysteria; additionally, he expended extraordinary time
and effort on his patient. No one has ever suggested that he acted im-
properly with Anna O., and nothing in his medical training or background adequately prepared him for the treatment onto which he inadvertently stumbled.

How did Bertha Pappenheim feel about the talking cure? No doubt
she felt abandoned by Breuer in her hour of need. There is no evidence
that she ever read "Fräulein Anna O." or realized the historical uniqueness surrounding her case. She suffered relapses after Breuer's departure,
required hospitalization, apparently "inflamed the heart" of another at-
tending psychiatrist (to quote Jones), and slowly recovered. She then began her long and distinguished career in social work—she was the first
social worker in Germany—in 1895, the year Breuer and Freud published
Studies on Hysteria.[6] Although she never married or had children, she did
give birth to the vast psychiatric literature that has been written on mental breakdown and recovery. Yet, her silence on the subject is difficult to
interpret, especially since she became a prolific author and wrote on a
variety of topics. She translated Mary Wollstonecraft's *A Vindication of
the Rights of Women,* wrote a play entitled *Women's Rights,* and authored
a collection of fairy tales, numerous short stories, humanitarian articles,
and travel pieces. An ardent feminist, she wrote: "If there is any justice
in the next life, women will make the laws there and men will bear the
children." The statement not only reveals indignation over the plight of
women but perhaps anger at the men in her life, including the male physicians who treated her. There may also be an element of revenge involved, as if to say: "Let Dr. B. bear his own child." Friends and colleagues admired her but were wary of her occasional nervousness, fits of
temper, and distant behavior. One of her mottoes, a biographer notes,
was: "To be severe is to be loving." No one can say whether she was
helped by Breuer's treatment, but after her recovery she had little use for
psychoanalysis. "Psychoanalysis in the hands of the physician is what
confession is in the hands of the Catholic priest. It depends on its user
and its use, whether it becomes a beneficial tool or a two-edged sword"
(quoted by Jensen, p. 289). It is ironic that Bertha Pappenheim, a devout
Jew, should compare the psychoanalyst to the priest; Freud made the same
comparison, arguing, however, that "In Confession the sinner tells what
he knows; in analysis the neurotic has to tell more" (*Standard Edition,*

XX, p. 189). Nevertheless, her analogy aptly describes the potential for good and evil within both spiritual and psychological approaches to human suffering.

To this day, the veil of obscurity surrounds not only the final stage of Breuer's treatment of Anna O. but virtually all accounts of the talking cure. The difficulty of writing a psychiatric case study may be seen in the fact that Freud published only five major case histories (excluding the brief sketches in *Studies on Hysteria*), dating from 1905 through 1918. They are, in the order of publication: *Fragment of an Analysis of a Case of Hysteria* ("Dora") in 1905, *Analysis of a Phobia in a Five-Year-Old Boy* ("Little Hans") in 1909, *Notes Upon a Case of Obsessional Neurosis* ("The Rat Man") also in 1909, *Psycho-Analytic Notes on an Autobiographical Account of a Case of Paranoia* (Schreber) in 1911, and *From the History of an Infantile Neurosis* ("The Wolf Man") in 1918. Two of the case histories are based on patients Freud either did not see or treated indirectly. The case of Schreber was based on an autobiographical memoir Freud came across, while the study of Little Hans was written from the notes supplied by the boy's father, a former patient of the psychoanalyst. Freud's case studies have become enduring psychiatric and literary classics, but they also reveal the paradigmatic difficulties of the genre. The problems fall under three main categories: medical confidentiality; belief; and the clinical phenomena of transference, countertransference, and resistance. Freud's psychiatric case studies offer an insight into the predictable and unpredictable problems that have subsequently vexed the novelists and playwrights writing about the talking cure.

Although psychiatric case studies often read like fiction, they are based upon actual patients. This obviously poses a major problem for the author, who must strike a compromise between truth and disguise. How much biographical information can the analyst reveal without disclosing the patient's identity? In *Studies on Hysteria,* Breuer and Freud conceded the constraints under which they were writing. It would have been a grave breach of confidence, they admitted, to publish material touching upon their patients' intimate lives. Consequently, the authors deleted some of the most important observations. Breuer's deliberate suppression of crucial information in "Fräulein Anna O." weakened both its literary richness and scientific credibility. One need not accept Robert Langs's extreme conclusion that the psychotherapeutic movement has its roots in complicity, lies, and evasions to agree that psychiatric case study literature has failed to disclose significant details of the therapeutic process.[7]

Freud's fullest account of the problem of confidentiality appears in *Dora*.

Conceding that the vagueness of information in *Studies on Hysteria* deprived researchers of the opportunity to test the authors' theory of hysteria, Freud vows to err in the opposite direction. "Whereas before I was accused of giving *no* information about my patients, now I shall be accused of giving information about my patients which ought not to be given" (*Standard Edition,* Vol. VII, p. 7). Obliquely hinting at Breuer's timidity, Freud insists on the physician's "duty" to publish all the facts about hysterical illness. Anything less than complete disclosure, he says, is "disgraceful cowardice." He acknowledges, though, that the complete discussion of a case of hysteria is bound to result in the betrayal of the patient's identity. To safeguard Dora's privacy, Freud makes several fictional changes, such as altering her name, place of residence, and other external details. In addition, he delayed publication of the case study for four years until he was convinced she would not accidentally come across the work. Nevertheless, Freud admits she would be upset if a copy of the case study fell into her hands. Freud returns to the subject of confidentiality in the introductory remarks of the *Rat Man,* telling us that he cannot give a complete history of treatment because that would compromise the patient's identity. "The importunate interest of a capital city, focussed with particular attention upon my medical activities, forbids my giving a faithful picture of the case" (*Standard Edition,* Vol. X, p. 155). He concedes, however, that deliberate fabrications in a case study are often useless and objectionable. If the distortions are slight, they are ineffective; if they are major, they destroy the intelligibility of the material. His conclusion is that it is easier to divulge the patient's most intimate thoughts (which usually do not cast light on his identity anyway) than to convey biographical facts.

But ambiguities over confidentiality still exist. Must the patient grant the analyst permission to write about his or her life? Medical ethics are unclear about this. Breuer did not have Bertha Pappenheim's permission to publish the precedent-setting "Fräulein Anna O." Despite his efforts to disguise her life, certain details in the case history, such as the date of her father's death and the beginning of therapy, made it possible for readers to infer her identity. Moreover, the Pappenheim family was prominent in Vienna, and many people knew about the young woman's breakdown and prolonged treatment by the eminent Breuer. Given the highly sensitive material found in a psychiatric case study, the author's freedom of expression is limited by confidentiality, ethics, and discretion.

Freud secured permission from the Rat Man, the Wolf Man, and Little

Hans's father, but not from Dora. In 1924, he mentions that when Dora visited another analyst in that year and confided that she had been treated by Freud many years earlier, the well-informed colleague immediately recognized her as the Dora of the famous case study. Nor did Freud have Schreber's permission to publish a case history of the former judge's *Memoirs of a Nerve Patient,* which appeared in 1903. Though Freud never treated him, there were still medical and legal uncertainties concerning the propriety of the publication of the book. In his *Memoirs,* Schreber declares his intention to publish the work even if his psychiatrist, Dr. Flechsig of Leipzig, brought a legal suit against him, presumably for defamation of character. "I trust," Schreber says, "that even in the case of Geheimrat Prof. Dr. Flechsig any personal susceptibilities that he may feel will be outweighed by a scientific interest in the subject-matter of my memoirs" (*Standard Edition,* Vol. XII, p. 10). Freud cites this passage and urges upon Schreber the same considerations the jurist requested of Flechsig. Freud did not know whether Schreber was still alive in 1911 when he was writing the case study (as it turned out, Schreber died a few months after Freud's monograph was published); but the analyst strongly believed that scientific knowledge took priority over personal issues.

The problem of confidentiality exists even when the author of a psychiatric case study is the patient. Just as the psychiatrist worries about preserving the patient's confidentiality, so does the patient feel obliged to respect the analyst's privacy and professional reputation. Freud's analysts in training, for instance, remained deferential toward him in their accounts of their experiences. Ironically, despite Freud's sallies into psychobiography—a genre he created in his book on Leonard da Vinci (1910)—he was uncompromising about his personal life, which he jealously guarded. Displeased by Fritz Wittels' biography of him, Freud expressed the opinion in a sternly worded letter that the biographer should wait until his "subject is dead, when he cannot do anything about it and fortunately no longer cares" (*The Letters of Sigmund Freud,* p. 350). When it came to his own life, then, Freud valued privacy over the dissemination of knowledge. The author of a psychiatric case study requires even more tact than the biographer. It is difficult for a patient to write openly and truthfully when he knows that other participants in the story will read the narration. Since psychological illness usually involves ambivalent feelings toward the closest members of one's family, the publication of a case history is bound to reopen painful family wounds. Both the analyst and his patient, then, must resort to fictional disguises, omissions, and evasions to protect the living protagonists and antagonists of the story. The question of sufficient disguise, moreover, may become problematic.

Another problem Freud confronted was over the nature of the psychiatric case study. Is it primarily a scientific treatise, designed to be read by other medical researchers, or a literary endeavor, written for a broader audience? The question reflects a fascinating division in Freud's character. He could never reconcile his scientific training with the artistic and philosophical elements of his personality. Nowhere is this conflict more evident than in his role as storyteller in the case studies. "It still strikes me myself as strange," he writes in *Studies on Hysteria,* "that the case histories I write should read like short stories and that, as one might say, they lack the serious stamp of science" (*Standard Edition,* Vol. II, p. 160). Yet Freud is disingenuous here, attributing the literary quality of the case studies to the nature of the material rather than to his artistic temperament. To describe a patient's psychiatric disorder, he adds, it is necessary to imitate the imaginative writer, who intuitively knows how to capture the workings of the mind. Unfortunately, few psychiatrists have needed to worry about the literary quality of their case studies, and it is strange to hear Freud professing horror at the thought that some readers will approach his case studies with anything other than scientific curiosity. "I am aware that—in this city, at least—there are many physicians who (revolting though it may seem) choose to read a case history of this kind not as a contribution to the psychopathology of the neuroses, but as a *roman à clef* designed for their private delectation" (*Standard Edition,* Vol. VII, p. 9). In rejecting "impure" motives for reading the psychiatric case study, Freud affirms the high seriousness of science. Yet he seems unduly embarrassed by the high seriousness of art—the aesthetic pleasure of reading and the sympathetic involvement with characters not terribly unlike ourselves. Freud's case studies are filled with the stuff of high drama: protracted family wars, twisted love affairs, unfulfilled hopes, broken promises, insoluble moral dilemmas. Few creative stories contain the involuted plots, demonic characterization, and racy dialogue of the *Rat Man* or the *Wolf Man*—their names alone seize our imagination and take their place among the world's enduring literature. The self-inflicted tortures of Freud's patients and their nightmarish settings make the case studies read like Gothic fiction. Appropriately, when Freud's name was mentioned for the Nobel Prize, it was more often for literature than for medicine.

It was not enough, however, for Freud to stimulate a reader's curiosity or fulfill his desire for aesthetic pleasure. Freud sought scientific truth, not artistic beauty (he took offense when Havelock Ellis maintained he was not a scientist but an artist), and he was vexed by the problem of converting intellectual skepticism into belief. How does the author of a psychiatric case study suspend the reader's disbelief? It is made difficult because psychoanalysis does not allow an audience to observe directly the unfolding drama of a patient's story. The talking cure remains enshrouded in mystery. "You cannot be present as an audience at a psychoanalytic treatment," Freud informs his audience of medical students in the *Introductory Lectures;* "You can only be told about it; and, in the strictest sense of the word, it is only by hearsay that you will get to know psychoanalysis" (*Standard Edition,* Vol. XV, p. 18). Yet hearsay is notoriously unreliable, as Freud well knew. Through the power of language the storyteller succeeds in spinning his web, and Freud never underestimated the ancient magical power of words to make one person blissfully happy and to drive another person to despair. Both the psychoanalyst and storyteller succeed or fail through their language. Freud remained pessimistic, though, about the power of language alone to create conviction in the disinterested reader, the "benevolent skeptic," as he wished his audience to be. In both *Little Hans* and the *Wolf Man* he remarks on the regrettable fact that no written account of psychotherapy can create the conviction achieved only through the actual experience of analysis. This, of course, creates a tautology. Why publish a case study if it cannot persuade the reader? The convert to psychoanalysis requires no further proof, while the cynic remains unconvinced. Is Freud's admission merely a defense against failure or an accurate statement about the unique validation required for psychoanalytic belief?

This question brings us to the unconscious projective tendencies unleashed by psychoanalysis and the interactional nature of the patient-analyst relationship. Any account of the talking cure must include the phenomenon of transference, one of the most central but misunderstood issues in therapy. Freud insisted that the recognition of transference is what distinguishes psychoanalysis from other forms of psychotherapy, including Breuer's early cathartic method, which sought symptom relief rather than an understanding of the underlying causes of mental illness. The patient sees in the analyst, Freud writes in *An Outline of Psycho-Analysis,* "the return, the reincarnation, of some important figure out of his childhood or past, and consequently transfers on to him feelings and reactions which undoubtedly applied to this prototype" (*Standard Edition,* Vol. XXIII, p. 174). The psychic mechanism behind transference is projection, in which a perception, fear, or drive is first denied and then displaced upon another person or object. Transference is usually ambivalent (a word coined by Freud's contemporary, the Swiss psychiatrist Eugene Bleuler), consisting of positive (affectionate) and negative (hostile) feelings toward the analyst, who generally occupies the role of a parental surrogate. Freud learned from experience that transference is a factor of undreamed-of importance, a source of grave danger and an instrument of irreplaceable value. The patient has both a real and an unreal or symbolic relationship to the analyst; the unreal relationship must be explored and traced back to its distant roots. The analyst in turn must guard against the tendency toward countertransference, which would hopelessly entrap the patient in the analyst's own confusion.

The narrative implications of transference and countertransference are far reaching. Both participants in therapy, the analyst and the patient, influence what is observed and felt. The observer's point of view always influences what is observed—a basic truth psychoanalysts have not easily conceded. The analyst's interpretation, for example, may be perceived as intrusive or aggressive and thus have undesirable consequences for the patient. The most important moments in therapy may remain unverbalized or concealed in an ambiguous silence. Freud himself remained contradictory on the analyst's proper stance, and many of his metaphors are profoundly misleading. In "Recommendations to Physicians Practicing Psycho-Analysis" (1912) he equates the analyst with the surgeon, "who puts aside all his feelings, even his human sympathy, and concentrates his mental forces on the single aim of performing the operation as skillfully as possible." He then uses an even more impersonal analogy, comparing the analyst to a telephone receiver, converting sound waves into electric oscillations (*Standard Edition*, Vol. XII, pp. 115–116). Not only are these bad analogies, evoking a mechanistic image of the analyst, Freud returns to them in his writings, as if he could not stress too strongly the analyst's objectivity and detachment. "The doctor should be opaque to his patients and, like a mirror, should show them nothing but what is shown to him" (*Standard Edition*, Vol. XII, p. 118). This is the same Freud whose discovery of unconscious projective mechanisms shattered the myth of human objectivity and its literary equivalent, the "ideal" reader.

Although many analysts still adhere to the blank-mirror image, more and more therapists are agreeing with Heinz Kohut's position that the analyst's introspective, empathic stance defines the psychological field. Earlier, Erik Erikson pointed out that Freud's discovery of transference leads to the conclusion that psychological investigation is always accompanied by a degree of irrational involvement on the part of the observer.[8] Freud's case studies demonstrate how transference and countertransference play a crucial role both in psychotherapy and in the narrations of the talking cure. Many of Freud's seemingly innocuous comments had unexpected literary and psychological implications. Breuer was certainly not alone in being entrapped in the emotional interlockings of psychoanalysis.

It was not unanalyzed affection that abruptly halted Freud's *Fragment of an Analysis of a Case of Hysteria,* as it had Breuer's "Fräulein Anna O.," but unconscious hostility. His only major case study on a woman, *Dora* reveals an aggressive and unempathic Freud, insensitive to the teenager's problems. Despite his candid acknowledgment of the inability to understand and control Dora's transference, Freud missed his countertransference toward her. A letter to Wilhelm Fliess in 1900 betrays his unrelenting pursuit of her illness. "I have a new patient, a girl of eighteen; the case has opened smoothly to my collection of picklocks."[9] There is more than a little arrogance here couched in an assaultive sexual image. Indeed, throughout the case study Freud attacks Dora's defenses; their relationship resembles a cat-and-mouse chase rather than a collaborative therapeutic alliance. One example will suffice. Freud interpreted one of Dora's acts, the opening and closing of a small reticule with her finger, as symbolic masturbation. One can hardly imagine the shock of a teenager hearing this interpretation in 1900. Moreover, for Freud to state explicitly this interpretation, instead of letting the patient hit upon it herself, would be considered by today's standards a gross deviation of technique. Dora soon began to play secrets with him, ambivalently encouraging his intellectual advances. One analyst has speculated that Freud's premature interpretations may have convinced the youth that he was a dangerous sexual adult who was attempting to seduce her.[10] Freud's responses apparently led her to believe that he was like her father and Herr K., both of whom were betraying her. Her father, for instance, was having an affair with Herr K.'s wife, and Herr K. was trying to seduce Dora. Additionally, Freud had treated Dora's father, and she may have perceived him as locked into a collusion with her father and all men. How could she trust the physician when he seemed to be doing intellectually what her father and Herr K. were doing sexually?

Freud's aggressiveness finally drove Dora out of therapy. When she returned after an absence of 15 months, expecting to resume treatment, Freud brusquely turned her away. One glance at her face convinced him, he writes, that she was "not in earnest" over her request. Instead of encouraging her to resume therapy and analyze her earlier flight, Freud reacted like a rejected lover and spurned her reconciliation. His rejection of Dora thus recalls Breuer's abandonment of Anna O. No wonder feminists have remained angry at Freud and psychoanalysis. "I do not know what kind of help she wanted from me," Freud writes without irony on the last page of the case study, "but I promised to forgive her for having deprived me of the satisfaction of affording her a far more radical cure for her troubles" (*Standard Edition,* Vol. VII, p. 122). According to Felix Deutsch, who briefly treated her, Dora later became embittered and obsessed by infidelities. Erikson has suggested that her bitterness may have been deepened by Freud's termination of treatment.[11]

Freud was more successful with the Rat Man. The analyst displayed remarkable compassion for the young man who was tortured by a love-hate ambivalence toward his deceased father. Yet even in this case study, with its dazzling exposition and resolution, Freud had to overcome problems caused in part by his Promethean quest for meaning. By contemporary standards, Freud exerted an excessively active role in seeking to untangle the origins of Paul Lorenz's obsessional neurosis. The patient believed that his father had access to his innermost thoughts and that no secret was safe from discovery. Imagine his horror upon learning that Freud could read his mind. Early in the story the patient attempts to describe the appalling fear that haunts his imagination. A brutal captain had told him of a particularly horrible custom practiced in the East, one so dreadful that Lorenz cannot verbalize it to Freud. Like Swift's satirical dialogue "Cassinus and Peter," in which the nervous hero cannot bring himself to relate to his college friend the "crime" that shocks humanity, Freud's case study builds up dramatic suspense through the patient's faltering dialogue. He simply cannot tell Freud the truth. Lorenz breaks off the narration, rises from the analytic couch, and begs Freud to spare him from the need to recite additional details. Freud replies that, although he is not sadistic and has no desire to torture the patient, Lorenz cannot circumvent the requirement that he tell everything on his mind, no matter how repugnant the thought may be. The dialogue proceeds as follows, with Freud playing the role of interrogator:

> I went on to say that I would do all I could, nevertheless, to guess the full meaning of any hints he gave me. Was he perhaps thinking

of impalement?—"No, not that; . . . the criminal was tied up
. . ."—he expressed himself so indistinctly that I could not immediately guess in what position—". . . a pot was turned upside down
on his buttocks . . . some *rats* were put into it . . . and they . . ."—he
had again got up, and was showing every sign of horror and resistance—". . . *bored their way in* . . ."—Into his anus, I helped him
out (*Standard Edition*, Vol. X, p. 166).

By filling in the patient's elliptical pauses and completing his unspoken
thoughts, Freud violated the technique of free association and unconsciously thrust himself into the center of Lorenz's story. As Mark Kanzer
points out, "the analyst was being seduced into the role not only of the
cruel officer, who told the story, but also of the rats which invaded the
victim's body." [12] In the transference neurosis that developed, Lorenz
imagined Freud to be participating in anal rape. In a sense this was true,
for Freud's eagerness to penetrate to the bottom of the mystery only intensified the patient's fear of violation. Despite the analyst's reassurance
that he was neither the patient's dead father nor the sadistic captain, who
was responsible for the precipitation of the illness, Lorenz thought otherwise, even calling him "Captain" on occasion. Freud did not discern
the basis in reality behind the patient's fear. Freud's questions did not
merely elicit the Rat Man's story but made him feel as if past tortures
were becoming present reality, with the psychoanalyst setting verbal traps
for the unsuspecting victim. Far from being a blank mirror, Freud became Lorenz's deadly antagonist, pursuing him into the most fearful places.
Indeed, the analyst was as compulsive as the patient in the examination
of every symptom of the illness. It was not simply a transference neurosis
from which Lorenz was suffering, as Freud mistakenly thought, but a
confusion of reality and delusion created by the analyst's unconscious imitation of the role of grand inquisitor. Lorenz defended himself against
each of Freud's oral interpretations with excremental outpourings. The
Rat Man's retaliatory anal transference fantasies were so abusive that Freud
included only a few of them in the published case study.

We know that Freud excluded many of the Rat Man's exclamations
because the psychoanalyst's original notes to the case study have been
preserved. Freud usually destroyed all the notes and original manuscripts
after a work was published, but, after his death, the notes to the *Rat Man*
mysteriously came to light. They reveal not only the violence of the Rat
Man's fantasy world but the pattern of attack and counterattack characterizing the relationship between analyst and patient. Each insight that

penetrated the Rat Man's defenses was converted into an expulsive transference fantasy involving the violation of Freud and members of his family. The following passage is typical of the case-study material Freud censored out of the published version:

> *Nov. 26*—He interrupted the analysis of the dream to tell me some
> transferences. A number of children were lying on the ground, and
> he went up to each of them and did something into their mouths.
> One of them, my son (his brother who had eaten excrement when
> he was two years old), still had brown marks round his mouth and
> was licking his lips as though it was something very nice. A change
> followed: It was I, and I was doing it to my mother (*Standard Edi-*
> *tion,* Vol. X, p. 286).

Unknown to the reader, beneath the surface narrative of the case study
there was an animated process of feeding and evacuation occurring between the two men, each intent to defeat the other's will. The more vigorously Freud offered his patient psychoanalytic morsels, the more violent were the Rat Man's expulsive movements. Freud also, in complete
violation of analytic technique, literally fed his patient. Nor could he understand why Lorenz suddenly expressed the wish to become slimmer.
Indeed, the herring Freud gave his patient, and which Lorenz did not
touch, was transformed into a transference fantasy in which the fish was
stretched from the anus of one woman to that of another—Freud's wife
and mother. Amidst these scatalogical attacks, Freud must have felt like
Gulliver in the land of the Yahoos. Yet the analyst remained remarkably
compassionate and good humored. Moreover, these were the fantasies of
only one patient, by no means his most disturbed. Freud analyzed hundreds
of people, each narrating confessions more fantastic than the next. Anyone coming across these notes would probably conclude that Freud was
the lunatic for allowing himself and his family to be shat upon with im-
punity.

It is easy to understand, for the reasons given above, why Freud omitted from the published account of the Rat Man's story the transference
fantasies described above as well as others, all of which were variations
on the same identity theme.[13] How could readers achieve a Coleridgean
suspension of disbelief when even the edited final version violated the laws
of order, decorum, and restraint? Was Freud treating human beings or
mad animals? What would prevent a reader from locating a published case
study and then seeking out Freud to cast further abuse on him—or his

family? Many of Freud's patients, in fact, were familiar with his writings. The Rat Man himself first read *The Psychopathology of Everyday Life* and then approached Freud for treatment. The analyst also gave the Rat Man and the Wolf Man inscribed copies of his books in appreciation of their importance to the psychoanalytic movement. Medical discretion required limits on the material he included for publication. He could not reasonably expect readers to distinguish the real Freud from the transferential figure conjured up by his patients' imagination.

Transference aside, there was a basis in reality for the Rat Man's fear of Freud's intrusiveness, and the analyst may have sensed this and decided to restrain this side of his personality from public view. Freud's observation of his beloved Goethe sheds light on his own desire for privacy. "Goethe was not only, as a poet, a great self-revealer, but also, in spite of the abundance of autobiographical records, a careful concealer" (*Standard Edition,* Vol. XXI, p. 212). As it was, many readers must have concluded that only a demented patient or pornographic writer could have conjured up the grotesque rat torture. Indeed, one researcher has discovered a possible link between the Rat Man's great obsessive fear and a similar rat torture found in Octave Mirbeau's notorious novel *Torture Garden,* published in 1899.[14] In suppressing, then, much of the transference material from the published story, Freud implicitly acknowledged the limits of analytic revelation. The precedent holds to this day. Narrations of the talking cure offer a more satisfactory account of the real analyst who guides the patient toward self-discovery than the symbolic or transferential analyst existing in the patient's imagination.

The Wolf Man posed different problems to Freud. Three separate versions of the case study exist: Freud's account, written shortly after the Wolf Man's treatment was ended in the winter of 1914 and 1915 and published in 1918; Ruth Mack Brunswick's reanalysis of the patient at Freud's request and her 1928 publication, "A Supplement to Freud's 'History of an Infantile Neurosis' "; and the patient's memoir, *The Wolf-Man,* published in 1971.[15] The Wolf Man is Freud's most illustrious patient, the only case study that has been followed from infancy to old age. Although the Rashomonlike differences among the three accounts are fascinating, a single issue confronts us here: the therapeutic misalliance resulting from the patient's privileged relationship to the analyst.

Freud called the Wolf Man a "piece of psychoanalysis," and an uncommon intimacy developed between the two men. Over the years, Freud befriended him in ways that left each awkwardly indebted to the other.

In his account, the Wolf Man concedes that a "too close relationship between patient and doctor has, like everything else in life, its shadow side"
(*The Wolf-Man,* p. 141). Freud certainly knew that friendship can impede
or destroy therapy. Without admitting that these boundaries were overstepped, the Wolf Man relates several incidents of his unique position to
Freud. The analyst told him, for example, not to follow his inclination to
become a painter and confided that his youngest son had also intended
to become a painter but then switched to architecture. Additionally, Freud
counseled him not to return to postrevolutionary Russia in a dangerous
and probably futile quest to regain his vast lost wealth. Freud continually
praised the Wolf Man and made him feel as if he were the "younger com-
rade of an experienced explorer setting out to study a new, recently discovered land." Freud said he was his best patient and that it would be
good if all his students could grasp the nature of psychoanalysis as soundly
as the Wolf Man did. The analyst shared with him information about his
family and colleagues, his taste for literature and art. Freud remarked at
the end of analysis that a gift from the patient would lessen his dependency on the doctor. Knowing Freud's love for archeology, the Wolf Man
presented him with a valued Egyptian figurine. Looking through a magazine 20 years later, he noticed a picture of Freud at his desk, with the
statuette still there. Freud later reanalyzed the Wolf Man (for what the
patient cryptically calls a "small residue of unanalyzed material") without
remuneration. Afterwards, Freud took up a collection from his followers
to subsidize the once-wealthy patient now unable to pay his rent.

The details relating to the analysis of the Wolf Man described above
appear harmless enough and irrelevant to the case study. Yet one of the
dangers of an analyst's affectionate overinvolvement with a patient is that
guilt may prevent the patient from acknowledging hostility. To quote the
Wolf Man's psychologically authoritative pronouncement, "resistances in
the transference increase when the patient looks upon the analyst as a father
substitute" (*The Wolf-Man,* pp. 141–142). What he fails to admit, though,
is the extent to which he seduced Freud into an extra-analytic relationship. The young man who gratefully accepted Freud's generous dona-
tions (and who, it turns out, was not honest about his financial situation)
later became haughty, as if, in Brunswick's words, "the gifts of money
from Freud were accepted as the patient's due, and as the token of a father's
love for his son" (*The Wolf-Man,* p. 282). The patient who respectfully
heeded Freud's advice not to return to Marxist Russia now blamed his
poverty on the analyst. The youth who eagerly received Freud's confi-

dence, repeatedly professing his veneration of the analyst, was now filled
with murderous violence toward the symbolic father. He even threatened
to shoot both Freud and Brunswick.

In short, since the Wolf Man had not worked through his transference
feelings toward Freud, he was now acting out infantile rage toward other
figures in his life. He also felt guilty about Freud's terminal cancer. He
tersely describes Freud's numerous operations and the prosthesis he wore
to replace part of the surgically removed jaw; he remains strangely silent,
however, over his psychological reaction to the analyst's disfigurement.
Brunswick reveals how the Wolf Man developed a hypochondriacal *idée
fixe* centering on his nose, which he feared would be amputated in unconscious imitation of Freud's jaw. The young man would compulsively
gaze into a pocket mirror he carried everywhere to make sure his nose
was still intact.

Pathos emerges from Brunswick's portrait of the Wolf Man who, with
his crippling obsessions, wounded pride, and blatant castration fear, walked
the streets of Europe examining his nose, like a mad character in a Gogol
story. But there are more ironies in the Wolf Man's life than one would
expect to find in fiction. Brunswick's analytic neutrality toward her famous patient is itself suspect.[16] In her reconstruction of the case, she correctly points out the Wolf Man's unresolved transference toward Freud,
and the ways in which the patient's acting out represented primitive
identifications with his parents. She fails to realize, however, that the Wolf
Man did indeed have a privileged status in psychoanalysis. To Freud, who
could play favorites, he was more than kin if less than kind. There is a
sad comedy in Brunswick's efforts to dethrone the Wolf Man from his
princely position to Freud, so that she could secure the father-analyst's
love and approval. How could she not feel sibling rivalry toward the man
who had greater access to Freud than she had? To add further confusion
to the story, both the Wolf Man and Brunswick were under treatment by
Freud at the same time. One can imagine the bewildering implications of
the analytic incest.

The case histories of Dora, the Rat Man, and the Wolf Man reveal
transference and countertransference complexities that escaped Freud's
attention. These complexities add a highly personal element to psychoanalysis, making it as much an art as a science, and requiring a narrative
point of view that encompasses the real and symbolic figures in the analyst's office. Freud refers to transference as the "battleground" on which
the patient's illness is exposed, fought, and won. But the battleground is

usually omitted from psychiatric case studies and literary accounts of psychological breakdown and recovery. In fact, Freud rarely discussed countertransference, believing that publication on this subject would seriously impair his effectiveness with patients familiar with psychoanalytic writings. To know too much about the analyst's personality, Freud feared, would deflect attention from the proper subject of psychoanalysis, the patient. He may have been right, but there was also a defensive element in Freud's silence. He had, after all, revealed an enormous amount of autobiographical material in *The Interpretation of Dreams*. In the decoding of his own dreams he exposed himself to relentless public scrutiny—demonstrated by the numerous biographies of Freud and book-length studies of his dreams.[17] There were times he must have felt more like a confessional poet than a detached scientist. Many of the dreams he narrated, such as Irma's injection and the botanical garden, dramatize Freud's grandiose ambitions, bitter frustrations over lack of success, and self-justifications. There were limits, though, to his willingness to open up his life to the reading public. None of his later books, including the deceptively entitled *An Autobiographical Study* (1925), repeats the candid self-analysis of the great dream book.

There are only a few scattered references to countertransference in Freud's writings, each suggesting the potential unruliness of the analyst's unconscious feelings. In a 1913 letter, he says that countertransference is one of the most troublesome technical problems in psychoanalysis. The analyst's effectiveness, he adds, depends upon the ability to control his own unconscious. At first he believed that the therapist must begin his professional career with a self-analysis, as Freud did, and continue it throughout his life. He remained convinced that no analyst goes further than his own self-insights or ability to overcome internal resistances. He later changed his mind about the adequacy of self-analysis and insisted on a training analysis conducted by an experienced senior analyst. Consisting of three to four sessions per week for several years, the training analysis remains the most indispensable part of psychoanalytic education. Erikson has compared the training analysis to monastic penitence, requiring total personal involvement.[18] By understanding his or her own projective tendencies, the future analyst is better able to experience the patient's feelings.

Since it was discovered by Freud, countertransference has received increasing theoretical and clinical attention. Instead of being viewed as an exclusively pathological phenomenon, as Freud conceived it, countertransference is now regarded as a natural complement or counterpart to the patient's transference.[19] The revelation of the analyst's human frailties may strike some people as proof of the failure of psychoanalysis, but to others it is an honest admission that analysts are not exempt from the problems besetting their patients. To become aware of these problems, moreover, is the first step toward overcoming them—an advantage those who are not trained psychoanalysts do not have. In a classic essay called "Hate in the Counter-Transference," D. W. Winnicott writes about the conditions under which a patient succeeds in eliciting the analyst's fear or hatred.[20] The analyst may feel overwhelmed by the patient's need for symbiotic merger, angered by the reduction into a narcissistic extension of the self, or seduced into emotional overinvolvement. In a lively article entitled "The Effort to Drive the Other Person Crazy," H. Searles argues that since one of the major defense mechanisms against intrapsychic conflict is reaction formation, the conversion of one instinct to its opposite, some therapists enter the profession to control unconscious wishes that run counter to therapeutic aims. His disturbing conclusion is that "desires to drive the other person crazy are a part of the limitlessly varied personality constellation of emotionally healthy human beings."[21] Few analysts are willing to make this statement in public, however; countertransference tends to be discussed only in professional journals that are seldom read by the layman. There are even fewer analysts who have written freely about their own training analysis (a remarkable exception is Tilmann Moser's *Years of Apprenticeship on the Couch*[22]). The unusually high suicide rate among psychiatrists and psychoanalysts suggests the presence of counterphobic motivation of many individuals who enter the field.[23]

Nowhere are the ambiguities of psychoanalysis more evident than in the concept of resistance. It seems wildly improbable to believe that a patient may struggle to retain his illness. In the first edition of *Dora,* Freud asserted that the motives for illness are not present at the beginning but are secondary consequences; later he changed his mind, concluding that the wish to fall ill is a major cause of psychological disorder. In a long footnote added in 1923 to the case study, Freud describes how the flight into illness represents an imperfect solution to mental conflict. Dora fell ill, for instance, in an attempt to detach her father's affection from a woman with whom he was having an affair. The Rat Man developed symptoms that prevented him from working, thus sparing him from an agonizing marital decision. Anna O.'s hysterical illness, an analyst has speculated, may have been a reaction to repressed hostility against her father and jealousy of her governess.[24] The motives for illness generally arise in childhood and later become a weapon for securing an advantage, such as parental affection or conflict avoidance. Because illness brings about certain advantages, the analyst may have difficulty in convincing the patient to devise more constructive solutions to psychic conflict.

But the concept of resistance easily lends itself to abuse. How does a patient know whether he is "acting out" a neurotic conflict or "working through" it?[25] In psychoanalytic terminology, the former is a manifestation of resistance while the latter is of resolution. Freud defines acting out as the discharge of anxiety through the involuntary repetition of an act, such as exhibiting incestuous drives or pathological defenses. Psychoanalysis evolved from Breuer's cathartic method, which aimed at bringing into focus the moment at which a symptom first occurred, then reproducing the mental processes involved for the purpose of symptom removal. Breuer and Freud called this process "abreaction." Since abreaction does not always lead to insight, Freud abandoned hypnosis as a therapeutic technique and devised the free-association method, a slower but more effective way to induce the patient to recall repressed material. He used the term "working through" to describe the process of overcoming internal resistance through intellectual and emotional self-discovery.

The problem, though, is the seductive appeal of the word. Anyone can invoke "resistance" to discredit another person's argument or point of view. Indeed, the term can be wielded by an analyst or anybody else to "rationalize" (another psychoanalytic term, coined by Ernest Jones, that can be easily abused) any self-serving point of view. As the history of the psychoanalytic movement regrettably demonstrates, analysts have not always resisted the temptation to employ *ad hominem* arguments when disagreeing with an esteemed colleague's theory. However, it would be equally unfortunate to dismiss the term because of its misuse. Erik Erikson's useful discussion of resistance clarifies many of the issues raised when applying psychoanalytic theory to history, biography, and literature. Erikson points out that Freud adopted the word not as a moral approbrium but as part of the physicalistic vocabulary of the age. Just as we would not expect to encounter electricity in a medium which "resists" conduction, so should we not expect the possibility of a "totally 'free' communication of memories or motives."[26] The psychobiographer thus frees the word from any connotations of a conscious, insincere, or fraudulent reluctance to tell the truth. There is resistance, then, in the nature of all inquiry.

Viewed in this way, resistance becomes the natural reluctance to reveal or discover troubling human truths.

Transference and countertransference undercut the traditional distinction between the outer and inner world, objectivity and subjectivity. The external world can be seen only through the internal world, but this perception inevitably alters the object in the mind's eye. Building upon the theory of the British analyst D. W. Winnicott, psychoanalytic literary critics have defined the text as a "potential space" or a "transitional object," in which there is an active interplay between objectivity and subjectivity, the external world of objects and internal world of readers.[27] The interactional nature of the patient-analyst relationship is analogous in some ways to the reader's reconstruction of the text in the literary process. The object is incorporated and transformed into a new creation consistent with the reader's unique identity theme. The difference is that the therapeutic process involves a double act of reading: the patient attempts to read the analyst as if he were a text ("reading" his mind, "interpreting" his motives, "locating" his authorial point of view), just as the analyst is seeking to decipher the patient's text. In one of the few articles published in a literary journal on the subject, Arthur Marotti has indicated how countertransference responses occur in literature, "especially in the critical interpreter who not only reacts immediately to literary works but also makes it his business to react to his reactions."[28] Psychoanalytic thinkers have been struck by the connection between Heisenberg's principle of indeterminacy and Freud's theory of transference. Just as the physicist's observations of subatomic particles alter the data, so does the analyst's presence influence the patient's responses. To date, literary critics have not adequately explored the role of transference and countertransference in fictional accounts of the talking cure.[29]

It is surprising that critics have not considered transference to any extent in light of the ubiquitous presence of the psychoanalyst in literature. Few twentieth-century figures have evoked more fascination than the mental healer, whose image "extends from the analyst's couch and from the meeting halls of modern faith healers and miracle men to the shrines of worship of ancient Greece and Judea, to the thatched-roof huts of the primitive shaman or witch doctor."[30] For many people, the analyst has replaced the priest as the healer of the diseased spirit or lost soul, though along with this overestimation comes inevitable hostility. One analyst has compared the mythic structure of psychoanalysis to the "Virgil-leading-Dante" pattern, in which the heroic introspective journey takes place not after death but in the shadowy dream world of the unconscious self.[31] The rich mythic symbolism of psychoanalysis undoubtedly owes its existence to Freud's imagination, which was stirred by the great mythic figures of antiquity.[32] Despite his aversion to publicity and his unusually quiet personal life, he remained convinced of his mission as destroyer of the world's peace. He conceived of himself as Prometheus stealing fire from the gods, Faust selling his soul to the devil in exchange for knowledge and power, Moses demonstrating superhuman restraint amidst betrayal and dissension. He chose as the motto for *The Interpretation of Dreams* a quotation from *The Aeneid: "Flectere si nequeo superos, Acheronta movebo"* ("If I cannot bend the Higher Powers, I will move the Infernal Regions").

Indeed, Freud's epigraph accurately foreshadows the antithetical image of the psychoanalyst in literature. Liberator and enslaver, healer and quack, ego ideal and repressive superego, the analyst serves as the object of intense ambivalence. Alternately worshiped and reviled, deified and damned, he evokes simultaneously the artist's fascination and contempt. The difference between the therapist and the rapist, Vladimir Nabokov never lets his readers forget, is a matter of spacing. Of the hundreds of fictional psychoanalysts, nearly all have been rendered into stereotypes. There are the lecherous analysts, such as Palmer Anderson in Iris Murdoch's *A Severed Head* and Adrian Goodlove in Erica Jong's *Fear of Flying,* eager to entice their attractive patients to bed; the deeply neurotic and conflicted psychiatrists, like Martin Dysart in Peter Shaffer's *Equus,* who regard their professional work as equivalent to emasculation; and the fraudulent therapists, such as Dr. Tamkin in Saul Bellow's *Seize the Day* and the sinister doctor who practices mythotherapy in John Barth's *The End of the Road.* The therapist usually dispenses bad prescriptions, smug morality, and dangerous advice. Sir William Bradshaw, the psychiatrist in Virginia Woolf's *Mrs. Dalloway,* embodies the artist's condemnation of the therapist. "Worshipping proportion, Sir William not only prospered himself but made England prosper, secluded her lunatics, forbade childbirth, penalised despair, made it impossible for the unfit to propagate their views until they, too, shared his sense of proportion. . . ."[33]

The bitterness in Woolf's tone reflects the dominant attitude among writers, who regard psychotherapy as a threat to free will, creativity, spiritual belief, and individuality. The "pecking party" in Ken Kesey's *One Flew Over the Cuckoo's Nest,* "release games" performed under the supervision of the diabolical Doktor Amalia von Wytwyl in Nabokov's *Bend*

Sinister, and "Ludovico's Technique" in Anthony Burgess' *A Clockwork Orange* all equate psychotherapy with brutal mind control. Not all therapists, of course, are treated with unmirthful contempt. Philip Bummidge ("Bummy"), the comic-turned-psychoanalyst hero of Bellow's zany play *The Last Analysis,* is not only a spoof of Freudianism but a parody of the self-help books that proliferated in the 1960s and 1970s and the language of psychobabble that has infected our contemporary culture. If, as Freud argues in *Jokes and Their Relation to the Unconscious,* caricatures represent the degradation of persons who command respect, even the Viennese analyst would have been startled by the unrelenting artistic debasement of his own profession. Only a handful of sympathetic and authentic analysts have been portrayed in literature; significantly, most of them have been women, such as Dr. Johanna von Haller in Robertson Davies' *The Manticore.* The majority of fictional analysts remain stereotypes, however, and (to paraphrase Mark Twain) have as much relation to genuine psychotherapists as the lightning bug has to lightning.

The nicknames of three representative analysts in the following chapters evoke the spectrum of attitudes toward psychotherapy, ranging from total rejection, through conditional acceptance, to enthusiastic support. Sir Harcourt-Reilly, the mysterious "Uninvited Guest" in T. S. Eliot's *The Cocktail Party* (1950), offers unorthodox clinical advice to his spiritually lost patients. A priest disguised as a psychiatrist, Eliot's hero betrays unmistakable hostility toward therapy as he guides Celia Coplestone to an ecstatic religious crucifixion. The play dramatizes the conflict between secular and spiritual approaches to mental suffering, leaving little doubt in the end about Eliot's mistrust of psychiatry. For Eliot, psychiatry remains an uninvited guest whose point of view is inimical to Christian salvation. He takes the same position toward psychological approaches to literature, a violation of the purity of the text. Mrs. Marks, "Mother Sugar" in Doris Lessing's *The Golden Notebook* (1962), is the Jungian psychoanalyst who helps Anna Wulf overcome a severe case of writer's block. Although Lessing treats psychoanalysis more sympathetically in *The Golden Notebook* than in *The Four-Gated City* (1969), Mother Sugar seems more interested in an arcane mythology than in understanding her patient's personal history. Furthermore, she dispenses sugar-coated myths that seem strikingly irrelevant to a contemporary society in which women are struggling for political and sexual freedom. Dr. Clara Fried, "Dr. Furii" in Joanne Greenberg's *I Never Promised You a Rose Garden* (1964), is the magical fairy godmother whose psychiatric power appears as purgatorial or volcanic fire to the schizophrenic Deborah Blau. Despite the novelist's efforts to avoid mythologizing the fictional analyst, we see an idealized portrait, with little hint that the main battleground in psychoanalysis lies in the transference relationship.

Apart from focusing on the relationship between the patient and analyst and the value of psychotherapy, these three literary works have another important element in common. In each case the writer suffered a psychological breakdown, entered psychotherapy, and later wrote an account of the talking cure in which the fictional analyst was loosely or closely based on the artist's actual therapist. Sir Harcourt-Reilly is roughly modeled on Dr. Roger Vittoz, the Swiss psychiatrist who treated Eliot during his nervous breakdown in the early 1920s, when he was writing *The Waste Land*. Mrs. Marks owes her origin to the Jungian analyst who treated Doris Lessing in the 1950s. And Dr. Fried is closely based on the distinguished American psychoanalyst Dr. Frieda Fromm-Reichmann, who successfully treated Joanne Greenberg at Chestnut Lodge in Maryland. Despite fundamental differences in genre, literary technique, clinical authenticity, and point of view, these three works dramatize protagonists who fall ill, seek professional help, and work out individual solutions to psychic conflict. The type of psychotherapy the characters receive varies radically from work to work, as do the characters' fates at the close of the book.

This does not imply that the autobiographical element necessarily predominates in these works, or that they are literal depictions of the authors' spiritual or psychological odysseys. The degree of autobiographical truth and clinical authenticity varies from story to story, as does the degree of literary success. Sometimes the character's fate at the end of a story is the opposite of the artist's in real life, thus confounding any one-to-one relationship between author and fictional projection. Additionally, although literary representations of mental illness are often based on personal experiences, the artist invokes a literary tradition which separates art from life. In *Madness in Literature,* Lillian Feder observes that while the madman of literature may be to some extent modeled on an actual character, the differences are at least as important as the similarities. The fictional character "is rooted in a mythical or literary tradition in which distortion is a generally accepted mode of expression; furthermore, the inherent aesthetic order by which his existence is limited also gives his madness intrinsic value and meaning."[34] It is admittedly risky, Feder cautions, to consider literary works as psychological autobiographies or to diagnose the psychic ills of fictive madmen. Without losing sight of these distinctions, we may note, as Feder does, that literary characters often reveal the artist's unconscious mental processes, in particular, attitudes toward psychological health and illness. A study of literary accounts of the talking cure can reveal much about the fascinating relationship between the creative and therapeutic process, and the crossfertilization of literature and psychoanalysis.

Of the nine creative writers studied here, seven have had experiences with mental illness serious enough to require hospitalization or prolonged treatment. More than a dozen fictional psychiatrists appear in the following pages, representing a variety of approaches to mental illness. *The Talking Cure* is, to an extent, an account of the changing forms of psychotherapy, or at least the ways in which the popular conception of psychotherapy has changed from its beginnings in the late nineteenth century. "The Yellow Wallpaper" (1892) is a chilling fictionalized account of Charlotte Perkins Gilman's breakdown in the 1880s and her harrowing experience with S. Weir Mitchell, the foremost American neurologist of his time and the originator of the well-known "rest cure." At the end of "The Yellow Wallpaper" the first-person narrator goes mad—unlike the author, who recovered from her devastating breakdown and went on to become a prolific author whose stories and outspoken feminist writings alerted other would-be patients to the evils of the Mitchell rest cure. F. Scott Fitzgerald acquired the clinical material for *Tender Is the Night* (1934) partly from his readings on psychiatry and also from his marriage to Zelda, whose incurable schizophrenia and repeated hospitalizations served as the background material for Nicole Warren. But Fitzgerald's psychiatrist-hero, Dr. Dick Diver, also embodies the novelist's own fears of dissipation and loss of creativity, themes he later wrote about in the autobiographical *The Crack-Up* (published posthumously in 1945).

The Bell Jar (1963) is Sylvia Plath's classic account of depression, suicidal breakdown, and electroshock therapy. The loving female psychiatrist who treats Esther Greenwood, Dr. Nolan, is based upon Plath's actual psychiatrist at McLean Hospital in Massachusetts, Dr. Ruth Beuscher. The recent publication of Plath's journals confirms the overwhelming importance of psychoanalysis to her life and art. Indeed, Plath's secret return to analysis in the late 1950s was partly responsible for the startling burst of creativity in her late poems. And the celebrated Dr. Otto Spielvogel of *Portnoy's Complaint* (1969) and *My Life as a Man* (1974) is modeled on the psychoanalyst who treated Philip Roth for many years, Dr.

Hans Kleinschmidt. Roth writes with a clinical expertise few creative writers can equal and, while his feelings toward psychoanalysis are typically equivocal, the therapeutic setting has given rise to many of his finest and most authentic stories. The remaining two creative writers, Vladimir Nabokov and D. M. Thomas, also figure prominently into any discussion of literary representations of psychoanalysis, though neither writer has undergone analysis. The lifelong enemy of the "Viennese witch doctor," Nabokov remains the supreme parodist of the psychiatric case study. On nearly every page of *Lolita* (1955), Humbert mocks the psychoanalytic approach to life and art; it is not Quilty who constitutes Humbert's secret adversary but Freud, whom the novelist obsessively slays in book after book. By contrast, Thomas' *The White Hotel* (1981) is an astonishing recreation of the Freudian case study, a novel that at once reconstructs the historical Freud and at the same time transcends purely psychological approaches to human suffering.

It seems particularly appropriate to begin and end a study of fictional accounts of psychotherapy with "The Yellow Wallpaper" and *The White Hotel,* respectively. Gilman was an exact contemporary of Bertha Pappenheim, and the two women led strikingly similar lives. Born a year apart, they suffered crippling breakdowns at the same time, were treated by eminent male physicians who failed them, and later became ardent feminists with no use for men. Gilman was one of the sharpest critics of Freud, who had, ironically—and unpredictably—warmly praised the Mitchell rest cure. Published three years before *Studies on Hysteria,* "The Yellow Wallpaper" brilliantly captures a young woman's irreversible descent into madness. Narrated with extraordinary restraint and clinical detachment, it succeeds where Breuer's "Fräulein Anna O." fails in dramatizing the oppressive social, political, and sexual forces responsible for the heroine's fatal entrapment in her Victorian ancestral house. And the stunning conclusion of Gilman's short story makes the ending of Breuer's medical treatise seem like a fairy tale, utterly divorced from reality. *The White Hotel* appeared exactly 100 years after Breuer's treatment of Anna O. In fact, the "Frau Anna G." section of Thomas' novel, written in the form of a Freudian case study, abounds in quotations from *Studies on Hysteria* and Freud's other writings, including his technical papers and massive correspondence. No novel better illustrates the symbiotic relationship between literature and psychoanalysis than *The White Hotel.* It is certainly not the last novel to employ an analytic apparatus to explore the depths of the human psyche, but it is hard to imagine a more profound example of the intricate art of those who practice Freud's "impossible profession." Thomas refers to the genuine Freudian case studies as "masterly works of literature"; in *The White Hotel* he has himself created one of the most remarkable novels in years.

As a genre, the literature involving psychiatric case studies raises questions that go beyond the territory of literary criticism: the definition of psychological health and illness, the relationship between suffering and creativity, adaptive versus pathological solutions to psychic conflict. Freud's equation of the artist with the neurotic has rightly angered writers.[35] Psychoanalysts continue to make unproven assertions of the artist's "narcissism," thus further provoking the writer's counterattack. Freud's theory of the neurotic artist not only singles out one class of people but lumps disparate individuals into the same group. It seems true, however, that certain individuals from widely differing backgrounds and occupations are capable of converting neurotic suffering into creativity. George Pickering has coined the term "creative malady" to describe the role of illness in otherwise dissimilar figures as Charles Darwin, Florence Nightingale, Mary Baker Eddy, Marcel Proust, Elizabeth Barrett Browning, and Freud. "The illness was an essential part of the act of creation rather than a device to enable that act to take place."[36] In many cases, the creative work and illness have a common source in mental torment. Psychological illness may promote scientific and artistic creativity by encouraging adaptive and integrative solutions to inner conflict. There are many reasons to write about mental breakdown, including the desire to exorcise old demons and ward off new ones. This does not imply, of course, that writing about breakdown guarantees protection against future illness, or that madness and creativity are interrelated, as many ancient (Plato) and contemporary (R. D. Laing) thinkers claim. As we shall see, Plath is an example of a writer for whom "dying is an art"—and whose art could not prevent her from prematurely dying.

Ironically, Freud suffered no less than many writers whose breakdowns receive greater public attention. His letters insist on the link between suffering and creativity. It is arguable that the first patient of psychoanalysis was not Bertha Pappenheim but Freud himself. "The chief patient I am busy with is myself," he confided to Fliess in 1897, implying that before he could heal others he had to understand himself. Long before he embarked upon the self-analysis that culminated in *The Interpretation of Dreams,* he complained about a variety of neurotic symptoms. In 1886 he wrote a letter to his fiancée detailing his genetic history, a "considerable 'neuropathological taint,' " as he called it (*The Letters of Sigmund Freud,* p. 210). Ernest Jones documents Freud's periodic depressions and fatigue, which later took the form of anxiety attacks. He also suffered from severe migraine attacks, fainting spells (most notably, in the presence of Jung), and the conviction he would die at a predetermined age. His stress was most severe during the 1890s, when his creativity was at its height. He candidly confessed his complaints to Fliess, who served as a father figure to him. The list of afflictions ranged from cardiac oppression to stomach trouble.[37] It was embarrassing for a neuropathologist to suffer from psychological problems, Freud admitted, and he did not know whether his ailments were physical or mental.

The impetus behind *The Interpretation of Dreams* was Freud's need to understand and master the unruly dreams provoked by his father's death. Out of Freud's loss came his most enduring achievement. The Fliess letters reflect the high drama surrounding this eventful period of Freud's life and the alliance of suffering and creativity. The letters written in the last six months of 1897 convey almost unbearable inner turbulence. His language assumes a mystical quality as he writes about the dark night of the soul. "I have been through some kind of a neurotic experience, with odd states of mind not intelligible to consciousness—cloudy thoughts and veiled doubts, with barely here and there a ray of light" (*The Origins of Psychoanalysis,* pp. 210–211). Moments of creativity alternated with frightening periods of emptiness. In October he seemed ready to collapse from the burden of introspection; he compared his state of mind to that of his patients. He emerged from self-analysis convinced that his illness was central to the discovery of his theories. He told Joseph Wortis years later that "Everybody has some slight neurotic nuance or other, and as a matter of fact, a certain degree of neurosis is of inestimable value as a drive, especially to a psychologist."[38] Not all of his neurotic symptoms disappeared after his self-analysis, as Jones misleadingly implies; nevertheless, Freud emerged healthier as a consequence of the period of intense introspection. He concluded in 1897 that he was "much more normal" than he was four years earlier.

Freud's neurotic symptoms do not invalidate his psychological theories any more than a writer's breakdown invalidates (or conversely, authenticates) his or her literary achievements. It would be unnecessary to say this were it not for the tendency of clinicians to perpetuate Freud's myth of the neurotic artist—and to remain silent about the neurotic psychoanalyst.[39] From the beginning of his career, Freud recognized that health and illness are highly subjective words. One of the themes of *The Inter-pretation of Dreams* is that neurotic characteristics appear in healthy peo-ple. "Psycho-analytic research finds no fundamental, but only quantita-tive, distinctions between normal and neurotic life; and indeed the analysis of dreams, in which repressed complexes are operative alike in the healthy and the sick, shows a complete identity both in their mechanisms and in their symbolism" (*Standard Edition*, Vol. V, pp. 373–374). He repeats this point in *Little Hans,* saying that no sharp line can be drawn between nor-mal and neurotic people. Individuals are constantly passing from the group of healthy people to that of the sick, while a smaller number make the journey in the opposite direction. And in "Analysis Terminable and In-terminable," one of Freud's last essays, he asserts that normalcy is a fic-tion. "Every normal person, in fact, is only normal on the average" (*Stan-dard Edition,* Vol. XXIII, p. 235).

If normalcy is a fiction, who is better able to explore the workings of the mind than the fiction writer? Not only did Freud generously pay trib-ute to the poets and playwrights who long ago discovered the uncon-scious self, he viewed the creative writer as the psychoanalyst's natural ally.[40] Nowhere is he more eloquent in his praise for literature than in "Delusions and Dreams in Jensen's *Gradiva*" (1907), his first extended published analysis of a literary work. He ingeniously demonstrates that in *Gradiva* the nineteenth-century North German novelist has presented a powerful and unerring psychiatric case study of a young man's delu-sional love for a woman who died during the destruction of Pompeii in the year 79. Rejecting the belief that writers should leave the description of pathological states to physicians, Freud insists that "no truly creative writer has ever obeyed this injunction." The analysis of the human mind is the creative writer's domain, Freud says, and from time immemorial the artist has been the precursor to the scientist. Creative writers are val-uable allies and their evidence is to be prized highly, "for they are apt to know a whole host of things between heaven and earth of which our phi-losophy has not yet let us dream" (*Standard Edition,* Vol. IX, p. 8). The allusion to *Hamlet* reminds us that Freud's most famous discovery, the Oedipus complex, was first revealed in a letter in which, in the same breath he postulates the idea of a son's love of the mother and jealousy of the father, he applies the insight to the plays of Sophocles and Shakespeare. The birth of psychoanalysis, then, is inseparable from the birth of psy-choanalytic literary criticism; for all of their differences, the analyst and artist look to each other for confirmation. Freud's conclusion in his essay on Jensen's *Gradiva* is that the "creative writer cannot evade the psychiatrist nor the psychiatrist the creative writer, and the poetic treatment of a psychiatric theme can turn out to be correct without any sacrifice of its beauty" (*Standard Edition*, Vol. IX, p. 44).

Elsewhere, it is true, Freud retreated from this position, and some of his statements are distinctly patronizing to the artist. In "Psychopathic Characters on the Stage," written a year or two before "Jensen's *Gradiva*," he frets over "sick art," fearing that the inept treatment of mental illness in literature may actually increase neurotic suffering. He implies that pathological characters should remain on the analytic couch, not on the theatre stage. (Outraged readers of "The Yellow Wallpaper" had the same reaction). He even seems ready to dismiss Hamlet as diseased. Freud's disturbing conclusion is that "If we are faced by an unfamiliar and fully established neurosis, we shall be inclined to send for the doctor (just as we do in real life) and pronounce the character inadmissible to the stage" (*Standard Edition*, Vol. VII, p. 310). Despite this contradiction, however, Freud envisioned the creative writer and analyst as collaborators, and he predicted a happy marriage between fiction and the psychiatric arts.

Thomas Mann also believed that the creative writer and the psychoanalyst are particularly well suited to explore the mysterious recesses of the mind. His observation about Hans Castorp in *The Magic Mountain* applies to all the writers in the following chapters, who regard illness not as an end in itself but as a means toward a higher goal. "What he comes to understand is that one must go through the deep experience of sickness and death to arrive at a higher sanity and health; in just the same way that one must have a knowledge of sin in order to find redemption."[41] Disease is thus a necessary precondition to knowledge and health. To the extent that the creative writer succeeds in portraying the fluctuating borders between normal and abnormal states of mind, the artist may even be considered a healer. This is close to Edmund Wilson's view of the artist in his influential essay "Philoctetes: The Wound and the Bow." Wilson interprets Sophocles' play as a parable of human character and the paradoxical fusion of sickness and health within the artist. Wilson regards the artist as both "the victim of a malodorous disease which renders him abhorrent to society" and the "master of a superhuman art which everybody has to respect and which the normal man finds he needs."[42] Like Mann, Wilson affirms the idea that "genius and disease, like strength and mutilation, may be inextricably bound up together." To write about illness in an illuminating and aesthetically pleasing manner is to transmute suffering into higher creativity. There are, of course, numerous qualifications to this view of art. The vast majority of people who suffer psychological breakdowns do not eventually write about their experiences. Suffering is rarely ennobling. Moreover, only a small number of literary narrations of the talking cure are sufficiently complex to warrant rereading.

Nevertheless, the creative writers who have experienced mental illness and undergone psychotherapy are often in a unique position to arrive at higher sanity and health. The catalyst for Mann's initiation into knowledge was, not surprisingly, Freud. In the Apollonian essay "Freud's Position in the History of Modern Thought," published in 1933 in T. S. Eliot's *The Criterion,* Mann argues that psychoanalysis has ceased to be merely a therapeutic movement and instead grown into a world view. In light of the catastrophic world events Mann could not foresee, and the gradual decline of psychoanalysis because of its failure to live up to the promises of its early enthusiasts, the novelist's optimism seem excessive. Yet Mann's affirmation of the ideal to which psychoanalysis remains committed still holds true half a century later:

> Its profoundest expertise in morbid states is unmistakably at work not ultimately for the sake of disease and the depths, not, that is, with an interest hostile to reason; but first and last, armed with all the advantages that have accrued from exploring the dark abysses, in the interest of healing and redemption, of "enlightenment" in the most humane sense of the word.[43]

It is in the spirit of Mann's insight that we apply psychoanalytic theory to literature of the talking cure, always remembering, as the distinguished psychoanalytic theoretician Heinz Kohut observed shortly before his recent death, that "Freud's writings are not a kind of Bible but great works belonging to a particular moment in the history of science— great not because of their unchanging relevance but, on the contrary, because they contain the seeds of endless possibilities for further growth."[44] Beset by controversies both within and outside the profession—Kohut's emerging self-psychology, for instance, has triggered off fierce debate in clinical circles—psychoanalysis remains, despite its imperfections, the most psychologically sophisticated explanatory system available, and indispensable for an understanding of literary representations of psychoanalysis. The warfare between the analyst and artist continues unabated, notwithstanding *The White Hotel:* Psychiatric journals still publish articles on neurotic or narcissistic artists, and novelists still portray rigid, repressive, or reductive analysts. Anna O.'s turbulent relationship to Breuer set a pattern that has been repeated countless times in life and literature. "Psycho-analysis brings out the worst in everyone," Freud sardonically declares in *On the History of the Psycho-Analytic Movement* (*Standard Edition,* Vol. XIV, p. 39), with more prophecy than he intends. But psychoanalysis can also bring out the best in everyone, and Freud continues to occupy a central position in contemporary literature. "No doubt fate would find it easier than I do to relieve you of your illness," D. M. Thomas' fictional Freud remarks to Lisa Erdman, echoing word for word the historical Freud's conclusion of *Studies on Hysteria,* "But much will be gained if we succeed in turning your hysterical misery into common unhappiness." Paradoxically, out of this hysterical misery and common unhappiness have come some of the most significant stories of our age. For a century now, Anna O.'s talking cure has seized the imagination of artists and analysts alike, and not even Freud could have foreseen the literary interest in the unending stream of characters narrating their adventures of lying on the couch.

TWO

The Unrestful Cure:
Charlotte Perkins Gilman
and "The Yellow Wallpaper"

I F CHARLOTTE PERKINS GILMAN'S name does not command the instant recognition of an Elizabeth Cady Stanton, Jane Addams, or Susan B. Anthony, it is not because her achievement was less. Social historians agree on the brilliance of her ideas and the extent to which her influential books helped to transform the condition of women in early twentieth-century America. The following judgments are representative. "The only systematic theory linking the demand for suffrage with the long sweep of history was that of Charlotte Perkins Gilman, the most influential woman thinker in the pre-World War I generation in the United States."[1] "Of all the great feminist writers, she made the finest analysis of the relation between domesticity and women's rights, perhaps the most troubling question for liberated women and sympathetic men today."[2] "Charlotte Gilman was the greatest writer that the feminists ever produced on sociology and economics, the Marx and the Veblen of the movement."[3] "It is hardly an exaggeration to speak of her as the major intellectual leader of the struggle for women's rights, in the broadest sense, during the first two decades of the twentieth century."[4] Two of her books, *Women and Economics* and *The Home: Its Work and Influence,* became immediate classics. The *Nation* called *Women and Economics* "the most significant utterance" on the women's question since John Stuart Mill.[5] She has been called the "most original and challenging mind" produced by the women's movement.[6] Not long before her death, she was placed first on a list of 12 great American women by Carrie Chapman Catt.[7]

The major source of the details of her life is *The Living of Charlotte Perkins Gilman: An Autobiography,* an absorbing book that raises more questions than it answers. In its wealth of information about the author's troubled childhood experiences, especially her relationship to a mother who refused to show affection to her and to a father who abandoned his young family, the autobiography casts much light on "The Yellow Wallpaper." The book also eloquently describes her lifelong battle with acute depression exacerbated by what can only be euphemistically called "psychiatry." Born on July 3, 1860, Charlotte Perkins was a great granddaughter of Lyman Beecher, the progenitor of the distinguished American family. Little else about her early life seemed auspicious. Although her parents appear to have been in love when they married in 1857, the marriage was short lived. In quick succession Mary Perkins gave birth to four children, two of whom died in early infancy. The first baby died "from some malpractice at birth" in 1858, a son was born in 1859, Charlotte in the next year, and a fourth child died in 1866. When the doctor forbade another child, the father deserted the family:

> There now follows a long-drawn, triple tragedy, quadruple perhaps, for my father may have suffered too; but mother's life was one of the most painfully thwarted I have ever known. After her idolized youth, she was left neglected. After her flood of lovers, she became a deserted wife. The most passionately domestic of home-worshiping housewives, she was forced to move nineteen times in eighteen years, fourteen of them from one city to another.[8]

Charlotte's father never did return. Her mother delayed 13 years before divorcing him, and even after the divorce she continued to wait for him until the end of her life. The daughter's account captures the pathos of the mother's story. "Divorced or not she loved him till her death, at sixty-three. She was with me in Oakland, California, at the time, and father was then a librarian in San Francisco, just across the bay. She longed, she asked, to see him before she died. As long as she was able to be up, she sat always at the window watching for that beloved face. He never came." To which the daughter parenthetically adds, "That's where I get my implacable temper" (*The Living,* p. 9).

The theme of a child waiting for a man who will never return, and the attendant bewilderment and rage, characterizes Charlotte Perkins Gilman's feelings toward her father in particular and men in general. "The word Father, in the sense of love, care, one to go to in trouble, means nothing to me, save indeed in advice about books and the care of them—which seems more the librarian than the father" (*The Living,* pp. 5–6).

But it is not only the absent father who is responsible for the daughter's traumatized youth. Equally ominous is the impact of an embittered mother who denies her child the parental love and attention she herself had been denied by her husband's desertion. Mother becomes both victim and victimizer. Despite the fact that the mother is described as a "baby-worshiper" who devoted her entire life to the children, she also inflicted upon them the pain and lovelessness from which she herself suffered. The most poignant moment in Gilman's autobiography occurs when she writes about a recurring childhood experience which, like a bad dream or Dickensian scene, permanently haunted her imagination. What makes the passage more astonishing is the daughter's absence of criticism, even years later, of the rejecting mother:

> There is a complicated pathos in it, totally unnecessary. Having suffered so deeply in her own list of early love affairs, and still suffering for lack of a husband's love, she heroically determined that her baby daughter should not so suffer if she could help it. Her method was to deny the child all expression of affection as far as possible, so that she should not be used to it or long for it. "I used to put away your little hand from my cheek when you were a nursing baby," she told me in later years; "I did not want you to suffer as I had suffered." She would not let me caress her, and would not caress me, unless I was asleep. This I discovered at last, and then did my best to keep awake till she came to bed, even using pins to prevent dropping off, and sometimes succeeding. Then how carefully I pretended to be sound asleep, and how rapturously I enjoyed being gathered into her arms, held close and kissed (*The Living*, pp. 10–11).

Deprived of paternal protection and maternal tenderness, forced to adopt both subterfuge and self-punishment to secure the little affection the mother reluctantly offered, and reared in an environment where the image of a baby must have symbolized the mother's entrapment, the child turned inward to fabricate a fairy-tale world that would supplant grim reality. In this inner world dwelled an all-loving mother and father who rescued rather than abandoned the children of the world. The element of wish fulfillment is unmistakable here as well as a rescue fantasy in which the dreamer becomes her own idealized parent, transmuting an anguished childhood into paradise. In this fantasy world lived a "Prince and Princess of magical powers, who went about the world collecting unhappy children and taking them to a guarded Paradise in the South Seas. I had a boundless sympathy for children, feeling them to be suppressed, misunderstood."

The comforting fantasy soon collapsed, however, destroyed by a Victorian mother who under the influence of a "pre-Freudian" friend forbade her child to indulge in the pleasures of the imagination. "My dream world was no secret. I was but too ready to share it, but there were no sympathetic listeners. It was my life, but lived entirely alone. Then, influenced by a friend with a pre-Freudian mind, alarmed at what she was led to suppose this inner life might become, mother called on me to give it up. This was a command. According to all the ethics I knew I must obey, and I did . . ." (*The Living*, p. 23). And so at the tender age of 13 she was forced to give up the "inner fortress" that had been her chief happiness for five years. "But obedience was Right, the thing had to be done, and I did it. Night after night to shut the door on happiness, and hold it shut. Never, when dear, bright, glittering dreams pushed hard, to let them in. Just thirteen . . ." (*The Living*, p. 24).

In later life, Charlotte Perkins Gilman held Freud responsible for the loss of her dream world. Of the many references to Freud in her autobiography and other writings, all are pejorative. She indicts Freud for offenses ranging from the violation of the human spirit to an unnatural emphasis upon sex. In a lecture called "The Falsity of Freud," she equates the psychoanalyst with evil and oppression. Her description of a friendship with another woman links Freud with psychopathology: "In our perfect concord there was no Freudian taint, but peace of mind, understanding, comfort, deep affection" (*The Living*, p. 80). In an essay called "Parasitism and Civilised Vice," she argues that a major obstacle to the advancement of women's rights is the "resurgence of phallic worship set before us in the solemn phraseology of psychoanalysis."[9] Toward the end of her autobiography, she recalls in amazement how "apparently intelligent persons would permit these mind-meddlers, having no claims to fitness except that of having read certain utterly unproven books, to paddle among their thoughts and feelings, and extract the confessions of the last intimacy." One of these "mind-meddlers" gratuitously attempted to psychoanalyze her in an effort to render her into the psychiatric case study she had fictionalized in "The Yellow Wallpaper":

> One of these men, becoming displeased with my views and their advancement, since I would not come to be "psyched," as they call it, had the impudence to write a long psychoanalysis of my case, and send it to me. My husband and I, going out in the morning, found this long, fat envelop with our mail. I looked at it, saw who it was from, and gave it to Houghton. "I don't want to read his stuff," I

said. "You look it over and tell me what it is about." This he did, to my utter disgust. "Burn it up, do," I urged. "I haven't the least curiosity to know what this person thinks is the matter with me" (*The Living,* p. 314).

Whoever this anonymous "psychoanalyst" was, he only confirmed her hatred of Freud and her belief that the Viennese doctor and his unholy disciples were antithetical to the women's cause and to the imagination itself. Who can blame her anger over this violation of privacy, a violation that may have reminded her, as we shall see, of her experience with S. Weir Mitchell? Yet Gilman also condemned Freud for other, less valid, reasons. She insisted that Freud was responsible for the widespread promiscuity of the age and the lowering of standards in sexual relations. She was, of course, Victorian in her horror of sex and glorification of chastity. The deemphasis of chastity, she was convinced, had debased human nature. She accused the Freudians of a "sexuopathic philosophy" that advocated as " 'natural' a degree of indulgence utterly without parallel in nature" (*The Living,* p. 323). Elsewhere in her writings she attacks the "present degree of sex impulse" as pathological, arguing instead for the suppression or redirection of the sexual instinct. In her female utopia, *Herland,* women conceive through parthenogenesis, virgin-birth. Men are no longer necessary and procreation is independent of the sex act. Like her exact contemporary Bertha Pappenheim, Gilman could see only the horror of sexuality.

Given these feelings, it is no wonder that the two subjects she was to spend most of her life writing about and trying to reform—marriage and motherhood—figured conspicuously in her mental breakdown. Her autobiography reveals the confusion and misgivings surrounding her decision to marry Charles Walter Stetson, whom she had met in 1882. Although she considered him "quite the greatest man, near my own age, that I had ever known," she knew intuitively that she should not marry the good-looking painter. Her experience with deprivation and denial prepared her for a life of continued abstinence. Unwilling to hurt his feelings, she postponed a decision for as long as she could. She defined her marital dilemma as a choice between love and work, the classic conflict of a woman. Only after Stetson had met with a keen personal disappointment did she consent to marry him. Her gloom deepened. A diary written during this time reflects depression and self-contempt. There is also a thinly veiled death wish. "Let me recognize fully that I do not look forward to happiness, that I have no decided hope of success. So long must I live. One does not die young who so desires it" (*The Living*, p. 84). The thought of a future filled with failure and guilt compels her to break off her narration: "Children sick and unhappy. Husband miserable because of my distress, and I—" Against this fearful backdrop Charlotte Perkins Gilman married Stetson in May 1884. A daughter Katherine was born in March 1885. Her breakdown followed immediately.

What seems so perplexing—and yet so characteristic—about the swift series of events leading to Gilman's collapse is the praise she bestows on her husband and child and her refusal to utter a word of reproach toward either of them. She insists that she and her husband were happy together both before and after the arrival of their child. From her descriptions, Walter Stetson seemed a woman's dream. "A lover more tender, a husband more devoted, woman could not ask. He helped in the housework more and more as my strength began to fail, for something was going wrong from the first" (*The Living*, pp. 87–88). The idealized description contrasts the bleakness of her diary. She uses a metaphor similar to Sylvia Plath's bell jar. "A sort of gray fog drifted across my mind, a cloud that grew and darkened." At first she attributes her growing nervousness to pregnancy, but when the baby is born the mother's health worsens. She tries repeatedly to convince us that her sickness was not due to the baby she mythologizes. "Of all angelic babies that darling was the best, a heavenly baby." The nurse's departure deepens the mother's grief, and neither the arrival of her own mother nor the move to a better house improves the situation. The chapter on "Love and Marriage" in the autobiography closes with these chilling words. "Here was a charming home; a loving and devoted husband; an exquisite baby, healthy, intelligent and good; a highly competent mother to run things; a wholly satisfactory servant—and I lay all day on the lounge and cried" (*The Living*, p. 89).

What caused the breakdown? The meaning of the illness mystified her even 50 years later. Although she could not define what it was, she knew what it was not. Angered by the accusation that her "nervous prostration" was merely a fanciful term for laziness, she insisted that it was not caused by a deficiency of will. Nor could she force happiness into her life, as one sympathizer urged. She was unable to read or write, get out of bed, or stop crying. The doctors ruled out a physical cause, for which she would have been grateful. An accusing voice within her kept shouting: "You did it yourself! You did it yourself! You had health and strength and hope and glorious work before you—and you threw it all away. You were called to serve humanity, and you cannot serve yourself. No good as a wife, no good as a mother, no good at anything. And you did it yourself!" . . . (*The Living*, p. 91).

She knew that marriage and motherhood were the problem although she did not know why. The evidence could not be more striking. From the moment she left her baby and husband to travel across the continent for a rest and change, she felt immediately better. "I recovered so fast, to outward appearance at least, that I was taken for a vigorous young girl. Hope came back, love came back, I was eager to get home to husband and child, life was bright again." But, within a month of returning home, she was depressed as before. The truth was inescapable. To preserve her sanity she had to leave her family and to repudiate society's most cherished values. It was at this time that she sought psychiatric help from S. Weir Mitchell. After a one-month rest cure she returned home, following his orders to "live as domestic a life as possible." She came perilously close to losing her mind. She made a rag doll at home, hung it on a doorknob, and played with it. "I would crawl into remote closets and under beds—to hide from the grinding pressure of that profound distress . . ." (*The Living*, p. 96). Again one is reminded of Sylvia Plath and her efforts to bury herself beneath the subbasement of her mother's house. In a moment of clear vision, Charlotte and her husband finally agreed on a divorce. "There was no quarrel, no blame for either one, never an unkind word between us, unbroken mutual affection—but it seemed plain that if I went crazy it would do my husband no good, and be a deadly injury to my child" (*The Living*, p. 96).

The fear of committing a deadly injury to her child would seem to be in light of psychoanalytic theory an unconscious repetition of the traumatic wound inflicted upon Charlotte Perkins Gilman when she was a child herself. The irony is stunning. The little girl's identification with the absent father, along with the aspiration for the glorious work that was a male privilege in a sexist society, was so intense as to compel her against her will to become her own father and, like him, to abandon spouse and baby. She could not express rage toward her husband because, as her biographer records, she had never been honest and open with him about her feelings.[10] The silent aggression she felt toward the father who abandoned her was now directed against herself. She fell desperately ill, overcome with confusion and guilt. Only by rejecting her own family, as her father had rejected his family 20 years earlier, could she free herself from the weakness and passivity that symbolized to her the condition of motherhood.

In her imagination babies came to be associated with death, bereavement, and abandonment. The deaths in infancy of two of Mary Perkins' four children indicated that, not only were the odds poor to have a healthy child, but the mother's life was also imperiled. Sex must have seemed irresponsible, procreation deadly. The act of childbirth probably evoked the fear of mutilation. The emotions Charlotte felt when she gave birth were appropriate for a funeral. Instead of rejoicing, she went into a period of mourning. The child drained her and threw her into a "black helplessness" with its "deadness of heart, its aching emptiness of mind." In becoming pregnant she was repeating her mother's dreadful mistake. Pregnancy implied maternal sacrifice bordering on suicide. "The surrender of the mother to the child is often flatly injurious, if carried to excess," she acknowledges in *Concerning Children,* and indicts motherhood as the ultimate human sacrifice:

> To put it in the last extreme, suppose the mother so utterly sacrifices herself to the child as to break down and die. She then robs the child of its mother, which is an injury. Suppose she so sacrifices herself to the child as to cut off her own proper rest, recreation, and development. She thus gives the child an exhausted and inferior mother, which is an injury to him. There are cases, perhaps, where it might be a mother's duty to die for her child; but, in general, it is more advantageous to live for him. The "unselfish devotion" of the mother we laud to the skies, without stopping to consider its effect on the child. This error is connected with our primitive religious belief in the doctrine of sacrifice,—one of those early misconceptions of a great truth.[11]

In contrast to mother's world, which symbolized death and martyrdom, father's world promised work, achievement, power. Charlotte's mother had placed two prohibitions upon her: She was to read no novels and to have no close friends. The first prohibition must have seemed incongruous in that Charlotte's father was a distinguished librarian, rising to be head of the San Francisco and Boston Public Library. Frederick Perkins, who "took to books as a duck to water," founded several influential newspapers and journals, introduced the decimal system of classification, and wrote a reference book called *The Best Reading* that became a standard work. Not only did his daughter carry on the father's achievements, she far exceeded them. She was an enormously prolific and successful writer, authoring the equivalent of 25 volumes of stories, plays, and verse. Her greatest single achievement was the writing, editing, and publishing of the *Forerunner,* a monthly magazine that lasted for seven years. *Women and Economics,* published in 1898, was translated into seven languages and went through seven English language editions. She wrote the first draft in 17 days, the second draft in 58 days. "To write was always as easy to me as to talk," she remarks, and her astonishing productivity would seem to indicate that she wrote and read effortlessly.

Nothing could be further from the truth. There were long periods of time when the act of writing or reading would throw her into black despair. To the end of her life she suffered from what she could diagnose only as a "weak mind." Often she could not read the easiest book or write the simplest letter. "When I am forced to refuse invitations, to back out of work that seems easy, to own that I cannot read a heavy book, apologetically alleging this weakness of mind, friends gibber amiably, 'I wish I had your mind!' I wish they had, for a while, as a punishment for doubting my word" (*The Living,* p. 98). No one could believe her mental distress nor the inexplicable nervous exhaustion that would cripple her mind and paralyze her will. "The natural faculties are there, as my books and lectures show. But there remains this humiliating weakness, and if I try to drive, to compel effort, the resulting exhaustion is pitiful" (*The Living,* p. 100). Nor did the self-torture long abate. She describes the landscape of her mind as a depleted library, bereft of the books so vital to its well-being:

> To step so suddenly from proud strength to contemptible feebleness, from cheerful stoicism to a whimpering avoidance of any strain or irritation for fear of the collapse ensuing, is not pleasant, at twenty-four. To spend forty years and more in the patient effort of learning how to carry such infirmity so as to accomplish something in spite of it is a wearing process, full of mortification and deprivation. To lose books out of one's life, certainly more than ninety per cent of one's normal reading capacity, is no light misfortune (*The Living,* p. 100).

"What is the psychology of it?" she asks mournfully. The answer, we suspect, lies in the library.

It is significant that twice in the autobiography she refers to the library as a symbol or symptom of the crippling psychological illness to which she was prone. "I say my mind is weak. It is precisely that, weak. It cannot hold attention, cannot study, cannot listen long to anything, is always backing out of things because it is tired. A library, which was once to me as a confectioner's shop to a child, became an appalling weariness just to look at" (*The Living,* p. 100). One page later she elaborates on the peculiar symptomatology of her illness. "For nearly all these broken years I could not look down an index. To do this one must form the matrix of a thought or word and look down the list until it fits. I could not hold that matrix at all, could not remember what I was looking for. To this day I'd rather turn the pages than look at the index." The autobiography reads like a Gothic horror story here; for the library, which had once enticed her as a confectioner's shop lures a hungry child, came to represent the feelings of betrayal and abandonment associated with her father's flight from the family into the world of the library and publishing. The price she paid for imitating her father's glorious male achievements was a lifetime of neurotic suffering, part of her paternal legacy. The father's distinguished professional career had included the introduction of the decimal system of classification. Years later his brilliant daughter found herself unable to read the index of a book.

Another symptom of her lifelong struggle against mental illness appears to be related to a childhood incident—the pain of correspondence. As a child she had pleaded with her absent father to write her letters. In the only letter from which she quotes in the autobiography, Charlotte implores him to write. First there is a request for money, then for personal news. "Please write a real long letter to me," the 12-year-old asks, repeating the request two sentences later. "I wish you would write to me often" (*The Living,* p. 22). In the same letter she complains that, whereas other people write to her brother, no one writes to her. She encloses two pictures in the hope that her father will reciprocate. Years later she found herself in the opposite position, dreading the letters sent to her by friends and admirers. She could not answer them. "Perhaps the difficulty of answering letters will serve as an illustration of the weakness of mind so jocosely denied by would-be complimenters":

> Here are a handful of letters—I dread to read them, especially if they are long—I pass them over to my husband—ask him to give me only those I must answer personally. These pile up and accumulate while I wait for a day when I feel able to attack them. A secretary does not help in the least, it is not the manual labor of writing which exhausts me, it is the effort to understand the letter, and make intelligent reply. I answer one, two, the next is harder, three—increasingly foggy, four—it's no use, I read it in vain, *I don't know what it says.* Literally, I can no longer understand what I read, and have to stop, with my mind like a piece of boiled spinach (*The Living,* p. 99).

The humiliating inability to answer her correspondence reflects a deep ambivalence toward a father who rejected his family to live quite literally in the library. The pattern of Charlotte's life consisted of escape from the woman's sanctuary of home and hearth into the father's exciting world of letters; but, no sooner did she achieve the success she had envisioned through dedication and hard work, than her neurotic suffering would return, driving her back to the mother's sickroom. She could not achieve success without imagining failure; to emulate father she had to abandon mother. The world of books and ideas remained antithetical to the world of people and emotions, and she could never integrate her paternal and maternal identifications. Her father remained impossibly aloof and uncaring. To recover from her breakdown, she left her husband and daughter to travel across the country to California, where she visited her father. He engaged a room for her and solemnly called upon her as if she were a distant acquaintance. She stayed for a few days and upon leaving politely extended an invitation to him. "If you ever come to Providence again I hope you will come to see me"; he replied: "Thank you, I will bear your invitation in mind" (*The Living,* p. 93). The offenses to which she confesses during her periods of mental illness were the identical crimes of which her father was guilty. "My forgetfulness of people, so cruel a return for kindness; an absentmindedness often working harm; many a broken engagement; unanswered letters and neglected invitations; much, very much of repeated failure of many kinds is due wholly to that continuing weakness of mind" (*The Living,* p. 102). Her father achieved success, fame, and independence but at the expense of love, responsibility, and loyalty. In fathering herself, she was tortured by the fear that she had to make the same sacrifice, with her husband and daughter as victims.

And her feelings toward mother? Filial loyalty prevented her from criticism, except when she describes the mother's rejection of the child's caresses. But even during this moment, when any other writer would have expressed righteous indignation and anger, she holds back, content to mythologize the mother's "heroic" determination to spare her child from future suffering. She could never admit that her mother was responsible for her own depression. As Patricia Meyer Spacks observes in *The Female Imagination,* "The force destroying beauty, hope, and love for her is in fact her mother, whose energy, as her daughter describes her, directs itself entirely toward rejection, suppression, denial."[12] Although she could not criticize her own mother, she could attack other mothers, as an amusing passage in the autobiography makes clear. Once, when she was feeling so ill that she should have been placed in a sanitarium, a brisk young woman greeted her with the words: "You don't remember me, do you?" Looking at her emptily, Charlotte "groped slowly about in that flaccid vacant brain of mine for some association." A memory arose. Speaking like a four-year-old child, she answers: "Why yes, I remember you. I don't like your mother." To the reader she adds: "It was true enough, but never in the world would I have said such a thing if I had been 'all there'" (*The Living*, pp. 101–102). She characterizes her behavior as "feeble-mindedness" bordering on "an almost infantile responsibility." Nevertheless, her rage toward mothers could not be totally repressed.

In fact, Charlotte Perkins Gilman spent a lifetime in critiquing motherhood. The attack was relentless. She condemned the cult of home and domesticity with a power that none of her contemporaries could rival. Many of the ideas that seemed so radical at the turn of the century are now taken for granted. She exposed the perniciousness of sex roles which confined women to housecleaning and babysitting, and she spoke out against the disastrous social and political consequences of the suppression of women's rights. At the heart of her attack was the worship of motherhood, "Matriolatry," as she bitterly called it. "Of all the myths which befog the popular mind," she writes in *The Home,* "of all false worship which prevents us from recognising the truth, this matriolatry is one most dangerous. Blindly we bow to the word 'mother'—worshipping the recreative processes of nature as did forgotten nations of old time in their great phallic religions."[13] Implicit in the last sentence is the aversion to sexuality that inevitably accompanies her attack. A more ferocious indictment of motherhood appears in *Women and Economics*. The shrillness of her language alerts us to the painful autobiographical elements she could not quite exorcise from the otherwise carefully reasoned argument:

> Human motherhood is more pathological than any other, more morbid, defective, irregular, diseased. Human childhood is similarly pathological. We, as animals, are very inferior animals in this particular. When we take credit to ourselves for the sublime devotion with which we face 'the perils of maternity,' and boast of 'going down to the gates of death' for our children, we should rather take shame to ourselves for bringing these perils upon both mother and child.[14]

To suggest that Charlotte Perkins Gilman's assault on home and motherhood originated from her own unhappy childhood, and that in attacking all mothers she was condemning her own mother, does not invalidate the prophetic truth of her ideas or the extent to which she reflected and shaped the growing women's movement. Nevertheless, we may question whether she was consciously aware of the early childhood events that influenced her writings. Carl Degler has noted the two central theses of *The Home*—that the "home crushed women" and that it was "dirty, inefficient, uninteresting and retrogressive." Yet, when he praises Gilman's book as a "model of the completely rationalistic analysis of an ancient human institution," he is underestimating the decisive role played by unconscious forces in shaping the tone and imagery of her attack.[15] Her opposition to the traditional family structure cannot be appreciated fully without an awareness of her own family matrix of maternal martyrdom and paternal abandonment. Nor can her account of madness in "The Yellow Wallpaper" be adequately understood without a recognition of her own struggle against mental illness and the obstacles she had to confront both in her personal and professional life. In exposing the "pathological" nature of human childhood, she was confessing both to her mother's failure and her own.[16] Poor mothering opened the gates of death to her, first as the innocent victim of her parents' union, then as the involuntary victimizer of her own daughter's childhood. Her final estimate of motherhood may be gleaned from the end of her book *Women and Economics*. Under the heading "Mother" and "Motherhood" appear her various indictments, with the appropriate page numbers: "criminal failure of," "a bad baby-educator," "result of servitude of," "not an exchangeable commodity," "disadvantages of," "deficiencies of," "the pathology of human," "unpreparedness for," "professions unsuitable to," "old methods of," "open to improvement," and "false perspective taught by primitive." These accusations are neatly arranged in a list appearing in—where else?— the Index. She was, finally, her father's daughter.

*   *   *

We are now almost ready to explore the details of Charlotte Perkins Gilman's breakdown, her experience with S. Weir Mitchell's "rest cure," and her fictional treatment of madness in "The Yellow Wallpaper." Her encounter with Mitchell takes on additional interest in light of the psychiatrist's fame as a novelist. Indeed, Mitchell's reputation as a psychiatrist and novelist was unsurpassed in his lifetime. Had he realized the implications of the therapeutic advice he gave to his then unknown patient— ". . . never touch pen, brush or pencil as long as you live"—he might have understood the personal and national calamity his psychiatry nearly wrought.

"Silas Weir Mitchell was almost a genius," E. Earnest begins in the Foreword to his book, "His contemporaries believed that he was one, an opinion Mitchell came to share."[17] Medical historians agree that he was the foremost American neurologist of his time. In 1874 he was unanimously elected as the first president of the American Neurological Association. For decades his medical treatises remained the standard textbooks on the subject: *Gunshot Wounds and Other Injuries of the Nerves* (1864), *Wear and Tear* (1871), *Injuries of Nerves and Their Consequences* (1872), *Fat and Blood* (1877), and *Doctor and Patient* (1888). His discovery of the nature of rattlesnake venom laid the foundation for important toxicological and immunological research. He was less a psychiatrist in the modern sense of the word than a neurologist, a "nerve doctor" to whom patients were referred suffering from mysterious motor and sensory disorders. "It was the neurologists rather than the psychiatrists who reintroduced 'physical' methods of treatment of psychiatric disorders; whereas the psychiatrists became more and more the explorers of personality reactions and the developers of methods of restoring patients to useful existence when the neurologists threw in the sponge."[18]

Mitchell's main contribution to neurology was the introduction into the United States of the "rest cure," also called the "Weir Mitchell Treatment." The rest cure consisted of prolonged rest in bed and isolation, overfeeding, and daily body massage. *Fat and Blood* contains a graphic description of the rest cure. "As a rule," notes Mitchell, "no harm is done by rest, even in such people as give us doubts about whether it is or is not well for them to exert themselves." His notion of rest contains little that a hypochondriacal patient would find attractive:

> To lie abed half the day, and sew a little and read a little, and be interesting as invalids and excite sympathy, is all very well, but when they are bidden to stay in bed a month, and neither to read, write, nor sew, and to have one nurse,—who is not a relative,—then repose becomes for some women a rather bitter medicine, and they are glad enough to accept the order to rise and go about when the doctor issues a mandate which has become pleasantly welcome and eagerly looked for.[19]

Normally the psychiatrist required the patient to remain in bed for six to eight weeks. During the first month, Mitchell did not allow her (he generally uses the female pronoun) to sit up, sew, write, or read. She cannot even use her hands except to brush her teeth. Although Mitchell does not use the word, the regimen is designed to "baby" the patient, to facilitate a total physical and emotional regression to the condition of infancy. ". . . the sense of comfort which is apt to come about the fifth or sixth day,— the feeling of ease, and the ready capacity to digest food, and the growing hope of final cure, fed as it is by present relief,—all conspire to make patients contented and tractable."[20]

The rest cure obviously worked on the symptoms of mental illness, not on the sources. At best, it could lead to a patient's temporary improvement. It was not psychotherapy: No effort was made to probe the dynamics of mental illness. Though Mitchell's rest cure coincided exactly with Anna O.'s talking cure, Freud's major discoveries were still several years away.[21] What seems most offensive about Mitchell's rest cure was its aim to make patients tractable. Most of the people he treated were women; those who did not passively submit to him provoked his ire. To his colleagues his treatment of women appeared protective and kind; to us his methods seem paternalistic and degrading. "Wise women choose their doctors and trust them," he writes in *Doctor and Patient*. "The wisest ask the fewest questions. The terrible patients are nervous women with long memories, who question much where answers are difficult, and who put together one's answers from time to time and torment themselves and the physician with the apparent inconsistencies they detect."[22] A nervous woman, he adds, "should be made to comprehend at the onset that the physician means to have his way unhampered by the subtle distinctions with which bedridden women are apt to trouble those who most desire to help them."[23] His portrait of the neurasthenic woman evokes an image of bitchy evil:

> I do not want to do more than is needed of this ungracious talk: suffice it to say that multitudes of our young girls are merely pretty to look at, or not that; that their destiny is the shawl and the sofa, neuralgia, weak backs, and the varied forms of hysteria,—that domestic demon which has produced untold discomfort in many a household, and, I am almost ready to say, as much unhappiness as the husband's dram. My phrase may seem outrageously strong, but only the doctor knows what one of these self-made invalids can do to make a household wretched. Mrs. Gradgrind is, in fiction, the only successful portrait of this type of misery, of the woman who wears out and destroys generations of nursing relatives, and who, as Wendell Holmes has said, is like a vampire, sucking slowly the blood of every healthy, helpful creature within reach of her demands.[24]

Ironically, both Mitchell and Charlotte Perkins Gilman agreed on the horror of this type of woman, and they even used similar metaphors of the "vampire" and "parasite" to describe her. But their agreement ended here. Mitchell aligned himself with the most conservative political and social positions in the country. He believed that women should not compete with men, intellectually or economically, and he maintained that women could not equal men in persistent energy or capacity for "unbroken brain-work." It would be better, he said, not to educate girls at all between the ages of 14 and 18 unless they were in unusually good health. ". . . our growing girls are endowed with organizations so highly sensitive and impressionable that we expose them to needless dangers when we attempt to overtax them mentally."[25] He did not worry about the dangers of undertaxing women.

Mitchell's other career was as a novelist. Although his fiction is almost entirely forgotten today, he was one of the most popular American novelists between 1885 and 1905. His Renaissance versatility prompted his contemporaries to view him as a Benjamin Franklin. A biographer notes that Mitchell's *Hugh Wynne* was compared to Thackeray's *Henry Esmond,* while his *Ode on a Lycian Tomb* was ranked with Milton's *Lycidas.* He translated the fourteenth-century poem *The Pearl* into modern verse, wrote a lively and controversial biography of George Washington, and created a children's story that went through 12 editions. Only after he established his medical reputation in the mid-1880s did he begin to write and publish fiction. He was 55 years old when his first novel, *In War Time,* was published in 1884. Other novels soon followed: *Roland Blake* (1886), *Characteristics* (1891), *Hugh Wynne* (1896), the immensely popular *Dr. North and His Friends* (1900), and *Westways* (1913), published one year before his death at the age of 85. In all there were 19 novels, several volumes of short stories, and three volumes of poetry. The bulk of Mitchell's art covers 6500 pages in the *Definitive Edition.*

Although Mitchell was obviously interested in psychiatric themes, he was not, oddly enough, a psychological novelist. Whether it was due to aristocratic restraint, neurological training, or simple incuriosity, he did not search very deeply for the psychological origins of his protagonist's conflicts and breakdowns. David Rein observes in *S. Weir Mitchell as a Psychiatric Novelist* that "in pursuing a psychological cause he was inclined to take a physiological direction."[26] Rein also remarks that, if one reads Mitchell's fiction in light of his psychiatric case studies, he is bound to be surprised and disappointed by what the novelist fails to include. "He created no characters exhibiting the more spectacular forms of hysterical illness such as he described in his medical writing."[27] Curiously, Mitchell makes a statement in *Doctor and Patient* that any psychoanalyst would endorse. "The cause of breakdowns and nervous disaster, and consequent emotional disturbances and their bitter fruit, are often to be sought in the remote past. He may dislike the quest, but he cannot avoid it."[28] This statement is untypical, however, of Mitchell's approach to character. Contrary to his own advice, he disliked the investigation into his patients' remote past and therefore avoided it. He remains silent on what we would consider today the root causes of mental illness—unempathic parents, identity problems, sexual conflicts, unconscious aggression.

Mitchell's aesthetic theory may be seen from this passage in *Doctor and Patient:* "The man who desires to write in a popular way of nervous women and of her who is to be taught how not to become that sorrowful thing, a nervous woman, must acknowledge, like the Anglo-Saxon novelist, certain reputable limitations. The best readers are, however, in a measure co-operative authors, and may be left to interpolate the unsaid."[29] Discretion and respectful vagueness should be the novelist's guiding principle. The psychiatrist had no desire to evoke medical realism in his fiction. "In older times the sickness of a novel was merely a feint to gain time in the story or account for a non-appearance, and the doctor made very brief show upon the stage. Since, however, the growth of realism in literary art, the temptation to delineate exactly the absolute facts of disease has led authors to dwell freely on the details of sickness."[30] Mitchell disapproved of those novelists interested in depicting illness and symptomatology. "Depend upon it," he exclaims, the modern novelist "had best fight shy of these chronic illnesses: they make queer reading to a doctor who knows what sick people are; and above all does this advice apply to death-beds."[31] Fortunately, not all novelists followed the doctor's orders here.

The basic facts of Charlotte Perkins Gilman's treatment with Mitchell come from two sources: a one-page article called "Why I Wrote the Yellow Wallpaper" published in a 1913 issue of *The Forerunner* and the chapter in her autobiography entitled "The Breakdown." Mitchell apparently never wrote about her in his psychiatric or fictional works. After suffering for about three years from a "severe and continuous nervous breakdown tending to melancholia—and beyond," she decided to visit Mitchell, "at that time the greatest nerve specialist in the country." She took the rest cure with the utmost confidence, prefacing the visit with a long letter in which she gave the history of the case in a way that a "modern psychologist would have appreciated." Mitchell thought the letter proved only self-conceit, perhaps because of what she called his prejudice against the Beechers. " 'I've had two women of your blood here already,' he told me scornfully." The psychiatrist seemed familiar with only two types of nervous prostration—that of the businessman exhausted from too much work and the society woman exhausted from too much play. He had difficulty in diagnosing her case although he did assure her there was no "dementia," only "hysteria." He ordered her to bed where she was fed, bathed, and rubbed. After about a month of the treatment he judged her cured and sent her home. She records his prescription along with her feelings at that time:

> "Live as domestic a life as possible. Have your child with you all the time." (Be it remarked that if I did but dress the baby it left me shaking and crying—certainly far from a healthy companionship for her, to say nothing of the effect on me.) "Lie down an hour after each meal. Have but two hours' intellectual life a day. And never touch pen, brush or pencil as long as you live" (*The Living*, p. 96).

She went home, followed his directions faithfully for three months, and nearly lost her mind. The mental agony was so unbearable that she would sit blankly, moving her head from side to side, to escape the pain. No physical pain was involved, not even a headache, "just mental torment, and so heavy in its nightmare gloom that it seemed real enough to dodge." Rejecting the psychiatrist's advice, she finally committed herself to work, work which is "joy and growth and service, without which one is a pauper and a parasite," thereby recovering a degree of her former health.[32]

Why did Mitchell's rest cure fail so miserably? The psychiatrist deified the worship of matriolatry which Charlotte Perkins Gilman feared and grew to despise. She was attempting to flee from the domestic prison of the mother's world—the parasitic world of abject dependency upon men, the depressing routine of endless drudgery, screaming babies, intellectual impoverishment, and helpless resignation. Mitchell's paternalistic therapy locked her into the mother's role, first by breaking her spirit and making her a baby again through the rest cure, then by imprisoning her with her own helpless baby. The rest cure could only deepen her psychic unrest; instead of helping her to accept the responsibilities of an adult or at least to understand her morbid fear of babies, Mitchell infantilized her further. His therapy deprived her of the opportunity to pursue her father's achievements and thus blocked her life-saving identification with the man who had fled from the home in quest of the magical world of ideas and books. Charlotte's health required neither childlike submission nor maternal self-sacrifice but the heroic challenge of Mitchell's own manly world. Two of the books she later wrote symbolize the direction of the therapy she needed: an escape from *The Home* in pursuit of *The Man-Made World*.

In contrast to Mitchell's dictum to return to her husband and presumably expand her family, Gilman chose the only form of pregnancy she could imagine—literary creation. From her agonizing labor with psychiatry was born "The Yellow Wallpaper." "It is a description of a case of nervous breakdown beginning something as mine did, and treated as Dr. S. Weir Mitchell treated me with what I considered the inevitable result, progressive insanity" (*The Living,* pp. 118–119). Midway through "The Yellow Wallpaper" the unnamed narrator refers to the psychiatrist to whom her physician-husband is threatening to send her. "John says if I don't pick up faster he shall send me to Weir Mitchell in the fall."[33] Clearly it is a threat. "But I don't want to go there at all. I had a friend who was in his hands once, and she says he is just like John and my brother, only more so!" ("The Yellow Wallpaper," p. 19). Gilman does not actually describe in detail her own encounters with her therapist, as later writers were to do—Doris Lessing, Joanne Greenberg, Philip Roth. There is little attempt to characterize the psychiatrist apart from naming him (though implicitly he is linked to the sinister husband). "The Yellow Wallpaper" represents an early and shadowy attempt to describe a psychiatrist in a work of fiction. As the therapist's role in the patient's healing process is expanded in later works, so, too, will be the depth of his or her characterization. Moreover, a therapy that involves no talking, as was the case with Mitchell's rest cure, can produce little characterization and dialogue.

Why, then, does Gilman name her psychiatrist at all? Probably for several reasons: the effort to establish medical authenticity, the willingness to acknowledge the autobiographical roots of the story, and the desire to recompense the doctor for his costly therapy. Far from suggesting the writer's flight from reality, or what Freud might call the neurotic's escape into fantasy, "The Yellow Wallpaper" prophesied the frightening outcome of Mitchell's psychiatry had the patient dutifully followed his advice. Gilman boldly reversed art and life: The eerie realism of "The Yellow Wallpaper" exposed the psychiatrist's rest cure as an evil fiction having nothing to do with reality.

It is interesting to compare the two accounts of mental illness in the autobiographical *The Living of Charlotte Perkins Gilman* and the fictional "The Yellow Wallpaper." There is no doubt about the greater truthfulness of art. The achievement of "The Yellow Wallpaper" lies in its ruthless honesty, accuracy, and power. Free from the constraints of hurting people in real life, the artist is free to imagine the unnerving details of her protagonist's story. In the autobiography, Gilman describes her husband as a patient and long-suffering man, the ideal spouse. She refers to his "unbroken devotion, his manifold cares and labors in tending a sick wife, his adoring pride in the best of babies . . ." (*The Living,* p. 97). Stetson becomes a husband less human than saintly, a heroic portrait like the one of Charlotte's mother. The following sentence is typical of her characterization of him. "He has worked for me and for us both, waited on me in every tenderest way, played to me, read to me, done all for me as he always does. God be thanked for my husband" (*The Living,* p. 88).

Gilman projects these qualities onto the narrator's husband in "The Yellow Wallpaper" but with a different emphasis. The husband displays solicitude but also incomprehension and insensitivity. Baffled by his wife's mysterious illness, he seems to aggravate the situation—indeed, she hints that he is responsible for her illness. "John is a physician, and *perhaps*— (I would not say it to a living soul, of course, but this is dead paper, and a great relief to my mind)—*perhaps* that is one reason I do not get well faster" ("The Yellow Wallpaper," pp. 9–10). The narrator's unconscious resentment of the husband momentarily surfaces here, allowing us to glimpse the truth. Nowhere in the autobiography is Gilman emboldened to voice a similar criticism, although that is the only inference a reader can draw. John's disbelief in the narrator's illness intensifies her suffering. "If a physician of high standing, and one's own husband, assures friends and relatives that there is really nothing the matter with one but temporary nervous depression—a slight hysterical tendency—what is one to do?" ("The Yellow Wallpaper," p. 10). He can urge only the platitudes of increased willpower and self-restraint. Whereas in her autobiography Gilman feels obligated to remain silent over her husband's role in her illness, in her art she can admit through the narrator to becoming "unreasonably angry" with him.

"The Yellow Wallpaper" also dramatizes the husband's prohibition against writing. "He says that with my imaginative power and habit of story-making, a nervous weakness like mine is sure to lead to all manner of excited fantasies, and that I ought to use my will and good sense to check the tendency. So I try" (pp. 15–16). Mitchell, we recall, had similarly prohibited his patient from writing. It is thus ironic that both the narrator's husband and Gilman's psychiatrist forbid their patients from the one life-saving activity, artistic creation. What proves therapeutic in Gilman's world is neither marriage nor psychiatry but art, and, when the narrator's husband deprives her of this activity in "The Yellow Wallpaper," her fate is sealed.

Opposed to the liberating world of art is the enslaving domesticity of the home. The woman remains isolated in the nursery of an old ancestral house, a "hereditary estate," that is part of an obscure national heritage. "The Yellow Wallpaper" foreshadows Gilman's more extensive assault on domesticity culminating several years later in *The Home*. Filled with "hedges and walls and gates that lock," the house reflects the alienation of nineteenth-century America, with its cult of domesticity and worship of children. The husband and wife live in the nursery at the top of the house, with barred windows for little children. The narrator's perception of the nursery slowly changes. In the beginning it seems like a big airy room to her, but after two weeks it becomes claustrophobic in its heavy bedstead, barred windows, and gate at the head of the stairs. The imagery identifies the home as a prison without escape. The woman rarely leaves the nursery, not even to look at her baby who is housed on a lower floor.

The most horrifying feature of the house, and the source of the story's great power, is the yellow wallpaper in the nursery. "It is dull enough to confuse the eye in following, pronounced enough to constantly irritate and provoke study, and when you follow the lame uncertain curves for a little distance they suddenly commit suicide—plunge off at outrageous angles, destroy themselves in unheard of contradictions" (p. 13). The wallpaper becomes a projection screen or Rorschach test of the narrator's growing fright. The chaotic pattern symbolizes her own unheard emotional contradictions: her need for security yet fear of dependency and entrapment; her acceptance of the American Dream (marriage, family, house) amidst the nightmare of reality; her passive acceptance of duty but rising protest. The narrator's perception of the wallpaper's suicide foreshadows her own self-destructive behavior. Indeed, the wallpaper functions as a Poesque black cat or telltale heart, the object upon which her madness is focused. There is a difference, however, between Poe's stories and Gilman's. The reader of "The Black Cat" or "The Tell-Tale Heart" soon learns that the first person narrator is crazy and can thus distance himself from the homicidal character. The reader of "The Yellow Wallpaper," by contrast, is far more sympathetic to the heroine and is almost seduced into sharing her increasingly psychotic point of view. The old ancestral house and its vision of America are enough to drive almost anyone mad. Yet, what we see in "The Yellow Wallpaper" is not simply an oppressive environment or a deranged woman but an organic connection between setting and character. Madness does not spring from nowhere. The story's richness lies in its ability to yield multiple meanings and points of view—psychological, sociological, historical. The house has rich symbolic meaning in "The Yellow Wallpaper": the domestic imprisonment of nineteenth-century women, the madness of the Mitchell rest cure, the isolation of rural America, the repression of the body. ("The human body as a whole is pictured by the dream-imagination as a house and the separate organs of the body by portions of a house," Freud tells us in *The Interpretation of Dreams.*[34])

Although critics have admired the complex symbolism of the yellow wallpaper, they have not sufficiently explored the relationship between the inanimate pattern and the narrator's mind, in particular, her fear of children. The violence of her imagery is striking. "There is a recurrent spot where the pattern lolls like a broken neck and two bulbous eyes stare at you upside down" (p. 16). Many of the images she uses to describe the wallpaper appear to be related to the "dear baby" whom she cannot bear to be with. Her only reference to the baby implies relief that "it" does not occupy the upstairs nursery where she and her husband live. "If we had not used it, the blessed child would have! What a fortunate escape! Why, I wouldn't have a child of mine, an impressionable little thing, live in such a room for worlds" (p. 22). True, she expresses love and concern for the baby, yet she is also solicitous toward her husband, and we know that behind this surface calm lies unconscious aggression. Is she similarly hostile toward her baby?

If so, we suspect this was not part of the author's conscious intentions. There is too much evidence, however, to ignore. The new mother's description of the wallpaper evokes an image of an insatiable child who seems to be crawling everywhere, even into the nursery which remains her only sanctuary. The unblinking eyes stare at her as if the baby demands to be nursed or held. "I get positively angry with the impertinence of it and the everlastingness. Up and down and sideways they crawl, and those absurd, unblinking eyes are everywhere" (p. 16). Her next free association is revealing. "I never saw so much expression in an inanimate thing before, and we all know how much expression they have! I used to lie awake as a child and get more entertainment and terror out of blank walls and plain furniture than most children could find in a toy-store" (pp. 16–17). Even as she renders the child into an inanimate object and consequently distances herself from its needs, the lifeless wallpaper assumes the characteristics of an angry child who grows increasingly demonic. She literally cannot escape from the baby because her imagination has projected it onto the landscape of her bedroom. Inanimate one moment and human the next, the baby evokes contradictory emotions within her—both tenderness and resentment. The baby also reminds the anxious mother of her own infancy. She tells us significantly that, when she was a child, the love and attention she craved were met with blank walls—just as her virtually motherless child meets with blank walls downstairs. The implication is that her present illness originates from an early childhood abandonment similar to the one her own child is encountering.

Tight-lipped about her own child, she speaks harshly about other children. The furniture in her bedroom had been scarred by the children of the previous owners. "I never saw such ravages as the children have made here" (p. 17). The room itself has been the victim of the children's vicious attack. The floor is "scratched and gouged and splintered," the plaster "is dug out here and there," and the great heavy bed "looks as if it had been through the wars" (p. 17). Later she returns to the oral imagery: "How those children did tear about here! This bedstead is fairly gnawed!" (p. 34).

The narrator's dilemma, then, is to escape from the voracious children who threaten to devour her body, just as they have gnawed upon the room. And indeed the other sub-pattern in the wallpaper reveals the figure of a strange woman skulking about the room. There is no doubt about her identity. "And it is like a woman stooping down and creeping about behind that pattern" (p. 22). By daylight the figure appears subdued, but at night she begins to crawl around. In the narrator's words, "You think you have mastered it, but just as you get well underway in following, it turns a back-somersault and there you are. It slaps you in the face, knocks you down, and tramples upon you. It is like a bad dream" (p. 25).

Interpreted according to dream logic, the wallpaper recreates the mother's inescapable horror of children and her regression to infancy. The pattern and sub-pattern mirror her terrified identification with the abandoned child and abandoning mother. The roles of victim and victimizer become hopelessly blurred. Who is escaping from whom? In fleeing from the image of the baby, the mother confronts its presence in the wallpaper located, appropriately enough, in the nursery of the old ancestral home.

Here, the mysteries of birth, marriage, procreation, and death are played out in her imagination. The decision to isolate herself from her baby betrays the contradictory wish to protect and harm it. The child's identity remains ambiguous, both innocent and evil. The wallpaper imagery evokes an appalling eruption of subhuman life, uncontrolled reproduction. It is not just one organism but an endless stream of growth. "If you can imagine a toadstool in joints, an interminable string of toadstools, budding and sprouting in endless convolutions—why, that is something like it" (p. 25). From the psychoanalytic point of view of object relations, the narrator cannot separate her identity from the baby's: She is both the hysterical mother searching for freedom and the insatiable child demanding attention. The angry child within the adult seems responsible for the mother's illness. Nor is escape possible from the sickening yellow substance that oozes from the wall. Its mysteriousness contributes to the indefinable sexual menace lurking throughout the house and penetrating the woman's body. The movement of "The Yellow Wallpaper" is suggestive of the wife's efforts to avoid sexual defilement, beginning with her abortive attempt to sleep in the room downstairs, with its single bed, and ending with the outraged husband's cry for an ax to break into the room where she has barricaded herself.

Despite the pre-Freudian world of "The Yellow Wallpaper" and Charlotte Perkins Gilman's subsequent condemnation of psychoanalysis, the story is startlingly modern in its vision of mental illness.[35] Anticipating Freudian discoveries, the story suggests that psychological illness worsens when it is not acknowledged as real and that the rest cure is antithetical both to the talking cure and to the therapeutic value of artistic creation. Moreover, "The Yellow Wallpaper" portrays mental illness as originating from childhood experiences. Unlike Breuer's "Fräulein Anna O.," "The Yellow Wallpaper" shows the social and political as well as psychological implications of madness. Gilman rejects not psychotherapy, which Freud was introducing, but pseudotherapy, which has always been with us. Gilman's narrator is one of the first in a long line of benumbed and bedeviled patients in American literature who search desperately for understanding but who, following the accepted medical advice of the time, lose their mind.

Gilman's achievement is that she is able to transform her narrator's bad dream into superb art. And here is where the literary brilliance of "The Yellow Wallpaper" comes into play. Although the narrator in the fictional story recalls the author's self-portrait in the autobiographical *The*

Living of Charlotte Perkins Gilman, "The Yellow Wallpaper" contains a shape and unity consistent with the demands of art. The difference between fiction and life lies in the greater narrative distance and formal control of art. In her autobiography, Gilman remains mystified by the origin and meaning of her breakdown; she eloquently describes the pain and confusion of a lifetime of neurotic suffering, but she is finally baffled by its significance. She depicts her illness as a digression to a life of struggle and work, rather than as a continuing conflict that compelled her to invent constructive solutions to the problems of her age.

Fiction empowered her to rework sickness into art. Dr. Mitchell had diagnosed her illness as hysteria not dementia; "I never had hallucinations or objections to my mural decorations," Gilman parenthetically adds in "Why I Wrote The Yellow Wallpaper."[36] But, for artistic reasons, she decided to confer deadly psychosis on her narrator. Although the woman begins with what her husband calls "temporary nervous depression—a slight hysterical tendency" (p. 10), she grows steadily insane until her situation is hopeless. In the beginning of the story, the narrator and the author are indistinguishable, but as the former becomes terminally insane, the latter remains firmly in control of the narrative, allowing the symbolic power of the wallpaper rather than authorial intrusions to expose the full horror. At the end, the narrator and author are worlds apart. Indeed, the technique of narrative distance and point of view is handled more confidently in "The Yellow Wallpaper" than in *The Bell Jar,* where Plath seems unable to imagine a character who is neither menacing nor locked into the bell-jar vision. We may continue to search for a full explanation of the bizarre events in "The Yellow Wallpaper," but this is secondary to witnessing a mind in the process of self-extinction. Moreover, there is no specific moment in the story when we can say that the narrator has suddenly become mad. It happens mysteriously, imperceptibly. The crackup is frighteningly appealing because it allows her to defy and mock a husband who has taken on the role of a jailor. Gilman succeeds admirably in sketching a man whose dialogue sounds well meaning but whose actions assume a diabolical quality. He prowls around the house in an effort to thwart his wife's escape. At the end he gains entry into his wife's bedroom, but then, in a cunning reversal of roles, he faints at her feet while she creeps over him.

The early readers of "The Yellow Wallpaper" keenly felt the story's horror, but not all of them were favorably impressed. William Dean Howells (who was a friend of both Gilman and Mitchell) admired the story.[37] However, when he submitted it to *Atlantic Monthly* for publication, Gilman received a rejection from the editor with an indignant note: "I could not forgive myself if I made others as miserable as I have made myself!" (*The Living*, p. 119). When it was published, the story provoked anger and ill will. A physician sent a protest to the Boston *Transcript* complaining of the "morbid fascination" of "The Yellow Wallpaper" and questioning whether stories of such "deadly peril" should be published at all. On the positive side, another physician wrote to Gilman to praise "The Yellow Wallpaper" for its delicacy of touch and correctness of portrayal. "From a doctor's standpoint, and I am a doctor, you have made a success. So far as I know, and I am fairly well up in literature, there has been no detailed account of incipient insanity." Thus began the claims and counterclaims for the story's psychiatric authenticity. In the same letter to Gilman, the physician wondered about her experience with mental illness. "Have you ever been—er—; but of course you haven't." Her reply was that she had gone as far as one could go and still return (*The Living*, pp. 120–121).

The real purpose of writing "The Yellow Wallpaper," she admits in her autobiography, was to reach S. Weir Mitchell and "to convince him of the error of his ways." Without denying the genuineness of her didactic aim, we can also speculate on the motive of revenge toward the psychiatrist who forbade her to touch pen, brush or pencil again for as long as she lived—which might not have been very long. "The Yellow Wallpaper" thus came into existence against the orders of a psychiatrist who almost blocked the development of a major American thinker and writer.[38] In writing "The Yellow Wallpaper" Gilman became a psychiatrist herself in the advice she offered to the nervous women who might be reading her story. She was not only shrinking her former psychiatrist to his proper size but also offering her readers the sympathy and understanding that the medical establishment could not give to women. There is justifiable pride in Gilman's voice when she speaks about the story's impact upon patients and doctors alike. "The little book is valued by alienists and as a good specimen of one kind of literature. It has to my knowledge saved one woman from a similar fate—so terrifying her family that they let her out into normal activity and she recovered."[39] Best of all was the story's effect on Mitchell. Although she had sent him a copy of "The Yellow Wallpaper" and received no acknowledgment, many years later she discovered that the famous specialist had indeed read the story and, as a result of it, altered his treatment of nervous illness. "If that is a fact," she boasts, "I have not lived in vain" (*The Living,* p. 121). As she concludes in "Why I Wrote the Yellow Wallpaper," "It was not intended to drive people crazy, but to save people from being crazy, and it worked."[40] No work of literature can accomplish more than this.

THREE

Tender Is the Night:
Fitzgerald's
A Psychology for Psychiatrists

Method of Dealing with Sickness Material

  (1) Read books and decide the general type of case
  (2) Prepare a clinical report covering the years 1916–1920
  (3) Now examine the different classes of material selecting not too many things
for copying
      (1) From the sort of letter under E
      (2) From the sort of letter under F
      (in this case using no factual stuff)
      (3) From the other headings for atmosphere, accuracy and material being
      careful not to reveal basic ignorance of psychiatric and medical training
      yet not being glib. Only suggest from the most remote facts. <u>Not</u> like
      doctor's stories.
          Must avoid Faulkner attitude and not end with a novelized Kraft-
      Ebing—better Ophelia and her flowers.

    F. Scott Fitzgerald, notes to *Tender Is the Night.*[1]

F. SCOTT FITZGERALD'S *Tender Is the Night* (1934) remains one of the most profoundly moving psychiatric case studies in American literature and, like Charlotte Perkins Gilman's "The Yellow Wallpaper," was born from the novelist's anguished experience with mental illness. Whereas Gilman was dramatizing her own breakdown and treatment with the Weir Mitchell rest cure, however, Fitzgerald was writing about his wife's psychiatric history and the extent to which he felt himself doomed through marriage. Zelda's mental illness was not only the "catalytic agent" in Fitzgerald's approach to *Tender Is the Night,* as Matthew J. Bruccoli has observed about the numerous revisions of the manuscript, but her tragedy "provided the emotional focus of the novel."[2] The Fitzgerald story was a double tragedy involving Zelda's incurable schizophrenia and Scott's worsening health and premature death at the age of 44. Their celebrated marriage in 1920 had collapsed just one decade later when Zelda suffered her first psychotic breakdown and her husband's alcoholism was destroying his work. Their final years involved a dark solitary journey which starkly contrasted the hope and excitement of their early marital life. Like Charlotte Perkins Gilman, the Fitzgeralds turned to literature in an effort to transmute suffering into enduring art; but unlike the author of "The Yellow Wallpaper," they could not achieve lasting therapeutic relief from their private horrors. Before exploring the vision of psychiatry in *Tender Is the Night*, we may review the major medical events Fitzgerald relied upon for the "sickness" material in his novel.

Their lives have been eloquently documented for us by their biographers. The three major books on Scott Fitzgerald are by Arthur Mizener, Andrew Turnbull, and most recently Matthew J. Bruccoli, and the life history of Zelda Fitzgerald by Nancy Milford.[3] The publication of Scott Fitzgerald's voluminous correspondence—more than 3000 letters have been located, perhaps half the number he actually wrote—has given us a more complete documentation of his life than that of any other twentieth-century American writer.[4]

We have a great deal of information about the factual details surrounding Zelda's breakdowns and psychiatric institutionalizations, although we know little about the inner causes of her madness. From the time of her first breakdown in 1930 to her death in 1948 in a fire which killed her and eight other female patients in Highland Hospital in Asheville, North Carolina, Zelda was in and out of psychiatric institutions. In all there were more than half a dozen, including Prangins Clinic on Lake Geneva in Switzerland, where she was treated by Dr. Oscar Forel, son of the world-renowned Swiss psychiatrist Auguste Forel. There was also the Phipps Clinic of Johns Hopkins University Hospital in Baltimore, where she was treated by the eminent American psychiatrist Dr. Adolf Meyer and others.[5] In a 1930 letter to Zelda's parents, Fitzgerald summarizes the diagnosis offered by Dr. Forel and the consulting psychiatrist, Dr. Eugene Bleuler, the world's leading authority on schizophrenia (which he actually named). In Fitzgerald's words, Bleuler "recognized the case (in complete agreement with Forel) as a case of what is known as *skideophranie,* a sort of borderline insanity, that takes the form of a double personality. It presented to him *no feature that was unfamiliar* and no characteristic that puzzled him."[6] Medically, the diagnosis would now make no sense in that schizophrenia is a psychosis, while "double personality," also called *Grande Hystérie,* is a neurosis. According to Fitzgerald, Bleuler was optimistic about the possibility of Zelda's recovery:

> He said in answer to my questions that over a field of many thousands of such cases three out of four were discharged, perhaps one of those three to resume perfect functioning in the world, and the other two to be delicate and slightly eccentric through life—and the fourth to go right down hill into total insanity.[7]

It is difficult to know whether the original diagnosis of Zelda's illness was incorrect or whether Fitzgerald was overly optimistic with Zelda's parents. In a letter to Nancy Milford in 1966, Dr. Forel offered a different account of his early diagnosis of Zelda. "The more I saw Zelda, the more I thought at the time: she is neither a pure neurosis (meaning psychogenic) nor a real psychosis—I considered her a constitutional, emotionally unbalanced psychopath—she may improve, never completely recover."[8] During her worst crises, she was delusional and paranoid. Several times she attempted to kill herself, by self-strangulation, among other means, and on at least one occasion Fitzgerald rescued her from certain death when she tried to throw herself in front of an approaching train. She also suffered from asthma attacks, colitis, and severe eczema. Forel acknowledged that he had not been able to psychoanalyze her for fear of disturbing the precious little stability she had. In a 1932 letter to her husband, Zelda wrote that "Freud is the only living human outside the Baptist Church who continues to take man seriously."[9] (Surely that was the only time Freud has been compared to that institution.) Nevertheless, there is no evidence to suggest that she received psychoanalytically oriented psychotherapy. It was not until two decades later that psychoanalysts were able to modify Freudian ideas to the treatment of psychoses, as Dr. Frieda Fromm-Reichmann successfully demonstrated in her work with Joanne Greenberg and others.

It was during 1932 when Zelda was hospitalized in the Phipps Clinic at Johns Hopkins after suffering a second breakdown that she began writing her autobiographical novel *Save Me the Waltz.*[10] She completed the manuscript in six weeks. A curious and uneven novel with powerful descriptive passages, *Save Me the Waltz* dramatizes a young woman's frantic commitment to become a ballet dancer in an effort to preserve her delicate psychic balance. In retrospect, the sheer intensity of her quixotic commitment to ballet (she began to study when she was too old to achieve real success) was probably a symptom of her later collapse.[11] Although *Save Me the Waltz* does not employ the apparatus of the psychiatric case study of *Tender Is the Night,* it is clearly about Zelda's breakdown and her criticisms of her celebrity husband. She even intended to name the heroine's husband "Amory Blaine" after the autobiographical hero of her husband's novel *This Side of Paradise.* Fitzgerald was incensed when he read the manuscript, which he felt not only attacked him personally but also exploited material he was using for *Tender Is the Night.* After the publication of *Save Me the Waltz,* Fitzgerald was again distressed by her plan to write a novel dealing with insanity—probably based on the Russian dancer Nijinsky's madness. According to Bruccoli, "Since Fitzgerald was treating psychiatric material in his novel, he charged that she was again poaching and insisted that she could not write about this subject until his novel was published."[12]

In *Some Sort of Epic Grandeur,* Bruccoli includes a revealing transcript of a bitter conversation in 1933 between the Fitzgeralds in the presence of Zelda's psychiatrist, Dr. Thomas Rennie. The angry discussion centered on Fitzgerald's demand that Zelda give up writing. He accuses her of being a "third-rate writer and a third-rate ballet dancer" who is "broaching at all times on my material just as if a good artist came into a room and found something drawn on the canvas by some mischievous little boy." He also refers to an agreement among her two psychiatrists at Johns Hopkins and himself over the inadvisability for her to write anything about her experience with insanity. His anger toward Zelda's fiction appears to have been motivated more by the jealous writer in him, fearful of his wife's literary success, than by the solicitous husband concerned for his wife's delicate mental health. Zelda's psychiatrist supported him:

> *Dr. Rennie:* We know that if you are writing a personal, individual study on a psychiatric topic, you are doing something that we would advise you right along not to do and that is not to write anything personal on psychiatric material.
>
> *Zelda:* Well, Dr. Rennie, didn't we discuss some time ago and didn't I say to you that I was miserable because I could not write short things? . . . And didn't we decide that it would perhaps be better to go on and write long things?
>
> *Dr. Rennie:* But didn't I also say very emphatically and haven't I said all along that for you to dabble with psychiatric material is playing with fire and you ought not to do it, and didn't you promise me really once that you would put the psychiatric novel away for five

years and would not touch it in that period? (*Some Sort of Epic Grandeur,* p. 350).

The circumstances were different, but it is hard not to recall the similar psychiatric advice Dr. Mitchell had given to Charlotte Perkins Gilman nearly four decades earlier: ". . . never touch pen, brush or pencil as long as you live." Zelda had to endure some of the other restrictions against which Gilman protested vigorously, including a strict regimen of rest and isolation and a husband who was often insensitive to her situation. And yet it would be unfair to place all the blame on Fitzgerald. The Fitzgerald correspondence affirms their love and concern for each other, and no one can study their lives without feeling deep sympathy for them. Their bad treatment of each other was followed by sincere penitence, grief, and renewed determination to make their marriage work. In 1932 Fitzgerald withdrew his objections to the publication of *Save Me the Waltz,* and he even wrote supportive letters on her behalf to his publisher, Max Perkins. Moreover, he later admitted that artistic creation had a therapeutic effect on Zelda by helping her to deal with her illness. He conceded to a psychiatrist in 1933 that writing the novel had improved her health. "She grew better in the three months at Hopkins where it was allowed and she grew apathetic in the two months at Craig House [a sanitarium in Beacon, New York] where she was continually disuaded."[13] Nevertheless, Zelda published no other novels.

Despite Fitzgerald's enormous difficulty in writing *Tender Is the Night,* he never seriously doubted the propriety of using Zelda's psychiatric experiences in his own novel. This was a writer's privilege, he felt, even if it intruded upon the private life of his family—as it certainly did. Indeed, he incorporated into his novel passages from letters that Zelda had actually written to him from the Swiss sanitarium in 1930.[14] In researching the material for *Tender Is the Night,* Fitzgerald rejected the idea of seeking psychiatric help for himself, although it had been suggested to him. According to Bruccoli, Zelda's psychiatrist, Dr. Meyer, "regarded the Fitzgeralds as a joint case and insisted that Zelda would not be cured unless Fitzgerald gave up drinking. The psychiatrist referred to him as 'a potential but unwilling patient.' But Fitzgerald refused to undergo psychiatric treatment; he thought that it would damage his writer's equipment."[15] Despite the popular fear that therapy destroys artistic creativity, as *Equus* and scores of other literary works claim, it is extremely unlikely that psychiatry would have harmed Fitzgerald's talents or anyone else's—

unless of course the advice was to give up writing. Far from availing himself of psychiatric help, Fitzgerald drifted in the opposite direction. In a letter to Zelda written after 1932, he rhetorically asked: "Is there not an idea in your head sometimes that you must live close to the borders of mental trouble in order to create at your best?"[16] He seems to have been describing himself as well.

The autobiographical elements of *Tender Is the Night* thus posed special difficulties for Fitzgerald. The objectivity needed to write the novel required emotional detachment, lest lucidity give way to self-pity; also, the clinical framework of the story demanded a degree of psychiatric authenticity. Apart from his experience with the psychiatrists who were treating Zelda and the clinical books he read on the subject, Fitzgerald had little help in creating the case study used in the novel. He knew the success of *Tender Is the Night* depended upon his ability to create a convincing psychiatrist and a credible therapeutic cure. Did the novelist succeed in finding a "method of dealing with sickness material?"

Fitzgerald believed so, and Zelda's psychiatrists agreed. To the editor of *Scribner's Magazine* he wrote, before pride gave way to embarrassment: "The psychiatrist at Hopkins says that not only is the medical stuff in [Part] II accurate but it seems the only good thing ever written on psychiatry and the—oh what the hell. Anyhow, that part's O.K."[17] Dr. Forel sent Fitzgerald a congratulatory letter from Switzerland in which he praised the novelist's ability to transpose reality into the world of fiction. Admitting that he was always on the defensive when he saw laymen approach subjects as complicated as psychiatry, Forel expressed relief that Fitzgerald had been accurate in his observations of Prangins Clinic.[18] This judgment was confirmed in a review presumably written by a practicing psychiatrist in *The Journal of Nervous and Mental Disease* in 1935. "For the psychiatrist and psychoanalyst the book is of special value as a probing story of some of the major dynamic interlockings in marriage. . . ." After praising Dick Diver's awareness of the "unconscious implications of the transference," the reviewer concludes by lauding *Tender Is the Night* as an "achievement which no student of the psychobiological sources of human behavior, and of its particular social correlates extant today, can afford not to read."[19]

In later years, however, critics have challenged Fitzgerald's understanding of psychiatry in *Tender Is the Night.* A brief discussion of the review appeared in 1961, written by a critic with a literary rather than psychiatric point of view. "It is not at all certain—or even likely—" that contempo-

rary students of psychology "will come away from a reading of Fitzgerald's novel with the same degree of enthusiasm voiced by the first of their
number in 1935."[20] The most authoritative judgment comes from Frederick J. Hoffman, who argues that the novel "is far more an account of
illusions clumsily and pathetically supported than it is a psychiatric ap-
praisal of modern ills." His conclusion emphasizes Fitzgerald's imperfect
understanding of psychiatry:

> There seems to have been something almost frantic about the writ-
> ing of *Tender Is the Night*, as though he were taking note of his own
> excesses in the course of describing those of his creatures. The novel
> is therefore a document of his own declining morale, his own suffer-
> ing, above all his terrible fright over the spectacle of his descent. Psy-
> chiatry was a part of his experience at the time; it became a part of
> his explanation of the world of the 1920s as he came then to see it.
> In so doing, he used his knowledge of psychiatry freely, as a layman
> would who had somehow to know enough about its functioning to
> comprehend what was happening to him and to the world in which
> he had always lived.[21]

With the exception of Hoffman, no literary critic has discussed one of
the most significant psychological questions in *Tender Is the Night*: Fitzgerald's use of the transference love relationship between Dr. Dick Diver
and Nicole Warren. Nor does Hoffman devote more than one sentence
to its importance. Of the few literary critics who use the term "transference," none defines the word in its precise psychoanalytic context.[22] Our
discussion of *Tender Is the Night* must therefore raise the following questions. How knowledgeable is Fitzgerald of the theoretical and clinical intricacies of transference love? Why does his psychiatrist hero catastroph-
ically disregard medical ethics to become romantically involved with his
schizophrenic patient? And why—contrary to autobiography—does Fitzgerald allow Nicole to recover, completely and permanently, from her severe mental illness while the novelist betrays a rigidly deterministic attitude toward Dick Diver's downfall?

*   *   *

Why is Dick, to begin with, a psychiatrist? He is not a psychiatrist in
the earlier versions of the story. Initially, the hero was a young Holly-
wood technician with the unlikely name Francis Melarkey; in a later version he became a famous motion-picture director called Lewellen Kelly.[23]
Autobiographical reasons doubtlessly influenced Fitzgerald's decision to

change the profession of his hero, but cultural reasons also came into play. In the four decades separating *Tender Is the Night* from "The Yellow Wallpaper" psychiatry had achieved an enormous national and international popularity, and, like the other writers in our study, Fitzgerald fully exploits the mythic possibilities. As with so many others of his generation, Fitzgerald shared in the myth of the psychiatrist as a modern magician, a miracle worker dwelling in the psychic landscape of life. It would be natural for the novelist to tap the imaginative possibilities of a psychiatrist hero. In addition to Dick Diver's impeccable credentials—a graduate of Yale College, Johns Hopkins Medical School, and an Oxford Rhodes Scholar—he is invested with the omniscience and omnipotence of a Godlike healer.

What are Dick's motives for becoming a psychiatrist? Fitzgerald offers a few intriguing clues here. In the beginning of Part II, he develops Dick's apparent good health and invulnerability, but the language becomes increasingly discordant, suggesting the hidden weaknesses and tensions that may have shaped his decision to become a psychiatrist. "Dick got up to Zurich on less Achilles' heels than would be required to equip a centipede, but with plenty—the illusions of eternal strength and health, and of the essential goodness of people; illusions of a nation, the lies of generations of frontier mothers who had to croon falsely, that there were no wolves outside the cabin door" (p. 117). The shrill tone and syntactical awkwardness foreshadow the instability of Dick's life: his illusion of health is exposed as a cruel delusion. His journey from the romantic French Riviera, in the beginning of the novel, to the obscure New York town, in the end, reflects the loss of strength and hope. But what exactly is the mystery of his fatal Achilles heel, and why does his idealism seem perilously close to cynicism? There is an instability about his identity that always threatens to force him out of character, both professionally and personally. Dick enigmatically hints at a counterphobic motive behind the decision to become a psychiatrist. "The weakness of this profession is its attraction for the man a little crippled and broken. Within the walls of the profession he compensates by tending toward the clinical, the 'practical'—he has won his battle without a struggle" (pp. 137–138).

Does this puzzling explanation imply that Dick Diver has become a psychiatrist to exorcise his own psychic wolves and demons? The evidence points in this direction. After observing that "a man is vulnerable only in his pride, but delicate as Humpty-Dumpty once that is meddled with," Fitzgerald adds: "Doctor Diver's profession of sorting the broken shells of another sort of egg had given him a dread of breakage" (p. 177). But is Dick's vulnerability the cause or effect of his work as a psychiatrist? The answer is essential if we are to determine Fitzgerald's vision of psychiatry in *Tender Is the Night* and the extent to which he interprets Dick as a victim of his profession. Fitzgerald's comment to Edmund Wilson supports the view that Dick has been victimized by his work. "I thought that, since his choice of a profession had accidentally wrecked him, he might plausibly have walked out on the profession itself."[24] By contrast, we suspect that Dick has become a psychiatrist to hold in check the inner forces ultimately leading to his ruin.

There is no ambiguity, however, surrounding Dick's preference for the theoretical over the clinical side of psychiatry. As opposed to the capable but unimaginative resident pathologist Franz Gregorovius, Dick is the brilliant theoretician—though regrettably we never glimpse his theorizings. Fitzgerald regards the clinical side of psychiatry as barely one step above nursing, and even when Franz persuades Dick to open a clinic with him, Franz uses the enticing argument that the experience will be good for his writing. "Consider it, Dick. . . . When one writes on psychiatry, one should have actual clinical contacts. Jung writes, Bleuler writes, Freud writes, Forel writes, Adler writes—also they are in constant contact with mental disorder" (p. 176).

Indeed, the emphasis upon Dick's career as the author of celebrated psychiatric texts suggests that he is less a physician than a writer—a writer of psychological breakdowns, as was Fitzgerald himself. To carry the similarity further, Fitzgerald uses the names of two of Zelda's psychiatrists (three, if we include Jung, whom Fitzgerald considered calling into the case), thus intimating the novelist's clinical attitude toward his wife's madness. The identification between Fitzgerald and his authorial writer is striking. It is also artistically dangerous in that the identification belies the incentive of increased narrative distance Fitzgerald hoped to achieve by making his protagonist into a physician instead of, like himself, a famous novelist. Indifferent to psychiatry, Dick invests all his energy and time into authorship. First there is *A Psychology for Psychiatrists,* with its ambitious if redundant title. Nicole observes that "the little book is selling everywhere—they want it published in six languages" (p. 159). Fitzgerald elaborates on Dick's writing career:

> On his two long tables, in ordered confusion, lay the materials of his book. Volume I, concerned with Classification, had achieved some

success in a small subsidized edition. He was negotiating for its reis-
sue. Volume II was to be a great amplification of his first little book,
A Psychology for Psychiatrists. Like so many men he had found that he
had only one or two ideas—that his little collection of pamphlets now
in its fiftieth German edition contained the germ of all he would ever
think or know (p. 165).

Interestingly, Fitzgerald confuses the highly limited and specialized demand for psychiatric textbooks with the greater commercial appeal of
novels. Few if any psychiatric studies have achieved the instant popularity
of *A Psychology for Psychiatrists,* including most of Freud's books. Yet, it
is biographically revealing that Fitzgerald projects his own fear of artistic
sterility onto his protagonist and then overcompensates by exaggerating
the popularity of Dick's books. The fear that a writer may have "only one
or two ideas" haunted Fitzgerald's life; Rosemary remarks that "Nobody
wants to be thought of forever for just one picture" (p. 24). Apart from
Dick there are two other artist figures in *Tender Is the Night,* the ruined
musician Abe North and the mediocre novelist Albert McKisco.

Another confirmation of Dick's identity as an artist is that his vocabulary derives not from the profession of psychiatry but from the world
of art—cinema, theatre, literature. "You and Rosemary aren't really alike,"
he tells Mrs. Speers, "The wisdom she got from you is all molded up into
her persona, into the mask she faces the world with. She doesn't think;
her real depths are Irish and romantic and illogical" (p. 164). Baby Warren's appreciation of his verbal energy reflects his gift for language, narration, pacing. "That's something you do so well, Dick. You can keep a
party moving by just a little sentence or a saying here and there. I think
that's a wonderful talent" (p. 216). Whenever Dick refers to a book, it
invariably involves a novel instead of a psychiatric text or case study. He
mentions Lewis Carroll, Jules Verne, Michael Arlen, and the author of
Undine. And like the novelist, Dick has a gift for setting: Abe North tells
Rosemary that Dick "invented" the French Riviera.

Dick's psychiatric expertise, by contrast, is less than convincing. One
of Fitzgerald's problems is the banality of Dick's medical advice to his
patients. Whenever the psychiatrist speaks, he sounds more like a mor-
alist than a therapist. "I won't lecture to you," Dick says to Nicole, and
then proceeds to do just that. ". . . it's only by meeting the problems of
every day, no matter how trifling and boring they seem, that you can
make things drop back into place again" (p. 185). Despite his immodest
aim to be a "good psychologist—maybe to be the greatest one that ever

lived" (p. 132), he remains indifferent to the distinctions in terminology among psychology, psychiatry, and psychoanalysis. Nor does Fitzgerald explain the dynamic basis of Dick's psychiatry except to note his avoidance of hypnosis. Yet, even here, the explanation is curious. Dick avoids hypnosis not because of its failure to bring repressed material to the surface but because of its perceived theatricality.

The question of psychiatric authenticity also occurs in Dick's understanding of Nicole's mental illness. Fitzgerald's description of Nicole's illness evokes Dr. Forel's diagnosis of Zelda. "She's a schizoid—a permanent eccentric," Dick tells Baby Warren, "You can't change that" (p. 151). Forel had considered Zelda "a constitutional, emotionally unbalanced psychopath—she may improve, never completely recover." So too does Dick's characterization of Nicole as a "schizophrene" or "split personality" recall Dr. Bleuler's diagnosis of Zelda. Fitzgerald cannot be faulted for the imprecision of Zelda's eminent psychiatrists; yet there is a deep pessimism toward Nicole's intellectual equipment that surprises us in light of her apparent recovery at the end of the novel. "A 'schizophrène' is well named as a split personality—Nicole was alternately a person to whom nothing need be explained and one to whom nothing *could* be explained. It was necessary to treat her with active and affirmative insistence, keeping the road to reality always open, making the road to escape harder going" (p. 191). The definition of Zelda's mental illness in *Tender Is the Night* implies that self-discovery and psychological insight are of little value in effecting any therapeutic cure. Fitzgerald views the psychiatrist as one who actively intervenes to prevent the patient from lapsing into insanity rather than one who, as Freud argues, adopts a more passive but analytical role as interpreter of the patient's symptoms and resistance to recovery. Despite the case-study approach of the novel, the descriptions of the sanitariums evoke an image of the rest cure rather than the talking cure. Patients and psychiatrists do not talk to each other; Nicole never seems to do anything. Her recovery at the end remains a mystery to us.

Toward Freud, Fitzgerald reveals a contradictory attitude of vague admiration and suspicion. Franz's statement that Dr. Dohmler had given Nicole "a little Freud to read, not too much, and she was very interested" (p. 131) conveys Fitzgerald's limited tolerance for psychoanalytic theory. Dick's decision to attend the "Psychiatric Congress" in Berlin confirms the novel's strong hostility toward psychotherapy. Fitzgerald satirizes, in the following passage, the motives of psychiatrists, condemning what he perceives to be the theatricality, hollowness, greed, and ineffectuality of the profession:

> He had no intention of attending so much as a single session of the congress—he could imagine it well enough, new pamphlets by Bleuler and the elder Forel that he could much better digest at home, the paper by the American who cured dementia praecox by pulling out his patient's teeth or cauterizing their tonsils, the half-derisive respect with which this idea would be greeted, for no more reason than that America was such a rich and powerful country (p. 194).

Dick's developing cynicism toward his own profession is primarily moral rather than intellectual; in the same paragraph he mocks the "dozens of commercial alienists with hang-dog faces, who would be present partly to increase their standing, and hence their reach for the big plums of the criminal practice, partly to master novel sophistries that they could weave into their stock in trade, to the infinite confusion of all values." Although Bleuler and Forel are spared from Fitzgerald's most withering criticism, the entire profession is condemned in the most categorical terms. It is as if the author of *A Psychology for Psychiatrists* has become disgusted with the entire field and is ready to denounce his own colleagues in a single jeremiad.

Oddly enough, Fitzgerald does not confront the one psychoanalytic concept that offers the greatest insight into Dick's catastrophic fall: transference love. The word "transference" appears three times in *Tender Is the Night,* each time in a clinical context. Referring to Nicole's growing emotional attachment to Dick, Franz exclaims: "It was the best thing that could have happened to her . . . a transference of the most fortuitous kind" (p. 120). Dr. Dohmler later uses the word in a similar context, warning Dick about the dangers of emotional involvement with his patient. But the tone of Dohmler's remarks suggests that, unlike Franz, he is more qualified in his endorsement of the term. ". . . this so-called 'transference' . . . must be terminated. Miss Nicole does well indeed, but she is in no condition to survive what she might interpret as a tragedy" (p. 139). The word also appears near the end of the novel when Nicole, falling in love with Tommy Barban, tries to detach herself from her husband. Feeling her old love for Dick reawakening, she "struggled with it, fighting him with her small, fine eyes, with the plush arrogance of a top dog, with her nascent transference to another man, with the accumulated resentment of years . . ." (p. 301). Additionally, the word appears three times in Fitzgerald's notes to *Tender Is the Night:* the hero " 'transfers' to himself and she falls in love with him, a love he returns"; "Only her transference to him saves her"; and "His hold is broken, the transference is broken. He goes away. He has been used by the rich family and cast aside."

References to transference confirm that Fitzgerald is using the term not in its dynamic psychoanalytic context—the projection of essentially primitive experiences and emotions onto other people—but in the more general sense of an absorption or incorporation of one individual by another in a shifting love relationship. Despite the mechanistic connotations, Fitzgerald's use of transference does coincide with the psychoanalytic definition to the extent that Dick cannot maintain emotional detachment from entangling human alliances. Dick's integrity and wholeness are constantly threatened by the "egos of certain people, early met and early loved," who undermine his independence:

> His love for Nicole and Rosemary, his friendship with Abe North, with Tommy Barban in the broken universe of the war's ending—in such contacts the personalities had seemed to press up so close to him that he became the personality itself—there seemed some necessity of taking all or nothing; it was as if for the remainder of his life he was condemned to carry with him the egos of certain people, early met and early loved, and to be only as complete as they were complete themselves. There was some element of loneliness involved—so easy to be loved—so hard to love (p. 245).

The language intimates a desire to love so intensely as to both engulf and be engulfed. Although the passage implies that the people who are oppressing Dick are figures from the present—Nicole, Rosemary, Abe North—psychoanalytic theory would suggest that these relationships are repetitions of much earlier relationships dating back to Dick's past. The pattern recalls the pre-Oedipal stage of the mother-child relationship when the form of nurturing creates the archetypes of identifications, the basis of future interaction. Dick's insatiable quest for love paradoxically drains him, rendering him broken and incomplete. Emotional involvement proves disastrous because it threatens the distinction between self and other. The loved object always becomes menacing to Dick because, in absorbing others, he finds himself absorbed, depleted, violated. At the center of the male-female relationship in *Tender Is the Night* looms the spectre of transference, with its ominous implications of the repetition-compulsion principle. Of all the characters who endanger Dick, it is Nicole whom Fitzgerald accuses of sapping his hero's strength and creativity. "He could not watch her disintegrations without participating in them" (pp. 190–191). To understand further the meaning of Dick's fear of absorption in *Tender Is the Night* we must explore the psychoanalytic theory of transference.

*   *   *

Freud's most complete definition of transference is given in *An Autobiographical Study,* published nine years before Fitzgerald's novel. Since it is impossible to improve upon Freud's description, we may quote it in full:

> In every analytic treatment there arises, without the physician's agency, an intense emotional relationship between the patient and the analyst which is not to be accounted for by the actual situation. It can be of a positive or of a negative character and can vary between the extremes of a passionate, completely sensual love and the unbridled expression of an embittered defiance and hatred. This *transference*— to give it its short name—soon replaces in the patient's mind the desire to be cured, and, so long as it is affectionate and moderate, becomes the agent of the physician's influence and neither more nor less than the mainspring of the joint work of analysis. Later on, when it has become passionate or has been converted into hostility, it becomes the principal tool of the resistance. It may then happen that it will paralyse the patient's powers of associating and endanger the success of the treatment. Yet it would be senseless to try to evade it; for an analysis without transference is an impossibility.[25]

Transference love arises when the patient becomes infatuated with the analyst. The love affair is fraught with dangers, Freud observes, and he proceeds to elaborate upon them as if he were indeed writing *A Psychology for Psychiatrists*. "This situation has its distressing and comical aspects, as well as its serious ones. It is also determined by so many and such complicated factors, it is so unavoidable and so difficult to clear up, that a discussion of it to meet a vital need of analytic technique has long been overdue. But since we who laugh at other people's failings are not always free from them ourselves, we have not so far been precisely in a hurry to fulfill this task."[26]

How is transference love related to a patient's resistance toward therapeutic cure? Precisely because the motivation behind this love and resistance to a cure is suspect. The motivation includes the patient's need to reassure herself of her irresistibility in the eyes of the analyst, the effort to make the analyst fall in love with her to lessen his authority and power, and the unconscious attempt to exaggerate her readiness for sexual surrender, so that when the love affair ends disastrously, as it inevitably must, the patient's original repressions will be rationalized or vindicated.

How, then, should the analyst confront a patient's love? Each alternative, Freud says, has its difficulties. Rarely do circumstances allow the analyst to marry his patient, even if he desires to, and besides, this would result in the breakdown of the therapeutic relationship—as *Tender Is the Night* illustrates. If the analyst breaks off therapy to defuse the affair, as Breuer did with Anna O., then this too would signal the collapse of the treatment. For the analyst to carry on an illicit affair with his patient would be unthinkable, both for reasons of morality and professional dignity. "If the patient's advances were returned it would be a great triumph for her, but a complete defeat for the treatment." What then must the analyst do?

He must, argues Freud, resist succumbing to whatever unconscious tendencies toward countertransference may be lurking within him. "He must recognize that the patient's falling in love is induced by the analytic situation and is not to be attributed to the charms of his own person; so that he has no grounds whatever for being proud of such a 'conquest', as it would be called outside analysis." Freud's papers on clinical technique, from which these passages come, are a model of lucidity, modesty, and probity—and in light of his warnings it is doubly ironic that so few fictional analysts have heeded his advice.

Once the analyst is in control of himself, he may direct the development of the patient's transference love:

> He must take care not to steer away from the transference-love, or to repulse it or to make it distasteful to the patient; but he must just as resolutely withhold any response to it. He must keep firm hold of the transference-love, but treat it as something unreal, as a situation which has to be gone through in the treatment and traced back to its unconscious origins and which must assist in bringing all that is most deeply hidden in the patient's erotic life into her unconsciousness and therefore under her control. The more plainly the analyst lets it be seen that he is proof against every temptation, the more readily will he be able to extract from the situation its analytic content. The patient, whose sexual repression is of course not yet re-

moved but merely pushed back into the background, will then feel
safe enough to allow all her preconditions for loving, all the phantasies springing from her sexual desires, all the detailed characteristics of her state of being in love, to come to light; and from these
she will herself open the way to the infantile roots of her love (*Standard Edition,* Vol. XII, p. 166).

Yet ambiguities continue to surround transference love. How does it
differ, for example, from genuine love? Freud's answer is surprising, for
he acknowledges the overlapping between the two forms of love. Although resistance is an element in transference love, it does not *create* the
love. Rather, the resistance exploits it. There may also be an element of
reality behind transference love, although the artificiality of the analytic
setting invariably colors the patient's feelings toward the therapist. Moreover, while observing that infantile determinants characterize transference love, Freud concedes that these elements also exist within genuine
love. "It is true that the [transference] love consists of new editions of
old traits and that it repeats infantile reactions. But this is the essential
character of every state of being in love. There is no such state which
does not reproduce infantile prototypes." What is different between the
two forms of love, Freud points out, is that transference love is provoked
by the analytic setting, intensified by clinical resistance to recovery, and
less concerned with reality than genuine love. The patient certainly cannot be expected to see this distinction, but the analyst must; otherwise,
the gravest consequences will occur.

One final observation must be noted. Freud insists that analytic treatment be conducted in a state of "abstinence," which is not limited to a
narrow sexual context. Insofar as it was a frustration that made the patient ill, "It is possible to observe during the treatment that every improvement in his condition reduces the rate at which he recovers and diminishes the instinctual force impelling him towards recovery."[27] Favorable
external changes in the patient's life may give the impression of effecting
a therapeutic cure while in reality retarding psychological progress. "Cruel
though it may sound, we must see to it that the patient's suffering, to a
degree that is in some way or other effective, does not come to an end
prematurely." The analysis should be carried out, Freud emphasizes, *"as
far as is possible, under privation—in a state of abstinence."* What example
does he cite of external changes endangering the complete recovery of a
half-cured patient? Apart from bodily infirmity, an unhappy marriage poses

a particularly severe danger. For by gratifying unconscious guilt, the un-happy marriage becomes a form of self-punishment in which the patient's neurosis takes on new symptoms or substitute gratifications.

*   *   *

One of the ironies of *Tender Is the Night* is that, had Dr. Dick Diver fully understood the psychoanalytic dynamics of transference love, he would have indeed been successful in writing the definitive *A Psychology for Psy-chiatrists*. And he would have immeasurably aided Nicole Warren's ther-apeutic recovery, succeeding where greater psychiatrists had failed. In-stead, Dick never does solve the meaning of Nicole's illness. His own research into psychology never progresses beyond *Studies on Hysteria*, which offers intriguing parallels to *Tender Is the Night*. Both Dr. Breuer and Dr. Diver find themselves in the presence of hysterical women who project their incestuous fantasies upon father figures. To be sure, Breuer's hasty retreat from Anna O.'s advances is in contrast to Dick's ambivalent sur-render to Nicole; yet, both women appear to be acting out imagined or real seduction fantasies. And in both case studies, treatment fails largely because of the psychiatrists' unawareness of the link between transference love and resistance. Dick's blindness to transference love deprives him of the most powerful instrument for Nicole's recovery. Worse, it ensnares him in a marital relationship built upon the similar psychological weak-nesses of husband and wife.

Dick's sin is that he is too loving and loved for his own good. No-where is Fitzgerald more successful than in portraying the complexity of his hero's dark love, with its lust for power and possessiveness. There is something terrible about Dick's need for adulation, a narcissistic hunger that can never be fulfilled. "Save among a few of the tough-minded and perennially suspicious, he had the power of arousing a fascinated and un-critical love. The reaction came when he realized the waste and extrava-gance involved. He sometimes looked back with awe at the carnivals of affection he had given, as a general might gaze upon a massacre he had ordered to satisfy an impersonal blood lust" (p. 27).

Dick's "impersonal blood lust" evokes the blood imagery surrounding Nicole and the "bathroom mystery" in which an unspeakable act is hinted at but never described. Waste, self-indulgence, and futility characterize Dick's carnivals of affection. His desire to "give a really *bad* party" iden-tifies him as the archetypal Fitzgerald hero. The motives behind the party call into question his attitude toward life. "Maybe we'll have more fun

this summer but this particular fun is over. I want it to die violently instead of fading out sentimentally—that's why I gave this party" (pp. 37–
38). The comment betrays his similar feelings about marriage: the need
to end love relationships with a bang, not a whimper; the assumption
that relationships with violent endings are less "sentimental" than those
which slowly fade or remain loyal and permanent; the hint, later magnified, of Dick's self-destructive tendencies. Fitzgerald returns to the dark
side of Dick's character, though the murky syntax and strained psychological interpretation do little to illuminate the problem. "And Lucky Dick
can't be one of these clever men; he must be less intact, even faintly destroyed. If life won't do it for him it's not a substitute to get a disease,
or a broken heart, or an inferiority complex, though it'd be nice to build
out some broken side till it was better than the original structure"
(p. 116). Oddly enough, when Fitzgerald does attempt to analyze—or
psychoanalyze—Dick's problem, the narrative distance breaks down and
the explanation only deepens the mystery. The novelist seems as bewildered and defenseless here as his character. Nor does Dick's next thought
cast further light on his situation. "He mocked at his reasoning, calling
it specious and 'American'—his criteria of uncerebral phrase-making was
that it was American. He knew, though, that the price of his intactness
was incompleteness." Cannot one be both intact and complete?

   Whence arises Dick's overwhelming need to love and be loved? The
novel offers a few clues. At the core of his unconscious feelings toward
psychotherapy lies a rescue fantasy in which he desires to cure his patients through love, not self-awareness. Hence the impossibility of clinical detachment from his female patients, even those who are strangers to
him. "Yet in the awful majesty of her pain he went out to her unre-
servedly, almost sexually. He wanted to gather her up in his arms, as he
so often had Nicole, and cherish even her mistakes, so deeply were they
part of her" (p. 185). The love from which his identifications spring contains both regressive and compulsive features, violating the necessary space
between self and other and compelling Dick's romantic attachments to
conspicuously younger women. Dick's natural protectiveness toward
women evokes his paternal nature, yet he fails to accept responsibility for
awakening sexual desires he cannot possibly fulfill. Paradoxically, there is
an infantile quality to his "father complex"; his paternalistic power over
women is one of the most dangerous aspects of his countertransference.
For example, he receives a letter from a woman recently released from his
clinic which "accused him in no uncertain terms of having seduced her

daughter, who had been at her mother's side during the crucial stage of the illness" (p. 187). Dick had "in an idle, almost indulgent way" kissed her, though he goes no further than this despite the girl's desire to deepen the affair.

Indeed, the pattern of Dick's romantic relationships invariably involves a much younger woman. *Tender Is the Night* opens in 1925, with Dick ten years older than his wife—a substantial difference (he is 34)—and 16 years older than Rosemary, with whom he later has an affair. Two additional incidents confirm the age inequality. When he is brought to the Italian courtroom at the end of Part II to face the charge of assaulting one of the carabinieri, the crowd confuses him with a native of Frescati who has raped and slain a child. Himself out of control, Dick yells: "I want to make a speech. . . . I want to explain to these people how I raped a five-year-old girl. Maybe I did—" (p. 235). In the penultimate paragraph of the novel, Fitzgerald hints at Dick's entanglement with a young woman who worked in a grocery store. According to Bruccoli, Fitzgerald had specified in the serial version of the novel that the clerk was 18, but he deleted her age in the final form of the story.[28] Dick's history thus seems to be a depressing pattern of recurring affairs with women half his age and younger.

Consequently, Dick has taken a prolonged "leave of abstinence"—to use the "Freudian slip" that Franz makes on two separate occasions. Franz has become increasingly critical of his colleague's decision to marry Nicole, and when Dick announces his plan to take a leave from the clinic—ostensibly to allow his troubled marriage to heal—Franz responds: "You wish a real leave of abstinence?" Without commenting upon the meaning of the slip of tongue, Dick replies: "The word is 'absence' " (p. 194). Franz's remark proves prophetic in that Dick's leave from home sets into motion his renewed and altered relationship with Rosemary. Later, Franz makes the identical verbal slip. "Why not try another leave of abstinence?" to which Dick again mechanically replies: "Absence" (p. 256). Franz's error continues to be prophetic; this time Nicole proves unfaithful.

These Freudian slips, which Fitzgerald deliberately structures into the novel, emphasize Dick's inability to control the transference love relationship arising both in and outside of therapy. They also suggest the incestuous nature of his love for Nicole and the others. Several critics have pointed out the importance of incestuous love in *Tender Is the Night*. In an essay published in 1952, D. S. Savage draws a parallel between Devereux Warren's incestuous relationship with his daughter Nicole and Dick

Diver's unconscious recapitulation of that earlier experience. "Since Nicole's condition is the consequence of physical seduction at the hands of her own father, it is impossible to evade the conclusion that Dick is unconsciously implicated in the very incestuous regression which is at the root of her psychopathic (schizophrenic) condition."[29] Robert Stanton published a similar interpretation in 1958. Exploring the subject of "Daddy's Girl," the film in which Rosemary stars, Stanton defines the incest motifs in *Tender Is the Night.* "The term 'incest-motifs' may seem ill-chosen at first, since most of these passages allude, not to consanguineous lovers, but to a mature man's love for an immature girl."[30] The critic draws three conclusions at the end of his essay. "First, these motifs function literally as one result of Dick's relationship to Nicole; they are symptoms of his psychological disintegration. Second, they both exemplify and symbolize Dick's loss of allegiance to the moral code of his father. Finally, by including such details as *Daddy's Girl* as well as Dick's experience, they symbolize a social situation existing throughout Europe and America during the Twenties."[31]

Other critics have confirmed these conclusions.[32] Biographical evidence also supports Fitzgerald's interest in incestuous love. "There is no help for it," D. S. Savage remarks, "what emerges most patently from Fitzgerald's biography is his character as a mother's boy."[33] He also cites Arthur Mizener's observation in *The Far Side of Paradise:* "His mother's treatment was bad for a precocious and imaginative boy, and as Fitzgerald confessed to his daughter after she had grown up, 'I didn't know till 15 that there was anyone in the world except me. . . .' "[34]

Incestuous love was obviously very much on Fitzgerald's mind not only in *Tender Is the Night* but in his story "Babylon Revisited," published in 1931, three years before the novel. Generally acknowledged as his finest short story, "Babylon Revisited" (whose title D. S. Savage suggests is an elided form of "Baby-land Revisited") is about a 35-year-old reformed alcoholic who seeks to regain custody of his 9-year-old daughter Honoria. The erotic dialogue between father and daughter is unmistakably incestuous; they are lovers in word if not deed. Charlie Wales, who has been indirectly responsible for the death of his wife, is a penitent sinner, yet the past returns to haunt him. Aware of the dangers of incestuous love, he is nevertheless devastated by the failure to regain Honoria at the end of the story. There is one passage that strikingly foreshadows the theme of "Daddy's Girl" in *Tender Is the Night:* "The present was the thing—work to do and someone to love. But not to love too much, for he knew the injury that a father can do to a daughter or a mother to a son by attaching them too closely: afterward, out in the world, the child would seek in the marriage partner the same blind tenderness and, failing probably to find it, turn against love and life."[35] It is not known whether Fitzgerald's ten-year-old daughter Scottie perceived this incestuous element in the story, but he did point out to her that she was the basis for the fictional daughter.[36]

There is a darker side to incestuous love. The notes to *Tender Is the Night* demonstrate that Fitzgerald had originally intended the story to deal with the subject of matricide, with the title *The Boy That Killed His Mother*. He must have felt terribly ambivalent about the subject. He began working on the matricide theme in 1925, discarded it in 1929, returned to it again in 1930, and finally abandoned it. Although he omitted the overt matricide element from *Tender Is the Night,* he did not entirely succeed in disguising the misogyny that underlies the story. In perceiving Nicole and Rosemary as images of "Daddy's Girl," Dick views them and the "Amazonian" Baby Warren as part of a conspiracy to drain his creativity and emasculate him. Dick's submerged hostility toward women may be interpreted, according to the dynamics of ego psychology, as a turning around or denial of incestuous love. Matricide and misogyny come into existence when sexuality and aggression are fused together, usually as a defense against incestuous love. The result is an intolerable ambivalence toward women—which exactly defines Dick's attitude toward the women in his life.

Fitzgerald's critics have been reluctant to acknowledge the presence of misogyny in his fiction, although they do concede that women are dangerous to his male characters. Matthew J. Bruccoli voices a representative opinion here. "Fitzgerald created a procession of female destroyers of men, but his judgment was not misogynistic. His women—even at their most destructive—are warmly attractive."[37] Yet misogyny, of course, can exist alongside of heroine worship. If Dick is only partly aware of the incestuous implications of his acting out, he is blind to his fear and mistrust of women. There are simply too many passages reflective of Dick's—and Fitzgerald's—anger toward women:

> Baby Warren shifted her knees about—she was a compendium of all the discontented women who had loved Byron a hundred years before, yet in spite of the tragic affair with the guards' officer there was something wooden and onanistic about her (pp. 151–152).

> Women are necessarily capable of almost anything in their struggle for survival and can scarcely be convicted of such man-made crimes as "cruelty" (p. 163).

> It would be hundreds of years before any emergent Amazons would ever grasp the fact that a man is vulnerable only in his pride, but delicate as Humpty-Dumpty once that is meddled with—though some of them paid the fact a cautious lip-service (p. 177).

> . . . the American Woman, aroused, stood over him; the clean-sweeping irrational temper that had broken the moral back of a race and made a nursery out of a continent, was too much for him (p. 232).

Fitzgerald can condemn Albert McKisco as a pretentious writer and Tommy Barban as a brutal soldier without condemning all men; but, by contrast, his attack on Baby Warren and to a lesser extent Mary North, Rosemary, and Nicole is generalized to include all women. The distinction is important. Even during the depths of Dick's self-degradation, Fitzgerald reminds us of the husband's anguish for his wife and the tragic consequences of a psychiatrist's love for his patient. Nicole, in contrast, can harden herself to Dick. Unlike him, she begins to "slight that love, so that it seemed to have been tinged with sentimental habit from the first. With the opportunistic memory of women she scarcely recalled how she had felt when she and Dick had possessed each other . . ." (p. 300).

Compared to Dick, all the women in *Tender Is the Night* remain harder, less vulnerable, armorial. The name he secretly whispers to himself—"Lucky Dick, you big stiff" (p. 116)—gives way to Fitzgerald's fear of unmanly softness as his hero drifts toward a nosedive. Indeed, Dick's nose actually is broken by a policeman, suggesting symbolic castration. Dick's name also has a phallic connotation; as one critic has pointed out about Fitzgerald, "in a fit of adolescent bravado he has consequently christened his hero with a name whose slang meaning amply conveys the author's contempt for softness."[38] And Leslie Fiedler has noted the fluid and shifting sexual distinctions in *Tender Is the Night,* including the inversion of roles. "Indeed, the book is shot through with a thematic playing with the ambiguity of sex: Dick Diver makes his first entrance in a pair of black lace panties, and homosexuals, male and female, haunt the climaxes of the novel."[39] Fitzgerald implies that between the time Dick met and married Nicole, and his acquaintance with Rosemary, his "spear had been blunted" (p. 201). The embodiment of phallic hardness in the novel is Rosemary's mother, whose last name—"Speers"—betrays the women's capture of an increasingly limp Dick.

Moreover, there is a curious coincidence behind the "Mary" element of three characters: Rosemary, who sees life from a rose-colored point of view; Mary North, whose successful remarriage after the death of her first husband arouses Fitzgerald's uneasiness; and Maria Wallis, who shoots to death an Englishman. Along with Nicole and Baby Warren, these women serve as a variation on the theme of Mary Magdalene, though without achieving final redemption. Dick becomes what Fitzgerald calls in the notes to *Tender Is the Night* a "spoiled priest," pursuing and pursued by the "legendary *promiscuous* woman."[40]

Fitzgerald's attitude toward Nicole fluctuates between sympathy and criticism. Although obviously a portrait of Fitzgerald's wife, Nicole—unlike Zelda—has been sexually traumatized by her father's advances. In inventing this detail, the novelist had difficulty in deciding whether it was rape or seduction. In the notes to the novel he views the incest with her father as nothing less than a rape: "at fifteen she was raped by her own father under peculiar circumstances—work out." In the novel, however, Nicole consents to sexual intercourse. The change is obviously significant in that now she must assume partial responsibility for the act, along with the consequent blurring of innocence. What Fitzgarald thus imagined initially as a rape now becomes Nicole's acting out of an infantile seduction scene. Yet Fitzgerald could have gone one step further by completely eliminating the objective basis of Nicole's seduction. If she had only imagined seduction, the novelist would have had to deal with her wishes and fears, and the extent to which her imagination had distorted reality into mental illness. This was precisely what Freud had to confront when he reluctantly gave up his seduction theory—the belief that his neurotic patients were actually seduced by their fathers—in favor of the idea that they only imagined incestuous acts.[41] Psychical reality need not correspond to objective reality, Freud taught us; fantasized seduction can seem as real as if it actually happened. We may question Fitzgerald's implication that the incest directly precipitated Nicole's schizophrenia. Indeed, she hardly appears schizophrenic at all. Unlike the female patients of other fictionalized psychiatric case histories—the heroines of "The Yellow Wallpaper," *The Bell Jar, I Never Promised You a Rose Garden*—Nicole rarely seems mentally ill to us and never psychotic except for perhaps a few moments. We certainly do not receive an inside account of her madness. The few symptoms she manifests suggest hysteria and obsession compulsion, especially during the "bathroom mystery."

However obscure the bathroom mystery must remain, it appears to have something to do with Nicole's menstruation, seduction, and horror of blood-stained sheets. Her swaying back and forth beside the bathtub may also hint at masturbation. Nicole seems to be obsessed with "blood lust" (Fitzgerald's simile to describe Dick's power to arouse a fascinated and uncritical love): the blood on the sheets of the dead black man, the blood from Dick's broken nose, and the menstrual blood of Rosemary when she and Dick make love for the first time, all seem thematically to coalesce around the bathroom scene. The entire drama has a play-within-a-play quality, reproducing the symbols and symptoms of Nicole's psychic conflict. Fitzgerald evokes a theme of the rites of passage through the expression "What time is it?" which becomes a major leitmotif in Part I. According to Freud, behind every neurotically inhibited activity lies an instinctual wish; Nicole's seduction fantasy evokes dread and desire. The hysteria during the bathroom scene may reflect the emotions accompanying her incestuous relationship with her father. Nicole's love for Dick has its source in her tangled feelings toward her father; but whereas she allows the father to seduce her, she reverses the situation with her psychiatrist. Despite Nicole's horror of sexuality, she proves to be the aggressor with Dick. It is she who is seducing him. Dick's command—"Control yourself"—becomes ironic in that he too conspires in the incestuous regression. The impossibility of purgation may be suggested in the "dirty bathtub water" scene in Part III, in which the childen appear implicated in the evil.

Nicole's desertion of Dick for Tommy Barban raises the question of the motives behind her present affair: Do these motives differ from those behind her attraction toward Dick when she was his patient? That is, is there an element of resistance in her transference love? She enters into her affair with Barban quite calculatingly, unlike the indecision and guilt with which Dick begins his affair with Rosemary. Before Nicole can commit herself irrevocably to the affair, she does a great deal of rationalizing, as Fitzgerald makes clear:

> Nicole did not want any vague spiritual romance—she wanted an "affair"; she wanted a change. She realized, thinking with Dick's thoughts, that from a superficial view it was a vulgar business to en-

ter, without emotion, into an indulgence that menaced all of them.
On the other hand, she blamed Dick for the immediate situation, and
honestly thought that such an experiment might have a therapeutic
value (p. 291).

Nicole's reasoning includes the desire both to hurt her husband and to
release herself from his power. Because she allies herself with the morally
hollow Barban (whose name suggests his barbarian qualities), we lose
sympathy for her. Why then does she commit herself to a man she does
not love? Barban offers her the possibility of rescue from an increasingly
destructive husband. She senses that the new union will complete the
therapeutic cure initiated by her preceding rescuer. The affair with Barban thus allows her to end the enforced dependency upon another man
and to exact a fitting revenge for his marital infidelity.

Although Fitzgerald recognizes the complex motives underlying Nicole's relationship to Barban, there is little evidence to suggest the novelist's awareness of her similar motives for loving Dick. This is not to
reduce Dick's generous character to Barban's, nor to debase her love for
Dick, but to suggest that Nicole's psychological needs dictate the nature
of her relationships with men. This returns us to the element of resistance behind her transference love for Dick. It is disingenuous for Fitzgerald to tell us that Nicole is thinking with Dick's thoughts in the passage above. Nicole's motives for pursuing Barban do not seem very
different from her initial pursuit of Dr. Dick Diver in the Swiss sanitarium: to effect a change in her life and to exert her sexual attractiveness
over a man. To this extent, Nicole has not changed at all—she is thinking
not Dick's thoughts but her own. In another sense, however, Nicole is
Fitzgerald's own creation, quite apart from her indebtedness to Zelda's
biography. Nicole's role as exploiter of men reaches back to Dick's deepest fears and ultimately Fitzgerald's as well.

The structure of Nicole's love relationships to the three men in her life—
father, husband, lover—reveals an element of aggression directed toward
the previous man, from whom the successful rival promises to free her.
Dick offers to rescue her from the mental illness triggered off by her father's
incestuous advances. Barban promises to liberate her from her husband's
incurable alcoholism. Love thus represents to Nicole an escape from an
unhappy situation engendered by the abandonment of an earlier man in
her life. She is astonishingly successful as a survivor. What we rarely see
in *Tender Is the Night* is the full-blown marital warfare that inevitably ac-

companies the subtle betrayal of love. The rage and painful recriminations found in the Fitzgerald correspondence are largely absent from the novel. That part of the story may have been too terrible for Fitzgerald to write.

As *Tender Is the Night* draws to a conclusion, we are left wondering about the reasons for Nicole's miraculous recovery and Dick's hopelessness. The novel is unclear here, but Fitzgerald implies that the patient's health depends somehow on the psychiatrist's dissipation, as if he has mysteriously absorbed her suffering and absolved her from guilt. Yet the "spouse" seems to be guilty of inflicting a lethal injury to the doomed protagonist. Just as the narrator's husband is responsible for the heroine's isolation and madness in "The Yellow Wallpaper," so does the wife seem responsible for the hero's self-destruction in *Tender Is the Night*. Fitzgerald's notes to the novel make clear that the patient's cure results in the psychiatrist's terminal illness, as if madness is contagious. "The Divers, *as a marriage* are at the end of their resources. Medically Nicole is nearly cured but Dick has given out and is sinking toward alcoholism and discouragement. It seems as if the completion of his ruination will be the fact that cures her—almost mystically."

The explanation for this probably lies in Fitzgerald's biography—his deep guilt over Zelda's illness, the fear she would not recover, and the wish to sacrifice himself for her sake. "I left my capacity for hoping on the little roads that led to Zelda's sanitarium," he wrote in his notebooks.[42] The hopelessness of her situation contributed to the bleakness of his. Why then does Fitzgerald grant Nicole complete and permanent recovery, contrary both to biography and to the pessimistic statements about schizophrenia earlier in the novel? The conclusion seems inevitable: in curing Nicole and condemning Dick, Fitzgerald is punishing himself for complicity in Zelda's illness.[43] He may also have been trying to heal Zelda's illness through the magic of fiction. But the element of wish fulfillment in *Tender Is the Night* may be viewed, psychoanalytically, as a denial of the novelist's unconscious aggression toward the woman perceived as responsible for the hero's collapse. Masochism and sadism, most therapists agree, are the sides of the same coin. There is one passage in the novel that ominously hints at Dick's death wish toward his wife. "Certain thoughts about Nicole, that she should die, sink into mental darkness, love another man, made him physically sick" (p. 217). This is one of the few clues that Dick's self-destructive behavior derives from guilt over his hostile feelings toward Nicole. But this idea is too terrifying for

Fitzgerald, and, like his fictional psychiatrist, the novelist retreats from these murky depths. Yet, Dick is literally killing himself over his "ambivalence" toward Nicole—ironically, it was Zelda's psychiatrist, Dr. Bleuler, who first coined the word.[44]

It is not Freud whom Fitzgerald and his fallen hero invoke at the end of *Tender Is the Night* but Christ. Releasing Nicole from the strangulation hold he has momentarily wished to exert, Dick "raised his right hand and with a papal cross he blessed the beach from the high terrace." Fitzgerald thus casts off his doomed hero, though not without conceding him a vestige of dignity and grandeur. Nicole's future with Tommy Barban remains uncertain: She seems destined to reenact a pattern of falling in and out of love in a futile effort to remain "Daddy's Girl." But Fitzgerald's main focus rests on Dick, who gives up psychiatry, we are told, for general medicine. Nor is this surprising. After all, Dick has never displayed an interest in parent-child relationships, the interpretation of dreams, symptomatology, ego defenses, or transference. The talking cure has never informed his therapy. Fitzgerald mentions the "big stack of papers on his desk that were known to be an important treatise on some medical subject, almost in process of completion." No longer practicing the art of psychiatry nor what had been for him the more valuable art of writing, the author of *A Psychology for Psychiatrists* succumbs in the end to his own shrinking vision, a victim of the love he never quite understands and the once heroic commitment to work that has now taken a permanent leave of abstinence.

FOUR

Religious Conversion or Therapy: The Priestly Psychiatrist in T. S. Eliot's *The Cocktail Party*

What is hell? Hell is oneself,
Hell is alone, the other figures in it
Merely projections. There is nothing to escape from
And nothing to escape to. One is always alone.

The Cocktail Party[1]

IN 1932, T. S. ELIOT delivered four broadcast talks over the BBC in which he discussed the major challenges to religious faith: communism, psychology, and science. Of the three, psychology posed the greatest threat to him. "It is only when the psychologists tend to persuade us, first that we are all ill in mind, next that we all need to acquire something of their science in order to understand each other and ourselves, and finally that psychology will supply that guide and rule of conduct which the Christian faith used to give, and still does give to some; it is only when these three assertions appear that the modern dilemma is engaged."[2] Distressed by the growing influence of psychology, Eliot warns against the loss of religious values. "Psychology is an indispensable handmaid to theology; but, I think, a very poor housekeeper." He singles out two harmful effects of modern psychology: the danger of invoking psychological determinism to rationalize crime, and the tendency to accept primitive instincts as more real than spiritual desires. Eliot mistrusts the Oedipus complex, in particular, which he views as seeking to explain original sin in terms of sexual drives. Up to a point, he concedes, psychoanalytic theory offers certain advantages. "To know oneself, that is good, and it is a lesson in humility to learn how primitive we are." But it does not follow, he continues, that all our suppressed desires should be satisfied or that the idea of sublimation is logically valid. " 'Sublimation' in effect means, I think, just substitution; and there is no substitute for anything." For psychology, then, to replace religion is highly dangerous. Eliot did not comment upon the opposite possibility, the belief that religion can be a substitute for psychotherapy in the treatment of mental illness.

It is clear from Eliot's writings that he identified Freud as the embodiment of the pernicious secularism assaulting age-old religious truths. In a four-page review of *The Future of an Illusion* published in his influential journal *The Criterion*, Eliot characterizes Freud's book as both shrewd and stupid. "The stupidity appears not so much in historical ignorance or lack of sympathy with the religious attitude, as in verbal vagueness and inability to reason."[3] Eliot criticizes Freud's definition of culture and illusion, correctly noting the psychoanalyst's refusal to question his boundless faith in science. Until the end of the review, Eliot wages a restrained semantic attack on psychoanalysis, in contrast to Freud's bold assault on religion. At the end, however, Eliot's restraint gives way to icy condescension in his attack on the inflated claims of the Freudians. "I have the impression that the real pundits of the real sciences, such as mathematical physics, are often less confident of anything than Freud is of everything. But it is naturally the adepts of the parvenu sciences, in their anxiety to affirm that their science really is a science, who make the most exaggerated claims for 'science' as a whole. This is a strange book." It should be remembered that Eliot had converted to Anglicanism in 1927, just one year before his review of *The Future of an Illusion*. In 1932 he again sharpened his attack on Freud, not only in the BBC broadcasts but in "Thoughts After Lambeth," where he returned to the "quantity of nonsense" generated by humanists and scientists over the subject of religion. "Dr. Sigmund Freud, with characteristic delicacy of feeling, has reminded us that we should 'leave Heaven to the angels and the sparrows'; following his hint, we may safely leave 'religion' to Mr. Julian Huxley and Dr. Freud."[4]

Eliot was no more able to leave psychiatry to the physicians, however, than Freud was willing to leave religion to the theologians. Eliot's mistrust of psychology—which he equated with psychiatry, psychoanalysis, and psychological approaches to literature—spans five decades of writing. Before we examine the conflict between religious conversion and psychotherapy in *The Cocktail Party,* it may be helpful to recall his efforts to purify literary criticism from what he called the "curious-Freudian-social-mystical-rationalistic-higher-critical interpretation of the Classics and what used to be called the Scriptures" (*Selected Essays,* p. 62). He viewed the modern dilemma as an Edenic garden overgrown not by scholarly neglect but by an excess of benign scrutiny. "A number of sciences have sprung up in an almost tropical exuberance which undoubtedly excites our admiration, and the garden, not unnaturally, has come to resemble a jungle" (*Selected Essays,* p. 62). To cut through the jungle to restore classical order and religious truth was Eliot's goal; to do this, he sought to show that psychiatry is as antithetical to spiritual concerns as psychological interpretation is to creative art.

Despite the enormous quantity of critical commentary on Eliot's work, surprisingly little has been written on his antipathy toward psychology. To be sure, he cannot be faulted for his insistence that a psychopathological approach to literature invariably reduces the imagination to disease, a position Freud implicitly held. Writing at a time when psychoanalysts failed to stress the creative aspects of art—the artist's ability to synthesize disparate elements and create an imaginative reality often superior to the scientist's material reality—Eliot vigorously warned against the danger of reducing an artist's work to the product of a neurosis. Baudelaire's *"ennui,"* he writes in a 1930 essay, "may of course be explained, as everything can be explained in psychological or pathological terms; but it is also, from the opposite point of view, a true form of *acedia,* rising from the unsuccessful struggle towards the spiritual life" (*Selected Essays,* p. 423). Instead of reducing spirituality to sexuality, Eliot chooses the opposite direction as he elevates anguished emotion into a higher or loftier religious preoccupation. Without ignoring Baudelaire's morbid temperament or intense personal suffering, Eliot affirms his knowledge of good and evil, his moral consciousness. Acknowledging Baudelaire's insistence upon the "evil of love" and his "constant vituperation of the female," Eliot remains uninterested in its causes. "In this there is no need to pry for psychopathological causes, which would be irrelevant at best; for his attitude towards women is consistent with the point of view which he had reached" (*Selected Essays,* pp. 429–430). As we shall see, Eliot's comments on Baudelaire's vision of the evil of love and the constant vituperations of the female reflect the identical point of view that informs his own vision in *The Cocktail Party.* Eliot engages in what can only be called rationalization when he observes that Baudelaire "was at least able to understand that the sexual act as evil is more dignified, less boring, than as the natural, 'life-giving', cheery automatism of the modern world." That sexuality could be dignified *and* natural, life giving *and* human, is a view that remains conspicuously absent from Eliot's world. In fact, he goes out of his way to legitimize the "objective," hence universal nature of Baudelaire's vision.

In another essay on the French poet, Eliot returns to the subject of psychopathology, strongly protesting Arthur Symons' assertion that Baudelaire's work is the "direct result of his heredity and of his nerves." Great art, affirms Eliot, transcends the personal problems that may burden the artist's life. Once again he protests that an artist's mental problems are irrelevant to the objectivity of his art. "We cannot be *primarily* interested in any writer's nerves (and remember please that 'nerves' used in this way is a very vague and unscientific term) or in anyone's heredity except for the purpose of knowing to what extent that writer's individuality distorts or detracts from the objective truth which he perceives. If a writer sees truly—as far as he sees at all—then his heredity and nerves do not matter."[5]

But despite Eliot's fear that a preoccupation with psychological questions deflects the reader's attention away from the text and onto the artist's life, he often acknowledged his fascination for the unconscious elements of art. This is one of the many curious inconsistencies in Eliot's attitude toward psychology. In "The Frontiers of Criticism" (1956), he acknowledges a definite role for the psychobiographer. "I do not suggest that the personality and the private life of a dead poet constitute sacred ground on which the psychologist must not tread. The scientist must be at liberty to study such material as his curiosity leads him to investigate— so long as the victim is dead and the laws of libel cannot be invoked to stop him."[6] He even goes so far as to suggest that the biographer have clinical experience, lest he practice armchair psychology on the artist's life. It is true that Eliot immediately qualifies his remarks in such a way as almost to rule out psychobiographical approaches to literature. Few literary critics, after all, are also trained clinicians. Nevertheless, it is surprising how often Eliot makes passing references, usually unexpectedly, to neurologists and pathologists. In "A Dialogue on Dramatic Poetry" (1928), one of Eliot's speakers affirms the value and mystery of verse drama. "The human soul, in intense emotion, strives to express itself in verse. It is not for me, but for the neurologists, to discover why this is so, and why and how feeling and rhythm are related" (*Selected Essays,* p. 46). A similar idea appears in his 1919 essay on *Hamlet*. "The intense feeling, ecstatic or terrible, without an object or exceeding its object, is something which every person of sensibility has known; it is doubtless a subject of study for pathologists" (*Selected Essays*, p. 146). Eliot's references to psychology are generally pejorative, as when he labels it an "alien or half-formed science" (*Selected Essays*, p. 347), but he sometimes uses the word in a more positive context. He esteems the two greatest masters of diction in French literature, Baudelaire and Racine, as the "greatest two psychologists, the most curious explorers of the soul" (*Selected Essays*, p. 290).

Eliot also praises Dante in psychological terms, and the great Italian medieval poet occasioned Eliot's remarkable excursion into depth psychology. Eliot's lengthy 1929 essay reveals a startling acceptance of psychoanalytic theory, at least to the extent that he understood it. Eliot touches upon many of the problematic religious and psychological issues that he explores more deeply in *The Cocktail Party*, including the Dantesque belief that "Hell is not a place but a *state;* that man is damned or blessed in the creatures of his imagination . . ." (*Selected Essays*, p. 250). Eliot begins by speculating whether the type of sexual experience Dante describes in the *Vita Nuova* as occurring at the age of nine could have actually happened to the poet. "My only doubt (in which I found myself confirmed by a distinguished psychologist) is whether it could have taken place so *late* in life as the age of nine years. The psychologist agreed with me that it is more likely to occur at about five or six years of age" (p. 273). Far from isolating literature from psychology, Eliot invokes a clinical authority to confirm his intuition. He also theorizes that the lady about whom Dante writes may have been a "blind for someone else, even for a person whose name Dante may have forgotten or never known"—in short, a Freudian screen memory. Unlike a Freudian approach to art, however, Eliot emphasizes not origins but final causes. He focuses, that is, on higher spiritual love rather than lower sexual drives. Yet he accepts the Freudian theory of sublimation and uses the word without major qualification. "At any rate, the *Vita Nuova,* besides being a sequence of beautiful poems connected by a curious vision-literature prose is, I believe, a very sound psychological treatise on something related to what is now called 'sublimation'" (p. 275). Similarly, in "Baudelaire In Our Time" Eliot speaks approvingly of the "sublimation of passion" toward which the French poet was always striving.[7]

In affirming the theory of sublimation, with its emphasis upon the dynamic transformation of sexual drives into spiritually higher or socially more acceptable activity, Eliot intuits a mysterious relationship between suffering and artistic creativity. The poet, he writes in "The Three Voices of Poetry" (1953), is oppressed by a burden which he must bring to birth in order to obtain relief. Or, to change the figure of speech, he is haunted by a demon, a demon against which he feels powerless, because in its first manifestation it has no face, no name, nothing; and the words, the poem he makes, are a kind of form of exorcism of this demon. In other words again, he is going to all that trouble, not in order to communicate with anyone, but to gain relief from acute discomfort; and when the words are finally arranged in the right way—or in what he comes to accept as the best arrangement he can find—he may experience a moment of exhaustion, of appeasement, of absolution, and of something very near annihilation, which is in itself indescribable.[8]

The metaphor of the creative process represents a striking revision of the old theory of the poet as catalyst that Eliot had enunciated in his celebrated essay "Tradition and the Individual Talent" (1919). "The poet's mind is in fact a receptacle for seizing and storing up numberless feelings, phrases, images, which remain there until all the particles which can unite to form a new compound are present together" (*Selected Essays*, p. 19). Eliot's former mechanistic view of the artist, reminiscent of Freud's comparison of the psychoanalyst to a catalytic agent, which sets into motion a process that must inexorably proceed along its own way, now gives way to imagery of confession and therapeutic relief. Psychology replaces chemistry.[9] Eliot's analogy of sulphurous acid has quietly vaporized into the familiar psychoanalytic cloud of guilt, repression, and suffering.

Writing as rescue dominates Eliot's later theory of artistic creation, with the artist engaged in a life or death struggle to master intolerable psychic conflict. The metaphor of exorcism dramatizes the central role of suffering in Eliot's life and art. The impetus behind artistic creation is not communication or pleasure but self-purgation. Literature thus becomes veiled confession, a working through of unresolved personal struggles. This theory of art, of course, runs counter to all the assumptions of the New Criticism which Eliot himself rigorously set forth, and which three generations of literary critics have accepted. Eliot affirms a romantic vision of art in opposition to the classical writers who, remaining detached from the creative process, neither suffer nor experience loss of life while occupied in the creation of art. There is little doubt about Eliot's uncomfortable affinity to the nineteenth-century Romantic poets he sought to repudiate. Moreover, Eliot's biography and art demonstrate the theory of creative malady in which intense neurotic suffering becomes the central driving force behind intellectual and artistic achievement. Eliot combines a mystical Christian belief in the creative process as a Dark Night of the

Soul with a contemporary psychoanalytic view of writing as an adaptive and integrative strategy, a counterphobic activity. Surely his intensely moving observation about Pascal has the most profound implications for his own life and art:

> We know quite well that he was at the time when he received his illumination from God in extremely poor health; but it is a commonplace that some forms of illness are extremely favourable, not only to religious illumination, but to artistic and literary composition. A piece of writing meditated, apparently without progress, for months or years, may suddenly take shape and word; and in this state long passages may be produced which require little or no retouch ("The 'Pensees' of Pascal," 1931, *Selected Essays,* p. 405).

Valerie Eliot erased any doubt about the autobiographical significance of this passage when she linked it to a section of "What the Thunder Said" in *The Waste Land.* According to his wife, "Eliot said he was describing his own experience of writing this section in Lausanne when he wrote in The 'Pensees' of Pascal. . . ."[10]

Indeed, Valerie Eliot's publication in 1971 of the transcript of the original draft of *The Waste Land* provides a fascinating glimpse into the history of T. S. Eliot's struggle against mental illness prior to and during the creation of the poem that revolutionized twentieth-century literature. Mrs. Eliot quotes several letters confirming the severity of the poet's fear of losing control, his efforts to seek psychiatric help, and the medical treatment he received in a Swiss sanitarium. The letters inevitably serve as a background to *The Cocktail Party,* offering a clue to Eliot's vision of psychiatry and his belief in the importance of religious conversion as the treatment of choice for personal suffering. Although *The Cocktail Party* lacks the medical authenticity of other plays and novels dealing with a protagonist's breakdown and recovery, it is now clear to us that Eliot had at least one major psychological collapse. His portrait of the psychiatrist in *The Cocktail Party* appears to be modeled upon the actual Swiss physician who treated him in 1921, nearly three decades before the publication of the play in 1950. Like Charlotte Perkins Gilman's fictional narration of her breakdown in "The Yellow Wallpaper," *The Cocktail Party* came into existence as a result of the writer's decision, however conscious, to recreate in disguised form the psychiatric experiences of an earlier period of his life.

What emerges from the published fragments of Eliot's early correspondence is a portrait of an artist oppressed by acute anxiety and the fear of impending psychological collapse. The letters do not throw much light on the precise causes of Eliot's breakdown, but they do indicate the severity of the crisis and his efforts to seek professional help. A letter written in 1916, when Eliot was 28, conveys the intense strain he was feeling at the time. He refers to "The Love Song of J. Alfred Prufrock" as a swansong, adding that "the present year has been, in some respects, the most awful nightmare of anxiety that the mind of man could conceive . . ." (p. xi). The voice of these letters contains a wryness that could not quite conceal the growing fear of silence which, A. Alvarez observes in *The Savage God*, may represent a form of suicide to the artist.[11] The fear may have seemed confirmed when, according to Ezra Pound, Eliot's doctors ordered him in 1918 "not to write any prose for six months" (p. xv)—a warning he fortunately disregarded, as Gilman had done years earlier.

Although we know less about Eliot's life than that of any other major twentieth-century American writer, we do have brief accounts of his life from friends and acquaintances. His stress during these years was heightened by a precipitous and ultimately disastrous marriage in 1915 to his first wife, Vivienne Haigh-Wood, who was also becoming seriously mentally ill. Bertrand Russell describes her as having "impulses of cruelty" toward her husband. "It is a Dostojevsky type of cruelty, not a straightforward everyday kind. . . . She is a person who lives on a knife-edge, and will end as a criminal or a saint—I don't know which."[12] Estranged from Eliot in 1932, she became permanently schizophrenic and was hospitalized in London shortly after World War II. She died in a mental home in 1947 when Eliot was midway through writing *The Cocktail Party*. According to Stephen Spender, Eliot believed his wife's unhappiness and illness were his own fault, although she had a history of psychological problems before her marriage.[13]

There are striking similarities between the Fitzgeralds and the Eliots. Both marriages were built upon a shaky foundation of mental illness in which the husbands blamed themselves for their wives' psychotic behavior. It may be that the women's eccentricity was symptomatic of the schizophrenia that developed in later life. The pattern of illness seemed to be one of crisis, breakdown, convalescence, and relapse, with both Zelda and Vivienne suffering from a multitude of neurotic and psychotic ailments. There can be little question that the unhappy marriages contributed to the husbands' guilt, depression, and withdrawal. Whatever fears of sexual inadequacy the men may have had before marriage, these fears apparently intensified later. Fitzgerald's doubts about his manhood show up in Hemingway's cruel portrait of him in *A Moveable Feast;* and Eliot's early poems reveal "not lack of libido," as one critic has remarked, "but inhibition, distrust of women, and a certain physical queasiness."[14] Both men remained devoted to their wives for as long as they could, but when it became apparent that their marriages were hopelessly destroyed, they made painful separations. Fitzgerald had contemplated divorce but died before he might have done so. Eliot abruptly detached himself from his wife in 1933. In 1957, he married his former secretary, Valerie Fletcher. By all accounts, this marriage provided him with much happiness in the remaining eight years of his life.

Eliot's health deteriorated sharply in 1921. His letters sketch the psychiatric odyssey that led him from London to Margate, an English resort area, and finally to Switzerland. To a friend, he admitted that he had seen a "specialist (said to be the best in London) who made his tests, and said that I must go away *at once* for three months quite alone, and away from anyone, not exert my mind at all, and follow his strict rules for every hour of the day" (*The Waste Land: A Facsimile,* p. xxi). The fear of mental illness haunted him. "I did not anticipate such a medical verdict, and the prospect does not fill me with anything but dread . . ." (p. xxi). He spent a month at Margate, but the rest cure did not help. "I went to this specialist on account of his great name," he wrote to Julian Huxley from Margate in October 1921, "which I knew would bear weight with my employers. But since I have been here I have wondered whether he is quite the best man for me as he is known as a nerve man and I want rather a specialist in psychological troubles" (p. xxii). In the same letter, he mentions that Ottoline Morrell had strongly advised him to go to Dr. Roger Vittoz in Lausanne for treatment. She told him that Huxley had also visited the physician. Eliot was reluctant to travel to Switzerland because of the expense, and he asked Huxley whether he thought the trip was worth it. Huxley answered the letter, apparently recommended the Swiss psychiatrist, and Eliot thanked his friend in the following note. "I shall go to Vittoz. . . . He sounds just the man I want. I am glad you confirm my opinion of English doctors. They seem to specialise either in nerves or insanity!" Shortly before his departure to Lausanne, he wrote to Richard Aldington: "I am satisfied, since being here, that my 'nerves' are a very mild affair, due not to overwork but to an aboulie [lack of will] and emotional derangement which has been a lifelong affliction. Nothing wrong with my mind—" (p. xxii).[15] A letter written from Switzerland to his brother in December 1921 offers us the only clue to the type of psychiatric treatment he received under the care of Dr. Vittoz:

> The great thing I am trying to learn is how to use all my energy without waste, to be *calm* when there is nothing to be gained by worry, and to concentrate without effort. I hope that I shall place less strain upon Vivien who has had to do so much *thinking* for me. . . . I am very much better, and not miserable here—at least there are people of many nationalities, which ᵀ always like. . . . I am certainly well enough to be working on a poem! (p. xxii).

Eliot's description offers few specific details of his therapy, but the research of Dr. Harry Trosman, a Professor of Psychiatry at the University of Chicago, provides us with the type of treatment Eliot probably received under the supervision of Dr. Vittoz. In his two articles on Eliot published in psychiatric journals, Dr. Trosman carefully discusses the events leading to Eliot's breakdown, his probable transference relationship to Vittoz, the extent to which the creation of *The Waste Land* contributed to the poet's reintegration following his collapse, and the psychological factors involved in his religious conversion.[16] According to Dr. Trosman, the Swiss psychiatrist evolved a method of psychotherapy based on a program of cerebral reeducation. "Vittoz believed that he could determine the workings of the cerebral hemispheres by feeling their vibrations through the patient's forehead with his hand. By assessing a patient's cerebral responses to simple tasks which he proposed, he believed he could monitor the disordered vibrations and gradually educate a patient to master his brain functions" (p. 713). Far from being a psychoanalyst, Vittoz was opposed to understanding unconscious factors which, he believed, endangered the patient's unity and integration. His mistrust of psychoanalysis doubtlessly reinforced Eliot's criticisms of Freud. Similarly, the psychiatrist's belief in Christ as a paragon of self-control must have appealed strongly to Eliot.

Vittoz succeeded in restoring Eliot's health but, in Dr. Trosman's view, it was the man rather than the method of therapy that was largely responsible for the patient's improvement. The psychiatrist served as an idealized father figure to Eliot whose real father, from whom he had been painfully estranged, died in 1919. Eliot probably invested a complicated transference symbolism onto Vittoz, who bestowed upon his patient both psychiatric and religious approval. "Vittoz preached a type of high-minded Protestantism with an emphasis on courage, sainthood, self-control and consideration of others, values reminiscent of the Unitarianism of Eliot's authoritarian grandfather whose presence permeated the St. Louis of Eliot's youth" (p. 713). Dr. Trosman does not discuss *The Cocktail Party,* but it is likely that Vittoz' combination of psychiatric and spiritual power provided Eliot with the model for the priestly Sir Harcourt-Reilly, who similarly preaches Christian values to his patients.

What was Eliot suffering from at the time of his breakdown? Dr. Trosman acknowledges the insufficiency of evidence from which to make a psychiatric diagnosis of Eliot's illness. Nor is it possible to understand fully the circumstances leading to Eliot's breakdown. Nevertheless, the psychiatrist offers several plausible observations in place of the tendency among most Eliot scholars simply to attribute his illness to overwork or mental exhaustion. "The predominant symptom complex was depression with exhaustion, indecisiveness, hypochondriasis, and fear of psychosis. His personality was vulnerable to specific injuries that disturbed his narcissistic equilibrium" (p. 712). Other symptoms apparently included compulsive defenses against emotions, the difficulty of integrating sexual and aggressive drives, and identity diffusion. Fear of unacceptable latent homosexuality may have also been a factor. Although Dr. Trosman does not elaborate on this, literary critics have long speculated on the homosexual implications of Eliot's poetry. John Peter suggested in 1952, for example, that *The Waste Land* was written in response to the death of Eliot's beloved friend Jean Verdenal, whom Eliot met in 1910 and who died in World War I.[17] More recently, James E. Miller, Jr., has written an ingenious booklength study that focuses on Eliot's tangled feelings toward Verdenal, whom Miller sees as the central love figure in Eliot's poem.[18]

To view Eliot's illness as a transitory narcissistic regression is not to pigeonhole the man into a convenient clinical category but to attempt to establish a link between the poet's illness, recovery, and the extent to which both his illness and recovery shaped the themes of his creative art. To be sure, it is admittedly dangerous to speculate on the mental illness of a man who guarded his privacy as carefully as did Eliot. Critics of psychoanalysis will argue that the entire medical model of mental illness—including symptomatology, causation, and treatment—remains an unproven myth no matter how much clinical evidence the analyst is able to amass from his patient. Eliot was himself part of the movement opposed to psychiatry, and his subsequent comments on psychotherapy remain predictably cool. The roots of his disapproval extend to many different sources, not simply to the fact that his therapeutic improvement failed to last very long. Less than three months after Eliot left the Swiss sanitarium, a friend reported that he was "going to pieces" again.[19] He never did enter another sanitarium, although in the summer of 1927 he and his wife attended a health spa near Geneva where they received hydrotherapy.[20] But Eliot's limited success with psychiatry does not entirely account for his sharp criticisms. In "The Frontiers of Criticism" (1956), he concurs with the antipsychiatric sentiment expressed by Aldous Huxley in a preface to the English translation of *The Supreme Wisdom,* a book written by a French psychiatrist. Contrasting Western psychiatry with the discipline of the West as found in Tau and Zen, Huxley comments that the aim of the former is "to help the troubled individual to adjust himself to the society of less troubled individuals—individuals who are observed to be well adjusted to one another and the local institutions, but about whose adjustment to the fundamental Order of Things no enquiry is made."[21] In contrast to this normality is a higher state of perfect functioning in which, notes Huxley, men are not merely adjusted to a deranged society. The fear is that, in ministering to the troubled individual, the psychiatrist may be promoting an unhealthy adaptation to a diseased society—a view upheld by contemporary psychiatrists both on the political left (R. D. Laing) and the political right (Thomas Szasz). Eliot cites Huxley's statement because it coincides with his own impression of Western psychiatry which, he believes, "is confused or mistaken as to what healing is for." The attitude of psychiatry, Eliot insists, must be reversed.

The complaints voiced by Eliot and Huxley raise important issues implicit not only in *The Cocktail Party* but in the antipsychiatric vision of such texts as *A Clockwork Orange, One Flew Over the Cuckoo's Nest,* and *Equus.* These works suggest that a spiritual or religious malaise lies at the root of mental illness. Society is at fault in these books, and Western psychiatry inadvertently conspires with the repressive social and political establishment to enforce a rigid conception of normality upon the benumbed citizens of the therapeutic state. Adjustment to an insane society is the height of madness, as *Catch-22* has taught us. But what if a spiritual crisis arises from or masks psychological illness? Can we treat the human spirit without ministering to the psyche? Eliot implies in *The Cocktail Party* that the major problem is not the sick individual but the spiritually impoverished society, fatally divorced from Christian values. Nevertheless, the play dramatizes a point of view that strikes us as far from healthy either from a religious or psychological perspective. Yet how does one judge health? Although the question ultimately demands a value judgment and is therefore inherently problematic, we may apply Freud's definition of health—the ability to love and to work—to the characters in *The Cocktail Party*. To what degree do they see reality clearly and freely choose their own fates? Does the play succeed in resolving the spiritual and psychological conflicts of the central figures? In the 1932 BBC broadcasts, Eliot warns of the danger of invoking psychological determinism to rationalize crime. Does he make the opposite error of invoking mystical religious determinism to rationalize the heroine's crucifixion at the end of the play?

The hero of *The Cocktail Party* is Sir Harcourt-Reilly, to whom the other characters refer as a great physician. Literary critics have rightly challenged the psychiatrist's medical authenticity.[22] However, they have not analyzed him to the extent they have scrutinized his three patients, Edward Chamberlayne, his wife Lavinia, and Celia Coplestone. As in *Tender Is the Night*, we should not be surprised to discover that the psychiatrist hero also turns out to be the secret patient and a reflection of the author himself. Much of the abundant criticism of the play has centered on the rich mythic and ritual origins of Reilly's identity, unfortunately ignoring the psychoanalytic implications of the psychiatrist's God-like behavior. Pursuing a hint offered by Eliot, Robert Heilman has demonstrated Reilly's mythic affinity to Heracles in Euripedes' classical play *Alcestis*.[23] Like Heracles, Reilly has the power to restore life to the dead: He revives the dying marriage of Edward and Lavinia and inspires Celia to give up her mundane human existence in favor of what Eliot sees as a glorious religious martyrdom. Reilly's mythic symbolism, however, clashes with his role as a modern psychiatrist. We may legitimately inquire into his ambivalence toward psychiatry and the meaning of his need to control omnipotently his patients' destinies. Both Lavinia and Celia assert in identical language that Edward is "on the edge of a nervous breakdown," but if we approach the play from the perspective of a psychiatric case study, which is after all the external framework of the play, we discover that Reilly also seems to be struggling against fragmentation, or at least betraying symptoms that coincide remarkably with those of his patients.

Lest we murder to dissect, however, we must acknowledge the danger of reducing literature to psychopathology and confusing literary analysis with a postmortem. The philosopher Abraham Kaplan has complained that "Psychiatrists suffer from a trained incapacity: the inability to distinguish symbols from symptoms." He warns against confusing aesthetic expression with psychological exposure. Quoting Stanley Edgar Hyman, he remarks that "When the interpretation is practiced by men of letters lacking in psychological training, they invite exposure themselves as 'amateur sexologists and Peeping Toms of criticism.' "[24] Kaplan's caveat certainly reflects Eliot's own critical precepts, but it does not invalidate the fact that literature serves as a revelation of the artist's conscious and unconscious intentions. Indeed, Kaplan's insight is double-edged: every act of interpretation reveals something about the interpreter, regardless of whether or not he has had psychological training. After counseling Edward and Lavinia, Reilly walks over to his office couch, in the middle of Act Two, and lies down. The gesture has subtle comic appeal, since he is the only character in the play to lie down on the analytic couch, the symbol of the talking cure. Several questions come to mind. How does Reilly serve as a projection screen for Eliot's own attitude toward psychological health and illness? To what extent does the fictional psychiatrist's inner world of object relations—including his fantasies, defenses, and perceptions—correspond to the symptoms of his patients and ultimately to the playwright's? And, finally, what are the dangers of a messianic psychiatrist? In *The Ego and the Id,* Freud cautions against the "temptation for the analyst to play the part of prophet, saviour and redeemer to the patient."[25] If Freud is right about the danger of succumbing to this temptation, what is the meaning of Dr. Reilly's unorthodox psychiatry in *The Cocktail Party?*

*   *   *

The best revelation into Reilly's character appears in the long speech he delivers to Edward early in Act One, before his identity as a psychiatrist is exposed. Informed by Edward that Lavinia has walked out on him, leaving the husband with a mystery about her disappearance, Reilly ("The Unidentified Guest") elaborates on what he calls the "loss of personality." The speech begins with an assertion of the mystery of human personality but quickly shifts to a description of dehumanization and reduction to object status:

> There's a loss of personality;
> Or rather, you've lost touch with the person
> You thought you were. You no longer feel quite human.
> You're suddenly reduced to the status of an object—
> A living object, but no longer a person.

It's always happening, because one is an object
As well as a person. But we forget about it
As quickly as we can. When you're dressed for a party
And are going downstairs, with everything about you
Arranged to support you in the role you have chosen,
Then sometimes, when you come to the bottom step
There is one step more than your feet expected
And you come down with a jolt. Just for a moment
You have the experience of being an object
At the mercy of a malevolent staircase.
Or, take a surgical operation.
In consultation with the doctor and the surgeon,
In going to bed in the nursing home,
In talking to the matron, you are still the subject,
The centre of reality. But, stretched on the table,
You are a piece of furniture in a repair shop
For those who surround you, the masked actors;
All there is of you is your body
And the "you" is withdrawn (p. 307).

If we interpret Reilly's speech from a psychoanalytic object relations approach, which emphasizes an individual's relationship to his own internalized objects rather than to actual external objects in the environment, and if we read the speech as if it were a dream whose logic operates according to the bizarre laws of primary process thinking that Freud disclosed in *The Interpretation of Dreams,* several key themes emerge. The loss of personality to which Reilly refers implies a fundamental split or defect in the ego, the self-regulating psychic agency which attempts to reconcile or mediate the instinctual drives of the id with the inhibiting functions of the superego. The movement from human to object status suggests dehumanization and the ego's failure to integrate intrapsychic conflict. The result is the fear of fragmentation, decomposition, annihilation—in short, breakdown. Although the source of the conflict remains shadowy, the tension seems to be embodied within an indefinable object that menaces the "you" in Reilly's speech. The exact nature of the menace remains ambiguous. On one level, the symptoms of the mysterious illness reflect depletion, loss of energy, emptiness—the ego's insatiable hunger for nourishment or replenishment. Reilly obliquely hints at this when he asks Edward to replenish his drink after the long speech. On another level, the fear of emptiness suggests the presence of an active force which is cruelly depleting the self. Psychological emptiness may be viewed in both ways, the absence of something desirable or, paradoxically, the presence of something harmful which threatens to empty the self.[26]

Significantly, the two extended analogies Reilly uses to describe the loss of personality both contain persecutory imagery. In the first example, he refers to the experience of falling down a flight of stairs and being "at the mercy of a malevolent staircase." It is unclear whether the evil is located within the staircase itself which has tripped up the patient or within the social mask he wears as a defense against the other people at the party. The breakdown results in paralysis. In the second example, Reilly speaks about a surgical operation in which a patient lies stretched on a table, like a piece of furniture in a repair shop. Far from leading to therapeutic recovery, the surgery mutilates the patient by violating his body and destroying his spirit. Again, it is unclear whether the evil is located within the act of surgery or in the sadistic surgeon. There is also an ambiguity in the positioning of the masked actors: Syntactically they seem part of the repair shop, while thematically they belong with the doctors in the operating room. What is clear, however, is that Reilly's patient is victimized by forces he can neither understand nor control.

The defense against these internalized persecutory objects is loss of feeling through dehumanization, the denial of emotion, and derealization, the belief that reality itself lacks meaning and value. It is astonishing how, throughout *The Cocktail Party,* none of the characters can openly express the aggressive emotions that inevitably accompany physical or psychological injury—rage, jealousy, hate. Reilly's speech emphasizes the need to submit passively to suffering. No protest is allowed. In the psychiatrist's world, one must stoically endure the fate of reduction to object status. Memory must be obliterated, since it serves as a reminder of past traumas. One has the sense of a past catastrophe which cannot be discussed or forgotten. Human behavior becomes little more than defensive role playing, the adoption of an "as if" personality to conform to the social expectations of others. To be sure, there is real pain in the characters' speeches, but the pain is expressed in abstract philosophical terms. Man is imprisoned in solitude and pain. Knowledge intensifies suffering. Life itself becomes unreal, illusory, hollow. One moment it is the world itself which has become poor and empty, the next moment it is the ego which is depleted and worthless. Confronted by internal and external dangers, the individual is easily overwhelmed. The man loses touch with himself, the partygoer stumbles down the malevolent staircase, the patient is penetrated by the surgeon. Reilly's imagery bespeaks of loss, horror, and degradation. In a brutal world, one can only stumble and fall.

There is also a submerged sexual element in Reilly's speech. According to *The Interpretation of Dreams,* a dream of ascending or descending a staircase is often symbolic of sexual intercourse. But we do not have to invoke a psychoanalyst's authority to demonstrate the suggestive nature of staircase imagery in Eliot's poems and plays. Leonard Unger points out that staircase imagery functions as a leitmotif in Eliot's writings: Of the five times in which the image appears in the *Prufrock* poems, four involve a "troubled encounter between a man and a woman."[27] Sexual anxiety, concludes Unger, characterizes the mood or context of these images. Indeed, stairs are hazardous and unreliable to Eliot's characters. The morbid sexuality contained in Reilly's image of tumbling down a staircase is reinforced in the next analogy of the surgical operation, in which a helpless patient is being stretched on a table. The patient finds himself "stretched on the table"—"like a patient etherised upon a table," we feel inclined to add. The image is, of course, Prufrockian, as scholars have realized. To cite Grover Smith: "Sir Henry continues with his comparison of Edward's discovery to the jolt at the bottom of the staircase. His image of the Prufrockian patient stretched on the table clarifies the state of Edward's soul: he is a 'piece of furniture in a repair shop,' and Sir Henry is the craftsman who must reassemble his smashed life."[28]

Must we assume, however, that Dr. Reilly is describing the state of Edward's soul and not his own? The Prufrockian image applies to patient and psychiatrist alike, just as Reilly's allusion to "shuffling memories and desires" (p. 365) echoes the "Memory and desire" in the opening lines of *The Waste Land*. Reilly is one of Eliot's most authorial speakers, and this lends greater significance to the fact that psychiatrist and patient share almost identical visions of the world. Neither man believes in "personality," and they seek ways to transcend the monotony of everyday existence. Their imagery reveals the precariousness of the self and the threat of persecutory attack. Both affirm the value of suffering, humiliation, and resignation. "Reality"—a favorite word in the play—is always a threat to be defended against through unquestioning submission to higher authority. Both speakers have one voice, using the same diction, syntax, and cadence. There are two kinds of discourse in *The Cocktail Party,* light comedy of manners conversation in which the characters engage in witty repartee and easy gossip, and anguished confessional speech filled with unconscious revelations of the artist's life. In Act One, Scene Two, Celia

asks Edward whether the returning Lavinia has prepared a trap for them.
Edward replies: "No. If there is a trap, we are all in the trap,/We have
set it for ourselves. But I do not know/What kind of trap it is" (p. 319).
In the beginning of Act Two, Reilly (who has been absent from the earlier scene) uses identical language to deny Edward's accusation of a trap.
"Let's not call it a trap./ But if it is a trap, then you cannot escape from
it" (p. 346). Eliot probably intended patient and psychiatrist to echo each
other here, and, throughout *The Cocktail Party,* each character delivers
major speeches which repeat the other's thoughts.

To appreciate the intense unconscious identification between patient
and psychiatrist, we may examine their attitudes toward love and marriage. Upon learning of Edward's separation from Lavinia, Reilly offers
him the following consolation. "You experience some relief/ Of which
you're not aware," the psychiatrist tells him. The next ten lines powerfully dramatize the nature of this relief:

> It will come to you slowly;
> When you wake in the morning, when you go to bed at night,
> That you are beginning to enjoy your independence;
> Finding your life becoming cosier and cosier
> Without the consistent critic, the patient misunderstander
> Arranging life a little better than you like it,
> Preferring not quite the same friends as yourself,
> Or making your friends like her better than you;
> And, turning the past over and over,
> You'll wonder only that you endured it for so long (p. 306).

Purporting to read Edward's mind, Reilly betrays his own vision of
marriage. He refers to a wife as the "consistent critic," the "patient mis-
understander" whose taste is antithetical to her husband's. It is the wife
and not the husband whom Reilly attacks. She rigidly controls life, dominates her husband, steals his friends. The best that Reilly can say in favor
of marriage is that it is an experience to be endured. What makes his speech
so disturbing is that these lines are among the most poetically convincing
in the play, suggesting the intensity of Eliot's hostility toward marriage.
Variations on this theme appear throughout the psychiatrist's speeches,
as in his chilling description of marriage and family life to Celia. "They
do not repine;/ Are contented with the morning that separates/ And with
the evening that brings together/ For casual talk before the fire/ Two people
who know they do not understand each other,/ Breeding children whom

they do not understand/ And who will never understand them" (p. 364). Reilly expresses similar disdain of marriage, later in the play, when he questions the wisdom of encouraging Edward and Lavinia to revive their cheerless marriage. "What have they to go back to," he asks Julia (one of the Guardians), "To the stale food mouldering in the larder,/ The stale thoughts mouldering in their minds./ Each unable to disguise his own meanness/ From himself, because it is known to the other" (p. 367).

Nowhere in *The Cocktail Party* does Reilly demonstrate sympathetic insight into marriage, bearing and raising children, sharing one's love for another person. "There is no reference to the possibility of either joy or glory," Lionel Trilling has complained about the play.[29] Nor does Edward offer a corrective point of view. He has lived with his wife for five years, but after a brief separation he can neither remember what she is like nor describe her to others. He falls back upon blaming Lavinia for his own unhappiness and identity loss, accusations Reilly fails to challenge. "We had not been alone again for fifteen minutes," Edward confesses to the psychiatrist, "Before I felt, and still more acutely—/ Indeed, acutely, perhaps, for the first time,/ The whole oppression, the unreality/ Of the role she had always imposed upon me/ With the obstinate, unconscious, sub-human strength/ That some women have" (p. 349).

Edward's hostility toward women must be recognized as misogyny, and, although Eliot uses elaborate defenses and disguises to conceal his own mistrust of women in *The Cocktail Party,* there is too much evidence to ignore. In fact, the psychiatrist's unconscious defenses against women and marriage give him away. He uses questionable logic that he passes off as profound psychological truth, as when he rationalizes Edward's inability to explain why he wants to return to his wife. "The fact that you can't give a reason for wanting her/ Is the best reason for believing that you want her" (p. 309). A real psychiatrist would, of course, wince at this explanation. Edward indulges in the same mystifying logic when he tries to explain to Celia (with whom he has been having an affair) how Reilly has changed his feelings toward his wife. "I have a very clear impression/ That he tried to persuade me it was all for the best/ That Lavinia had gone; that I ought to be thankful./ And yet, the effect of all his argument/ Was to make me see that I wanted her back" (p. 322).

Sometimes Reilly will agree with a perceptive remark but then perversely reach the opposite conclusion. When Lavinia correctly fears that what she and Edward have in common "Might be just enough to make us loathe one another," Reilly concludes: "See it rather as the bond which holds you together" (p. 356). Several times the psychiatrist maddeningly contradicts himself. After cataloguing the horrors of marriage, he answers Celia's alarmed question of whether marriage is the best life by responding: "It is a good life" (p. 364). Without seeing any irony or contradiction in his remarks, he tells her that neither existence, grim marital domesticity or joyous Christian martyrdom, is superior to the other.

Reilly's most conspicuous error is his mistrust and abuse of psychiatry. He makes extraordinary efforts to deny his patients' psychological problems, voicing Eliot's thesis that "The single patient/ Who is ill by himself, is rather the exception" (p. 350). The psychiatrist pretends to encourage his patients' confessional disclosures, but when Edward actually attempts to begin a therapeutic dialogue, Reilly retreats on the grounds that such disclosures are a "luxury." In fact, Reilly repeatedly closes off potentially useful exchanges. Edward has been literally dying to talk to someone about his unhappy life; but no sooner does he begin to open up about his past, than the psychiatrist warns him not to "strangle each other with knotted memories" (p. 330). Reilly confides to a friend that he has kept Edward waiting for several days, since it was "necessary to delay his appointment/ To lower his resistance" (p. 345). It is the psychiatrist, though, who resists the talking cure. During the psychiatric interview, Edward tries to focus on the origins of his disbelief in his own personality, but just as he recalls his childhood experiences, Reilly peremptorily cuts him off:

> I always begin from the immediate situation
> And then go back as far as I find necessary.
> You see, your memories of childhood—
> I mean, in your present state of mind—
> Would be largely fictitious; and as for your dreams,
> You would produce amazing dreams, to oblige me.
> I could make you dream any kind of dream I suggested,
> And it would only go to flatter your vanity
> With the temporary stimulus of feeling interesting (p. 348).

Reilly condemns psychiatry as nothing less than the deadly art of mind control. He rejects nearly all the assumptions of modern psychotherapy: the belief that childhood experiences shape adult behavior; the recognition that dreams are a reflection of inner reality; the existence of transference, countertransference, and resistance; the importance of empathic mirroring. Mistrusting his profession, Reilly assumes that all psychiatrists are intent on manipulating their patients and exerting limitless power over them. Recall his Prufrockian metaphor of a patient stretched on a table while doctors perform a sinister operation on the anesthetized body. "All there is of you is your body/ And the 'you' is withdrawn."

The countertransference implicit in Reilly's earlier speech to Edward now becomes clearer to us. Foreshadowing Peter Shaffer's ambivalent psychiatrist in *Equus,* who reduces psychiatry to castration, Eliot's therapist unconsciously reveals contradictory urges: the wish to penetrate and to be penetrated, to humiliate and to be humiliated, to control omnipotently and to be controlled. The difference between Edward and Reilly is not their state of mind but their situation. Whereas Edward remains fearful and passive, on the verge of psychic disintegration, Reilly has inexplicably managed to achieve reintegration. His choice of profession suggests counterphobic motivation. Unlike the patient, the psychiatrist has converted weakness into apparent strength. This is the reason Reilly intuitively grasps Edward's point of view. Yet the psychiatrist's own psychic health seems precarious in the rigidity of his defenses. It is no wonder that he almost drives his patients crazy.

Indeed, to the extent that Reilly's therapy demands blind submission to higher authority, we must question the psychiatrist's prescription for health. Reilly's intense overidentification with Edward's state of mind suggests that he is both the Prufrockian patient stretched on the dissecting table and the Godlike psychiatrist who promises to release the patient from an oppressive personality. Reilly diagnoses everyone, patients and others alike, as spiritually ill, and the only prescription for cure is to be "transhumanised," Eliot's term for redemption through suffering. There are several paradoxes surrounding Reilly's therapy. Rejecting the manipulation and mind control associated with psychiatry, he nevertheless exerts omnipotent control over his patients' destinies, including what turns out to be a glorified death sentence for Celia. Despite his repudiation of dream interpretation on the grounds of its excessive subjectivity, he never questions the religious assumptions he imposes upon his patients. Preaching humility and resignation, he tolerates no dissent. The salvation he offers is based on absolute submission to religious authority—although Eliot studiously avoids any reference to God. Whereas Fitzgerald's Dr. Dick Diver attempts to heal his patients not through the expansion of their self-insight but through the physician's love and Christlike martyrdom, Eliot's Sir Harcourt-Reilly encourages his patients to transcend personality and submit themselves to religious authority. Tragically, the psychiatrist affirms the loss of personality from which Edward and the others suffer. Reilly insists that the pretense of human knowledge, psychological and otherwise, must be abandoned. Instead of analyzing his patients' destructive defenses, in this case, the reliance upon dehumanization and derealization, the psychiatrist urges renewed repression and self-abnegation.

The issue here is not religious as opposed to psychiatric approaches to human unhappiness, nor the mythic versus medical origins of Reilly's identity. Eliot's hero alarms us because of the rigidity and harshness of his value judgments, the rapid shifts between overidealizing and devaluating, and the erratic nature of his empathy. He dichotomizes reality in terms of redemption and damnation, omnipotent control and fragmentation. There is no capacity for ambiguity or ambivalence in his imagination: Inflexible control is the only defense against chaos. Personality is evil and must be transcended; the ego is weak and must be subordinated to God; relationships are painful and must be denied. What is missing from Reilly's personality is the broad middle range of human emotion.

Can we infer the psychiatrist's past on the basis of the countertransference he brings into his therapeutic sessions? Without divulging specific details about his life, Reilly makes several observations which hint at deep disappointment and pain over past relationships. In one of his most revealing speeches, he talks about the necessity to approach close relatives and friends as if they were strangers. This is less painful, he says, than to maintain the pretense that they are not strangers. "The affectionate ghosts: the grandmother,/ The lively bachelor uncle at the Christmas party,/ The beloved nursemaid—those who enfolded/ Your childhood years in comfort, mirth, security—/ If they returned, would it not be embarrassing?" (p. 329). Surely one can imagine emotions other than embarrassment in this situation—deep feelings of love and gratitude and joy as well as the inevitable sadness of personal loss. One suspects that Reilly is concealing something here, perhaps idealizing the past excessively. If his ghosts are truly "affectionate," why does he express the wish to harden himself to them? We defend ourselves against painful memories, not happy ones. Overidealization nearly always disguises disappointment and pain. Significantly, Edward agrees with the psychiatrist that "There are certainly things I should like to forget." "And persons also," Reilly quickly adds, not only missing the opportunity to open a potentially crucial therapeutic exchange but actually reinforcing the patient's illness. The psychiatrist's advice is that "You must face them all, but meet them as strangers" (p. 330). What Reilly seems to be advocating throughout *The Cocktail Party* is not only repression but the defense of isolation of feeling—the denial of one's emotions, especially the aggressive and unruly emotions of anger, jealousy, bitterness.

Insofar as Reilly succumbs to what Freud calls the analyst's temptation to play the role of prophet, saviour, and redeemer to his patients, we may call him messianic. But the word is not nearly precise enough to describe the structure of his unconscious fantasies and defenses, a structure which appears to indicate in Reilly's case a narcissistic personality disturbance. Although there is sharp disagreement among contemporary psychoanalytic theoreticians over the meaning and treatment of narcissism, including whether the grandiose self reflects a developmental fixation of an archaic though normal primitive self (the view of Heinz Kohut), or whether the grandiose self is pathological and thus clearly different from normal infantile narcissism (the view of Otto Kernberg), all analysts agree upon the crucial importance of narcissism as a personality structure. We may cite Kohut's definition here. "In the narcissistic personality disturbances . . . the ego's anxiety relates primarily to its awareness of the vulnerability of the mature self; the dangers which it faces concern either the temporary fragmentation of the self or the intrusions of either archaic forms of subject-bound grandiosity or of archaic narcissistically aggrandized self-objects into its realm."[30] Kohut speaks about the ego's inability to regulate self-esteem, the sudden rapid shifts between anxious grandiosity, on the one hand, and extreme self-consciousness, hypochondria, and shame, on the other hand. As a consequence of severe deprivation of maternal love, the child develops a grandiose self based upon a compensatory image of perfection and reinvents his parents, so to speak, into an idealized parent imago. The child thus recreates his insufficiently loving parents into omnipotent figures who function as transitional self-objects, extensions of himself. Kohut postulates two major types of narcissistic transference relationships (and their corresponding countertransference relationships): the idealizing transference, based upon the therapeutic mobilization of the idealized parent imago; and the mirror transference, arising from the mobilization of the grandiose self.

Kohut's "psychology of the self," as it has come to be called, has intriguing implications to the relationship between transference and countertransference in *The Cocktail Party*. The play reveals a consistent pattern of merging with an omnipotent idealized object. Reilly's patients accord him respect and obedience as though he were a God: They defer to his authority, carry out his orders, incorporate his power. In Kohutian terms, the patients narcissistically transform Reilly into an omnipotent self-object, and the psychiatrist eagerly accepts their idealizing transference. Edward's feelings of emptiness, worthlessness, and fragmentation are counteracted by his merging with Reilly's omnipotence. The psychiatrist clearly functions as an idealized father figure to the patient. Reilly neither questions his magical power to restore life to his patients nor acknowledges the limitations of his psychiatric art. Kohut distinguishes between the analyst's ability to accept the patient's idealizing transference when offered and the analyst's indulgence in or craving for idealization. Only the former response, Kohut argues, is analytically permissible.

Reilly's countertransference reveals a dependency upon omnipotent control and inability to tolerate indecisiveness or dissent. He sternly reprimands Edward and Lavinia for their attempts to work out their own diagnosis and treatment. "But when you put yourselves into hands like mine/ You surrender a great deal more than you meant to./ This is the consequence of trying to lie to me" (p. 353). The reverse side of Reilly's omnipotent countertransference is his subordination to God, the spiritual healer with whom the psychiatrist has an idealizing transference. Reilly submits blindly and totally to divine authority, never allowing himself to voice doubts about religious truths. Interestingly, Kohut observes that the idealizing transference relationship in a narcissistic disturbance may manifest itself through "the expression of vague and mystical religious preoccupations with isolated awe-inspiring qualities which no longer emanate from a clearly delimited, unitary admired figure."[31] This accurately describes the way in which Edward, Lavinia, and Celia accept Reilly's proclamations, invested with a religious and mystical aura. There is also a parallel between the devout worshiper's relationship to his God, the incarnation of perfection, and the child's perception of the idealized parent. This does not imply that religion may be reduced to infantile wish fulfillment, as Freud concluded, but that the patients' deification of the psychiatrist in *The Cocktail Party* is analogous to the idealizing parent-child relationship that Kohut speaks about in his clinical work.

Celia Coplestone's attitude toward Reilly is no less complex than Edward's. Both patients suffer from symptoms of identity diffusion, emptiness, and derealization. Her opening words to Reilly contain telltale denials which the psychiatrist stubbornly refuses to analyze. "Well, I can't pretend that my trouble is interesting," she says, "But I shan't begin that way. I feel perfectly well./ I could lead an active life—if there's anything to work for;/ I don't imagine that I am being persecuted;/ I don't hear any voices, I have no delusions—/ Except that the world I live in seems all a delusion!" (p. 359). Analysts speak of the importance of a patient's opening words in therapy: Celia can't make up her mind whether she or the world is worthless. She contradicts herself from moment to moment. After asserting her own worthlessness, she reverses herself, expresses well-being, and then deprecates the world the emptiness of which she invokes to rationalize her inability to work. Most blatant is her denial of feelings of persecution and delusion—a denial that soon gives way to her projection of persecutory and delusional impulses upon an alien world. She admits that her two major symptoms include an "awareness of solitude" and a "sense of sin," then claims that she "should really *like* to think there's something wrong" with her because if not, "then there's something wrong,/ Or at least, very different from what it seemed to be,/ With the world itself—and that's much more frightening!" (p. 359). With Reilly's immediate approval she concludes that her problems are not individual but universal (not psychological, that is, but spiritual), thus disavowing the need for psychiatric help. Curiously, she rules out feeling "sin in the ordinary sense" regarding her adultery with Edward. She claims that immorality is not part of her generalized sense of sin and denies hurting Edward's wife. "I haven't hurt *her*./ I wasn't taking anything away from her—/ Anything she wanted" (p. 361). Celia is right but in an unexpected sense: Edward's wife never does seem very interested in him.

Paradoxically, both Edward and Celia would rather confess their sins than try to understand them. What crime has Celia committed to warrant her crucifixion? And why does her psychiatrist express satisfaction upon learning of the details of her martyrdom? Like Reilly, Eliot believes he is treating the heroine of *The Cocktail Party* sympathetically, yet, she bears the brunt of the playwright's violence. What, then, can be the source of the aggression responsible for the violent death of a saintly woman who denies any wrongdoing to others and whom the other characters in the play apparently revere? She seems to be in flight from something or someone; the flight ends in religious crucifixion but also could have culminated in suicide or madness. Perhaps no character in literature has offered a vaguer confession than Celia. "It's not the feeling of anything I've ever *done*,/ Which I might get away from, or of anything in me/ I could get rid of—but of emptiness, of failure/ Towards someone, or something, outside of myself;/ And I feel I must . . . *atone*—" (p. 362). She hints at disappointing the expectations of other people but then characteristically

internalizes her failures. Yet what lies beneath Celia's chronic self-accu-
sations? "If one listens patiently to a melancholic's many and various self-
accusations," Freud writes in "Mourning and Melancholia,"

> one cannot in the end avoid the impression that often the most vio-
> lent of them are hardly at all applicable to the patient himself, but
> that with insignificant modifications they do fit someone else, some-
> one whom the patient loves or has loved or should love. Every time
> one examines the facts this conjecture is confirmed. So we find the
> key to the clinical picture: we perceive that the self-reproaches are
> reproaches against a loved object which have been shifted away from
> it on to the patient's own ego.[32]

Sexuality and aggression are the two topics conspicuously absent from
any of the cocktail-party conversations in the play or from Reilly's psychiatric interviews. This does not necessarily prove the existence of repressed sex and violence in Eliot's characters; nevertheless, Celia's speeches
reveal persecutory imagery, displaced aggression, and incestuous fantasies. Her self-reproaches hint at rage toward the lover who abandoned
her. Edward's physical appearance to her changes twice as she gazes upon
him early in the play. "I looked at your face: and I thought that I knew/
And loved every contour; and as I looked/ It withered, as if I had un-
wrapped a mummy" (p. 326). If looks could kill, in other words, Edward
would be dead. Celia's morbid perceptions of Edward, it seems, disguise
murderous thoughts.

There is no object constancy in any character in *The Cocktail Party:* Love
dissolves into hate; good images deteriorate into bad ones; memory yields
emptiness. Edward serves as the object of Celia's reproaches. She compares his voice to the "noise of an insect,/ Dry, endless, meaningless, inhuman," and then develops the unflattering image. "You might have made
it by scraping your legs together—/ or however grasshoppers do it. I
looked,/ And listened for your heart, your blood;/ And saw only a beetle
the size of a man/ With nothing more inside it than what comes out/
When you tread on a beetle" (pp. 326–327). Interpreting her speech according to the rules of the dream work, we find the characteristic elements of displacement, condensation, and symbolization. Edward is the
beetle she longs to squash. The image of scraping his legs together—"or
however grasshoppers do it"—may suggest his sexual inconsequence. Celia is certainly disgusted by the interior of Edward's body. Her pestilen-
tial image of Edward coincides with Reilly's allusion to marriage and hu-

man procreation—husband and wife "Breeding children whom they do not understand." Celia's sadistic threat to tread on the beetlelike Edward elicits his masochistic reply: "Tread on me, if you like."

Significantly, Edward's mistress and wife both stress his passivity, ineffectuality, and infantility. "You look like a little boy who's been sent for/ To the headmaster's study," Celia tells him (p. 331). Lavinia's reproach is more damaging. "Oh, Edward, when you were a little boy,/ I'm sure you were always getting yourself measured/ To prove how you had grown since the last holidays" (p. 340). Reilly also cruelly casts doubt on Edward's potency. "To men of a certain type," the psychiatrist tells him, "The suspicion that they are incapable of loving/ Is as disturbing to their self-esteem/ As, in cruder men, the fear of impotence" (p. 355). Edward silently accepts the humiliation. Lavinia, by contrast, seems invulnerable. "I have never known anyone in my life/ With fewer mental complications than you," Edward bitterly tells his wife. "You're stronger than a . . . battleship. That's what drove me mad" (p. 352). The numerous allusions to Edward's sexual inadequacy and unmanliness lead to the conclusion of castration fear, with both his wife and mistress serving as castrating women. Like his more famous literary relative, J. Alfred Prufrock, whose seductive love song is drowned in a sea of *femmes fatale,* Edward lies etherized upon his death bed, lacking the strength to force the moment to its terrible crisis.

Edward's fear of sexual mutilation may explain the ease with which he is able to renounce his affair with Celia. Her comparison of Edward to a squashed beetle suggests both his fear of annihilation and the specific threat she poses to him. Not surprisingly, Edward easily convinces Peter Quilpe, who is also romantically interested in Celia, to avoid entangling alliances with her. Edward congratulates his rival "on a timely escape." Edward gives up his claims upon Celia because she has never meant very much to him in the first place. Indeed, Edward is temperamentally repelled by women. We remember his chilling characterization of Lavinia's formidable power—the "obstinate, unconscious, sub-human strength/ That some women have." Why then does Edward remain masochistically attached to his emasculating wife? This is one of the central weaknesses of *The Cocktail Party,* which never adequately justifies the continuation of the Chamberlaynes' cheerless marriage. Their oversolicitousness toward each other in Act Three confirms Eliot's inability to imagine a joyful marriage, and the oblique allusions to Lavinia's pregnancy do little to offset Reilly's prior dismissal of procreation.

Reilly also renounces his claims upon Celia but in a different way. Whereas Edward's mistrust of Celia expresses itself through devaluation ("There's no memory you can wrap in camphor/ But the moths will get in," he sadly tells Peter Quilpe), Reilly uses overvaluation or idealization, which attempts to create through fantasy a perfect love object that will resist the disappointments of reality. In narcissistic personality disturbances, idealization is the primary psychic mechanism to ward off anxiety and maintain the grandiose self. Idealization is not a pathological defense, but the difficulty arises when a person shifts back and forth between virulent devaluation and impossibly lofty idealization, thus forming an identity around a rigid grandiose self which cannot tolerate weakness or its own aggression. The insatiable hunger for perfection leads only to perpetual unhappiness and depletion. Narcissistic hunger, as suggested earlier, may be viewed either as the absence of nourishing internalized objects or the presence of poisonous objects residing in the self. *The Cocktail Party* dramatizes emptiness as a plenitude of persecutory objects. Reilly makes the same point (though he uses traditional mystic religious imagery instead of contemporary psychoanalytic concepts) when he refers to his patients as "A prey/ To the devils who arrive at their plenitude of power/ When they have you to themselves" (p. 356). Celia similarly speaks of the need to harden herself to these demons lest they overpower her. Her solution to inner horror is to reject the human condition and to prepare herself for the purgatorial suffering that will allow her to merge ecstatically with an omnipotent authority. And Reilly's solution to his own inner horror is to confer sainthood status on Celia and then offer her to God.

From a clinical point of view, Celia and Reilly are stuck in an idealizing relationship between transference and countertransference. Both patient and psychiatrist strive to maintain an image of the other's perfection, as if the only way to escape fragmentation is through merging with the other's grandiosity. Each character conceals painful truths from the other. Celia does not allow herself to express aggressive and libidinal drives, because they would destroy the psychiatrist's idealization of her. Reilly does not acknowledge these drives within himself, since they would shatter the patient's idealization of him. She renders him into a God, while he elevates her into a saint. The absence of any clinical or narrative distance between them suggests the extent of their merging. Each recreates or fictionalizes an idealized self to heal a narcissistic injury. They also act out Oedipal fantasies. By encouraging Celia to reject the imperfect human world for a spiritually perfect kingdom that lies beyond death, Reilly expresses the wish to preserve the purity of the original love object, the maternal imago. But preservation demands rejection. By urging Celia to remove herself from the world, Reilly is thus eliminating temptation—repudiating his own incestuous fantasies and insuring that no other man will possess her. He literally idealizes her to death.

The psychosexual implications are intriguing. On an oral level, the psychiatrist is merging with the patient in a mystical union, incorporating her magical goodness. On an anal level, he is sadistically killing her off and casting her away. On a phallic level, he is sublimating his incestuous drives by offering her to the highest authority, God the father, to whom he devoutly submits himself. Similarly, Celia receives pathological gratification from this misalliance cure.[33] Her martyrdom becomes clearer once we understand that Reilly gives her only two choices, both involving death: ignoble suicide or religiously sanctioned crucifixion. Religious penance allows her to gratify a self-destructive superego the aggression of which has been expressed in symptoms of emptiness, derealization, paranoia. By rejecting secular love for spiritual union, she is able to gratify libidinal drives while punishing herself for being human. Religious martyrdom allows her to convert rage into altruistic surrender.

The Cocktail Party reveals the contradictory wish both to destroy and then retrieve the abandoned love object, renunciation followed by restoration. It is the two-stage process Freud viewed as the structure of every neurosis and psychosis. "In neurosis a piece of reality is avoided by a sort of flight, whereas in psychosis it is remodelled. Or we might say: in psychosis, the initial flight is succeeded by an active phase of remodelling; in neurosis, the initial obedience is succeeded by a deferred attempt at flight."[34] In Eliot's play, the psychiatrist's messianic fantasies form a perfect fit with the patient's conviction of the absolute worthlessness of human life. Jacob Arlow and Charles Brenner have provided an ego psychology interpretation of the relationship between delusions of world destruction and messianic fantasies. "One need only assume that in the case of the messianic patient, the patient's own role has changed from that of a mere observer of the destruction about him to that of an active savior, rescuer, or restorer of life and health to those threatened by the destructive forces which seem to him to be raging everywhere."[35] The messianic Reilly functions as the savior and restorer to life of the troubled patient whose entire relationship to the world of objects is unstable and threatened by mass destruction.

We are stunned, furthermore, by the violent intensity of the disturbance of the world of objects in *The Cocktail Party*. Following her psychiatrist's orders, Celia withdraws from society to devote herself to missionary work in a remote part of the world. During a heathen uprising,
she is crucified "very near an ant-hill," her body presumably devoured—
psychic incorporation with a vengeance. Reilly expresses no dismay upon
learning the details of her crucifixion. Quite the opposite: The expression
on his face, according to Lavinia, is one of "satisfaction." The psychiatrist
agrees and acknowledges that, from the first time he saw Celia, he could
intuit her violent death. She was, he claims, a woman "under sentence of
death." Significantly, he affirms not the goodness of Celia's life but the
sanctification of her death. What is shocking, though, is the gruesome
violence of her ending. E. Martin Browne, the director of *The Cocktail
Party*, reports that Eliot originally had written a more explicit description
of the crucifixion. In Eliot's words, Celia was to be "smeared with a juice
that is attractive to ants."[36] Eliot was persuaded to omit the grisly detail
from the play, but the feeling of horror persists in *The Cocktail Party*,
which is subtitled "A Comedy."

Perhaps the most controversial question in Eliot's drama is the meaning and value of Celia's religious crucifixion. The history of the literary
criticism of the play reflects bitter disagreement.[37] To be sure, the audience's attitude toward her martyrdom will depend upon the religious
convictions one brings to the play as well as attitudes toward psychiatry,
humanism, and eschatology. *The Cocktail Party* raises a host of problematic questions concerning the relationship between religious conversion
and psychological health and the issue of free will versus determinism.
Eliot's characters repeatedly assert the importance of choice; Reilly insists
upon the triumphant free will leading to Celia's saintly ending. Yet Reilly
is characteristically evasive here: He manipulates her into martyrdom and
then disclaims all responsibility for her actions. His proclamations have
an incurably deterministic ring, acceptable only to those who can reconcile Celia's freedom with religious predestination.[38]

Throughout *The Cocktail Party*, Reilly has been displaying bad faith
toward his patients, profession, and religion. Nowhere does he question
his own motives or resistance to the fundamental principles of any truthful therapy: insight, structural change, and growth. In interpreting his
patients' suffering as a sign of the pervasive religious malaise of the time,
Reilly is offering what Freud would call a secondary revision, a coherent
but false decoding of a dream or symptom. One can imagine a different

ending to Eliot's play, in which Celia goes off to another sanitarium to receive less expensive psychotherapy. Critics remain divided over the artistic justification of her death. Stephen Spender has argued, for example, that her death does not strike one as aesthetically inevitable. "Much of the fascination of these plays is that they make one think about the author; but that betokens some measure of failure."[39]

Indeed, despite Eliot's insistence that a work of art must be divorced from history, biography, and psychology, it is impossible not to think about the relationship between Eliot's psychiatric experiences and *The Cocktail Party*. Scholars may wish to explore two particular links between Eliot's life and art: Edward and Lavinia consult a psychiatrist after five years of marriage, the length of time Eliot was married to Vivienne before he began treatment with Dr. Vittoz; and midway through the writing of *The Cocktail Party*, Eliot's estranged wife died in a mental hospital, an event that must have brought to the surface his complicated feelings toward her. How could he not feel guilt, anguish, mortification, and probably relief upon learning of her death? Bertrand Russell's characterization of Vivienne as a "person who lives on a knife-edge, and who will end as a criminal or a saint"[40]—has relevance to the saintly Celia, whose threat to tread on the passive lover who has abandoned her culminates in saintly martyrdom.

Eliot might argue, though, that, in applying psychoanalytic theory to *The Cocktail Party*, we have been performing a literary autopsy on his characters that fully justifies the playwright's mistrust of Freud. Perhaps, but it is significant that Eliot viewed every act of interpretation, psychoanalytic or otherwise, as an unwarranted intrusion or violation of the text. "Comparison and analysis need only the cadavers on the table," he writes in "The Function of Criticism," "but interpretation is always producing parts of the body from its pockets, and fixing them in place (*Selected Essays*, p. 33). Any literary interpretation was illegitimate to Eliot. The most influential literary critic of his age, he sanctioned evaluation and analysis, not interpretation—as if meaning could be divorced from evaluation. This position led him to dubious assertions, as when he states in the same essay that "any book, any essay, any note in *Notes and Queries*, which produces a fact even of the lowest order about a work of art is a better piece of work than nine-tenths of the most pretentious critical journalism, in journals or in books." Facts cannot corrupt, he claims; "the real corrupters are those who supply opinion or fancy." How astonishing this claim is in light of the colossal theoretical turmoil of our own age. Even when

Eliot softened his objections to literary interpretation, as he did in his "Introduction" to G. Wilson Knight's *The Wheel of Fire,* he remained disheartened by the pluralistic nature of meaning. He views all interpretation as Satanic rebellion, an inevitable falling away from truth and innocence. He invokes the metaphor of demonism to explain the misguided quest for meaning, and he justifies literary interpretation not because of its power to illuminate the text but because of the futility to repress the instinct for knowledge. His reluctant and saddened conclusion is that it is necessary to "surrender ourselves to some interpretation of the poetry we like."[41] The act of interpretation, in other words, is analogous to an intrusive authority seeking to extract the creative essence from the artist's life and work. Additionally Eliot's mistrust of literary interpretation recalls Edward's horror of exposure or violation, a Prufrockian dread of the body or text being probed, dissected, castrated.[42] "After such knowledge, what forgiveness?"

There would seem to be a correlation, then, between Eliot's theory of aesthetics, grounded upon the attempt to avoid literary subjectivity by removing the interpreter from the text, and the "loss of personality" from which the characters suffer in *The Cocktail Party.* The assumption that literary interpretation is a violation of the text, resulting in dangerous fragmentation and loss of belief, coincides with the fear of mutilation and narcissistic injury seem in many of Eliot's speakers—Prufrock, Gerontion, the speaker in *The Waste Land,* and Edward in *The Cocktail Party.* There is a consistency between Eliot's essentially Protestant approach to literary criticism, calling for a direct communion with the text, and Reilly's rejection of clinical distance in favor of mystical union. Similarly, the papal element in Eliot's proclamations of taste and orthodoxy in literature parallels Reilly's position as high priest of psychiatry. The text must not be corrupted by the reader's opinion or fancy, just as Celia's purity must not be compromised by imperfect human existence. Eliot's theory of art and vision of psychiatry rule out the idea that both the literary text and the therapist function as transitional objects, transformed by reader and patient alike into their unique identity theme and characterological structure.[43] Yet this is precisely what happens, despite Eliot's intentions. His literary pronouncements call attention to his personal suffering, just as his fictional psychiatrist serves as a projection screen of the artist's earlier breakdown and recovery.

A psychobiographical approach cannot prove conclusively that Eliot's theory of the "impersonality" of art and the "loss of personality" in *The*

Cocktail Party both came into existence as a defense against the artist's narcissistic injury. Correlation is not causation. Mental functioning is always multiply determined, moreover, as Robert Waelder has pointed out.[44] Nevertheless, Eliot's writings reflect both the symptoms of a man continually struggling against psychic fragmentation and, more importantly, the successful restitutive efforts he made to resist future breakdowns. Although *The Cocktail Party* reveals signs of the playwright's narcissistic injury, the existence of the play demonstrates the artist's struggle toward health and the therapeutically beneficial nature of artistic creation. Art was, for Eliot, a way to heal a narcissistic injury, a method to achieve a magical fusion with the great tradition of literature.

We cannot say, finally, whether Eliot's treatment with Dr. Vittoz proved to have more than a temporary salutary effect on his life and art or whether, had he undergone treatment with a psychoanalyst skilled in narcissistic personality disturbances (and Freud, it must be remembered, did not believe analysts could treat narcissism), Eliot's suffering would have been diminished. It is clear, though, that Eliot's mental breakdown in 1921 and psychiatric odyssey provided him with at least the theme and the apparatus of the psychiatric case study for the play he was to write nearly three decades later. The marriage of religion and psychiatry in *The Cocktail Party* remains as shaky as the Chamberlaynes' union, however, and it is unfortunate that Eliot misunderstood both the theory and practice of psychoanalysis. "There is always an implicit psychology behind the explicit antipsychology," Erik Erikson reminds us.[45] This remains especially true of Eliot's life and art. We do him a grave injustice by accepting at face value his repudiation of psychology, because we must then ignore his determined efforts to heal himself through art and religion. The artist who suffers a breakdown and subsequently writes about it, in however disguised form, would seen to be engaged in a counterphobic activity, transmuting illness into psychic and literary health. Replaying his own breakdown and recovery, Eliot rejected nonspiritual forms of psychotherapy and affirmed the only cure he could believe in, religious conversion. Out of his creative malady came *The Cocktail Party,* a striking example of how "some forms of illness are extremely favourable, not only to religious illumination, but to artistic and literary composition."

FIVE

"If Writing Is Not an Outlet, What Is?": Sylvia Plath and *The Bell Jar*

[He] helped me up on the wall, and in my tight skirt, I tried to step over the spikes; they pierced my skirt, my hands, and I felt nothing, thinking from the great distance that I might at last lie on a bed of spikes and not feel it, like the yogi, like Celia Copplestone [sic], crucified, near an anthill, at last, peace, and the nails went through my hands. . . .

The Journals of Sylvia Plath[1]

SYLVIA PLATH'S identification with Celia Coplestone's crucifixion is but one of the many striking similarities between the worlds of *The Cocktail Party* and *The Bell Jar*. Despite the extensive research on Plath's work, little has been written about her fascination with psychiatry and its importance to her life and art. Until recently, we have had few clues into the nature of Plath's mental illness that culminated in her suicide in February 1963 at the age of 30 or the details of her psychiatric treatment in 1953, after her first breakdown and suicide attempt. *The Bell Jar*, published in England one month before her death, describes the events leading up to Plath's initial collapse. However, we learn surprisingly little about Esther Greenwood's experiences with Dr. Nolan, the sympathetic female psychiatrist who treats and apparently cures the autobiographical heroine. The nature of the doctor-patient relationship has remained enshrouded in mystery, and even Plath's biographer, Edward Butscher, has been unable to offer much information about this important subject.

Within the last few years, however, the publication of two major autobiographical volumes—Plath's massive correspondence, *Letters Home* (1975), and *The Journals of Sylvia Plath* (1982)—has deepened our understanding of the gifted writer who committed suicide during the height of her creative powers. Her journals confirm the intimate relationship between the creative and therapeutic process. Not only was Plath in psychiatric treatment, and more than once with the same psychiatrist, but the therapy lasted longer and was more valuable to her life and art than anyone has publicly suggested. She understood the theory and practice of psychoanalysis better than any of the writers we have discussed— Charlotte Perkins Gilman, F. Scott Fitzgerald, T. S. Eliot—and her psychiatric experiences were more positive and insightful than those of her predecessors. Psychotherapy allowed her to discover and verbalize the severe repressed conflicts of her "murderous self," and she used the material of her own analysis for the themes of her art. Rather than implying, as A. Alvarez does in *The Savage God,* that her fierce creativity was responsible for the infernal vision at the end of her life, we may view her art—as we viewed Eliot's—as an attempt to master and work through her psychological conflicts, to heal through the creation of literature the deep injuries that had brought her into therapy.[2] To this extent, *The Bell Jar* resembles *The Cocktail Party.* Both writers suffered major breakdowns, and their psychiatric odyssey provided them with the theme and the medium of the case study for their later works. And yet there is also an obvious difference between the two artists. The mocking irony of *The Bell Jar* is that even as it dramatizes Esther Greenwood's collapse and apparent recovery, autobiography intrudes to remind us of the failure of therapy and art to sustain Sylvia Plath's life.

Aurelia Schober Plath's introduction to her daughter's 500-page correspondence, containing 696 letters Sylvia wrote to her mother between the years 1950 and 1963, offers a biographically revealing, though highly selective, sketch of the early years of the artist's life. The most striking detail of the mother-daughter relationship was the element of symbiotic fusion. "Throughout her prose and poetry, Sylvia fused parts of my life with hers from time to time."[3] In the "Introduction" Mrs. Plath acknowledges the wish behind the preservation of her daughter's letters. "Throughout these years I had the dream of one day handing Sylvia the huge packet of letters. I felt she could make use of them in stories, in a novel, and through them meet herself at the varied stages in her own development . . ." (p. 3). We can already see a symbiotic element working here: the mother functions to mirror her daughter's life, to receive and give back Sylvia's reflection, to subordinate herself to and participate vicariously in Sylvia's brilliant career. Later in the "Introduction," Mrs. Plath returns to their symbiotic relationship. "Between Sylvia and me there existed—as between my own mother and me—a sort of psychic osmosis which, at times, was very wonderful and comforting; at other times an unwelcome invasion of privacy. Understanding this, I learned, as she grew older, not to refer to previous voluntary confidences on her part" (p. 32). In light of this, it is interesting that mother and daughter revealed so much about each other in print.

But this creates many problems, including the issue of confidentiality. Would Sylvia have consented to the publication of her private letters and journals, with their often scathing references to family and friends? Mrs. Plath must have agonized over this question, for in releasing her daughter's personal writings, the mother exposed herself and others to the intense public scrutiny she had previously avoided. Any biographical or psychoanalytic approach to Plath must by necessity cause pain to the survivors, if only because she mercilessly caricatured them in her writings and quite often alienated them in her life. Nor was her aggression limited to art. She was filled with hostility toward those closest to her, and the publication of her letters and journals invariably opens up the wounds of those who witnessed and participated in the tragedy. In studying her biography, one inevitably must confront her family life, "with its twisted tensions, unreasoning loves and solidarity and loyalty born and bred in blood" (*The Journals*, p. 26). In writing about a young woman who took her own life, one becomes aware of those who loved her who were also symbolically killed in the process. Plath herself seemed to invite her own victimization, even by the reader: we are placed in the position of the "peanut-crunching crowd" in "Lady Lazarus" who "Shoves in to see/ Them unwrap me hand and foot—/ The big strip tease."[4] In approaching Plath's life and art, the reader thus may find it unusually difficult to maintain a balance between sympathy and criticism, and it is even harder to separate her psychic reality from objective truth.

The central event in Sylvia Plath's life was the traumatic death of her father in 1940 when she was eight years old. Otto Plath was a Professor of Entomology at Boston University and an authority on bumblebees, on which he had written a well-known textbook. Born in Grabow, Germany, he emigrated to the United States when he was 16 and entered a Lutheran seminary in Wisconsin. Growing disenchanted with religion, he left the seminary and decided to pursue a teaching career. He met Aurelia Schober in 1929, when she was a graduate student at Boston University. She was surprised when he told her that he had married 14 years ago, that he and his wife had separated, and that he had not seen her for 13 years. After securing a divorce, Plath married Aurelia in 1932. Sylvia was born nine months later and a brother, Warren, followed in 1935. Otto Plath began to fall ill shortly after the birth of his son. He was ill for years before he was diagnosed as suffering from diabetes mellitus. The tragedy was that the condition could have been controlled if treated promptly, but because of a morbid fear of cancer from which he thought he was suffering, Plath had refused to consult a physician until it was too late. After examining him and concluding that an amputation of a gangrenous leg was necessary, the surgeon murmured to Mrs. Plath: "How could such a brilliant man be so stupid." His condition continued to deteriorate after the amputation. Immediately after his death Sylvia presented her mother with a paper on which was written: "I PROMISE NEVER TO MARRY AGAIN. Signed:————" (*Letters Home*, p. 25). The mother signed the note at once and never did remarry.[5]

But why would a child require that her mother promise never to remarry unless the marriage was so perfect that it could never be duplicated—or so troubled that the child did not wish to have another father like the one who passed away? Otto Plath remains an enigmatic and contradictory figure to us. He was evidently a loving and devoted husband and father, respected by his colleagues, and hardly the monstrous Nazi his daughter mythologized in "Daddy." Indeed, he was a confirmed pacifist in his political views. Nevertheless, despite the generally admiring portrait of him that emerges from the introduction to *Letters Home,* Mrs. Plath allows herself to express a few quiet criticisms of her husband and their marriage. There were authoritarian aspects of his temperament that his wife and family had to appease. A trained English teacher, Mrs. Plath had to yield after marriage to her husband's wish for her to become a fulltime homemaker. Professor Plath's preoccupation with the book he was writing demanded absolute control and order in their small apartment. "The seventy-plus reference books were arranged on top of the long sideboard; the dining table became his desk. No paper or book was to be moved!" During their first year of married life everything had to be "given up for *THE BOOK.* After Sylvia was born, it was *THE CHAPTER"* (pp. 12–13). He became increasingly rigid and authoritarian.[6] "Despite the fact that he was only sixteen when he arrived in the United States, the Germanic theory that the man should be *der Herr des Hauses* (head of the house) persisted, contrary to Otto's earlier claims that the then modern aim of 'fifty-fifty' appealed to him" (p. 13). Realizing that, if she wanted a peaceful home, she would have to become "more submissive," even though it was not her nature to be so, the wife reluctantly yielded to his attitude of "rightful dominance."

It was against this background of a stoical mother anxious to keep the peace and an increasingly ill father unable to adapt to a more democratic society that Sylvia Plath spent the earliest and most crucial years of her life. There was never a time when the children's father was not ill, and consequently the family had to adjust its behavior. ". . . it was heart-breaking to watch a once-handsome, powerfully built man lose his vigor and deteriorate physically and emotionally. Appealing to him to get med-ical diagnosis and help only brought on explosive outbursts of anger." To protect her husband and children from each other, Mrs. Plath had to create an "upstairs-downstairs" household, "partly so their noisy play and squabbling would not upset him, but mostly so that he would not frighten them, for he now occasionally suffered intense cramping spasms in his leg muscles, which would cause him to moan in pain" (p. 18).

Given the intolerable situation, Sylvia must have felt a multitude of tangled emotions: love, hate, rage, confusion, guilt. The distinguished father whom she loved was also the fearful and violent man who, in re-fusing to call in a physician after years of terrible suffering, in effect killed himself and forever ended the family's security and well-being. The om-nipotent Germanic father, author of *Bumblebees and Their Ways,* suc-cumbed to a gangrenous infection brought on by accidentally stubbing his toe against the base of his bureau, stung to death, as it were, by his own carelessness. No wonder his daughter's faith was shattered. Upon learning of his death, Sylvia said: "I'll never speak to God again!" It was as if her father and God were mysteriously fused together and lost for-ever. The man she could not understand in life she began to mythologize in death. In her poems she could not decide whether to kill him again, as in "Daddy" and "Lady Lazarus," or to dig up his bones, as in "Full Fathom Five," "Electra on Azalea Path," and "The Colossus." The father's suffering infected the entire family.

After her father's death, Sylvia began to develop a lifelong tendency toward sinusitis, one of the father's physical symptoms, and during the last two years of his life Mrs. Plath developed a duodenal ulcer, which Sylvia analyzed in her journals as a Victorian woman's fear of her hus-band.[7]

Unable to direct her rage and feelings of abandonment toward the ab-sent father, Sylvia lashed out at her long-suffering mother. But the explosion was delayed, triggered only years afterwards, as the perplexed mother implies in the following incident in *Letters Home*. Because an autopsy had been performed on her husband's body, Mrs. Plath decided not to allow the young children to attend the funeral. "What I intended as an exercise in courage for the sake of my children was interpreted years later by my daughter as indifference. 'My mother never had time to mourn my father's death'" (p. 25). The scene is dramatized in *The Bell Jar*, though with a more sinister interpretation of the mother's point of view. Characteristically, the differing accounts of the mother-daughter relationship can hardly be reconciled.

Indeed, Mrs. Plath remains as enigmatic as her husband and certainly more instrumental in the formation of her daughter's character. In *Letters Home* she speaks briefly about her father's catastrophic business losses in the 1920s as a result of unwise stock-market investments. Consequently, "my father, broken in spirit and blaming himself most unjustly for his very human error, handed over the reins of management to my mother to the extent that my five-years-younger sister and my thirteen-years-younger brother grew up in a matriarchy" (p. 3). The daughter who grew up in a matriarchy later was forced to be both mother and father to her children after the death of her husband, who also made a human—and catastrophic—error. Mrs. Plath's comments about herself in *Letters Home* reflect a strong and determined personality concealed behind a quiet, restrained exterior. Sylvia's feelings toward her were obviously complicated by the fact that Otto Plath was old enough to be Aurelia's father (Mrs. Plath was 21 years younger than her husband, who was only four years younger than her own father).[8] In marrying her husband, Mrs. Plath may have been searching for a strong father figure to replace her own father, "broken in spirit"—a pattern that was certainly true of Sylvia's relationship to *her* husband, Ted Hughes. The biographical evidence suggests a compulsion to repeat a condition here. In this instance, it is an unconscious reenactment of painful marriages. In relating how uncritical Sylvia was of her during her high-school years, Mrs. Plath repeats a remark made by her 15-year-old daughter: "When I am a mother I want to bring up my children just as you have us." Mrs. Plath then adds parenthetically, "This charitable attitude, however, was not to last, and I was vividly reminded of my own hypercritical judgment of my parents throughout *my* undergraduate years at college!" (p. 37). In being disappointed first by her father and then by her husband, Mrs. Plath would almost inevitably feel hypercritical to men; and Sylvia shared this attitude, for she too was deeply hurt first by her father, whose death she interpreted as an act of abandonment, and then by her husband, who walked out on her and their two small children in late 1962, just months before she took her own life. History thus seemed to be repeating itself for both mother and daughter, a fact which must have terrified Sylvia, who resented her mother's self-sacrificial life.

But when does self-sacrificial behavior become self-destructive? This was perhaps the central question Sylvia Plath grappled with throughout her life. The enormity of her split between the "good" and "bad" mother is astonishingly dramatized in her correspondence and journals, respectively, which reveal her contradictory feelings toward the major figure in her life. In the hundreds of letters she wrote to her mother, there is scarcely a word of criticism much less hypercriticism. We see only the "good" daughter dutifully writing to the "good" mother. The only hint of criticism appears in a paragraph written to her brother in May 1953, three months before her suicide attempt. The paragraph begins innocuously enough but soon becomes ominous in its implications:

> One thing I hope is that you will make your own breakfasts in the a.m. so mother won't have to lift a finger. That is the main thing that seems to bother her. You know, as I do, and it is a frightening thing, that mother would actually Kill herself for us if we calmly accepted all she wanted to do for us. She is an abnormally altruistic person, and I have realized lately that we have to fight against her selflessness as we would fight against a deadly disease (*Letters Home*, p. 112).

Only by labeling the mother "abnormally altruistic" can the daughter allow herself to criticize her. And yet behind the overidealization lie hostility and a thinly veiled threat. Whatever truth there may have been in Sylvia's perception of a self-destructive mother, she is speaking about herself in encoded form. For it is Sylvia who will soon attempt suicide as an act of defiance against an impossibly demanding mother whose image of perfection the daughter cannot possibly satisfy. In the letter, however, Sylvia places the responsibility for this "suicide" on her brother, whose self-indulgence she imagines as the cause of the mother's death. A few pages later in *Letters Home*, Mrs. Plath chillingly reports how one morning during the fateful summer of 1953 she noticed partly healed gashes on her daughter's legs. "Upon my horrified questioning, she replied, 'I just wanted to see if I had the guts!' Sylvia's next words are crucial. "Oh,

Mother, the world is so rotten! I want to die! *Let's* die together!" (p. 124). In her imagination, one suicide inevitably led to two.

Sylvia's ideas concerning suicide are confirmed in her journals. The quarrel with her mother was based on the belief that Mrs. Plath's "selfless love" prevented the gratification of the daughter's healthy wishes—ambition, pride, sex, power. Selfless love became associated with domesticity, childbearing, poverty, submission—in other words, the fate of being a woman in a rigidly male-dominated society. Both Charlotte Perkins Gilman and Sylvia Plath equated maternal love with self-denial, self-sacrifice, and ultimately self-destruction, and it is no coincidence that their writings are filled with matricidal and infanticidal imagery. In reacting against their own mothers, they were, of course, rejecting their own unhappy childhoods in which they had both lost a father. And yet one of the ironies Sylvia could not or would not see was that, after her father's death, the mother was thrust into the position of being both the "nurturer" and the "provider"—and that this duel role required strength, courage, and determination. The situation would seem to suggest that Sylvia's mother had, through necessity, overcome the obstacles that prevented most mothers from also having careers outside the family during the 1950s. Yet Sylvia's anger toward her mother increased in later years.

Paradoxically, Sylvia's anger derived from the fear that her mother was not too weak but too strong—controlling, smothering, omnipotent. *The Journals of Sylvia Plath* leads to the conclusion that Sylvia's intense self-hatred originated from a deeply repressed rage toward a rejecting mother, and that the mother-daughter symbiotic relationship prevented Sylvia from developing inner boundaries between self and other, resulting in a lack of identity. As early as 1950 or 1951 (the beginning of the published journals), we see evidence of the theme of fusion with the maternal object which, psychoanalysts tell us, reflects the child's failure to enter the necessary separation and individuation stage of personality development, a stage which occurs when the child is between 18 months and three years old.[9] Speaking about herself in the third person, Plath writes: "But with your father dead, you leaned abnormally to the 'humanities' personality of your mother. And you were frightened when you heard yourself stop talking and felt the echo of her voice, as if she had spoken in you, as if you weren't quite you, but were growing and continuing in her wake, and as if her expressions were growing and emanating from your face" (*The Journals,* p. 26). It is as if the child is merely a narcissistic extension of her mother. Threatened by the lack of identity and autonomy, the child cannot live apart from her mother—but she cannot permanently live with her mother, since the child's personality is devoured (her space violated). As the child grows up, it becomes increasingly difficult to maintain the symbiotic relationship. Rebellion—as Plath describes in *The Bell Jar*—may prove unsuccessful in effecting the desired separation. Since the embattled self has a tenuous existence in a symbiotic relationship, its own annihilation may imply the destruction of the maternal love object—the fusion of suicide and matricide. This possibility is darkly hinted at in a July 1953 journal entry, just weeks before Sylvia's suicide attempt. "You saw visions of yourself in a straightjacket, and a drain on the family, murdering your mother in actuality, killing the edifice of love and respect built up over the years in the hearts of other people" (p. 87). This is the last entry before her breakdown; there is then a gap of two years in the journals, which is, unfortunately, the period of greatest interest to readers of *The Bell Jar*.

Only years later, in the late 1950s, does Plath begin to write about her "murderous self." "Its biggest weapon," she realizes, "is and has been the image of myself as a perfect success: in writing, teaching and living" (p. 176). The driving compulsion behind Plath's life and art was the quest for perfection that would mask an insecure and deficient self-image. At the center of the problem was the need to free herself from her mother, as the editor of *The Journals of Sylvia Plath* observes. "They had a symbiotic, deeply supportive union of great complexity in which it may not always have been easy to feel a separate person, an individual self . . ." (p. 265). The material that follows in the published journals, which Mrs. Plath acknowledges, in a brief note, was extremely painful for her to release, betrays an unrelenting assault on the symbiotic mother-daughter relationship. Despite the fact that, in the editor's words, "some of the more devastating comments" have been omitted from publication, the comments are devastating enough in their attack on the bad mother.[10] In addition, the reader frequently confronts "omissions" indicating the Editor's deletion of even more scathing material that has been censored out of the text, presumably to protect the survivors of the story.[11]

Throughout her journals, we see Sylvia's point of view, with its inevitable subjective coloring and often solipsistic thinking; there is one remarkable moment, however, when she reports on her *mother's* dream. The entry is dated December 12, 1958, the beginning of approximately six months of analysis with the psychiatrist who had originally treated her in the fall of 1953. Here is the mother's dream, as narrated by Sylvia in third person:

> It was her daughter's fault partly. She had a dream: her daughter was all gaudy-dressed about to go out and be a chorus girl, a prostitute too, probably. [Omission] The husband, brought alive in dream to relive the curse of his old angers, slammed out of the house in rage that the daughter was going to be a chorus girl. The poor Mother runs along the sand beach, her feet sinking in the sand of life, her money bag open and the money and coins falling into the sand, turning to sand. The father had driven, in a fury, to spite her, off the road bridge and was floating dead, face down and bloated, in the slosh of ocean water by the pillars of the country club. Everybody was looking down from the pier at them. Everyone knew everything (*The Journals*, pp. 268–269).

Dream interpretation is notoriously risky and fraught with difficulty, and it is hard enough to analyze the diarist's (or patient's) dream. But how do we interpret the mother's dream, which is filtered to us through the memory of the patient? We cannot even be sure that this is indeed the mother's dream, although two other details corroborate this: in Plath's poem "Electra on Azalea Path," written in 1959, she elaborates on the father's death, saying "My mother dreamed you face down in the sea." [12] In a later entry in the journals (December 27, 1958), Sylvia returns to her mother's dream and offers an extended analysis.

To understand the dream, we would need to have the dreamer's free associations, which we do not have here; yet, we do have Sylvia's associations and analytic commentary, and with these we can begin to decode the meaning. Moreover, since we are dealing with a symbiotic relationship, we should not be surprised to find a merging of identities. Sylvia's interpretation, arising from a session with her psychiatrist, emphasizes the fear that her mother holds her responsible for Otto Plath's death. "I have lost a father and his love early; feel angry at her because of this and feel she feels I killed him (her dream about me being a chorus girl and his driving off and drowning himself" (*The Journals*, p. 279). It is the Freudian theory of the omnipotence of thought, the irrational belief that unconscious wishes, in this case the daughter's repressed aggression toward her father, may actually cause a person's death. If the object of these murderous thoughts does indeed die, the child is overwhelmed with guilt and may accuse herself of being responsible for the death. Sylvia's interpretation of the dream explores the ambivalent feelings both the mother and daughter harbor toward the husband-father, whose memory continues to terrify both women nearly two decades after his death. Each woman seems to hold the other responsible for his death. On the same day she records her mother's dream, Sylvia writes: "He was an ogre. But I miss him. He was old, but she married an old man to be my father. It was her fault. [Omission.]" (p. 268). Interestingly, in the mother's dream it is the daughter, with her shameless seductiveness, who is responsible for Otto Plath's death. The Oedipal element is striking: The daughter's sexuality inflames the father and drives him to madness and suicide. The mother futilely attempts to placate the wrathful husband but her own sexual enticement, the empty money bag, is contemptuously rejected. The dream ends with the husband-father drowning himself in his own rage and the mother sinking into oblivion. The last two sentences convey the deepening horror of public disclosure of the family tragedy, a fear that may also disguise the wish for public vindication.[13]

If the woman in the dream is the mother running desperately to rescue her husband and daughter from a fatal collision, the dreamer is also the daughter searching frantically for lost innocence and youth. Sylvia's dreams during this time reflect the quest for parental love and approval. "I dreamed often of losing her," she writes about her mother in the December 27, 1958 journal entry, and she also dreams of losing a husband who inescapably reminds her of her father. Her unhealthy dependency on Ted Hughes, to whom she subordinated her literary and professional aspirations, repeats her mother's submission to Otto Plath. Sylvia's dreams return obsessively to the symbiotic relationship of a mother and daughter, and, in a variation on the theme, she imagines herself giving birth to her mother. "Magical fear Mother will become a child, my child: an old hag child" (p. 287). During her first pregnancy, when she expected to give birth to a boy, she dreamed that her father had come to life again and that her mother was also having a son. "This son of mine is a twin to her son," the bewildered Sylvia writes in October 1959; "The uncle of an age with his nephew. My brother of an age with my child. Oh, the tangles of that old bed" (p. 325).

Like Kafka's intensely moving *Letter to His Father,* these sections of *The Journals of Sylvia Plath* record the efforts to sort out the most wrenching emotions a child can feel toward a parent and to effect a reconciliation with her mother. In confessing to her inadequacies and fears, Sylvia drops the masks to reveal her most closely guarded secrets. She also wins the reader's respect and sympathy, for there is none of the facile self-praise that mars *Letters Home* or the mask of innocence disguising subtle malice that characterizes her persona in *The Bell Jar.* No one can read her journals without feeling the horror and loneliness of her life. And yet her journals are not unrelentingly bleak. To acknowledge the depths of her rage seemed to be liberating to her, and, however painful her self-analysis was, it also provided her with relief from her suffering. "Have been happier this week than for six months," she says at the beginning of her therapy. "It is as if R.B. [her psychiatrist], saying 'I give you permission to hate your mother,' also said, 'I give you permission to be happy.' Why the connection? Is it dangerous to be happy?" (p. 276). We overhear her brooding repeatedly over the link between her suicidal despair and defective mothering. "WHAT DO I EXPECT BY 'LOVE' FROM HER? WHAT IS IT I DON'T GET THAT MAKES ME CRY? I think I have always felt she uses me as an extension of herself; that when I commit suicide, or try to, it is a 'shame' to her, an accusation: which it was, of course. An accusation that her love was defective" (p. 281). She refers to reading Freud's "Mourning and Melancholia" and discovering an exact description of her suicidal feelings and the reasons for her writer's block: "a transferred murderous impulse from my mother onto myself: the 'vampire' metaphor Freud uses, 'draining the ego': that is exactly the feeling I have getting in the way of my writing: Mother's clutch" (p. 280). The way to escape her depression, she realizes, is to refuse to allow her mother to control her life. How is this done? "Talking and becoming aware of what is what and studying it is a help."

The person with whom Sylvia Plath did the most talking, and with the greatest therapeutic results, was the sympathetic female psychiatrist she first began to see during the end of 1953. *Letters Home* offers a few glimpses of her initial experience with psychiatrists prior to her breakdown. In her mother's words, "The first psychiatrist unfortunately reminded Sylvia of a handsome but opinionated date she felt she had 'outgrown,' and did not inspire her with confidence" (p. 124). He was presumably the source of "Dr. Gordon" in *The Bell Jar*, whom Esther immediately detests because he fails to conform to her image of a kind and omniscient father figure. He prescribes a series of electroshock treatments that Esther experiences as an electrocution. Another psychiatrist prescribed sleeping tablets, which Mrs. Plath carefully locked in a steel case. On August 24, 1953 Sylvia ingested about 40 pills and buried herself beneath the crawl space of her mother's house in Wellesley, Massachusetts. On the third day of her disappearance, Mrs. Plath and her son heard a moaning and discovered the unconscious woman. Like Lazarus, with whom she closely identified, she seemed to be resurrected after three days near death. After spending two weeks at the Newton-Wellesley Hospital, she was transferred to the psychiatric wing of the Massachusetts General Hospital for an additional two weeks and then sent to the renowned McLean Hospital in Belmont, where she responded well to psychotherapy. She received insulin therapy, as well as another series of shock treatments, and then entrusted herself to the psychiatrist in whose faith she never wavered.

An element of mystery has surrounded the sympathetic female psychiatrist who treated Plath. Called "Dr. B." in *Letters Home,* Dr. Nolan in *The Bell Jar,* and "Dr. Ruth Jones" (a pseudonym) in Edward Butscher's biography, she soon became the good mother for whom Sylvia was always searching. The references to her in *Letters Home* abound with praise. "I do love her," Sylvia writes to her mother in 1954, "she is such a delightful woman, and I feel that I am learning so much from her" (p. 140). In a letter beginning "Dearest of Mothers," Sylvia writes in 1956: "My whole session with Dr. B. is responsible for making me a rich, well-balanced, humorous, easy-going person, with a joy in the daily life . . ." (p. 215). In *Letters Home,* it is true, Sylvia told her mother only what Mrs. Plath wanted to hear, and consequently her reliability is always suspect. Nevertheless, there is no reason to question her unfailing praise of her loving psychiatrist. She tells her mother how her excellent tutor at Cambridge University, Dr. Dorothy Krook, is going to become her "mentor in the poetic and philosophic realm just as Dr. B. is in the personal and psychological" (p. 255). She also speaks about dedicating her first book of poems to her psychiatrist. This is the last reference to her therapist in *Letters Home,* though at the end of the volume Mrs. Plath adds that during the months preceding her daughter's death, Sylvia had received supportive letters from her beloved Dr. B.

The publication of *The Journals of Sylvia Plath* has given us a great deal more information about Sylvia's treatment with her psychiatrist and the relationship between the creative and therapeutic process. The editor reveals that perhaps the most important element of Plath's recovery in 1953 was her relationship to Dr. Ruth Beuscher, "an extraordinary therapist who played an important role in Plath's life, both at the time and for years afterward" (p. 88).[14] Without telling her mother or husband (whom she had married in June 1956), Sylvia had returned to therapy in December 1958. The effect was dramatic. "It gave rise to her first major work several months later: 'Poem for a Birthday' " (p. 266). About 40 pages of the journals, covering the period from December 1958 to late May or early June 1959, document her responses to her sessions with Dr. Beuscher and the working through of her feelings toward her family and herself. This section of her journals, preceded by Mrs. Plath's explanatory note authorizing the release of the highly personal—and painful—material, begins with Sylvia's determination to make the most out of her analysis. "If I am going to pay money for her time & brain as if I were going to a supervision in life & emotions & what to do with both, I am going to work like hell, question, probe sludge & crap & allow myself to get the most out of it" (p. 266). Frequency of treatment was about once a week, and the fee was $5 an hour—"Enough, considerable for me. Yet not outrageous, so it is punishment" (p. 286). Since Plath did not tell her mother or husband that she was entering therapy again, we may assume she feared their disapproval; consequently, an element of secrecy may have surrounded the analysis. Therapy lasted until around June, when she and her husband went on a three-month tour of the United States, followed by her stay at Yaddo, the writer's retreat in Saratoga Springs, New York. There is no clear indication in the journals when or why Sylvia ended therapy, or her final evaluation of its effect on her.

So far as we can tell, Dr. Beuscher has never publicly commented upon or written about her clinical experiences with Sylvia Plath—medical confidentiality would have made this unlikely. Unlike Dr. Frieda Fromm-Reichmann's treatment of Joanne Greenberg, which the German-born psychiatrist wrote about, in disguised form, in her two medical texts, Dr. Beuscher has refrained from publishing any material on her famous patient. From *The Journals of Sylvia Plath* we learn only her present name—Ruth Tiffany Barnhouse. A glance at the *American Psychiatric Association Biographical Directory* supplies us with background information and her psychiatric orientation.[15] Born in France in 1923, she received her medical degree from Columbia University in 1950 and did her psychiatric residence at McLean Hospital from 1953 to 1955. Plath thus must have been one of her first patients, and only nine years younger than her psychiatrist. In 1959 she was appointed clinical assistant professor of psychiatry at Harvard University, a position she has held until recently. A deeply religious woman, she received a Th.M. in Spiritual Direction from Weston College of Theology. Her articles have appeared in theological as well as psychoanalytic journals. In 1976 she coedited *Male and Female: Christian Approaches to Sexuality,* and in 1977 she published *Homosexuality: A Symbolic Confusion,* a book that demonstrates her sensitive and enlightened approach to controversial social issues.[16] Although she apparently did not study at a psychoanalytic institute, her orientation is psychoanalytic, more Jungian than Freudian, and her writings reveal an

extraordinary synthesis of religious, psychoanalytic, and feminist insights.[17]

It is clear from the journals that during Sylvia's second period of treatment with Dr. Beuscher, she was beginning to make major breakthroughs, intellectual and emotional, in her self-understanding. Contrary
to inferences based upon *Letters Home* and *The Bell Jar*, she was beginning to dislodge the masks she had worn all her life.[18] Few aspects of her
personality went unexamined. She was able to trace back the writer's block
from which she was suffering at this time to her ambivalence toward her
mother, whose love and approval seemed to be contingent upon success.
In a crucial passage in the journals, the psychiatrist's voice merges into
the patient's as Sylvia probes her inability to write:

> Dr. B.: You are trying to do two mutually incompatible things this
> year. 1) spite your mother. 2) write. To spite your mother, you don't
> write because you feel you have to give the stories to her, or that she
> will appropriate them. (As I was afraid of having her around to ap-
> propriate my baby, because I didn't want it to be hers.) So I can't
> write. And I hate her because my not writing plays into her hands
> and argues that she is right, I was foolish not to teach, or do some-
> thing secure, when what I have renounced security for is nonexistent
> (p. 280).

Sylvia's analysis dramatically freed her from writer's block, and many
of the poems she wrote during 1959 were better than anything she had
yet written. Several of these poems—"Electra on Azalea Path," "The Bee-
keeper's Daughter," "Man in Black," "The Colossus," and "Poem for a
Birthday"—are filled with the same anguished familial themes that she
was working through in her analysis. Ironically, many of her best poems
reflect the image of the artist as a "bad" daughter who expresses rage toward mother and father. In this way, Sylvia could use the creative process
to extricate herself from the dilemma that was causing her writer's block.
She could spite her mother by writing about her—using her art, that is,
to reject the rejecting mother. This would enable the poet to achieve the
success that would both conform to, yet defy, the mother's perfectionist
standards.

There were also breakthroughs in her understanding of men. During
her analysis she visited her father's grave, presumably for the first time,
and felt tempted "to dig him up. To prove he existed and really was dead"
(p. 299). He was dead, yet she resurrected and mythologized him in her

poems. Her recognition of the "Electra" complex came from this time, and, while it may be argued that this was not a real insight but a flirtation with one of the clichés of a post-Freudian era, she began to examine the meaning of her often-seductive behavior toward men and traced it back to the wish to regain her lost father. She also began to explore her ambivalence toward men and, despite the fact that she was a physically attractive woman, her poor body image.[19] Identifying women with weakness, passivity, and incompleteness, she yearned to be a man, so that she could merge with his strength and freedom. Her dreams, though, were often preoccupied with images of deformity, mutilation, and death, reflective of her fear of fragmentation. In one of her most-poignant journal entries, she asks: "If I really think I killed and castrated my father may all my dreams of deformed and tortured people be my guilty visions of him or fears of punishment for me? And how to lay them? To stop them operating through the rest of my life?" (p. 301). Castration fear is a particularly strong motif in her writings and may derive from biological, psychological, and cultural sources. The sexism of the 1950s was no less oppressive than that of Charlotte Perkins Gilman's era, and the cult of domesticity made it difficult for many women to achieve self-fulfillment and wholeness. Otto Plath himself embodied the belief in male supremacy, and his own disfigurement and death may have seemed a fitting end to some of his more authoritarian ideas.

By current standards, where psychoanalysis usually lasts for many years, Plath made remarkable therapeutic progress in a short time. Almost immediately upon reentering analysis, she began to question nearly every aspect of her life. To judge from her journals, she was, characteristically, a "perfect" patient. Rather than seeking merely symptomatic relief, she accepted the challenge to discover the root causes of her conflicts and to heal herself through insight, change, and growth. The image of psychotherapy we see in the journals evokes the slow but steady process of self-discovery and the controlled regression to childhood experiences. There are revelations and blinding flashes of insight, to be sure, but they are earned, hard won. The insights are often followed by days of darkness and despair. Progress in psychotherapy is measured not by magical purgation and rebirth, as *The Bell Jar* curiously dramatizes, but by the agonizingly slow development of ego strengths: the ability to tolerate frustration and imperfection, the renunciation of pathological modes of gratification, the capacity for reality testing and problem solving. There was an intense intellectual struggle without "intellectualizing," the separation of ideas from dangerous emotions, and she was going through what her psychiatrist elsewhere called a "corrective emotional experience," which is generally played out in the transference relationship.[20] She was investigating not only the Oedipal components of her personality, such as her competition with men, but the more significant pre-Oedipal issues of separation and individuation, breaking out of the symbiotic union with the mother. There were, of course, areas she did not adequately explore, and her psychiatrist raised two questions that, in retrospect, Sylvia failed to work through: her feelings toward her husband and children. When asked by Dr. Beuscher whether she would "have the guts" to admit she made the wrong choice in a husband, she replied: "nothing in me gets scared or worried at this question" (p. 270). And to the question whether pregnancy would bring her peace of mind, she remained uncharacteristically silent, able only to paraphrase the analyst's thought. "I would, she says, probably have a depression after my first baby if I didn't get rid of it now . . ." (p. 291). Both questions proved to be more complicated than Sylvia suspected.

The journals also confirm Sylvia's positive transference relationship with her psychiatrist and the need to create a healthier symbiotic fusion with the therapist than she was able to achieve with her mother. At one point she parenthetically refers to the growing erotic love for Dr. Beuscher: "am very ashamed to tell her of immediate jealousies—the result of my extra-professional fondness for her, which has inhibited me" (pp. 304–305). This was an indication, perhaps, of latent homosexual love. In light of the early death of her father and the fact that she grew up in a house dominated by strong women, this is certainly not unexpected. What is surprising, though, is that Esther's "evil-Double" in *The Bell Jar,* Joan Gilling, is a lesbian, and the novel betrays a strong aversion to homosexual love. Esther is repelled by Joan's sexual advances, and there is only one moment in the story which offsets the pattern of homophobia. When Esther asks Dr. Nolan "What does a woman see in a woman that she can't see in a man?" the psychiatrist succinctly answers: "Tenderness." The suicide of Esther's alter ego at the end of the story symbolizes the repudiation of the novelist's homosexual and suicidal impulses.[21]

Contrary to the impression given by *The Bell Jar,* however, the journals reveal a passionate need for womanly love, and Dr. Beuscher was able to accept Sylvia's ardent admiration. Warm, supportive, empathic, the psychiatrist functioned as a Kohutian mirror by receiving and reflecting back the patient's idealizing transference. Sylvia's initial judgment of her at the beginning of therapy never wavers. "I believe in R.B. because she is a clever woman who knows her business & I admire her. She is for me 'a permissive mother figure.' I can tell her anything, and she won't turn a hair or scold or withhold her listening, which is a pleasant substitute for love" (pp. 266–267). The therapist listened, interpreted, but did not tell the patient what to do. Dr. Beuscher's management of Plath was apparently free from any disturbing countertransference or attempts to disrupt the therapeutic frame through excessive closeness or distance.[22] There is no condescending dismissal of the patient's complaints, as in "The Yellow Wallpaper," nor incestuous acting out, as in *Tender Is the Night,* nor a glorified death wish, as in *The Cocktail Party.* The psychiatrist was able to handle the patient's negative transference when it arose and analyze it.[23] At one point, for example, Sylvia writes about her anger when the psychiatrist changed an appointment. "She does it and is symbolically withholding herself, breaking a 'promise,' like Mother not loving me, breaking her 'promise' of being a loving mother each time I speak to her or talk to her" (p. 277). There is also a nightmare preceding one of her visits to the psychiatrist in which Sylvia fears the doctor will lock her out or pretend not to be at home. Within a short time, though, she was able to understand much of this negative transference and control it. She worked through her anger so that when the therapist was late for a session, the patient did not feel threatened. She talks about her "hunger" for the psychiatrist's praise and the magical power of her therapeutic art. Her desire to study psychology and pursue a Ph.D. in clinical psychology was an effort to incorporate Dr. Beuscher's omnipotence. In the psychiatrist's words, "You are never the same afterwards: it is a Pandora's box: nothing is simple anymore" (p. 281).

The Pandora's box of psychoanalysis enabled Plath to overcome her writer's block and to begin to make the imaginative leaps that were to secure her artistic fame. With the help of Dr. Beuscher, she was able to affirm the therapeutic impulse behind her art. "If writing is not an outlet, what is? . . ." (p. 292). There were times, of course, when she questioned the value of psychotherapy and whether her psychiatrist could help her to write or, equally important, help her to write well. Psychotherapy cannot improve the quality of art nor tell us much about aesthetics, why *Hamlet* succeeds while other plays dealing with the Oedipus complex fail. Freud's own conclusion—"Before the problem of the creative artist analysis must, alas, lay down its arms"[24]—reminds us of the limits of psychoanalysis to explain the forever mysterious creative process. Yet far from endorsing the view that literature and psychotherapy must necessarily re-main antithetical to each other, as so many writers have maintained in the mistaken belief that therapy destroys creativity, Plath remained in-debted to her psychiatric experiences and profited from them. In affirm-ing that "Writing is my health" (p. 327), she recognized that both the creative and therapeutic process allowed her to express her volatile emo-tions and to achieve a degree of mastery over them. In the end her strength and determination failed, and she succumbed to indescribable horror; yet, even toward the end of her life, she remained hopeful that artistic expres-sion would be therapeutic. She told a friend that *The Bell Jar* was "an autobiographical apprentice work which I had to write in order to free myself from the past."[25] The exorcism ultimately failed to rescue her from the bell-jar vision, but the novel does offer us an insight into the writer's illness and the extent to which both her conflicts and defenses shaped the texture of her art.

Rather than arbitrarily divorcing Sylvia Plath's art from her life, as many critics have done in an attempt to make her into a "mythic" writer, can we discover a meaning to Esther Greenwood's breakdown in *The Bell Jar* that would be consistent with our increased understanding of Plath's bi-ography and also help to explain the novelist's conscious and uncon-scious fictional strategies in the story?[26] The interpretation would not imply that *The Bell Jar* is an example of pathological art—by definition art can-not be pathological—but that it reflects, like Eliot's *The Cocktail Party,* the signs of an individual struggling against psychic fragmentation and the restitutive efforts toward health and wholeness. Both *The Cocktail Party* and *The Bell Jar* are products of a creative malady, a striking confirmation of how, in Eliot's words, "some forms of illness are extremely favourable, not only to religious illumination, but to artistic and literary composi-tion." But what is the nature of this illness, its origins and dynamics, and the literary choices to which it gives rise?

*   *   *

Neither *Letters Home* nor *The Journals of Sylvia Plath* offers a diagnostic category of the writer's illness beyond a few vague references to "depres-sion."[27] A more contemporary interpretation would suggest "pathologi-cal narcissism." The subject of narcissism, as we discussed in *The Cocktail Party,* remains highly controversial even within analytic circles. It is im-portant to distinguish healthy narcissism (which Freud called primary narcissism, the infant's oneness with the world), from pathological narcissism, a secondary process in which the individual seeks to gain in later life the genuine love that was lacking in childhood. Not all analysts accept the classification of pathological narcissism. Heinz Kohut rejects the term and constructs an alternate explanation based on developmental arrests.[28] The theory will almost certainly undergo major revision in the future. Psychiatric classification is notoriously subjective, culturally determined, and shifting. It represents at best a working hypothesis or useful fiction for the understanding and treatment of mental disorders. Few literary critics are sympathetic to the idea of diagnosing a fictional character or placing him on the analyst's couch. A novel as undisguisedly autobiographical as *The Bell Jar*, however, may justify a clinical approach. Moreover, it is hardly possible to explore the novel without an understanding of Esther's conflicts and defenses. The work of Dr. Otto Kernberg, a leading theoretician in the area of pathological narcissism, has a striking relevance to Plath's novel. In its presentation of Esther's distorted internalized object relationships, the genetic-dynamic features of her breakdown, and the novelist's adoption of fictional strategies based upon primitive defense mechanisms, such as merging and splitting, *The Bell Jar* reveals a remarkably accurate portrait of a phenomenon that has far-reaching literary, cultural, and psychiatric implications. What follows is first a summary of Kernberg's discussion of the narcissistic personality and then the application of this theory to *The Bell Jar*.

In *Borderline Conditions and Pathological Narcissism* (1975), Kernberg characterizes patients with a narcissistic personality structure as presenting "an unusual degree of self-reference in their interactions with other people, a great need to be loved and admired by others, and a curious apparent contradiction between a very inflated concept of themselves and an inordinate need for tribute from others."[29] Other features include a shallow emotional life, an inability to empathize with others, a restlessness or boredom with life, and an excessive need to envy or idealize other people. To an extent, everyone has suffered from these problems from time to time, and there is probably no one who has escaped narcissistic injury. What distinguishes the narcissist, clinically, is the degree and duration of these injuries. The need to idealize is inseparably related to the impulse to devalue. The narcissist usually turns against those people whom he formerly idealized, because they failed to supply him with sufficient admiration. There is thus a tension between overvaluation and devaluation. One is elevated to a pedestal only to be cast off later. Grandiosity, self-centeredness, and emotional coldness characterize the narcissist, who attempts to control and possess other people in an exploitative or parasitic manner. The narcissist's haughty and grandiose behavior is a defense against paranoid traits related to the projection of inner rage, which is central to his pathology. Both the narcissist and the borderline personality, another category of patients, present similar defensive organization, including a reliance upon splitting, denial, projective identification, and omnipotence. Unlike the borderline patient, the narcissist usually functions well in society because he can control impulses better, mask rage, and sublimate. But this may lead to a vicious circle. The narcissist's success allows him to receive the admiration from others which, in turn, only heightens his grandiosity. For this reason, the prognosis for treatment remains guarded.

How does pathological narcissism arise? Kernberg offers an object relations approach based on the work of earlier theorists, most notably, Edith Jacobson.[30] In the early stages of normal development, there is a differentiation between self and object images, leading to the formation of identity. Severe frustrations with early objects, however, especially disruptions in the mother-child bond, may bring about a dangerous refusion of self and object images, resulting in identity diffusion—the loss of ego boundaries.[31] In contrast to other psychoanalytic theoreticians, Kernberg proposes that a process of refusion of the internalized self and object images takes place in the narcissistic personality. The ideal (or perfect) self, ideal object, and actual object merge together as a defense against intolerable reality, with a devaluation and destruction of all other inner and outer objects that are less than perfect. Identity is thus created around what Kohut, the proponent of the other major approach to narcissism, calls the "grandiose self," an inflated self-image which comes into existence as a protection against cold or rejecting parents. Kernberg observes that "chronically cold parental figures with covert but intense aggression" contribute to the development of pathological narcissism. These parents, especially the mother, function well on the surface but nevertheless demonstrate callousness, indifference, or nonverbalized aggression toward the child. To protect himself against this intense aggression and deprivation, the child retreats into himself and creates a grandiose self in defiance of reality.

In time, the narcissist becomes entrapped in his delusions of grandiosity, and his suffering increases. Rejected, he cannot prevent himself from rejecting. Because he cannot tolerate weakness or imperfection, he rejects other people as "mere mortals." He cannot genuinely love or establish warm relationships. The terrible irony is that behind the narcissist's self-love lies the absence of love, just as behind his grandiosity lies self-contempt. The grandiose self may be overwhelmed, resulting in a psychotic breakdown—blurring of ego boundaries, loss of the ability to test reality, regression to more infantile modes of behavior. Feelings of self-hatred, arising from a punitive and accusatory superego, may drive him to suicide. Superego function remains poor, according to Kernberg, because it contains derivatives of primitive, aggressive, and distorted parental images. Unlike other analysts (including Freud), who maintain that narcissistic patients do not form transference relationships, Kernberg argues that they do, but of a special type. "What appears as distance and uninvolvement on the surface is underneath an active process of devaluation, depreciation, and spoiling. The undoing of this transference resistance typically brings about intense paranoid developments, suspiciousness, hatred, and envy" (pp. 247–248). Indeed, one of the narcissist's central problems is the inability to tolerate aggression. He perceives other people as lifeless, shadowy persecutors who are endowed with sinister powers. To deal with his own virulent aggression, he adopts primitive splitting defenses, such as projective identification, in which he projects his rage upon others with whom he then actively identifies. His attitude toward others, Kernberg says, is "either deprecatory—he has extracted all he needs and tosses them aside—or fearful—others may attack, exploit, and force him to submit to them" (p. 233).

Not only does *The Bell Jar* accurately portray the major elements of Kernberg's theory of the narcissistic personality, the story dramatizes one of the most paradoxical features of narcissism, the widening gulf between the achievement of success and perfection, on the one hand, and loneliness and despair, on the other. As a narrator Esther succeeds in conveying the horror of her collapse and the depletion of her spirit. However, as an interpreter of her thoughts and feelings, she usually remains silent, making it difficult for us to determine the extent of her knowledge of herself, both before and after her breakdown. Indeed, narrative distance remains problematic in *The Bell Jar* and, unlike the introspective journals, it is often hard to locate Plath's attitude toward her narrator.

Until her breakdown during the summer of 1953, Esther has led an exemplary life. She speaks proudly about her successful career and the envy it has engendered in others. She describes a life of ferocious competition where only the very best can attain the American Dream. "All my life I'd told myself studying and reading and writing and working like mad was what I wanted to do, and it actually seemed to be true, I did everything well enough and got all A's, and by the time I made it to college nobody could stop me" (p. 34). The ambiguity of "working like mad" becomes increasingly ominous, as does the hint of aggression in the words "nobody could stop me." Nobody could stop her, that is, except herself. Inextricably, she begins to break down, to drop out, to punish herself for an unspecified crime. Her only explanation is that she has worked too hard and has not known when to stop—a "nonexplanation."[32] Whereas she had always looked down on her mother's coed college, filled with people who could not get scholarships to the prestigious eastern schools, now she believes that the "stupidest person at my mother's college knew more than I did" (p. 140). The condescending reference to her mother's college, and thus to the mother herself, alerts us to Esther's perfectionist standards as well as her tendency to perceive life in terms of success or failure.

Esther candidly acknowledges her former "perfect" character (or, in Kernberg's language, the grandiose self) but she never reaches a more disquieting insight, her devaluation of others. Readers of *The Bell Jar* may be persuaded to accept Esther's harsh judgment of the world, and the novel powerfully satirizes American society of the 1950s, with its woman haters, "baby-making" machines, and McCarthyist hysteria. The glittering artificiality of the Amazon Hotel in New York, where Esther and the other magazine contest winners are staying, becomes a metaphor of a wasteland culture. Like *The Catcher in the Rye,* to which it remains indebted, *The Bell Jar* exposes the phoniness, superficiality, and corruption of adult society.

The world of sanity seems more terrifying than the world of madness, and when the bell jar descends upon Esther, it is difficult to tell how if at all the world has changed to her. But there is a problem with the novel's persistent devaluation of the world. As we suggested about Eliot's depiction of reality in *The Cocktail Party,* the reader begins to mistrust the consistently acidic portraits of human nature. Nearly everyone seems pathological to Esther, and she condemns others for faults within herself. She criticizes women for being fashion conscious, for example, but her own descriptions of people begin and end with their physical appearance. Often she makes value judgments on the basis of what she perceives to be their deformed body image. Her characterization of a woman giving birth evokes the image of Gothic horror. She accuses Buddy Willard of hypocrisy, his mother of puritanical fanaticism, his father of abandonment. She feels no gratitude toward her literary patron, Philomena Guinea, who later provides her with the funds for a private psychiatric hospital. Those whom Esther does not deprecate, like Betsy, are "innocent," as if they are not part of human nature. Characters speak "mercilessly" or with a "brutal promptitude." They "hiss," a recurring verb. A nurse "affirmed with relish" the news that Esther and the others are suffering from food poisoning. Facial expressions betray sinister meaning. Buddy has a "queer, satisfied expression" on his face when he tells her that she has broken her leg in a skiing accident. And the nurses walk around the hospital with "conspiratorial grins."

Certainly no one would deny that the world can be and often is an evil place, yet it is equally obvious that sincerity and compassion also exist, often alongside cruelty. Rarely does Esther acknowledge the good within people. Her world is dark and fearful, and human nature seems as corrupt as the contaminated food she eats. Part of the bell-jar vision is the hypercriticism that prevents her from discovering the unique joys in life, joys that are as real as sorrow. The depth of her cynicism reflects the grimness of her vision. She cannot imagine a man and woman in love without the relationship becoming exploitative or parasitic. She cannot understand how people might freely choose to have a baby and experience pleasure from it. She cannot contemplate love without feeling hate or think about work without becoming competitive. Nor can she pursue experience without having it become poisonous and dead. Attuned to the false self, she denies the possibility of a true self. Every attempt at friendship leads back to a solipsistic point of view. People look good only from a distance, but the moment they approach Esther notices their flaws. When men come close to her, they "sink into ordinariness." She sees reality as shadow without substance and, like the characters in *The Cocktail Party,* she is always on the verge of fragmentation and decomposition. Her tenuous identity dissolves when she looks into a mirror. "I felt myself melting into the shadows like the negative of a person I'd never seen before in my life" (p. 11).

Esther remains on the surface passive throughout the novel, more sinned at than sinning. Like so many heroes and heroines who have experienced psychological breakdowns, she appears Christlike in her suffering and more sensitive than those who have never broken down. And yet beneath her mask of innocence lies virulent aggression directed, appropriately enough, at her parents.[33] Replaying her journals, Plath recreates in *The Bell Jar* a mother whose "sweet, martyr's smile" conceals a coldness that is eerily reproduced in her daughter's personality, and a father whose premature death becomes the archetype of primeval loss. Kernberg's description of a narcissistic patient's mother accurately characterizes Mrs. Greenwood. She is practical, efficient, hardworking, but also nonverbally spiteful. Plath allows us to feel little sympathy for Mrs. Greenwood despite the terrible loss *she* has suffered and her years of bitterness. "My mother had taught shorthand and typing to support us ever since my father died, and secretly she hated it and hated him for dying and leaving no money because he didn't trust life insurance salesmen" (pp. 42–43). Both mother and daughter feel anger toward the man whose death is perceived as an act of abandonment, even betrayal.

Even before his death, however, the marriage appeared lifeless and loveless. Mrs. Greenwood confides to Esther the fact that no sooner were they married and on their honeymoon than her husband casually informed her that they could "stop pretending and be ourselves" (p. 94). From that day on her mother never enjoyed a minute's peace. Despite the affection a man may show to his wife, he secretly wants her to "flatten out underneath his feet." All the marriages in *The Bell Jar* are deadly and dehumanizing, and Esther's rejection of marriage is clearly a rejection of her parents' union. No camaraderie exists between mother and daughter, no sympathy born out of mutual suffering. Esther experiences her as harsh and rejecting. Seeing her mother asleep, Esther perceives the pin curls on her head "glittering like a row of little bayonets." She has a fantasy of murdering the sleeping woman. "The piggish noise irritated me, and for a while it seemed to me that the only way to stop it would be to take the column of skin and sinew from which it rose and twist it to silence between my hands" (pp. 137–138).

Paradoxically, Esther's central fear, maternal abandonment, is also her wish. In her mind matricide and suicide are fused, and she cannot kill one person without killing two. Additionally, the wish to slay the mother reflects the belief that the mother will slay her. Matricide and infanticide are thus inseparably joined, as in "The Yellow Wallpaper." Chapter Thirteen of *The Bell Jar* opens with a discussion of Ibsen's *Ghosts,* in which a young man discovers he has a brain disease inherited from a syphilitic father. At the end of the play he goes mad, and the mother debates whether to kill him. Esther's preoccupation with the play suggests her identification with the insane victim. She too awaits attack from her mother. While speaking to a sailor, she confesses that she is an orphan, and in the hospital she has a fantasy that her mother and brother will abandon her. Yet, Esther becomes furious when her mother does visit her. Of all the visitors in the hospital, "My mother was the worst. She never scolded me, but kept begging me, with a sorrowful face, to tell her what she had done wrong. She said she was sure the doctors thought she had done something wrong because they asked her a lot of questions about my toilet training, and I had been perfectly trained at a very early age and given her no trouble whatsoever" (p. 228).

As in *The Journals of Sylvia Plath,* we are confronted with the difficulty of verifying the daughter's interpretation of the mother in *The Bell Jar.* Are we dealing with psychic or historical reality? Is Esther's illness responsible for the distorted perception of the mother, or is her self-hate a correct evaluation of the rejecting mother? Who is driving whom crazy? Twice in the novel Esther describes her mother as reproachful: "She looked loving and reproachful, and I wanted her to go away" (p. 194); "My mother's face floated to mind, a pale, reproachful moon . . ." (p. 267). We can dismiss Esther's self-conscious disclosure that she had been perfectly toilet trained at an early age, but it is harder to dismiss the suspicion that the daughter's self-destructive behavior derives from the mother's self-sacrificial personality. One of the technical achievements of *The Bell Jar* is the indefinable hostility surrounding the mother's character. It is as hard for us to locate the problem in the mother-daughter relationship as it is for Esther. Ironically, Mrs. Greenwood's silent reproaches are reproduced with a vengeance in her daughter's personality. The climax of the story occurs when Esther expresses to Dr. Nolan her hatred of her mother. Not even then, however, does Esther realize that her own martyrdom is part of her mother's bitter legacy. Esther remains, tragically, her mother's daughter.

Esther is also her father's daughter. Her feelings toward him are no less contradictory than those toward her mother. Early in the story she refers to her German-speaking father, dead since she was nine, who came from "some manic-depressive hamlet in the black heart of Prussia" (p. 36). The reference to psychopathology links the father and his birthplace to a diseased state of mind, part of her paternal legacy. She rejects both him and his Germanic culture. Significantly, her anger toward him is converted to idealization elsewhere in the story. In the presence of the father surrogate, Constantin, whom Esther tries unsuccessfully to seduce, she asserts that she felt happier than she had been since she was nine years old, "running along the hot white beaches with my father the summer before he died" (p. 82). She is struck by the thought that she was "only purely happy" until his death.

Unlike the journals, there is little suggestion in *The Bell Jar* that the father was an "ogre" or that the daughter may have felt responsible for his death. The joyous image of Esther running along the beach with her father the summer before his death sharply contradicts the mother's terrified dream Sylvia narrates in analysis, which ends with the father's drowning caused in large part by the daughter's gaudy seductiveness. We thus receive a highly selective portrait of the novelist's life, especially in its softened father-daughter relationship. Plath retains the biographical incident in which the daughter visits her father's grave. "I thought it odd that in all the time my father had been buried in this graveyard, none of us had ever visited him" (p. 186). The mother remains the scapegoat. Because Mrs. Greenwood had not allowed Esther and her brother to attend the funeral, the father's death seemed unreal for all these years. "I had a great yearning, lately, to pay my father back for all the years of neglect, and start tending his grave. I had always been my father's favorite, and it seemed fitting I should take on a mourning my mother had never bothered with" (p. 186).

In *The Bell Jar*, then, the theme of family betrayal is central to Esther's illness, with each member of the family hurting and being hurt by the others. The roles of victim and victimizer become hopelessly confused. Mrs. Greenwood's neglect of her husband's grave represents her payment for his years of absence. By being unable to visit her father's grave, Esther in turn has been forbidden to engage in the necessary mourning that will allow her to expiate her guilt and grief over his death. Esther's ambivalence toward him is intense, and there is a telling ambiguity in her "great yearning, lately, to pay my father back for all the years of neglect." Until now, the daughter has shut the father from her mind, as the mother seemingly has done. However, because Esther has not been able to talk about her feelings toward him, she has remained unable to integrate the good father with the bad one. Thus, she has mythologized him into an omnipotent Daddy while at the same time reviling his black heart—and her own black heart. Even the verb she uses, "to pay him back," confirms the indebtedness and resentment she feels toward him, the love and hate.

Rather than filling a deep void in her, Esther's discovery of her father's grave intensifies her suicidal urge. Immediately after she visits the grave, she breaks down in tears and then calmly proceeds to bury herself beneath the crawl space of her mother's house.[34] This section of *The Bell Jar* is almost completely autobiographical. Psychoanalytically, the suicide attempt represents an acting out of infantile rage and a desire to merge with the buried father. Plath's description of the self-burial contains sexual imagery, with Esther penetrating and being penetrated by the dark earth. Once buried, she feels her head rise, "like the head of a worm" (p. 192).[35] In attempting suicide, Esther also seems to be incorporating the bad mother. The pre-Oedipal imagery evokes a poisonous breast as Esther swallows the sleeping pills that will destroy her insides. Her descent into the black earth may also symbolize the Hadeslike journey into her father's forbidding Germanic roots. The early reference to the "manic-depressive hamlet in the black heart of Prussia" foreshadows Esther's account of self-burial. She "crouched at the mouth of the darkness, like a troll"; once buried, she regards the eerie silence "as black water." The description of her rescue conjures up the image of a child or animal returning to the mother's body. Esther's helpless cry suggests that the object of her search has been not only the father, who remains unresurrected, but the mother, the most primitive object of the child's quest for oneness and security. For it is the word "mother!" that Esther hears herself instinctively uttering as rescue finally comes.

Esther's suicide attempt thus represents a regression to an infantile state in which the young woman reenacts her primitive longings for fusion with the maternal and paternal love object. Given her rage toward mother and motherhood, however, she remains mistrustful of children. The image of a baby "pickled in a laboratory jar" haunts her imagination, as if the fetus itself is imprisoned in its own bell-jar vision. And indeed Plath's journals and novel both suggest that mental illness arises from unresolved childhood conflicts. Like "The Yellow Wallpaper," which dramatizes a young mother's unsuccessful efforts to escape from the insatiable demands of her baby, *The Bell Jar* portrays babies as fat voracious creatures who drain their mother's strength. Esther devotes an entire paragraph to a description of an issue of *Baby Talk*, containing the feeding of babies; she is repelled by their monstrous appetite. She broods over her aversion toward children and implicitly decides to remain childless. "Why was I so unmaternal and apart? Why couldn't I dream of devoting myself to baby after fat puling baby like Dodo Conway? If I had to wait on a baby all day, I would go mad" (p. 250). Earlier in the story, she says that children make her sick. There are several unintentional ironies here. Although Esther imagines babies as voracious and cannibalistic, she herself seems eternally hungry for nourishment, unable to fill the "profound void of an empty stomach" (p. 86). Her image of a healthy overnourished baby may represent a denial of her fear of a sick undernourished one. She rightly resents a society in which women are required to choose between a family or a career, yet during her breakdown she becomes more and more like the child she had feared and thus a drain on her own mother's already depleted resources. Despite statements like "I felt pure and sweet as a new baby" (p. 22) early in the story, Esther does not usually associate childhood experience with purity and sweetness. Rather, children are parasitic to her.

Significantly, Esther cannot avoid returning to her own childhood experiences as *The Bell Jar* relentlessly carries her backward into time. Wherever she goes, she sees an image of her mother. Plummeting down the ski slope, she sees her entire past returning; the disastrous journey ends with a broken leg and the return to her mother. Lying on a hospital bed, she drinks a cup of hot milk given to her by a nurse; Esther tastes the milk luxuriously, "the way a baby tastes its mother" (p. 226). In light of Margaret Mahler's pioneering work in developmental theory and identity formation, the separation and individuation theme in *The Bell Jar* remains distorted and unstable, fluctuating between fusion and loss of ego boundaries, on the one hand, and matricidal and suicidal fantasies, on the other. In a startling authorial slip at the beginning of the story, Esther breaks the chronology to refer to her own baby, but it is impossible to reconcile her coldness toward children with the mature decision to become a mother. In fact, one must turn to the journals, not to the novel, to understand Plath's positive feelings toward motherhood, and her desperation when she was unable to conceive.[36] Yet, Plath never did resolve her ambivalence toward motherhood, and Esther's disclosure seems totally out of character.

What emerges, then, from a psychoanalytic interpretation of *The Bell Jar* is a portrait of a woman whose narcissistic personality structure originates from a matrix of rigid maternal control and paternal loss. Her underlying struggle against identity diffusion may be traced to pre-Oedipal difficulties of separation and individuation. This is admittedly a dry and perhaps reductive analysis.[37] It does not account for the popularity of the novel, Plath's ability to implicate the reader into Esther's harrowing world. The reader certainly does not have to be "narcissistic" to identify with Esther's feelings of emptiness, self-absorption, and persecution. To judge from the horrified reactions of Plath's family, friends, and teachers upon reading *The Bell Jar,* the reader feels more sympathy toward Esther than the real-life characters felt toward the novelist, whom they accused of distorting reality and betraying their trust. This is the prerogative of the novelist, of course, to shape aesthetic reality and to subordinate biographical details to artistic truths.

Esther's psychological health remains, however, a legitimate subject of inquiry. Her defenses only widen her intrapsychic split; for, even as she rejects grandiosity and perfectionism, she retains a magical belief in the Lazarus myth of rebirth through death, which increases her vulnerability to suicide. Kernberg's discussion of the dangers of a sadistic superego and its sanction of self-aggression is particularly relevant to *The Bell Jar.* "Self-destruction, originally expressing primitive, pregenital aggression, may become an ego ideal and gratify the patient's sense of omnipotence in that he no longer needs to fear frustration and suffering (suffering is now an enjoyment in itself)" (p. 169). This may explain the orderly manner in which Esther plans her suicide, the methodical efforts to control her feelings and environment. Her refusal to allow herself to feel pain, and her tendency toward dehumanization and derealization, recall Celia Coplestone in *The Cocktail Party,* with whom Plath closely identifies in her journals. Both vulnerable women seek to merge with an omnipotent object to restore their wounded self-esteem. Celia's struggles culminate in her religious crucifixion and merger with Christ; Esther's breakdown unites her with a more secular healer, Dr. Nolan, whose psychiatric power contains none of the destructive excesses of Eliot's Sir Harcourt-Reilly.

Oddly enough, *The Bell Jar* reveals surprisingly little about Esther's treatment with Dr. Nolan, far less about the psychoanalytic process than Plath records in her journals. In fact, were it not for the journals, it would be impossible to infer the extent of Plath's experience with and understanding of psychotherapy. Dr. Nolan is the only major sympathetic character in *The Bell Jar.* She quickly establishes a loving relationship with Esther and becomes the good mother for whom she has always been searching. The emotional climax of the novel occurs when Esther confesses her repressed hostility toward her mother. " 'I hate her,' I said, and waited for the blow to fall. But Doctor Nolan only smiled at me as if something had pleased her very, very much, and said, 'I suppose you do' " (p. 229). It is an important but by no means sufficient insight into Esther's illness. The other components—the symbiotic relationship with the mother, the blurring of boundaries between the self and objects, the use of primitive defenses, the ambivalence toward the father—remain unanalyzed. It is certainly not necessary for a novelist to be a psychologist, even in a story striving for the authenticity of a psychiatric case study. Nevertheless, *The Bell Jar* might have been a better novel if Plath had transmuted the rich analytic material in her journals into her fiction. Of the four writers we have studied thus far, Plath had the greatest familiarity with modern depth psychology and, unlike Fitzgerald, who went out of his way to research the clinical material for *Tender Is the Night,* Plath already had pages and pages of intensely moving and remarkably insightful journal entries. And certainly other writers were by this time publishing accounts of their own psychotherapy—H. D.'s *Tribute to Freud,* for example.[38]

Dr. Nolan remains a shadowy figure in the novel. Esther's admiration for her suggests, on a transference level, the need to merge with an omnipotent object and to incorporate her magical power. The fictional psychiatrist functions, like her real-life counterpart, as a Kohutian mirror in accepting Esther's idealizing transference and supplying her with the empathic "food" to satisfy her intense object hunger.[39] There is no suggestion that behind Esther's idealization of Dr. Nolan lies primitive rage, as Kernberg's theory of pathological narcissism would predict. We can only speculate on the reasons for the incomplete portrait of the therapist. In writing *The Bell Jar,* Plath knew that Dr. Beuscher would eventually read the novel; indeed, Plath had considered dedicating a book to the psychiatrist. The novelist may have feared writing anything that would undercut, compromise, or devalue the doctor's identity—fears that did not prevent her, however, from attacking the other real-life characters in the story. But these people were perhaps less vital to her psychological health, and she probably did not want to do anything that would foreclose future sessions with her analyst. The idealized portrait of Dr. Nolan lacks complexity, however, and little of the actual drama of Plath's own psychotherapy appears in *The Bell Jar,* including the valuable therapeutic alliance between the two women.

Curiously, whereas in real life Plath was able to incorporate the psychiatrist's power so that it became part of her own self, in the novel we do not see this healing process. The traditional pattern of psychotherapy, the one-step-forward-two-steps-backward process that occurs in *I Never Promised You a Rose Garden,* is missing from *The Bell Jar.* Esther's apparent therapeutic recovery is achieved not through psychotherapy, as we might have expected, but through the destruction of Joan Gilling, her *Doppelgänger.* And it is here that we can best see the confluence of literary and mythic conventions, on the one hand, and unconscious psychological defenses, on the other. Although introduced very late into the novel, Joan occupies a central position. "Joan was the beaming double of my old best self, specially designed to follow and torment me" (p. 231). The two women torment each other through their ferocious competition. They strive for Buddy Willard's affection, compete over the severity of their mental illness, and vie for the attention of their female psychiatrists. Both women share the same problems of separation and individuation; Joan is identified with voracious orality. She hovers over Esther "like a large and breathless fruitfly—as if the sweetness of recovery were something she could suck up by mere nearness" (p. 243). The main difference between them, as previously noted, is that Joan is a lesbian. Esther inadvertently attracts the attention of women she fears and mistrusts. ". . . the famous woman poet at my college lived with another woman—a stumpy old Classical scholar with a cropped Dutch cut. And when I had told the poet I might well get married and have a pack of children someday, she stared at me in horror. 'But what about your *career?*' she had cried" (pp. 247–248). Ironically, Esther does not really wish to have a pack of children—she is as horrified at the idea as the women she criticizes.

Plath's decision to kill off Joan Gilling represents the attempt to resolve two of the most conflicted subjects in her life: suicide and homosexuality. The chronology of events in the novel confirms a link between Esther's initiation into heterosexuality and Joan's death, which speeds Esther's recovery. But there are aesthetic and psychological problems with the suicide. Although the use of the *Doppelgänger* relationship has a long and rich tradition in literature, dating back to early German Romantics such as E. T. A. Hoffmann and Jean Paul Richter, Plath herself had written perceptively elsewhere that reconciliation rather than destruction of mirror images contributes to psychological health. In her excellent Smith College honors undergraduate essay, "The Magic Mirror: A Study of the Double in Two of Dostoevsky's Novels," she discusses the *Doppelgänger* motif, offers a persuasive psychological explanation, and affirms the duality of human nature. "This reconciliation does not mean a simple or monolithic resolution of conflict, but rather a creative acknowledgment of the fundamental duality of man; it involves a constant courageous acceptance of the eternal paradoxes within the universe and within ourselves."[40]

Despite this insight, Plath rules out reconciliation between the two mirror images in *The Bell Jar*. We cannot take Joan's character seriously, much less her suicide, and, since she has not been the cause of Esther's breakdown, why should her suicide release Esther from the bell-jar vision? Why, then, did Plath err here? Perhaps because she was also influenced by unconscious motives, namely, her tendency toward projective identification or the projection of aggression onto another individual and then the active identification with the person who has been persecuting her. Analysts view projective identification as a primitive defense against intrapsychic rage and thus less healthy than higher level defenses which seek to strengthen ego functions, such as impulse control and anxiety tolerance. Instead of witnessing, at the end of *The Bell Jar,* an earned reconciliation between Esther Greenwood and Joan Gilling, the good and bad selves, we see further splitting and disintegration. Contrary to the novelist's intentions, Joan's suicide casts Esther's fate into deeper ambiguity. Plath imagined only two solutions to the problem of insanity, as Murray Schwartz and Christopher Bollas have shown, self-destruction and rebirth.[41] Neither solution represents a realistic understanding of the therapeutic process.

The conclusion to *The Bell Jar* raises additional issues that suggest the extent to which psychological factors influenced artistic decisions. Plath's biographer argues that Joan Gilling's suicide is the "only purely imagined event in the book."[42] If so, the novelist's preoccupation with suicide severely limited her freedom to imagine a more successful ending to the novel. The imagination that created *The Bell Jar* was highly dependent upon a precarious defense system consisting of splitting, projective identification, and merging. Too often, these primitive defenses limited the artistic choices in her fiction. As a result, the novel lacks the inventive power of more mature literary works. Joan's suicide, one could argue, is influenced less by the tradition of the *Doppelgänger* than by the novelist's unconscious defensive strategies—a disturbing idea in its deterministic implications. Ironically, the woman upon whom Plath modeled Joan Gilling did not actually take her own life; in a mocking twist of fate, she became a psychologist.

The tragedy of Sylvia Plath's death is that despite her superficial portrayal of psychotherapy in *The Bell Jar* and the misleading idea that a therapeutic cure derives from the Lazarus motif of rebirth through death, a pattern that works better in ritual and myth than in actual life, her journals affirm a more authentic and heroic struggle for self-understanding and recovery. There is a danger of heroicizing the vision of death that appears in her final poems. The last poem she ever wrote, "Edge," reveals an almost total repudiation of life. Even the poet's children are imagined as dead, coiled like a white serpent at an empty pitcher of milk. One of Plath's most sensitive critics speaks of the perfect transcendence in the poem, the calm and noble death of the tragic heroine.[43] Yet, even at the very end of her life, Plath did not entirely abandon hope of rescue, and her suicide becomes more distressing when we realize that she was not a tragic heroine but a woman fighting desperately for survival. In the last paragraph of the last letter in *Letters Home,* she mentions her renewed efforts to cope with the gloom enveloping her life in England, where she was living with her two small children. One week before her death, she wrote to her mother: "I am going to start seeing a woman doctor, free on the National Health, to whom I've been referred by my very good local doctor, which should help me weather this difficult time" (p. 500). As far as we can tell, even as she planned her suicide, she made attempts to get in touch with her psychotherapist. Alvarez, the source of much of our knowledge of the last weeks of Plath's life, reports that a few days before her death she had sent a letter to the doctor requesting an appointment. The therapist's letter was delivered to the wrong address, however, part of a pattern of bad timing and poor luck. When she was found, only moments after she had gassed herself by placing her head in an oven—a bitter parody of maternal domesticity—a note was discovered next to the body, with the words and appropriate phone number: "Please call Dr. ———."[44]

SIX

I Never Promised You a Rose Garden:
The Limits of the Fictional Psychiatric Case Study

ANYONE READING *The Bell Jar* who lacks familiarity with Plath's *Journals* is bound to form a mistaken impression of the talking cure. Plath's desire to preserve the confidentiality of her relationship with Dr. Beuscher and the need to idealize her psychiatrist both contributed, we suspect, to the incomplete portrayal of psychotherapy in the novel. Confidentiality and transference issues always prove problematic in literature based on case studies, whether the author is the analyst who conducted the treatment or the patient whose recovery is the subject of the story. Freud was vexed by these constraints and assumed, as he writes in the introduction to *Dora,* that other physicians would read his case histories not as a contribution to the understanding of psychopathology but as a *"roman à clef* designed for their private delectation."[1] Freud did not anticipate, however, the possibility that both patient and analyst might eventually write accounts of the same experience from different points of view, the narration of one complementing and perhaps contradicting the other. The situation becomes particularly troublesome when both parties are writing without the other's awareness or consent. A full-scale war may erupt, as we shall see in the case of Philip Roth, involving, among other issues, the preservation of the patient's anonymity and the impossibility of resolving fundamental differences in analytic interpretation. But other problems may occur when the participants are aware of each other's account of therapy and even have contemplated collaborating on the writing project.

A case in point is the best-selling novel *I Never Promised You a Rose Garden,* a powerful description of a young woman's battle against schizophrenia. The novel has sold more than 5 million copies, been made into a film, and has become required reading for medical and psychology students as well as literature students. The novel has earned its author the Frieda Fromm-Reichmann Award from the American Academy of Psychoanalysis in 1967, the first nonphysician to receive that honor.[2] When the story was first published in 1964, the author used the pseudonym Hannah Green to conceal her identity. Growing tired of the pseudonym and sensing the irony of maintaining a double identity even after she was cured of schizophrenia, the novelist disclosed her real name—Joanne Greenberg.[3] Nor is it a secret any longer that the affectionate portrait of the fictional Dr. Fried, the psychoanalyst who successfully treats Deborah Blau in *Rose Garden,* is based upon Dr. Frieda Fromm-Reichmann, who treated Joanne Greenberg at Chestnut Lodge Sanitarium in Rockville, Maryland. What remains unknown, however, is that long before the novelist wrote her story, the analyst had published accounts of it as a case study (though without disclosing the name of her patient) in her two medical textbooks: *Principles of Intensive Psychotherapy,* published in 1950, and *Psychoanalysis and Psychotherapy,* appearing posthumously in 1959.[4]

A comparison of the novel to the psychiatric case study reveals significant differences of interpretation, emphasis, and characterization. An interesting story in itself, *Rose Garden* conceals a still more fascinating story in the pages of Frieda Fromm-Reichmann's clinical study. These differences, moreover, may suggest the limits of any autobiographical or semi-autobiographical narration of an author's breakdown and recovery.

Published only one year after *The Bell Jar, Rose Garden* closely resembles Plath's novel in many of the external and internal details of the protagonists' breakdowns. Born in 1932 to immigrant fathers, Sylvia Plath and Joanne Greenberg struggled to assimilate their parents' American and East European cultures. Growing up against the backdrop of World War II, the girls keenly suffered discrimination, one because of her German origins, the other because of her Jewish roots. In both novels, the parents of each child share similar personality traits. The fathers have strong, often violent, tempers while the mothers maintain a surface calm that is experienced by their daughters as coldness and rejection. Despite different economic backgrounds and family history, Esther Greenwood and Deborah Blau form their identity around the theme of martyrdom and regard themselves as victims of personal and historical persecution. Unable to express their feelings of anger and injustice, they turn inward and reject the external world. Esther's breakdown begins in college while Deborah's psychotic break occurs earlier, in high school. Each attempts suicide and is then hospitalized, Esther for a couple of months, Deborah for a couple of years. In both novels there is a contrast between an unsympathetic male psychiatrist and a sympathetic female psychiatrist. Dr. Nolan and Dr. Fried become the loving mother figures for whom Esther and Deborah have been searching, respectively. Like "The Yellow Wallpaper" and *The Cocktail Party*, *The Bell Jar* and *Rose Garden* are born out of the writers' experience with mental illness, and the novels may be viewed as acts of exorcism. Closely following autobiography, the two novelists create fictional narrators who break down, attempt suicide, and then are restored to health at the end. The heroines' recovery contrasts other less fortunate women who either commit suicide in the story or are condemned to permanent madness, victims of an uncaring society and questionable psychiatric procedures such as lobotomy and electroshock. Employing psychiatric case studies to dramatize the process of breakdown and recovery, *The Bell Jar* and *Rose Garden* fall into the category of the *Bildungsroman,* an autobiographical novel about the growth and education of the artist.

There are also significant differences between the two novels. Unlike *The Bell Jar,* which does not convincingly demonstrate the dynamics of therapeutic cure, *Rose Garden* remains one of the most psychologically sophisticated literary representations of mental illness. Deborah's rage is analyzed, traced back to its distant origins, and successfully worked through. The third-person authorial narrator is judicious in her characterizations, balancing sympathy and criticism. She enters into the world of insanity without losing sight of the world of health, and narrative distance is handled expertly. Like Esther's bell-jar vision, Deborah's psychotic Kingdom of Yr comes into existence as a defense against terrifying reality. Soon Yr becomes more frightening than the world it has replaced, and we can experience its nightmarish as well as seductive qualities. In its realistic depiction of psychoanalysis, *Rose Garden* adopts a mythic pattern of rebirth through death, as does *The Bell Jar*. Unlike Plath's story, Greenberg offers an earned resolution of the protagonist's madness. The resolution derives not from the adoption of primitive defenses, such as splitting and projective identification, but from the integration of the good and bad self. As with Flora Rheta Schreiber's *Sybil,* a remarkable study of multiple personality, *Rose Garden* presents us with a "whodunit of the unconscious." In contrast to earlier literary portrayals of the talking cure,

Greenberg's story dramatizes the paradoxical idea of a "good, healthy illness."

The roots of Deborah's schizophrenia, like those of nearly all patients suffering from severe mental illness, extend backward to her childhood. Born in 1932 to well-meaning middle-class parents, she spends her early years in apparent calm. On the surface she seems little different from any other child. The problem lies precisely in Deborah's surface deception. Her crippled Jewish immigrant grandfather, filled with anger that distorts his vision, teaches her to deceive the world by pretending to an inhuman perfection and self-control she obviously lacks. Viewing himself as both a cripple and outcast, the embittered grandfather sees Deborah as the means for his own redemption. Unexpectedly, however, Deborah internalizes her grandfather's anger and martyrdom and develops her identity around the image of damnation. Against a backdrop of anti-Semitism experienced at a camp during the time of World War II—madness on a cosmic level—she comes to regard herself as an enemy Japanese soldier. Or in the clinical language of the personality tests she takes, Deborah suffers from a "typically schizophrenic pattern with compulsive and masochistic component."[5]

Another major cause of Deborah's illness is an operation performed on her at the age of five to remove a tumor growing in her urethra. The first symptom of the tumor is an embarrassing incontinence for which she is punished by a stern governess. Even worse are the feelings of violation and impurity arising from the "wrongness inside her, in the feminine, secret part," along with the lies and callousness of her doctors. " 'Now just be quiet. This won't hurt a bit,' they had said, and then had come the searing stroke of the instrument. 'See, we are going to put your doll to sleep,' and the mask had moved down, forcing the sick-sweet chemical of sleep" (p. 45). The insensitivity of the surgeons and the location of the tumor horrify the child. Far from feeling cured by the surgery, she believes the tumor is still lodged within her, punishing her for an unspecified crime. Her self-hatred is magnified by a troubled relationship with her inarticulate father and by the normal Oedipal instincts that seem malignant to both of them. As Deborah explains to her psychiatrist:

> He was always frightened of the men—the men lurking to grab me from dark streets; sex maniacs and fiends, one to a tree, waiting for me. So many times he shook warnings into me. Men are brutes, lusting without limit. Men are animals . . . and I agreed in myself. One time he was scolding me for having seen an exhibitionist on the

> street. Because I had attracted the man's attention my father some-
> how connected me with having done something. He was full of rage
> and fear and he went on and on as if all such men were bound by
> laws like gravity to me alone. I said to him, "What do they want
> with me, broken into and spoiled already. I'm not good enough for
> anyone else." Then he hit me very hard because it was true (p. III).

Deborah is not actually seduced by her father, as Fitzgerald conveys
with the "Daddy's Girl" motif in *Tender Is the Night*. Nor does she search
out father figures to seduce, as do Nicole Warren and Esther Greenwood. But she does regard herself as sexually violated, and behind the
fear lies a concealed wish. In all three novels, *Tender Is the Night, The Bell
Jar,* and *Rose Garden,* unresolved Oedipal feelings—"the tangles of that
old bed," as Plath writes in her *Journals*—strongly contribute to the formation of the heroines' madness. These feelings shape their relationships
to all men.

The birth of a sister also proves upsetting to Deborah, not only because she feels displaced in her parents' affection, but because the intense
sibling rivalry culminates in an imagined near murder of the infant. "The
sick are all so afraid of their own uncontrollable power!" Dr. Fried thinks,
"Somehow they cannot believe that they are only people, holding only a
humanized anger!" (p. 46). As with *The Bell Jar,* we see how Deborah's
overestimation of her unconscious powers—the "omnipotence of
thought"—leads to the irrational belief that she has caused the death or
near death of a family member. While this phenomenon, according to
Freud, applies to all people, it is especially true for psychotics, who consistently overestimate their destructive powers. Thus, Deborah fears that
her own malignant essence, what she calls *nganon* or "Deborah-rot," will
fatally infect those who come too close. Only late in the novel does Dr.
Fried convince her that what she had misremembered as an attempt to
murder her sister was only harmless jealousy.

Neither the events nor explanations underlying Deborah's schizophrenia appear remarkable from a literary or psychological point of view. The
real artistic triumph of *Rose Garden* lies elsewhere, in the startling descriptions of Deborah's retreat from reality into the inner kingdom of Yr
that defines the space of her psychotic break from the normal world. To
imagine this self-created universe, the novelist uses mythological themes
and symbols: a pantheon of dark gods, incantatory chants of seduction
and damnation, metaphors of darkness and chaos, descent into an abyss,
and a gradual reemergence into light. Deborah's gods have Latinate names,

speak in Miltonic rhythms of defiance, and embody Dantesque horrors. The ruler of Yr is Anterrabae, the god who evokes images of Satan and Icarus in his thunderous plunges into the pit of madness. Lactamaeon, the black god, alternately moans in horror and hurls execrations. The Collect symbolizes the "massed images of all the teachers and relatives and schoolmates standing eternally in secret judgment and giving their endless curses" (p. 22). The Censor must preserve the mysterious secrets and voices of Yr from the outside world. Upuru is the punishing god, Imorh is the Awaited Oncoming Death. The mythological kingdom has its own secret language and code. "Suffer" is the Yri metaphor for greeting, "tankutuku" means unhidden, "nelaq" signifies eyeless, and "Deborah" means "The Always Deceived."

As *Rose Garden* progresses, we discover, along with Deborah, the psychological explanation of the origin of Yr, but the power of the novel lies less in the analytical decoding than in the terrifying immersion into her psychotic reality. Although Yr originates as a defense against a threatening environment, the psychic landscape eventually becomes more oppressive than the external world. Deborah begins as the queen of the alluring kingdom but soon becomes its slave. The novel moves downward as she descends into a fearful pit suggestive of a Dantesque Inferno, Christian Hell, and Freudian unconscious. Amidst Dr. Fried's gentle but persistent questioning, Deborah discovers the origins of Yr. The gods personify the various figures and events in her life. The Collect embodies the tyrannical self-criticism of her mind, the superego. Upuru arises from the punishing tumor operation and the frightening memory of the hospital. Lactamaeon incarnates her father's violence, while Anterrabae originates from a long-forgotten book, Milton's *Paradise Lost,* which she had seen in her grandfather's study. Through analysis, Dr. Fried persuades Deborah to renounce the kingdom of Yr, with its private allurements and imaginative landscapes, for the everyday reality of the world.

Critics have noted, however, that the healthy reality Deborah tentatively embraces at the end of *Rose Garden* seems less aesthetically powerful than the psychotic world she repudiates. Certainly this is an old problem for artists: evil appears more fascinating than good, sickness more interesting than health. Yet if there are Laingian hints that the sick are more creative and less dishonest than the healthy, we remain convinced at the end that Deborah's search for insight, trust, and compassion can be fulfilled in the "normal" world, where she has the freedom to choose how she wants to live her life. In Yr there is no choice or responsibility, only eternal punishment. Another criticism of *Rose Garden* is that we fail to see any character in Deborah's life who contains the terrible intensity of the Yr gods. Neither the father nor the maternal grandfather seems sufficiently cruel or terrifying to explain the demonic power of Deborah's inner torturers. And the mother's role in the daughter's flight into Yr remains curiously undeveloped. Once again, as in *The Bell Jar*, it is difficult to separate psychic reality from objective reality. Also, as we shall see, although *Rose Garden* offers one of the most authentic descriptions of the relationship between the patient and analyst found anywhere in literature, the stormy therapeutic sessions containing the interactions of transference and countertransference are largely missing from the novel.

The clue to Deborah's reintegration into society lies in the character of Dr. Fried, the beloved "old mental garbage-collector" (p. 248) who serves as psychoanalyst and exorcist. A tiny, gray-haired, plump woman who looks more like a housekeeper than a famous doctor, she is nicknamed "Furii" or Fire-Touch, the Yri word suggestive of her fearsome power over Deborah. Mistrustful of hypnotism, medication, shock therapy, social adjustment without inner change, and easy therapeutic reassurances, Dr. Fried affirms the power of dynamic psychology, psychoanalysis with certain minor modifications, for the treatment of psychotics. Defining herself to Deborah as a "representative of and fighter with you for this present world" (p. 241), she succeeds where the others have failed. She alone understands the elementary principles of mental health that the others in Deborah's life have forgotten or never learned. Unlike Deborah's father, who calls her "unhappy" rather than sick, and unlike her family and teachers, who have been telling her for years that there is nothing wrong with her, Dr. Fried acknowledges her sickness and thus initiates the process of recovery. Unlike the others in the hospital, Dr. Fried knows how to maintain the proper distance from her patients—neither too close nor remote.

Rose Garden powerfully dramatizes the shaky defenses erected against the "crazy" patients by the "healthy" who are only slightly less ill. During Deborah's treatment, two nurses crack up shortly after leaving their psychiatric affiliation and become patients in mental hospitals. One sadistic attendant, Hobbs, commits suicide while another attendant, a religious fanatic named Ellis, hovers on the brink of losing control. Even the doctors erect defenses through intellectualization of their patients' illnesses. Dr. Royson, whom Deborah calls "Snake-Tooth," can painstakingly analyze the Latinate roots of Yri but never overcome his professional coldness. But Dr. Fried is different. The symbolism of her name foreshadows her therapeutic triumph: Deborah is freed by the analyst's insights and compassion. And Dr. Fried's name returns us to Joanne Greenberg's real psychoanalyst, Dr. Frieda Fromm-Reichmann.

Frieda Fromm-Reichmann's contribution to psychiatry involved the demonstration of the effectiveness of psychoanalysis for psychotic patients. Unlike Freud, who was pessimistic about the application of psychoanalysis to the cure of the psychoses, she remained optimistic about the possibility of curing even severely ill patients. She showed that transference relationships could be established, that the psychotic's communications could be understood, and that the patient's hidden resources could be tapped. Along with Harry Stack Sullivan, probably the foremost American psychiatrist of the age, she maintained that there is a potential toward health even in severely regressed patients. "In some mental patients, a spontaneous wish for change and recovery is found. In others, such a wish can be aroused on the basis of their tendency toward health, unless life has so little in store for them that they cannot be expected to become interested in being able to cope with its vicissitudes" (*Psychoanalysis and Psychotherapy,* p. 22). She helped to elevate the mental patient from the ranks of an object of therapy to a partner of the therapist, and she affirmed an attitude of respect and equality between doctor and patient—an attitude strikingly different from the inequality of earlier doctor-patient relationships.

Psychotic patients, however, required modification of psychoanalytic techniques. Frieda Fromm-Reichmann pioneered these changes and thus helped to achieve the widening scope of psychoanalysis. She believed analysts should be "thrifty" with interpretations for fear of intellectualizing their patients. She repeated Freud's warning that "The psychoanalyst's job is to help the patient, not to demonstrate how clever the doctor is." She urged the patient to play an active role in therapy, and she minimized the use of free association, fearing it would disturb the psychotic's inner disorder. She also stressed the multiple meaning of symptomatology, the principle of overdetermination, in which a symbol in a dream or symptom of an illness may have several different meanings. If a symptom persists after its meaning has been unraveled, additional meanings must be discovered until the symptom disappears.

To appreciate Frieda Fromm-Reichmann's influence on *Rose Garden* and the extent to which the psychiatric case study has been transmuted into fiction, we may compare the doctor's account in *Psychoanalysis and Psy-*

chotherapy (p. 204) with the novelist's description in *Rose Garden* (p. 106). The influence begins with the title of the novel:

> One exuberant young patient, the daughter of indiscriminately "encouraging" parents, was warned against expecting life to become a garden of roses after her recovery. Treatment, she was told, should make her capable of handling the vicissitudes of life which were bound to occur, as well as to enjoy the gardens of roses which life would offer her at other times. When we reviewed her treatment history after her recovery, she volunteered that this statement had helped her a great deal, "not because I believed for a moment that you were right, Doctor, but because it was such a great sign of your confidence in me and your respect for me, that you thought you could say such a serious thing to me and that I would be able to take it."

> "Look here," Furii said. "I never promised you a rose garden. I never promised you perfect justice . . . and I never promised you peace or happiness. My help is so that you can be free to fight for all of these things. The only reality I offer is challenge, and being well is being free to accept it or not at whatever level you are capable. I never promise lies, and the rose-garden world of perfection is a lie . . . and a bore, too!"

Psychiatric realism defines both passages. The historical and fictional analysts demythologize their role during the therapeutic process, declining to act like tragic heroes, Christlike saviors, or demonic Fausts. The doctors wisely attach limits both to their own power and to the role of psychiatry. The patient's cure will not transform the world nor restore order or sanity to society. In Frieda Fromm-Reichmann's words, the psychotherapist "should know that he is not called upon to fulfill any noble, magic mission. More skeptical of all types of would-be and as-if attitudes than the rest of us, the schizophrenic will definitely react unfavorably to a therapist with alleged missionary and similar Godlike attitudes" (*Psychoanalysis and Psychotherapy,* p. 173). In Joanne Greenberg's words, "Esther and Jacob sat together in the office, waiting, Dr. Fried saw, for reassurance and for peace. She wanted to tell them bluntly that she was not God. There were no sure promises and she could not be a judge of what they had done or not done to their daughter to bring her to this battlefield" (*Rose Garden,* p. 108). This vision of psychotherapy is antithetical to that seen in *Tender Is the Night* and *The Cocktail Party,* in which Dick Diver and Sir Harcourt-Reilly function not as trained psychiatrists but as Christlike saviors who offer Messianic love or religious consolation. Dr. Fried's clinical insight represents a more modest but appropriate treatment for mental illness. The psychiatric authenticity of *Rose Garden* does not become apparent until the novel is contrasted to earlier fictional representations of mental illness, which reveal distorted characterizations of the therapeutic process.

Additionally, we see a new approach to the patient-analyst relationship not seen in earlier fictional representations of psychotherapy, not even in the contemporaneous *The Bell Jar*. There is little exchange between Esther and Dr. Nolan apart from the patient's vague admission that she hates her mother, an admission that remains curiously anticlimactic. But in *Rose Garden,* the heroine's illness is taken seriously and treated with the precision and expertise accorded organic illness. For the first time, a patient's symptoms are analyzed not as a symbol of a universal religious or historical malaise but as a manifestation of an inner and potentially curable conflict. The psychiatrist promises at the beginning of treatment that she will not eliminate the patient's symptoms without her consent; Deborah will not be rendered defenseless against anxiety. This part of the novel also reflects Frieda Fromm-Reichmann's actual treatment of Joanne Greenberg, as a comparison of the psychiatric case study and *Rose Garden* suggests:

> A patient shouted at the psychiatrist during their first visit, "I know what you will do now! You'll take my gut-pains, and my trance, and my withdrawal states away from me! And where will I be then?" The psychiatrist first asked for a description of the three pathological states, the loss of which the patient allegedly feared. The patient's answer made it possible for the psychiatrist to demonstrate to her the attempt at escaping anxiety, which all three of the states had in common. Subsequently, her anxiety regarding the psychiatrist's role as a foe rather than as a co-worker was labeled as such, and the historical roots for this interpersonal attitude and expectation could be scrutinized. After that the patient was told that her symptoms would not be taken away from her but that, in all likelihood, she herself would wish to dispose of them when she learned to understand enough about her anxiety to make it decrease. Also the patient's attention was drawn to the fact that she had made her symptoms known immediately to the psychiatrist. It was suggested that this seemed to indicate that, perhaps without realizing it, she was just as desirous of losing her symptoms as she was anxious, within her awareness, at the prospect of being deprived of them (*Psychoanalysis and Psychotherapy,* p. 190).

> They went into a sunny room and the Housekeeper-Famous-Doctor turned, saying, "Sit down. Make yourself comfortable." There came a great exhaustion and when the doctor said, "Is there anything you

want to tell me?" a great gust of anger, so that Deborah stood up quickly and said to her and to Yr and to the Collect and to the Censor, "All right—you'll ask me questions and I'll answer them—you'll clear up my 'symptoms' and send me home . . . *and what will I have then?*"

The doctor said quietly, "If you did not really want to give them up, you wouldn't tell me." A rope of fear pulled its noose about Deborah. "Come, sit down. You will not have to give up anything until you are ready, and then there will be something to take its place" (*Rose Garden,* p. 23).

In the description of the treatment we have a striking confirmation of the similarity between the psychiatric case study and the novel, a cross-fertilization of two essentially different yet similar disciplines and art forms. The psychiatrist uses the patient's actual speech in the case study and then, several years later (at least 12, since this section of *Psychoanalysis and Psychotherapy* first appeared in a book published in 1952), the novelist repossesses the language for her own story. The difference between these two passages is not content but form: The novelist condenses the material, dramatizes the scene, and endows the psychiatrist with dialogue. The novelist also deemphasizes the pedagogical quality of the psychiatric case study without sacrificing the power of illumination. In the novel we have direct access to the patient's inner life, the psychotic kingdom of Yr, that refuses to yield its privileged position to the external world. In both accounts, the psychiatric case study and the novel, the therapist assures the patient that she will not be violated or left defenseless. Nothing will be taken away from her except, if she desires, the terror. This fundamental tenet of psychotherapy regrettably gets lost in literature, which often portrays illness as allied with creativity. At the end of Peter Shaffer's *Equus,* the deeply ambivalent psychiatrist promises to deliver Alan Strang from madness but only by destroying his passion and imagination. "Passion," says Dr. Dysart, "can be destroyed by a doctor. It cannot be created."[6] By contrast, Dr. Fried simply promises to help Deborah help herself, allowing the patient to liberate her own passion and creativity from the oppressive Yr gods.

Curiously, however, not all of the pertinent details of Joanne Greenberg's therapy appear in *Rose Garden.* For a fuller account of the patient's illness and stormy relationship with her analyst, we must turn to Frieda Fromm-Reichmann's two medical texts, *Psychoanalysis and Psychotherapy* and *Principles of Intensive Psychotherapy,* both of which contain revealing clinical vignettes of the same patient. To demonstrate, it is necessary to quote an extended passage from *Principles of Intensive Psychotherapy* (pp. 176–177) and then to contrast this full and lively narration to the fragmentary clues in *Rose Garden:*

An eighteen-year-old schizophrenic girl complained about severe persecutory ideas, to the effect that she could not bear to have anyone standing or walking behind her. Something frightful would happen to her, perhaps a stab in the back or, at any rate, something terrible, the thought of which made her shudder. She was paralyzed and could hardly move whenever there was someone behind her or whenever she sensed that there might be someone back of her. She did not dare to go downtown because there always seemed to be someone right behind her. Questioned about the actual experience which the patient might consider as the first one of its kind, she said that she could not remember. But she did volunteer the information that, as far back as she could remember, her father had warned her against men who might persecute her and rape her. This happened long before the patient knew what "rape" was and what men might "do" to women. Further investigation of and associations to her fantasies regarding rape and regarding her persecutory delusions disclosed that the form of the patient's persecutory ideas were due neither to her fear of nor her secret wish for rape only, as one might have easily suspected. Eager to safeguard against therapeutic operations with any partial interpretive truth, the psychiatrist asked for further associative memories to the patient's delusions. The patient recalled eventually that at the time of Hitler's invasion of Czechoslovakia her father had condemned, with great affect, "the stab in the back" done to the Czechs. She was too young to know that father was referring to people and thought he was talking about the checks in the tablecloth on the breakfast table. It was at the breakfast table and while reading the morning paper that her father had these emotional outbursts which were incomprehensible to the patient. Also during breakfast her father would scold the patient severely for various types of infantile misdemeanors about which he had just been told.

Another associative memory came from a later period of the patient's life. Her parents would find out that she had taken money from them, that she had bought hair ribbons or sweets against their wishes, that she had teased her baby brother or the dog, or that she had antagonized the maid. Her father would throw a temper tantrum and say that she was betraying her parents and the training they had given her. The use of the word "betraying" reminded her of her father's using the word "betrayal" in connection with "the stab in the back" to the Czechs.

As a result of a condensation of these memories, the patient experienced her persecutory delusions to the effect that she dreaded that someone behind her would "stab her in the back"—betray her, rape her—as she allegedly had stabbed in the back, that is, betrayed, her parents when she had stolen pocket money or when she had committed any of the other above-mentioned childhood sins. Father had reacted the same way, namely, with a heavy temper outburst, to both types of stabs in the back, hers and the one done by Hitler to the Czechs. Besides, the Czechs had been the "checks" of the tablecloth to her, and father had thrown temper tantrums about her, too, when she misbehaved. So the temper tantrums about the "checks," about her earlier and later childhood sins, together with the fear of rape with which her father had imbued her, were condensed into the patient's formulation of her persecutory delusion of being "stabbed in the back" by someone who was behind her.

The psychiatrist's artful narration is extraordinary in its thematic unity, compression, symbolic richness, and moral ambiguity. The patient's fear of "the stab in the back" may be interpreted in different ways and on different levels: the sociopolitical madness of Hitlerism, the insidiousness of racial or nationalistic fervor, the irrational anger of a hot-tempered father, the paranoid schizophrenia of an adolescent. Yet the patient is not merely an innocent victim of her father's (or Hitler's) wrath. Insofar as she is guilty of childhood crimes, however minor, she too becomes the aggressor, the stabber, the criminal, thus unconsciously imitating her father's (and Hitler's) acts of violence. Consequently, in the psychiatric case study, she plays the dual role of victim and victimizer, betrayed and betrayer. She is paralyzed with ambivalence as she acts out the psychoanalytic maxim that wishes and fears are often inextricably related. Her symptoms reveal a bewildering condensation of wishes, fears, and defenses: confused Oedipal feelings, regression, identification with the aggressor, paranoia, and displaced aggression.

What emerges from the case study is a portrait of a self-flagellating young woman whose ambiguous moral identity evokes contradictory emotions from the reader. We sympathize with the daughter's suffering but also feel for the father's grief. We are torn between sympathy and judgment, pity and disapproval. As we begin to criticize the father for his violent outbursts and defective parenting, we remember that he, too, is human and caught up in the madness of World War II. Indeed, he and his parents had left Poland during World War I; how could he not feel rage and perhaps guilt for the continued destruction of his birthplace? Despite our natural sympathy for his daughter, the victim of forces she can neither understand nor control, we remind ourselves that she must also accept a degree of responsibility for her infantile behavior and the fact that she is driving her family crazy. Neither the father nor the daughter is entirely blameless in the psychiatrist's narration. Both characters are caught up in a terrible family drama in which each stabs the other in the back. The psychiatrist refuses to favor one character at the expense of the other or to reduce the complexity of the story.

To appreciate the psychological and moral complexity of Frieda Fromm-Reichmann's case study, we need only recall earlier literary representations of mental illness. In "The Yellow Wallpaper," the narrator is viewed more as a victim than as the potential victimizer of the beloved baby whose presence she cannot bear to suffer. The infanticidal imagery hints at the diffuseness of the mother's rage and her inability to escape from intolerable reality. In *Tender Is the Night,* Nicole Warren's schizophrenia is seen as the result of the incestuous union with her father instead of, as clinical experience would predict, the product of much earlier disruptions in the mother-daughter relationship. Celia Coplestone's protracted struggle against psychotic fragmentation and derealization in *The Cocktail Party* is perceived as a precursor to her special calling as a saint, rather than as a deep narcissistic injury that can be healed through a less manipulative therapy. In *The Bell Jar,* Esther's breakdown is presented as a martyrdom and crucifixion, instead of as a mode of behavior concealing virulent aggressive feelings toward her family and herself.

Oddly enough, many of the rich details in Frieda Fromm-Reichmann's case study are omitted from *Rose Garden,* to the novel's loss. A passing reference to the "checks-and-the-poles" appears in the novel but with narrowed focus:

> The instincts of these hating children [at camp] were shared, for Deborah heard sometimes that a man named Hitler was in Germany and was killing Jews with the same kind of evil joy. One spring day before she left for camp she had seen her father put his head on the kitchen table and cry terrible, wrenching men's tears about the "checks-and-the-poles." In the camp a riding instructor mentioned acidly that Hitler was doing one good thing at least, and that was getting rid of the "garbage people." She wondered idly if they all had tumors (p. 50).

Whereas in the psychiatric case study the patient acts out roles of victim and victimizer, in the novel she appears only as an innocent and passive martyr, almost Christlike in her suffering—in short, very much like Esther Greenwood. Greenberg reduces the father-daughter tension, softens the father's character, and internalizes Deborah's violence, rendering it harmless to everyone except herself. We are struck by the similarity to *The Bell Jar*. These fictional changes in *Rose Garden* heighten our sympathy toward Deborah but also diminish the complexity of her character. Interestingly, the novelist splits off the paranoid characteristics of Deborah and projects them onto another woman in the hospital. In Frieda Fromm-Reichmann's case study, the patient herself fears the "stab in the back" while, in Joanne Greenberg's novel, the persecutory fear dwells within Lee, a more violent and sinister character than Deborah. "Lee could not allow anyone to be behind her, and she didn't like to stand against the wall the way the others did, so she had to keep circling relentlessly to 'keep everyone properly placed.' Without allegiance or loyalty, but because of a mysterious sense of fitness, Deborah began to follow Lee, the ptolemaic sun circling her planets" (p. 106).

Why did the novelist omit this rich material from *Rose Garden*? There are genetic and biographical explanations that come into play not only in *Rose Garden* but in perhaps all fictionalized accounts of psychological breakdown. To maintain reader sympathy and identification, the author of a fictionalized psychiatric case study tends to create innocent heroes or heroines whose violence is internalized, not externalized. Who among us feels more sympathy for a victimizer than for a victim? A suicidal character awakens greater pity in us than does a homicidal character, and there is probably more mystery surrounding the former than the latter. The paradigm behind most accounts of madness and recovery is the timeless religious and mythic metaphor of death and rebirth, with both "cure" and "redemption" awaiting those who are worthy. "How many of the dead could be raised?" (p. 246) the narrator in *Rose Garden* asks about the patients of D Ward, containing the most seriously disturbed patients, who, like Lazarus, are waiting to be reborn. As we have seen, the Lazarus theme also figures prominently in *The Bell Jar* and in Plath's poetry. Indeed, the majority of fictionalized psychiatric case studies contain "innocent" patients, ranging from Chief Bromden and McMurphy in *One Flew Over the Cuckoo's Nest* (victims of a "matriarchy") to a host of other fictional and nonfictional accounts of madness: *The Snake Pit, Autobiography of a Schizophrenic Girl, The Three Faces of Eve,* and *Sybil.* Even in Anthony Burgess' *A Clockwork Orange,* Alex's viciousness is more than offset by the horrors of the psychiatric brainwashing he undergoes. "Ludovico's Technique" transforms Alex from a thug into an ironic Christ symbol, a "true Christian," in the words of the doctor, "ready to turn the other cheek, ready to be crucified rather than crucify, sick to the very heart at the thought even of killing a fly."[7]

Another generic determinant of the fictionalized psychiatric case study involves the need for heroism and fairy-tale status for those who recover from a severe breakdown. Because mental illness is so mysterious, terrifying, and unpredictable, there is the tendency to confer heroic status on the survivors, to see them as initiates who possess secret knowledge. Kurtz's dying words in *Heart of Darkness*, "The horror! The horror!", evoke the oxymoronic "exalted and incredible degradation" of those who plunge into the abyss. Deborah's affinity to the adolescent heroine in popular literature, however, imposes artistic constraints, as critics have pointed out:

> None of the violence on Deborah's part is directed at anyone other than herself, and the general absence of sexual motives and experience from her story—even though it seems likely that such experiences would comprise a significant element of her psyche—give her the aspect of the "innocent." Not even her most repulsive actions, such as her continued self-mutilation, are sufficient to remove our sympathies from her, and in this respect she is not unlike many other adolescent heroines in popular fiction.[8]

In addition, a strong didactic element characterizes this genre. The novelist aims implicitly for a clear-cut resolution of the protagonist's mental illness, at the expense of the ambiguities that often remain unresolved in the greatest imaginative literature.

There are also biographical constraints on the novelist's freedom to describe the intimate details that may appear without difficulty in a psychiatric case study of an anonymous patient. Joanne Greenberg presumably omitted many details from *Rose Garden* for the same reason she and Sylvia Plath used pseudonyms: to protect herself and her family from embarrassing public scrutiny, and perhaps to avoid stirring up the distressing memories of the past which contributed to the formation of the former illness. Can anyone be blamed for the wish to avoid reopening the wounds which must intimidate even the healthiest writers, those who, in Hemingwayesque language, are strong at the broken places? The difficulty lies in reconciling the conflicting demands of confidentiality and revelation, private life and impersonal art. Reconciliation becomes impossible when, as in the example of *Rose Garden*, the patient's psychiatrist has first published a substantial account of the story, thus creating a narration against which the novelist's later version may be read and judged.[9]

Nowhere is the problem of portraying the analyst more apparent than in the incomplete portrait of the doctor in *Rose Garden* and other fictional psychiatric case studies. Although we see a far more authentic and lively picture of the therapist in *Rose Garden* than in *The Bell Jar*, the figure of Dr. Fried remains highly idealized. She is not merely an admirable doctor but a paragon, a woman of inexhaustible courage and strength. Her private life never intrudes upon her professional duties; her inner consciousness never interferes with the patient's story. If we could see more of her private life and learn more about her inner consciousness, we would have a more satisfying grasp of her life. Dr. Fried's human frailties are asserted but not demonstrated, and she endears herself to us when she confesses her imperfections to Deborah. Part of the problem lies in the restriction of the doctor's point of view. She appears only in a clinical setting, thus depriving the reader access to her life apart from her treatment of Deborah. Moreover, she functions less as a character than as the instrument of the patient's recovery. The novelist's traditional interest in character for the sake of character is absent from *Rose Garden*, as if the subject were off limits.

Nor is the relationship involving transference and countertransference adequately explored. *Rose Garden* presents us with a few tantalizing glimpses of Dr. Fried's personal life, but the novel does not show us the image of the analyst existing within the patient's imagination. The interaction between the patient and analyst, we have been suggesting, contains real and symbolic elements. To cite Freud's observation, the patient sees in the analyst the "return, the reincarnation, of some important figure out of his childhood or past. . . ."[10] In addition, problems with countertransference pose greater difficulties with psychotic patients because the analyst must serve as a representative of and bridge to reality. The fusion and confusion of the analyst's real and imagined presence make the relationship between transference and countertransference infinitely complicated in therapy and no less problematic in literary representations of the talking cure.

As with Esther's relationship to Dr. Nolan, only the patient's attitude of positive transference toward the therapist appears in *Rose Garden*. We do see glimpses, admittedly, of Deborah's fear that the analyst will deceive or betray her. On one occasion, for example, Deborah cannot help project her fear of maternal loss on to the therapist. Despite Dr. Fried's assurance that she will return from an extended professional conference in Zurich, the young woman interprets the absence as an act of abandonment. Immediately after Dr. Fried's departure, Deborah initiates a series of ugly skin-burning incidents involving stolen cigarettes and matches. To Dr. Fried, Deborah's burning herself is symptomatic of self-hatred and displaced aggression toward the doctor. The patient disagrees with this interpretation, though, and the novel remains ambiguous here. Apart from these isolated moments of Deborah's anger and mistrust, nothing occurs in the novel to suggest the stormy therapeutic interviews between patient and doctor.

"Stormy therapeutic interviews"—the words come from Frieda Fromm-Reichmann's case study, and we do not have to speculate on the intense negative transference that is missing from *Rose Garden*. The story is told in great detail in *Psychoanalysis and Psychotherapy* and includes both the skin-burning incident and a related symptom, skin-pulling. According to the psychiatrist's narration, the patient emerged from a severe schizophrenic disturbance for which she was hospitalized for two years at Chestnut Lodge and treated for another two years as an outpatient. Eventually she became free of all psychotic symptomatology except one symptom: She would pull off the skin of her heels to the point of producing open wounds. In response to the doctor's comment on the favorable changes that had taken place as a result of therapy, the patient developed an acute anxiety state which helped to illuminate one meaning of the compulsive symptom. Like the earlier skin-burning, the skin-pulling enabled the patient to maintain a continuity between sickness and health, past and present. Further investigation revealed that the localization of the symptom was determined by "mischievously ridiculing memories of her mother's coming home from outings to prepare a meal for the family, going into the kitchen, removing shoes and stockings but not coat and hat, and walking around the kitchen on bare feet."

None of this appears in *Rose Garden*, and consequently the novel is less successful than *The Bell Jar* in dramatizing the antagonistic mother-daughter relationship. On a transference level, the self-mutilating nature of the skin-pulling expresses resentment toward the psychiatrist whose Yri name in Greenberg's novel, "Furii" or "Fire-Touch," symbolizes the "fearsome power that had seared Deborah's arm with an invisible burning" (p. 105). The patient's self-mutilation thus represents displaced aggression toward the therapist, whose interpretations are experienced as intrusive and incorrect. "In her judgment," writes Dr. Fromm-Reichmann, "I misevaluated the other act of self-mutilation from which she suffered during her psychotic episodes, the compulsion to burn her skin. The patient thought of it as a means of relieving unbearable tension, whereas she felt that I thought of it only as a serious expression of tension. In maintaining the skin-pulling, while otherwise nearly recovered, she meant to demonstrate to me that skin injuring was not a severe sign of illness" (*Psychoanalysis and Psychotherapy,* p. 206).

But symptoms have multiple meanings, as do symbols in a dream, and another meaning of the skin-pulling is the patient's fear of closeness, the effort to peel away an unhealthy dependency on mother and analyst. In the psychiatric case study, we discover, as we do not discover in the novel, the fact that the patient's imaginary kingdom has arisen as a means to exclude the prying parents from the young woman's life:

> During the treatment period after the dismissal from the hospital, the patient tried for quite a while to avoid the recognition of her hostility against me and the realization of her dependent attachment to me, which she resented, by trying to cut me out of her everyday life. She did so, repeating an old pattern of living in two worlds, the world which she shared with me during our therapeutic interviews and her life outside the interviews, during which she excluded me completely from her thinking. Previously, the patient had established this pattern with her parents by living for eleven years in an imaginary kingdom which she populated by people of her own making and by the spiritual representations of others whom she actually knew. They all shared a language, literature, and religion of her own creation. Therapeutic investigation taught us that the patient erected this private world as a means of excluding her prying parents from an integral part of her life. It was her way of fighting her dependence on them and of demonstrating how different she was from them in all areas where she disliked and resented them (*Psychoanalysis and Psychotherapy,* pp. 206–207).

After a few stormy therapeutic interviews, the patient discovered that her periods of readmission to the hospital, when she regressed to the old symptom of skin-burning, indicated her dependency on and resentment of mother and doctor. Dependency forced her to return to the hospital; resentment compelled her to burn her skin. Through analysis she learns that the exclusion of the analyst from her life was a repetition of the exclusion of the parents from her private kingdom. "After that, she saw, too, that her resentment against me was also a revival of an old gripe against her parents; they had a marked tendency to make her out to be dumb, as I tried to do, in her judgment, by inflicting upon her my mis-evaluation of the skin burning. They kept her for many years in a state of overdependence, as I had done, too, by virtue of our therapeutic relationship" (*Psychoanalysis and Psychotherapy*, p. 207).

Like Esther's retreat into the bell-jar vision, Deborah's escape into the kingdom of Yr originates in part from the need to flee from an intrusive parent. The destructive mother-daughter symbiotic relationship is central to both novels, with pre-Oedipal issues of separation and individuation coming into play. Both heroines are paralyzed by the confusion of wish and fear: the desire to remain dependent upon mother and the fear that dependency will result in loss of freedom and autonomy. As in "The Yellow Wallpaper," it is the internalized mother, the mother within the daughter, from whom Esther and Deborah are attempting to escape. But, in rejecting the biological mother, the daughters are searching for higher spiritual mothers with whom to merge. Had Plath remained in psychoanalysis, she would have had to work through these identity conflicts and experience them emotionally in the transference relationship, just as Joanne Greenberg did with Frieda Fromm-Reichmann. The patient's separation from the analyst is almost always painful (patients speak of this as a period of mourning), just as the child's separation from the parents is fraught with emotion. Nevertheless, the process of separation is essential for health.

Significantly, the story of the patient's separation from the analyst seldom appears in literary representations of the talking cure. Nor do many writers choose to include any description of the relationship between transference and countertransference. Usually it is the analyst, not the patient, who is willing to write about this hidden story and, even then, only reluctantly, fearful that the public will seize upon this as evidence of the ineffectiveness of psychoanalysis.

Frieda Fromm-Reichmann's uniqueness was her willingness to admit to the analyst's fallibility and in particular to her own mistakes. Her two medical texts offer eloquent proof of a statement by Harry Stack Sullivan she was fond of quoting: "We are all much more simply human than otherwise." Far from accepting the mythic status accorded to the analyst, she demythologized the role and stressed her failures as well as successes. In *Principles of Intensive Psychotherapy*, we hear her saddened admission of a schizophrenic woman whose reasonably good therapeutic prospects she damaged through noncommital talks and inappropriate setting. In *Psychoanalysis and Psychotherapy*, she tells how an assaultive patient, unable to endure the analyst's blundering question about her past violence, struck her in the face with a cup from which she was drinking. "In retrospect, I consider this act of violence wholly justified from the patient's point of view. She had every reason to interpret my question as an implied reference to her assaultiveness; it made me another of those people who labeled her a violent person" (p. 214). In appropriate settings she could mime a patient's over-solicitous mother or domineering wife, as Joanne Greenberg has commented upon elsewhere.[11] She also could confess to countertransference with certain patients. She was more than willing to accept responsibility for failure, as she admits in italicized print in *Psychoanalysis and Psychotherapy*. "*If the schizophrenic's reactions are more stormy and seemingly more unpredictable than those of the psychoneurotic, I believe it to be due to the inevitable errors in the analyst's approach to the schizophrenic, of which he himself may be unaware, rather than to the unreliability of the patient's emotional response*" (p. 119).

If Joanne Greenberg had included the tempestuous therapeutic sessions in *Rose Garden,* they would almost certainly have enriched the novel and resulted in a more intellectually satisfying presentation of Deborah's illness and recovery. There also would have been a greater aesthetic and psychological tension between patient and analyst and a more complete picture of the vicissitudes of therapy, including the intensity of the patient's resistance to regaining her health. The multiple meaning of Deborah's schizophrenic symptomatology would have strengthened the detectivelike quality of the novel. The reader would have been thrust into the analyst's position of tracking down the scattered and distant clues to the psychological thriller. And since psychotherapy with the schizophrenic patient is a hotbed for the analyst's positive and negative difficulties with countertransference, we might have been allowed a glimpse into the unspoken story—the extent to which the patient's anxiety or loneliness may become contagious to the therapist, for instance, or the analyst's tendency to be seduced into sharing the patient's madness.

The discovery of the medical source of Joanne Greenberg's novel thus reveals the difficulty of writing a story based upon the author's psychological breakdown and therapeutic recovery. And a comparison of the psychiatric case study to the novel points to the limits of literary representations of the talking cure. Despite the intimate relationship between the creative and therapeutic process and the extent to which novels like *The Bell Jar* and *Rose Garden* remain indebted to the writers' own therapy, the unique requirements and ground rules of psychoanalysis often make it hard for patients to write about their personal experiences. Why?

Because the analyst is required to maintain a strict distance from the patient and to refuse to talk about his private life or feelings to the person lying on the couch. This is, in a sense, unfair, but the patient-analyst relationship is exempt from notions of social equality. Psychoanalysis limits the patient's efforts to come to know the analyst or to encounter him in nonanalytic settings. Indeed, the analyst is trained to interpret the patient's inquiry into his private life as a subtle form of resistance, an unconscious attempt to thwart the process of self-discovery by undermining the analyst's distance and authority. *Tender Is the Night* reveals the catastrophic consequences of a patient's seduction of her therapist. The seduction may be sexual or intellectual. Countless novels offer additional evidence of the ambivalence directed toward the person who investigates the secrets of the psyche. The analyst's privileged position deepens his mystery to outsiders and thus perpetuates the fascination and mistrust surrounding psychoanalysis. For analysis to succeed, though, the patient must agree to restrict his contact with the therapist and to interpret his curiosity as symbolic of forbidden wishes, to be analyzed but not acted out.[12]

The restriction of the patient's imaginative freedom to enter into the analyst's character is helpful for therapy but harmful for literature. Although the patient is not medically or legally constrained by the rules of confidentiality, as the analyst is, the patient turned novelist almost invariably adopts clinical assumptions about the proper focus of attention in a story about the talking cure. There are several ways in which the patient-analyst relationship limits the novelist's freedom to imagine the visible and invisible details of his therapeutic experiences. First, the novelist's exploration of the analyst's life may compromise his privacy and professional career, impairing his effectiveness with future patients.[13] Although this did not happen in *Rose Garden,* which was published seven years after Frieda Fromm-Reichmann's death, the fear of compromising the analyst's privacy may be seen in *Sybil,* where the author presents an admiring but highly restricted portrait of Dr. Cornelia Wilbur, a leading authority on multiple personality.[14] Second, the novelist may question his own motives in imagining hence "analyzing" the therapist's character. If the effort to penetrate the analyst's mind during therapy betokens resistance, can the patient turned novelist entirely escape this fear during writing? Finally, the patient's affection for the analyst (assuming therapy was successful) culminates in the natural desire to pay him back through loving art, but this may work against realistic characterization. Analysis cannot succeed unless the patient has the freedom to project his hostility on to the therapist and work through the transference relationship. Similarly, art cannot fully succeed unless the writer has the imaginative freedom to enter into the lives of both participants, patient and analyst, in the therapeutic drama. To date, this has not been accomplished, neither by writers like Sylvia Plath and Joanne Greenberg, who wish to repay their psychiatrists through loving art, nor by a writer such as Philip Roth, who repays his analyst through an angry act.

I do not mean to disparage *I Never Promised You a Rose Garden* but to appreciate for the first time the unique generic and biographical difficulties from which the novel blossomed. The title aptly cautions us not to expect too much from life, neither perfect justice nor complete truth. Ironically, the exclusion of the stormy therapeutic scenes, especially those moments when Deborah's violence toward the doctor must have seemed demonic, creates a rosier impression of the therapeutic process than occurred in reality. And the omission of the emotionally volatile relationship of transference and countertransference transforms the psychoanalyst into the mythic figure Frieda Fromm-Reichmann passionately warns against in her medical texts. It is as if these angry or emotionally charged clinical sessions were too terrible to be contained within the novel or, paradoxically, too "fictional," calling for a suspension of disbelief worthy of *The Inferno* or *Paradise Lost*. *Rose Garden* ends with Deborah's affirmative words "Full weight," suggestive of her steady progress ahead; yet, the words conceal an intriguing irony whose meaning is revealed only in the context of Dr. Fromm-Reichmann's case study.[15] The complexity of psychoanalysis is such that a full narration of the talking cure is impossible. The principle of indeterminacy always limits the observer's point of view, and the transactional nature of the patient-analyst relationship results in a forever changing communicative flow. The best we can hope for is an approximation or partial fiction of health emerging from sickness, heroism arising from therapeutic battle, art awakening from the shrinking vision.

SEVEN

Doris Lessing's Antipsychiatry

THE SPECTACULAR SUCCESS of psychoanalysis in *I Never Promised You a Rose Garden* sharply contrasts the failure of therapy in Doris Lessing's fictional world. Indeed, the two novelists reveal the central ambiguity of psychiatry, its capacity for good and evil. The enormous growth of the profession in the twentieth century has brought with it enormous problems, and the growing pessimism about psychiatry is as conspicuous as the optimism of a generation ago. The "triumph of the therapeutic"—to use Philip Rieff's expression—has created a new secular mythology in which the psychiatrist, replacing the priest or shaman, is both exalted and feared for his almost limitless power.[1] "The psychiatrist is the most important nongovernmental decision maker in modern life," writes the author of a recent book detailing the uses and abuses of psychiatric power.[2] In an age of skepticism and disbelief, the psychiatrist is viewed as the final authority on mental health and illness. He has the power to institutionalize people, often against their will, to confer "patient" status with all the privileges and liabilities associated with loss of responsibility, and to influence decisions that touch upon nearly every aspect of society from childrearing to moral standards.

In the last two decades psychiatrists have become increasingly critical of verbal therapy, the talking cure, and the pendulum is now swinging in the direction of organic or "medical" approaches to mental illness: a heavy reliance upon drugs like tranquilizers, barbiturates, and the phenothiazines, and more drastic approaches such as electroshock and electroconvulsive therapy. Herein lies a major dilemma. Is it the psychiatrist's task to liberate a patient from a restrictive society, encourage his adaptation to a healthy society, or compel his submission to a totalitarian society? In a science that is notoriously filled with value judgments (and sometimes filled with notoriously bad judgments), is the psychiatrist a progressive or reactionary figure? What are the limits of his power?

For more than a quarter of a century, Doris Lessing has wrestled with the questions posed above in her fiction. She has established herself as the most eloquent voice in the growing antipsychiatry movement. Like the other subjects to which she repeatedly returns—Marxism, feminism, mysticism—her attitude toward psychiatry has remained essentially constant. Her characters are particularly vulnerable to mental breakdowns, and they embark upon odysseys that lead them to the doorstep of psychiatry and, if they are lucky, beyond. They are endlessly medicated, tranquilized, psychoanalyzed, and institutionalized. The unfortunate characters, dependent upon conventional psychiatrists, lose their minds and become burned out shells, victims of what Lessing calls a Dark Age approach to mental illness. The fortunate ones, relying on different therapeutic guides, work through their madness to achieve higher understanding and creativity.

Lessing's view of psychiatry can be easily seen in the anecdotal "Afterward" to *Briefing for a Descent Into Hell* (1971). Subtitled "A Small, Relevant Reminiscence," the "Afterward" describes Lessing's experience with the psychiatric community. She tells how she once wrote a story for a film based on a close friendship with a man whose senses were different from the normal person's. The point of the film, Lessing says, is that the "hero's or protagonist's extra sensitivity and perception must be a handicap in a society organised as ours is, to favour the conforming, the average, the obedient." The film-makers were puzzled by the script and asked the same question: "What is wrong with the man in the film?" Startled by the inappropriateness of the question and because the real-life original had been contradictorily diagnosed by the medical establishment, Lessing decided to send the script to two doctors. One was the consulting psychiatrist at a teaching hospital attached to a large university, the other a neurologist working at a large London teaching hospital. She asked the eminent authorities to diagnose her fictional character as if he were a real patient. Their verdict? "They were kind enough to do so, taking trouble over it, and time. But their skilled and compassionate diagnoses, while authoritative, were quite different from each other's. They agreed about nothing at all."[3]

Lessing's fictional therapists confirm this bewildering subjectivity. They display a wide range of attitudes and approaches toward mental illness, and frequently they are less benign than the two actual psychiatrists who responded to Lessing's query. They include the nonmedical Jungian analyst, Mrs. Marks, in Lessing's masterpiece, *The Golden Notebook.* Her pet name, Mother Sugar, indicates a "whole way of looking at life—traditional, rooted, conservative, in spite of its scandalous familiarity with everything amoral" (p. 5). They also embrace the bland-looking Dr. Lamb in *The Four-Gated City,* who skillfully "explodes" the benumbed Martha Quest, as well as the anonymous Doctor X and Doctor Y in *Briefing for a Descent Into Hell,* who disagree violently on the best therapeutic stratagem for curing Professor Charles Watkins' amnesia. Only Mrs. Marks is sympathetically portrayed, not because of her professional training or point of view, but because she remains a caring woman who is able to listen empathically to Anna and offer pragmatic advice. As Lessing's psychiatrists become more medical, they become more dangerous to their patients. Doctor X's refrain in *Briefing for a Descent Into Hell*—"E.C.T. should be attempted"—echoes the punitive philosophy inherent in Lessing's psychiatric community.

In the autobiographical *A Small Personal Voice* (1974), Lessing acknowledges that the fictional Mrs. Marks is based on the novelist's actual psychotherapist. The decision to write on psychiatric themes, Lessing adds, was less a matter of conscious choice than inner necessity. When she began *The Golden Notebook* in the 1950s, she was in analysis and, like her fictional heroine Anna Wulf, able to transmute her therapeutic experiences into art. Her feelings toward her analyst were deeply ambivalent:

> My own psychotherapist was somewhat like Mrs. Marks. She was everything I disliked. I was then aggressively rational, antireligious, and a radical. She was Roman Catholic, Jungian, and conservative. It was very upsetting to me at the time, but I found out it didn't matter a damn. I couldn't stand her terminology, but she was a marvelous person. She was one of those rare individuals who know how to help others. If she had used another set of words, if she had talked Freud talk, or aggressive atheism, it wouldn't have made a difference.[4]

The analyst was helpful, not through the art of psychotherapy, the validity of which Lessing rejects, but through the act of friendship—the ability to empathize and offer insights that are not necessarily psychoanalytic. In a letter to a critic, Lessing has described her therapy as "paying for a friend, which I needed desperately, to counterbalance certain very destructive things in my life. I think usually what people are doing when

they are in analysis or therapy or whatever, is paying for a friend."[5] Not
that Lessing portrays an extra-analytic relationship in *The Golden Notebook*. There is no violation of the patient-analyst relationship, and Anna
remains a model patient. Nevertheless, she is able to reject the analyst's
interpretations without dismissing Mrs. Marks's goodwill.

Unlike other novelists, such as Plath and Greenberg, Lessing shows little interest in symptomatology or the dynamics of transference. Nor is
she interested in revealing the particulars of her own therapy. Indeed, the
structure of *The Golden Notebook* makes autobiographical inferences difficult and, apart from a few suggestive comments Lessing makes in *A Small
Personal Voice* about her parents' struggle against mental illness, we cannot discuss her fiction in terms of her actual therapy, as we did in *The
Bell Jar* and *I Never Promised You a Rose Garden*.[6] An extremely intelligent writer who remains committed to ideas and their moral consequences, Lessing writes about psychotherapy with authenticity. Nevertheless, one senses that she has now become indifferent to the lively
exchanges between patient and analyst that the author of *The Golden
Notebook* popularized two decades ago. "For the last twenty years I have
been closely involved with psychiatrists and mentally ill people. I did not
make a deliberate choice in the matter, but I started a process which is
now common. Twenty years ago it was considered unusual to have a psychiatrist. Now, almost everyone I know has had a breakdown, is in psychoanalysis, or pops in and out of mental hospitals. Mental illness is part
of the mainstream" (*A Small Personal Voice*, p. 69).

Lessing has always criticized the politics of psychoanalysis. Although
she does not endorse the Marxist claim that therapy is counterproductive
(an idea her early characters occasionally echo), she does regard the inherent differences in the patient-analyst relationship as analogous to political inequality. And inequality can become exploitation. She identifies
all forms of psychotherapy with an antidemocratic spirit: patient and analyst are locked into rigid roles, the former submitting blindly to the clinical dogmas of the latter. She views the psychiatrist as the apologist of a
treatment designed to perpetuate a repressive sociopolitical structure. For
a novelist who believes that mental illness and psychological breakdown
are potentially curative in overcoming the false dichotomies of society,
Lessing nevertheless views therapists as reactionary figures. Psychiatry remains, in her judgment, irrevocably opposed to social enlightenment, political reform, and personal transcendence. Far from guiding a patient
through a breakdown, the analyst—as the word implies—contributes to

his fragmentation. The talking cure becomes a coping cure, leading to conformity and obedience.

Lessing also condemns the medicopsychopathological model of illness. (The one exception is Stalin, whom Anna concedes in *The Golden Notebook* was "clinically insane.") She rejects the effort to diagnose or classify mental illness, arguing that such labeling is meaningless and dehumanizing. She remains skeptical of symptomatology on the grounds that it reduces a person to patient status. And she remains firmly opposed to Freud. "The Freudians describe the conscious as a small lit area, all white, and the unconscious as a great dark marsh full of monsters. In their view, the monsters reach up, grab you by the ankles, and try to drag you down. But the unconscious can be what you make of it, good or bad, helpful or unhelpful. Our culture has made an enemy of the unconscious" (*A Small Personal Voice*, p. 67). She also remains dubious of Jungian analysis, fearing entrapment in its quaint mythic system. In her more recent novels she has rejected the entire concept of mental illness, shunning the words "neurosis" and "psychosis" in favor of a non-clinical and non-pejorative "craziness."

There are, however, contradictions in Lessing's vision of psychological breakdown. Her repudiation of psychopathology and its schema of neurosis and psychosis would seem to ally her with Thomas Szasz, whose influential *The Myth of Mental Illness* does away not only with nebulous psychiatric classification but also with the existence of mental illness. Lessing would certainly endorse Szasz's impassioned efforts to point out and correct the injustices that have been perpetrated in the name of psychiatry: involuntary institutionalization, the widespread use of medication, electroshock, and—the most invasive of all therapies—the leucotomy or prefrontal lobotomy.[7] Unlike Szasz, Lessing affirms the power of unconscious forces, and her characters inexplicably lose control. Moreover, her mysticism remains alien to Szasz's rationalism. The metaphor of "plugging into madness" evokes a malevolent frequency or wavelength "in the air" which compels her characters to break down. This concept of mental illness is much closer to that of R. D. Laing, the other outspoken leader of the antipsychiatry movement. Laing regards psychosis as a potentially reparative process, a journey through inner space, that can lead to higher creativity and mental functioning. As with Laing's patients, Lessing's protagonists go mad in highly stylized ways. Madness and mysticism are almost identical phenomena in Lessing's world.

But there is an obvious danger in romanticizing mental illness: Few psychotics behave as well as Lessing's, and if psychosis is potentially creative to some people, it is nevertheless destructive to most people. Additionally, there has been a shift in Lessing's assumptions of reality. Her early fiction grows out of the tradition of social realism, with all its assumptions of normative consciousness. Her later fiction dramatizes characters who possess telepathic powers suggestive of an evolving human consciousness, an idea Lessing has acquired from her reading of Sufi philosophy.[8] Paradoxically, although she argues (along with Szasz) for a demystification of mental illness, she seems to have embraced (along with Laing) an older, demonological model of madness.

Lessing's interest in psychology begins as early as *Martha Quest* (1952), Volume I of the five-volume *Bildungsroman, Children of Violence,* which traces the heroine from her early childhood in fictional Zambesia (Southern Africa) in the first quarter of the twentieth century to her death at the end of the war-ravaged century. A sprawling canvas filled with hundreds of events and characters, the *Children of Violence* series documents Lessing's belief that civilization is moving inexorably toward nuclear holocaust. This is precisely what happens in *The Four-Gated City* (1969), the final volume in which atomic warfare has decimated the planet and produced an odd species of mutants who embody the hope for future regeneration. Even as a young woman, Martha is interested in psychology, hoping to discover in it an explanation of the terrifying destructiveness of human nature. Others in her life also are enamored of psychological theory. Her friend Solly Cohen "was in love (there is no other word for it) with psychology; he passionately defended everything to do with it, even when his heroes contradicted each other" (*Martha Quest,* p. 18). Martha eagerly devours these volumes only to emerge from her readings saddened by the oppressive determinism of the "numerous sects who agreed on only one thing, that it was the first five years of life which laid an unalterable basis for everything that followed" (p. 19).

In Volume II, *A Proper Marriage* (1954), Martha reluctantly continues her study of psychology, disappointed by the novelists who depicted women in literature according to what male authors believed. ". . . there always came a point where Martha turned from the novelists and tale tellers to that section of the bookcase which was full of books called *The Psychology of . . . , The Behaviour of . . . , A Guide to . . . ,* with the half-formulated thought that the novelists had not caught up with life . . ." (p. 322). Once again her reading of psychology yields nothing fruitful. Instead of illuminating the complexity of human nature or the mystery of inner life, the psychology texts reinforce the bias of male authors. The association of psychology with stale psychologisms continues in the next two volumes of the *Children of Violence* series, *A Ripple from the Storm* (1958) and *Landlocked* (1965).

Lessing's most profound exploration of psychological breakdown is made in *The Golden Notebook* (1962), regarded as "the most considerable single work by an English author in the 1960s."[9] Here Lessing first begins to write about the theme of breakdown as a method to heal the false dichotomies and divisions of the self. The structure of *The Golden Notebook* is unusually complex, consisting of a novel within a novel—a 60,000 word conventional short novel called *Free Women* which serves as the skeleton or frame. (The entire novel is huge, nearly one-quarter of a million words long.) *Free Women* is divided into five sections, each separated by stages of the four notebooks: Black, Red, Yellow, and Blue. Anna Wulf keeps four notebooks instead of one because of a need "to separate things off from each other, out of fear of chaos, of formlessness—of breakdown" (p. vii). At the end of Lessing's novel Anna's fragments come together to produce a new creation, the Golden notebook, in which her inner tensions have been reconciled and healed, revealing the triumph of the second theme, unity. In the inner Golden notebook Anna and her male counterpart Saul Green break down and are then reunited. From this experience arises a new Anna, strengthened and healed. There are actually two Annas in Lessing's novel, one "real" and the other "fictional." The real Anna is writing the notebooks, and she has also written a novel called *Frontiers of War,* which she has grown to hate. The other Anna is the central character of *Free Women.* Only toward the end of Lessing's story, do we realize that *Free Women* has been written by the real Anna. The discovery is astonishing because Anna has been suffering from writer's block and repeatedly claims to have given up art, a problem that leads her into psychoanalysis with Mrs. Marks. The fictional Anna is thus the literary creation of the real Anna, who, in turn, is a fictional creation of Doris Lessing, the supreme creator playing off reality and illusion.

Anna enters psychoanalysis because of a paralyzing inability to feel emotion and because of growing cynicism of the psychological impulse behind her writing. The two problems are related. Her emotional paralysis appears to be a defense against the disturbing dreams she calls "joy-in-destruction," suggestive of unconscious aggression. Anna is the first fictional protagonist we have seen who enters therapy specifically because of an inability to write. Foreshadowing Roth's *My Life as a Man, The*

Golden Notebook painstakingly analyzes the relationship between artistic creation and psychopathology. Anna's inner violence produces numbness and self-alienation; her writings, including diary entries, autobiographical recollections, and novel, reflect her troubled state. She sees her art as a reflection of the artist's divided consciousness and society's hopeless fragmentation. She coldly dismisses the emotions behind *Frontiers of War* as nostalgia, a word she equates with sentimentality, and she condemns her novel for containing the same nihilistic longing for dissolution from which wars are made. She criticizes herself for being too fragmented to write the kind of novel which interests her, a book "powered with an intellectual or moral passion strong enough to create order, to create a new way of looking at life" (p. 61). Yet she also mistrusts herself for the artistic urge to shape a story into a coherent work of fiction instead of reproducing the raw incidents of life. Unwilling to falsify experience, she vows to give up writing.

Although Anna repudiates art, she cannot prevent herself from transmuting her conflicts into literature. Her mistrust of psychoanalysis appears in her proliferation of fictional therapists based upon her ex-lover Michael, a psychiatrist with whom she lived for five years. In the Yellow notebook, devoted to stories based upon her experiences, Anna works on a manuscript called *The Shadow of the Third* in which her alter ego, Ella, is writing a novel about suicide (paralleling the theme of suicide in *Free Women*). Ella is having an affair with a psychiatrist, Dr. Paul Tanner, who embodies Anna's divided consciousness and ambivalence toward therapy. Later, in *The Shadow of the Third*, Ella has an affair with another psychiatrist, Cy Maitland, who specializes in leucotomies. Both Paul Tanner and Cy Maitland are fictional images of Michael, a "witch-doctor," whose decision to return to his wife devastates Anna and sends her into deep depression.

The "Shadow" in the title of Anna's manuscript in the Yellow notebook refers to the Jungian concept of the unconscious side of personality. Lessing's experience with Jungian analysis informs the psychology of *The Golden Notebook,* and a basic knowledge of Jungian terminology is helpful for an understanding of the novel. In Jungian theory, the shadow complements the conscious self and may be in harmony or disharmony with it. Jung defines the shadow as the hidden personality fragment which has been split off from the conscious self. It is often perceived as the " 'negative' side of the personality, the sum of all those unpleasant qualities we like to hide, together with the insufficiently developed functions and the content of the personal unconscious."[10] Another Jungian concept Lessing uses in *The Golden Notebook* is the anima and animus. The anima is the female side of man, the mother in him; the animus is the male side of woman, the father in her. Psychological health and balance, Jung maintained, requires the positive acceptance of the element of the opposite sex within the self, the integration of male and female. The process of integration Jung called individuation, a "coming to self-hood" or "self-realization." Accordingly, Ella and Paul Tanner are deeply split individuals, and their relationship betrays their inability to live with each other or with themselves. Idealistic and cynical, generous and cruel, Paul is a walking contradiction. His inner split reflects Ella's (and Anna's) self-division. Neither Ella nor Paul is able to reconcile the antinomies of human existence and the male/female split within each individual.

Paul Tanner serves as a projection screen in the Yellow notebook, not unlike the role of the yellow wallpaper in Charlotte Perkins Gilman's short story. He reflects the conviction of his creator, Anna Wulf, and *her* creator, Doris Lessing, that no coherent system of thought can hope to describe or resolve the irrationality of human nature. When Ella tries to imagine Paul's wife, whom she has never seen, she becomes wildly jealous and possessive, almost as if she were another person. Only by projecting herself into another character does Ella/Anna recognize the shadowy underside of human personality. Under Paul's questioning, Ella admits to truths she has never realized. She sees the discrepancy between her idealized portrait of herself and the actual portrait, which she finds reprehensible. Just as Paul's negative personality increasingly disturbs Ella, who finds herself less emotionally stable than she imagined, so does Paul become another person, a "self-hating rake, free, casual, heartless" (p. 207). His split toward psychiatry echoes Anna's ambivalence toward art. He takes his work with his patients seriously, but he makes fun of the jargon he uses. And he seems to have a perverse desire to mock the truths he holds most dear. Condemning himself and his profession, Paul asks Ella: "What sort of a doctor is it who sees his patients as symptoms of a world sickness?" (p. 212). The judgment coincides exactly with the viewpoint of the two novelists of *The Golden Notebook,* Anna Wulf and Doris Lessing.

Interestingly, although Anna has had an affair with a psychiatrist, she does not see her therapist, Mrs. Marks, as an extension of Michael. Nor is Mrs. Marks a self-divided figure, as are Anna's fictional therapists, Paul Tanner and Cy Maitland. Lessing thus avoids the solipsistic danger of creating a therapist in the author's own image, a problem other writers, including Fitzgerald, Eliot, and Plath, failed to solve. Mrs. Marks is neither schizoid nor self-mocking. In a novel that dazzlingly juxtaposes illusion and reality, she maintains a remarkably consistent identity. A cultivated and articulate therapist, and a "most intelligent wise old woman," Mrs. Marks has a dry ironic style that never interferes with the compassion she feels for Anna. Her silence is as impressive as her speech. The office in which her patient sits three times a week reflects dignity and taste. The walls are covered with reproductions of masterpieces and, along with the statues, the office resembles an art gallery—a setting which gives Anna pleasure.

Like the incomplete portrait of Dr. Fried in *I Never Promised You a Rose Garden,* Mrs. Marks is not a fully developed literary creation—and for perhaps the same reason. Because Mother Sugar is based on Lessing's own therapist, the novelist probably did not wish to compromise the privacy or speculate on the inner life of the "good, kind, infinitely generous woman."[11] Lessing does not idealize Mrs. Marks, however, and Anna resents the therapist's detachment and impersonality. Because the analyst does not doubt her own profession nor question the theoretical assumptions of her work, she appears close minded to Anna. And her impersonality maddens Anna, who tries to force the analyst outside of her professional role. She succeeds twice in momentarily breaking Mrs. Marks's equanimity, but even when the analyst's wry smile turns to a frown, she maintains self-control. Like Dr. Fried, Mrs. Marks functions less as an autonomous character than as an instrument of therapy, voicing a traditional Jungian point of view. At the end of *The Golden Notebook* she remains unchanged by her experience with Anna.

Mrs. Marks is especially interested in the psychoanalysis of writers, and her sessions with Anna constitute one of the most serious discussions in literature about the relationship between creativity and neurosis. The two women predictably disagree over the question of art. "I became a psychotherapist because I once believed myself to be an artist" (p. 234), Mrs. Marks cryptically remarks, implying a vicarious participation in the creative process. (Was she at one time an artist?) Her office certainly looks like a shrine to art, and her understanding of mythology is formidable. Despite her reverence for art, however, she maintains that the "artist writes out of an incapacity to live" (p. 62). She thus repeats Freud's error that the artist is a neurotic who, failing to make his dreams come true in the real world, escapes into art as a substitute gratification. Anna rightly objects to this view of creativity and to the magisterial tone of Mrs. Marks's pronouncements. ". . . this business about art and the artist has become so debased, the property of every sloppy-minded amateur that any person with a real connection with the arts wants to run a hundred miles at the sight of the small satisfied nod, the complacent smile" (p. 62). The remark anticipates Roth's *My Life as a Man* in which he also takes issue with psychoanalysts who make definitive pronouncements over the creative process. In Anna's judgment, Mrs. Marks cannot help voicing clichés that diminish the dignity of art.

Anna also objects to the analyst's subordination of personal conflicts to the collective unconscious, a process that devalues history in favor of myth. Implicit in the Jungian analyst's view of the timelessness of art is a conservatism toward human nature that carries over to sociopolitical issues. Anna complains, with considerable justification, that her own psychoanalysis has never moved outside the realm of primitive myth. From her experiences she is forced to conclude that psychoanalysis is "essentially a process where one is forced back into infantilism and then rescued from it by crystallising what one learns into a sort of intellectual primitivism—one is forced back into myth, and folk lore and everything that belongs to the savage or undeveloped stages of society" (p. 468). She accuses the analyst of practicing a form of mythotherapy (though not the type found in John Barth's existential novel *The End of the Road*).[12] No matter what dream or emotion or conflict Anna dredges up in therapy, Mrs. Marks will locate its mythic origins or find a mythic analogue, thus impersonalizing the patient's unique experience. "As far as you are concerned, I've gone beyond the childish, I've transmuted it and saved it, by embodying it in myth. But in fact all I do, or you do, is to fish among the childish memories of an individual, and merge them with the art or ideas that belong to the childhood of a people" (pp. 468–469). Individuation, Anna continues, is nothing more than the discovery of the universality of experience, a process which, she fears, denies the uniqueness of the individual and the possibility of breaking through or transcending the present. When pressed to elaborate on the possibility of further development of the human race, Anna says, foreshadowing *The Four-Gated City:* "*Yes,* there's a hint of something—there's a crack in that man's personality like a gap in a dam, and through that gap the future might pour in a different shape—terrible perhaps, or marvellous, but something new . . ." (p. 473). Rejecting Mother Sugar's efforts to diminish pain by encapsulating it in primitive myth, Anna prefers to endure her suffering.

How valid are Anna's criticisms here? Is she rationalizing, as she has done about the writer's block to which she admits only at the end of the novel? Or is she, as we suspect, accurately reflecting Lessing's condemnation of psychoanalysis? Anna expresses the mistrust of many patients who find themselves in an ontological no-win position in psychotherapy. On the one hand, they fear they can manipulate the analyst by telling him what he wishes to hear, thus "confirming" the truth of psychoanalysis. On the other hand, they believe that the analyst will dismiss as "rationalization" or "denial" their legitimate doubts about an interpretation. This is what Mrs. Marks appears to do, accusing Anna of "using our experience together to re-enforce your rationalisations for not writing" (p. 474), a charge the patient bitterly denies. Analyst and patient reach an uneasy standoff here, though it is clear that Lessing's sympathy lies with Anna's point of view. On at least one issue, however, Anna is incorrect—the assumption that "Psychoanalysis stands or falls on whether it makes better human beings, morally better, not clinically more healthy" (p. 470). Psychoanalysis has moral implications, of course, and ideally it makes individuals more aware and therefore more sensitive to moral concerns. Nevertheless, it is not identical with moral philosophy or religion, neither of which has been conspicuously successful in improving human nature.

In Mrs. Marks's defense, she has an uncanny ability to read Anna's mind, especially the intuition that the writer has been keeping a diary of her experiences in therapy. Mrs. Marks is also prophetic in the belief that Anna will soon write fiction again. The analyst's patience is extraordinary, and she tirelessly affirms Anna's creativity and independence as a free woman. When Anna meets the psychological chameleon Saul Green, who functions as her symbolic counterpart, male-female, brother-sister, she remembers how Mother Sugar " 'taught' me about the obsessions of jealousy being part homosexuality. But the lesson at the time seemed rather academic, nothing to do with me, Anna. I wondered if I wanted to make love with that woman he was with now" (p. 587). Many of the analyst's other insights prove valuable to Anna, including the recognition that the unconscious can be benevolent as well as malevolent, that "All self-knowledge is knowing, on deeper and deeper levels, what one knew before" (p. 239), and that the process of writing a diary will represent the beginning of the unfreezing or releasing of the writer's block that holds Anna captive.

Readers looking to *The Golden Notebook* for an unambiguous statement about the relationship between the creative and therapeutic process will doubtlessly be disappointed, however. Many of Anna's objections to psychoanalysis coincide with her suspicion of art, further complicating Lessing's position. Anna sees the creative and therapeutic process as the endeavor to turn the formless into form, naming the ineffable. Both the artist and analyst universalize experience and make use of the repetition-compulsion principle, in which painful experiences are repeated over and over again in an effort to master the anxiety underlying them. "Literature is analysis after the event" (p. 228), Anna realizes, as psychoanalysis is. The end result, she says, is that "all the pain, and the killing and the violence is safely held in the story" where it cannot hurt her (p. 470). Contrary to logic, the conclusion depresses her.

Does therapy cure Anna's writer's block? Without endorsing the validity of Mrs. Marks's psychoanalytic theory, Lessing affirms the analyst's enthusiastic support of Anna and by implication the therapeutic value of art. Anna's diaries allow her to focus on her feelings and defuse her self-destructiveness. Throughout her sessions with Mrs. Marks, Anna has denied suffering from writer's block, and it is significant that she admits the problem not to her analyst but to Saul Green near the end of the Blue notebook. Although the admission confirms the analyst's diagnosis, Anna's major insights derive not from therapy but from the act of writing, which forces her to be introspective. Immediately after the admission, Anna buys the Golden notebook, which represents the working through or integration of her conflicting selves. In naming her private demons, she is able to achieve a degree of mastery over them. Both literature and psychoanalysis imply the act of naming, the creation of useful fictions by which to live. Like the heroine of the *Children of Violence* series, with whom she has so much in common, Anna undertakes a quest into the deepest recesses of the unconscious self. If she is appalled by the selfishness of the "I, I, I, I," the naked ego, she also realizes she is ultimately responsible for her own actions, including sickness or health. "I haven't done time with the witch-doctors not to know that no one does anything to me, I do it to myself" (p. 622).

Curiously, despite Anna's long psychoanalysis (from January 1950 to April 1954), neither she nor Mrs. Marks explores the most crucial psychological determinant of personality development: the parent-child relationship. Recent psychoanalytic research has stressed the decisive importance of the mother's role in the formation of child development and the extent to which early patterns of mothering are reproduced when the child becomes an adult and bears children. Studies in the area of identity formation and the process of separation and individuation have confirmed the importance of concepts which Freud and the other early psychoanalytic pioneers insufficiently emphasized: mirroring, empathy, healthy self-love. Whereas Freud asserted the biological inferiority of women, and consequently reinforced destructive cultural biases, modern analysts—influenced by the feminist movement—are more sensitive to the growing number of women who choose both parenthood and career, a synthesis which has been harder for women to achieve than men. (Men have obviously enjoyed greater cultural opportunity than women to fulfill Freud's definition of psychological health, the ability to love and work.) Yet how does a daughter growing up in a traditional society reject her mother's values in favor of a more self-fulfilling role involving both love and work? The daughter's struggle for independence is fraught with anxiety and guilt, Esther Menaker has observed, for she must counteridentify with her mother to achieve a more positive self-image:

> This tendency to counteridentification, to a sometimes almost conscious decision not to repeat the life-style or personality of a parent, is particularly common among little girls who have repudiated the traditional feminine role as their mothers have lived it. Clinical experience with young women in recent years has made it clear that a major factor in this repudiation is the little girl's experience of her mother's unhappiness, her lack of fulfillment, her bitter feeling that life has cheated her and, above all, her low opinion of herself. In this depreciated self-image, the mother has accepted the male-oriented social attitude toward woman as an inferior, as a second-class citizen.[13]

Lessing's refusal to discuss Anna's relationship to her parents in *The Golden Notebook* becomes more conspicuous in light of the wealth of material revealed about other aspects of her life, including the parental surrogates in the novel: Molly, the Communist party, and the men in whom she merges her identity.[14] Indeed, it is impossible to believe that not once during her four-year analysis does Anna comment upon her parents. Nevertheless, no critic has pointed out this huge gap in her therapy. Significantly, the few comments Anna makes about her parents are expressed, not during psychoanalysis, but in her fiction—the completed novel *Free Women* and the uncompleted manuscript *The Shadow of the Third*. Only through the protective disguise of fiction does Anna (and Lessing) allow herself to touch upon this most troubling of subjects. Since we cannot be certain whether the parents of the "fictional" Anna or Ella coincide exactly with the parents of the "real" Anna, we must be especially cautious about making autobiographical inferences from the novelist's art.

The form of *The Golden Notebook* defends Anna against autobiographical exposure and the accusation of basing her art entirely upon her life. *The Shadow of the Third* is a more exaggerated version of her life than either the notebooks or *Free Women;* yet, it is also a more revealing and truthful portrait of the severity of her fears. Similarly, Lessing cannot be equated with the "real" Anna, at least not in any literal or obvious way. (Lessing has apparently never suffered from writer's block, for example, nor did her mother die early, as does Anna's.) The novelist thus stands twice removed from the artist heroines of *Free Women* and *The Shadow of the Third.* Lessing remains the mysterious figure behind the veil, always eluding the reader's sight. Many of the distinctions among the two Annas and Ella are more apparent than real, however, and we can discern major similarities of personality and artistic vision uniting the fictional writers with their creator.

The only time Anna thinks about her mother in *Free Women* occurs early in the novel during a heated discussion with Molly, who tends to dominate her friend. Stung by Molly's insensitivity to her problem with writing, Anna manages to avoid counterattacking her friend—a counterattack that would have been a repetition of ancient battles with her mother. "Anna nearly said, stubbornly, 'But I'm not an extension of you,' but knew it was something she might have said to her mother, so stopped herself. Anna could remember her mother very little; she had died so early; but at moments like these, she was able to form for herself the image of somebody strong and dominating, whom Anna had had to fight" (pp. 41–42). Although we learn nothing else about Anna's mother in *Free Women,* there is the suggestion of a troubled relationship—an intrusive mother who regards her daughter as an extension of herself. In the notebooks, Anna's discussion of Maryrose's mother may be relevant to her own mother, as well as a foreshadowing of Mrs. Quest in *The Four-Gated City.* "I remember Maryrose's mother, a dominating neurotic woman who has sapped all the vitality out of the girl, a woman of about fifty, as vigorous and fussy as an old hen. . . . When she was there Maryrose sank into a state of listless irritation, a nervous exhaustion. She knew she ought to fight her mother, but did not have the moral energy" (p. 99).

Two of the most severe obstacles to a child's happiness are the loss of the mother and rejection by the father. Anna suffers from this double blow. Bereft of the mother from an early age, the daughter has been raised by a father whose rejection of her must have been devastating. In *The Shadow of the Third*, Anna writes about Ella's grim relationship with her father, an embittered ex-Indian army officer now in retirement. Stunned by a question from Paul Tanner, Ella admits her father never liked her—an admission Anna makes for the first time. " '*Like* me?' The question was startling to Ella. Not once had she asked herself whether her father liked her. She turned to Paul in a flash of recognition, laughing: 'What a question. But you know, I don't know?' And added, in a small voice: 'No, come to think of it, and I never have, I don't believe he does, not really' " (p. 191). Although she does not idealize her father, as Esther Greenwood does in *The Bell Jar*, she fails to express the keen disappointment one might expect from a rejected child.

Later, in *The Shadow of the Third*, Anna elaborates on Ella's feelings toward her long-dead mother and remote father. Visiting him, Ella learns for the first time about her parents' unhappy marriage. The story of the marriage remains obscure, with Ella's mother emerging (like Paul Tanner's wife) as the shadow of the third figure in Anna's imagination. "Your mother was altogether too good for me," the father enigmatically begins. Under questioning, he admits his wife was frigid, sexless. "She didn't give a damn about me, but she was jealous as a sick cat" (p. 462). Instead of trying to help her overcome her sexual repulsion, he looks elsewhere for satisfaction, "buying himself" a woman. The father coldly thwarts Ella's wish to learn more about her parents. Not only does he deny any connection to his dead wife, he disclaims kinship with his living daughter. He remains emotionally withdrawn, uncaring, unresponsive. He characterizes all people, including Ella's child, as "cannibals," waiting to devour the father. "People are just cannibals unless they leave each other alone" (p. 464). Accusing Ella of being a "modern woman," he abruptly ends the conversation. Another visit with him proves equally unsatisfactory. Each story she imagines about her father contains the same pattern of defeat, death, and bitter irony.

Ella's dream of a disintegrating house may symbolize a repetition of her parents' disintegrating marriage and homelife. Anna struggles with many of the conflicts that defined Ella's parents' unhappy marriage. The sexual frigidity of Ella's mother shows up as a generalized numbness, loss of feeling, and anesthesia within Anna. Indeed, Anna enters analysis because of her inability to feel pleasure or pain. Writing about herself in the third person, she observes, during the beginning of therapy: "Anna Wulf is sitting in a chair in front of a soul-doctor. She is there because she cannot deeply feel about anything. She is frozen" (p. 234). Unlike Ella's mother, who remains frigid throughout her life, Anna enters into satisfying sexual relationships. And yet both Anna and Ella are sexually repelled by their husbands shortly after marriage. (Anna's unhappy marriage to Max Wulf may be a repetition of the failure of her parents' marriage.) An unselfish and generous person, Anna becomes wildly jealous (like her mother?) of the wife of her ex-lover Michael. In *The Shadow of the Third*, she tortures herself by imagining the invisible woman to whom Michael keeps returning. In the Blue notebook, Anna also feels a strong jealousy toward Saul Green, who leaves her for other women. "I am mad, obsessed with a cold jealousy which I have never experienced before" (pp. 575–576).

It is impossible to prove that Anna's jealousy and emotional block are part of her maternal legacy, but it seems logical that in profound ways she is her mother's daughter, and thus the product of a psychosocial background that could be usefully explored in analysis. Since mental illness is often a family affair, in which there is a reciprocal interaction of the social and familial environment, on the one hand, and the development of pathology, on the other, we need to know specific information about the mother-daughter relationship. Was the mother available or absent to the daughter? Was Anna able as a child to separate successfully from the mother? If not, this might help to explain her identity diffusion in later life and the need to lose herself in symbiotic relationships with other men and women. Was Anna disappointed by her mother and consequently filled with bitterness and aggression? If so, this might account for the "return of the repressed" in later life, along with the fear that she must conceal her anger at all cost, lest it destroy the love object, whether it be a parent, Michael, or her own daughter. At what age did Anna's mother die, and what was her response to the death? Maternal loss is one of the underlying patterns in *The Golden Notebook* and most likely the origin of Anna's separation anxiety. Was the mother replaced by another woman in the family, or was Anna forced to mother herself, a role she conscientiously performs for her own daughter Janet, who is also raised by a single parent? In short, to appreciate Anna's predicament and the courageous struggle to become a free woman, one must know something about her family history and the enigmatic figure in her life who is conspicuously missing from the patient's analysis and the writer's biography.

So too is Anna her father's daughter, and there seems to be a relationship between the father's cynicism and the corrosive nihilism from which the daughter suffers. "Nothing is more powerful than this nihilism," Anna writes in her notebooks, "an angry readiness to throw everything overboard, a willingness, a longing to become part of dissolution" (p. 64). The statement is a philosophically more profound version of the father's deadly bitterness. The father's dominant response to life—to retreat into a safe place where emotions cannot touch him—is also the daughter's characteristic defense against pain. Anna retreats so deeply into herself, in fact, that she denies the existence of emotions—the presenting symptom she brings into analysis. The pattern of defeat, death, and grim irony links Ella and Anna to their fathers. Additionally, one of Ella's revelations is the discovery that her father writes poetry, "poems about solitude, loss, fortitude, the adventures of isolation" (p. 465). These are subjects similar to the ones Anna writes about. Unlike Anna, the father does not wish to be published. After writing poems, the father locks them up, uninterested in sharing them with other readers. Yet Anna, we remember, suffers from writer's block, which does not seem very different from the old man's embittered silence. Moreover, after Michael abandons Anna, she enters into masochistic relationships with other men who reenact the father's rejection of her.

Nowhere in *The Golden Notebook* is there evidence to suggest that Anna's parents were warm, empathic, loving. Indeed, there is striking evidence to the contrary. "The consequence of the parental self-object's inability to be a joyful mirror to a child's healthy assertiveness," Heinz Kohut has argued in *The Restoration of the Self,* "may be a lifetime of abrasiveness, bitterness, and sadism that cannot be discharged. . . ."[15] It is hard to avoid the conclusion that the severe problems which drive Anna into therapy—the extreme detachment from herself and others, the feelings of isolation, apathy, and inferiority, and the diffuse rage and anxiety—are the consequences of her parents' flawed empathic quality. Clinical experience would suggest that Anna's sadomasochistic feelings derive from narcissistic injuries suffered at the hands of chronically cold parents. Anna's problems of low self-esteem, self-mockery, dependent relationships with uncaring men, and fears of fragmentation imply an unstable self, which, in Kohutian terms, originates from the inability to merge with healthy, loving parents (omnipotent self-objects). The child's narcissistic vulnerability need not derive from a single traumatic event, such as the death of a parent, although Anna's mother obviously dies when her daughter is young, but from a family environment of faulty empathic mirroring. Far from compensating for this severe maternal loss by offering his daughter an affirmative mirroring of life, the father allies himself with negation and death, thus reinforcing the daughter's crushing rejection. It is no wonder that Anna sees darkness everywhere.

Oddly enough, although Lessing meticulously analyzes the violence and chaos of Anna's emotions and the extent to which they reflect the madness of the twentieth century, the novelist evades the question of the patient's personal history, the complicated interlockings connecting one family generation to another. *The Golden Notebook* chronicles the history of war throughout Anna's century but not the warfare of her own family. Nor does Lessing trace Anna's self-aggression to its personal antecedents. For instance, Anna has a recurrent nightmare about destruction which, under pressure from Mrs. Marks to name it, she calls "joy-in-spite." The dream manifests itself in different forms and images, beginning as a peasant wooden vase, then looking like a species of elf or pixie, and then transforming itself into an "old man, almost dwarf-like, infinitely more terrifying than the vase-object, because he was part human" (p. 477). There are further transformations of the dream which the Jungian analyst interprets mythically, preferring to deal with primitive gods and goddesses than with the significant figures in Anna's life. The weakness of Mrs. Marks's interpretation is that it ignores Anna's private myth system; for by transmuting the patient's dreams into ancient myths and the collective unconscious, the Jungian analyst neglects the personal experiences which give birth to Anna's dreams. The problem with Anna's analysis, in other words, is that she universalizes the meaning of her conflicts before she particularizes them. It is like engaging in dream interpretation without first knowing the dreamer's free associations; the effort is doomed to failure. Symbols have different meanings to different people and unlike Jung, who made little effort to discover the dreamer's free associations, Freud insisted that analysis could not succeed without this knowledge.

An important unexplored area in *The Golden Notebook* is the link between Ella's father, whom we may infer as the reflection of Anna's father, and the cruel old man in the dream who represents "pure spite, malice, joy in a destructive impulse" (p. 477). At times male and other times female, the figure in the dream is lively despite having a wooden leg, crutch, hump, or other deformation. The creature embodies "purposeless, undirected, causeless spite" (p. 478). A later dream of the dwarfed malicious man assumes a more explicitly sexual meaning. "He had a great protruding penis sticking out through his clothes, it menaced me, was dangerous, because I knew the old man hated me and wanted to hurt me" (p.

562). Anna becomes the old-man/woman-dwarf figure and, along with her counterpart Saul Green, ritualistically descends into a "cocoon of madness" to live out sadomasochistic fantasies. Persuaded by Mrs. Marks to "dream the dream positively," Anna achieves wholeness through integration of the anima and animus, the female and male elements of the psyche.[16]

A Freudian interpretation of the nightmare of "joy-in-spite" would explore the possibility that Anna's dream of a malevolent old man symbolizes her anguish over a father who disappointed her, first by denying her the parental love necessary for a child's well-being, then by openly excluding her from his life. The father's body deformity may reflect both an actual war injury, which rendered him unfit for further duty ("He got unfit for the army and was in the administration for a time," Ella vaguely tells Paul [p. 190]), and Anna's fears of the annihilation of the self. The "great protruding penis" in the dream has an obvious Oedipal symbolism; yet, the pre-Oedipal longing to merge with the father's power has an emotional no less than sexual significance. Given the fact that Anna has spent the greater part of her adolescence living alone with her father (in the notebooks she says she has lived with him through the age of 15), we can assume his decisive impact upon her and the consequences of her emotional estrangement. In a rare admission to her analyst, Anna refers to the feeling of "violent repulsion and shame and curiosity" she experienced when she saw her father naked, along with her wish to see him dead (p. 474). Mrs. Marks remains curiously uninterested in pursuing this theme, and Anna does not expand upon it. The subject of the child's sexuality and aggression toward the father is of the greatest importance in Anna's troubled life, however, and therefore deserves the highest priority in her psychoanalysis. And since the repetition-compulsion principle informs the structure of *The Golden Notebook,* it becomes imperative to determine the extent to which Anna's life repeats her parents' lives. Once this knowledge is gained, the daughter can then realistically hope to break the vicious circle of family history.[17]

Interestingly, Anna is a better parent to her daughter Janet than her own parents were to her; yet, once again we learn surprisingly little about the mother-daughter relationship. It is almost as if Anna's feelings toward Janet are too personal or private for Lessing to describe fully. Anna makes a significant observation about motherhood but does not fully elaborate upon it. "The control and discipline of being a mother came so hard to me, that I can't delude myself that if I'd been a man, and not forced into self-control, I'd have been any different" (p. 334). Anna's struggle against a dominating mother is not repeated in the next generation, and her relationship with Janet is non-conflicted. There are a few clues, though, to suggest Anna's ambivalence toward her. In the beginning of the Blue notebook, she records a "feeling of unreality" coming over her in January 1950 in the presence of her young daughter. When Janet asks her mother to play with her, Anna cannot respond. She acts like a machine, divorced of feeling, and she experiences the schizoidlike detachment that frightens her. In analysis she admits to experiencing hostility toward Michael, who has been making unfair demands on her, but she does not also consider the possibility of tension toward her daughter. Mrs. Marks unfortunately allows the discussion to wander into the area of art, which is not the crucial issue of Anna's diary entry. It would be remarkable to assume that a daughter who has been denied love by her parents could herself be a model mother to her child without experiencing the usual or unusual problems of being a parent. Anna slips into mild depression when Janet leaves home for school, reminding her of the void in her life before her daughter was born. Yet this only emphasizes her love for Janet. In a world of inconstancy and disappointment, Anna's single-minded devotion to Janet is extraordinary. "I don't care about anyone in the world except Janet," she writes in the Blue notebook (p. 544), able to preserve at least one area in her life from chaos, pain, and confusion.

There is a surrogate child in *The Golden Notebook* who embodies Anna's destructive feelings toward motherhood and children: Molly's son Tommy. He is in both the notebooks and in *Free Women,* but there is no "biographical" explanation for the fact that Anna has him attempt suicide in her novel. In the "real" notebooks, for example, Tommy does not appear to be suicidal. Yet, there is a psychological explanation for Anna's decision to blind him in her art. In *Free Women: 2,* Tommy begins to read Anna's notebooks without her permission. "Anna tensed herself and sat quiet; she could not endure that anyone should see those notebooks and yet she felt that Tommy had a right to see them: but she could not have explained why" (p. 265). She feels violated by the intrusion and enraged to the point where she wishes to hurt an object, Tommy. "She told herself that his state of mind had infected her; that she was being invaded by his emotions; marvelled that what appeared in his face as gleams of spite and hatred appeared in his voice briefly as shrillness or hardness—should be the outward signs of such a violent inward storm . . ." (p.

266). Asked by Tommy why she keeps four notebooks instead of one, she says the result would be chaos. Almost immediately after Tommy glances at the notebooks, he attempts suicide by shooting himself in the head. He lives but is permanently blinded.

Since these details have no basis in objective reality, Tommy's symbolic self-destruction may represent a projection of Anna's ambivalence toward children, the fear that her innermost thoughts (which she can express only in highly encoded fictional form) will have a lethal effect on her child. Tommy is the "bad" child in the same way that Janet is the "good" child. Significantly, although *Free Women* is written after the completion of Anna's psychoanalysis and thus after the resolution of her writer's block, the novelist still splits up her feelings toward children. This strengthens the suspicion that Anna's emotional block has been a defense against destructive feelings she will not allow herself to verbalize. The woman who has been bitterly rejected by her parents is horrified at the possibility of similarly hurting her own child. To preserve the good object, she must also create a bad object to keep the two separate. Tommy is literally blinded by Anna's emotions, a striking confirmation of Freud's theory of the omnipotence of thought. The bad mother in Anna may well be the internalization of her own mother whom she cannot bring herself to talk about in psychoanalysis. Ironically, Tommy's blindness has the effect of artificially healing his own divided personality, but it is a false resolution which Lessing unambiguously rejects.

Despite the fact that Anna's ambivalence toward children never emerges during therapy, she unconsciously recognizes the split. In the last section of *Free Women,* she records a dream she often has had about two children. "One was Janet, plump and glossy with health. The other was Tommy, a small baby, and she was starving him. Her breasts were empty, because Janet had had all the milk in them; and so Tommy was thin and puny, dwindling before her eyes from starvation" (p. 651). Once awake, she can find no reason for the dream of having starved Tommy, yet Anna Wulf the novelist darkly realizes the split in the feelings toward the child. Anna achieves therapeutic relief not from psychoanalysis but from the act of fiction, a process allowing her to verbalize truths too painful to admit even to a sympathetic analyst.

Another crucial issue that fails to show up in Anna's psychoanalysis is the origin of her identity as an artist. From an early age she has played the "game" of inventing the world. "I used at night to sit up in bed and play what I called 'the game.' First I created the room I sat in, object by object, 'naming' everything, bed, chair, curtains, till it was whole in my mind, then move out of the room, creating the house, then out of the house, slowly creating the street, then rise into the air, looking down on London . . ." (p. 548). Not content to stop with London, the young Anna would create the world, continent by continent, ocean by ocean, even as she would hold on to the contents of the house and imagine the swarming life in a drop of water. Anna's game of inventing the universe, creating life out of nothing, is a metaphor of the artistic process. As a young child, she was developing the imaginative powers that would later be essential to the artist. The game also represents the mind's effort toward unity and wholeness, an escape from the claustrophobia of her room. Frederick Karl has characterized Lessing's fiction as the "literature of enclosure."[18] The room suggests both a desire to seek refuge from external onslaughts and the fear of nightmarish repetition, destiny inexorably repeating itself. In the inner Golden notebook, Anna makes a revealing connection between her terrifying childhood nightmares and the game of invention. ". . . before I slept each night I lay awake, remembering everything in the day that had a quality of fear hidden in it; which might become part of a nightmare. I had to 'name' the frightening things, over and over, in a terrible litany; like a sort of disinfection by the conscious mind before I slept. But now, asleep, it was not making past events harmless, by naming them, but *making sure they were still there*" (p. 616).

By naming and recreating the universe the artist can escape from the constraints of reality and restore order to a fragmented inner world. Anna's inventive powers thus preserved the child from psychic extinction. Art functions as a counterphobic activity, an act of exorcism. Yet, later in her life, Anna has a terrible fear that her writings not only falsify reality but contain a violence that will literally blind the reader—as happens to Tommy. Again we wonder about the events occurring during Anna's unreconstructed childhood: why she had to retreat into the claustrophobic world to escape from intolerable reality.

Anna's reluctance to communicate to her analyst the ambivalence she feels toward her parents and child reflects, no doubt, Lessing's mistrust of psychoanalysis. Apart from whatever biographical decisions compelled Lessing not to divulge her own therapy to the reading public, there were literary concerns. In a revealing exchange with Mrs. Marks, Anna acknowledges that although the analyst has helped her to break down shame and guilt, the reader who has not undergone a similar experience cannot be expected to accept unthinkable ideas like Oedipal drives. The person reading about this feeling, Anna says, "without the subjective experience, the breaking down, would be shocked, as by the sight of blood or a word that has associations of shame, and the shock would swallow everything else" (p. 474). Lessing raises several of the fundamental limits of the fictional psychiatric case study that we have been exploring in the literature of the talking cure: the difficulty of suspending disbelief, the problem of writing about intimate subjects without engaging in sensationalism, and the delicate issue of confidentiality and discretion.

Lessing also recognizes that intellectual knowledge does not always produce emotional change in the patient or a sense of conviction in the reader. Insight is not enough for emotional change; it must be validated by the process of working through. Freud's unwavering faith in knowledge as power has been modified by contemporary analysts who emphasize the importance of empathic mirroring and the growth of self-esteem. "Early deficits in the development of healthy narcissism cannot be corrected by insight into these processes *alone*," Esther Menaker remarks, "but require actual support from the therapist in the form of affirmation and acceptance of the patient's total personality."[19] The deficits in the formation of Anna's healthy narcissism are restored not mainly by the empathic Mother Sugar but by the novelist's alter ego, Saul Green. And since Saul Green is Anna's literary creation, it is the artistic process which provides the empathic self-mirroring that heals the artist's narcissistic injury. Art alone is therapeutic for Anna and by implication Doris Lessing. By contrast, psychoanalysis is deemed inartistic and consequently devalued.

Lessing does provide us with one clue, however, that suggests a fascinating psychoanalytic link between Anna Wulf and the heroine of the last volume of *Children of Violence*. The clue involves an outline for a future novel that Anna jots down in *The Golden Notebook*. The novel is to be based on a story Mother Sugar tells her about a patient who entered therapy because he was in deep distress. Finding nothing wrong with him, the analyst asks to see the members of his family. One by one, Mrs. Marks interviews them and judges them perfectly normal. Then the mother comes. "She, apparently 'normal,' was in fact extremely neurotic, but maintaining her balance by passing it on to her family, particularly to the youngest son. Eventually Mother Sugar treated the mother, though there was terrible trouble getting her to come for treatment. And the young man who had come in the first place found the pressure lifting off him" (p. 536). The point of the story, as Mrs. Marks defines it, is that often the most normal member of a family may be the sickest. Due to a strong personality, he or she manages to survive largely because the illness is expressed through weaker family members. Mental illness is often a family affair, as we suggested earlier. Anna considers transmuting Mrs. Marks's anecdote into a short novel but nothing comes of it. Nor is there an explicit family relationship in *The Golden Notebook* that falls into this pattern. But in *The Four-Gated City,* we see a striking example of this family constellation and, not surprisingly, it involves the *Bildungsroman* heroine Martha Quest and her severely disturbed mother.

*   *   *

In the 17-year interval between the first and last volumes of the prodigious series, Lessing's extraordinary heroine has grown and matured. She has also accelerated the voyage into madness, both as observer and participant, that Lessing views as characteristic of the psychic landscape of the century. Like Anna Wulf, Martha becomes increasingly hostile to all forms of psychotherapy, including Jungian analysis. Her suspicions are confirmed when she decides to read up on psychology before visiting Dr. Lamb. "The two great exemplars, forming as they did the two faces or poles of the science, or art, were easy. 'Freud' and 'Jung' were easy" (p. 222). Martha examines so many psychology texts that she emerges from her independent study with the equivalent of a university course. Her reading convinces her of only one essential fact: "That these practitioners of a science, or an art, agreed about absolutely nothing." The conclusion foreshadows the "Afterward" to *Briefing for a Descent Into Hell,* where Lessing uses identical language to emphasize the hopeless confusion of psychiatry.

Hence the maddening diagnoses of Martha's friend, Lynda Coldridge, who for years has been labeled, categorized, and victimized by the psychiatric establishment. The novelist's language sounds like a parody of *DSM-3,* the latest reference guide to psychiatric nosology. "Lynda had been diagnosed by a large variety of doctors: there had been a large variety of diagnoses. She was depressed; she was a manic depressive; she was paranoid; she was schizophrenic. Most frequently, the last. Also, in another division, or classification, she was neurotic; she was psychotic. Most frequently, the latter" (p. 193). When Martha asks Dr. Lamb to define Lynda's schizophrenia, he equivocates, confessing that "there are different theories." Nor is he willing to define the diagnosis he has attached to Martha: "manic-depressive, with schizoid tendencies" (p. 237). Martha suppresses an old joke: "If that's depression, then where's the mania?"

Dr. Lamb is not an evil man, but he embodies the potential for evil that has accompanied the unrestrained growth of modern psychiatry. A pleasant middle-aged man with thoughtful eyes and dry wit, he is "not a bad sort of chap," as Mark Coldridge neutrally observes. The psychiatrist has a "strong guarded face" and "armoured look" which give him an impenetrable appearance to his patients. Lessing's anger toward the psychiatrist arises not from his bland character but from the unlimited power invested in him by an unquestioning society. Even the cynical Martha finds herself succumbing to this power as she asks herself how the image of the infallible doctor has developed historically. She asks, Why do Dr. Lamb's medical degrees give him the right to make Godlike pronouncements? And how did people cope with their problems a hundred years ago before the birth of this secular religion and brave new world?

In *The Golden Notebook* Lessing sympathetically portrays Anna's therapist without endorsing Jungian psychoanalysis, but in *The Four-Gated City* all the therapists are cold, rigid, unempathic. Martha is infuriated by Dr. Lamb's language, dogma, and the purring "Hmmm" of his responses. Although Lessing does not identify his psychiatric orientation, he seems ominously Freudian in his preoccupation with Martha's sexuality. Witness the psychiatrist's following remark, with its accusatory tone and baiting quality. "And of course, the other reason you are sleeping with Mark is because you are saying to me, I don't find you attractive, Dr. Lamb, I have another man" (p. 242). Martha snaps back, "Rubbish!" The doctor's empathic failure is appalling, as is his sexual stereotyping. He calls Martha's intelligence "masculine" in anticipation of the sexism of the Freudian analyst Mrs. Johns, who cannot imagine that a woman may commit herself to a political movement without losing her femininity.

Why then does Martha visit Dr. Lamb? Quite simply, because she has nowhere else to go for help. Her breakdown occurs immediately after she receives a series of letters from her mother, announcing her intention to travel to England from Africa for a visit. Mrs. Quest's letters throw Martha into turmoil. Each letter has the same structure, beginning with "My darling girl" and ending with "Your loving mother." In between are pages of "reproof, reproach, hatred." A study in abnormal psychology, Mrs. Quest is poisoned by racial hatred, religious fanaticism, and morbid fear of sexuality. All women are "filthy pigs" to her, including her daughter. Like the mother Mrs. Marks mentions to Anna in *The Golden Notebook,* the strong-willed Mrs. Quest is normal on the surface but severely disturbed underneath. She passes along her illness to her self-effacing daughter.

Lessing implies that Mrs. Quest's neurotic pattern of self-martyrdom has undermined Martha's health and weakened her self-esteem. Long-forgotten childhood and adolescent conflicts continue to cripple the mother-daughter relationship, despite Mrs. Quest's ineffectual denial:

> This business of illness—and had not her whole life been involved with it?—was not as simple as it seemed. As for Martha's being ill, Mrs. Quest had unpleasant memories that went back to her adolescence. The old lady could not quite remember the incident, the words, but lying awake at night rehearsing conversations that had taken place (might have taken place?), she heard herself saying: That's not true, you are always accusing me. How can I make you ill? Why should I want to make you ill? All I want is to look after you, what is my life for if it isn't to sacrifice it, for you . . . (p. 279).

Not only does Lessing offer a more extended treatment of the embattled mother-daughter relationship in *The Four-Gated City* than in *The Golden Notebook,* but May Quest seems to be the oppressive mother whom Anna Wulf cannot remember during psychoanalysis. Indeed, Mrs. Quest has a catastrophic influence on her daughter's life and has been symbolically dead and unavailable for years, again recalling Anna's long-dead mother. Whenever Martha allows herself to think about the tormented childhood years with her mother, the 35-year-old daughter breaks down in tears, infantilized. "Martha heard herself crying. She wept, while a small girl wept with her, Mama, Mama, why are you so cold, so unkind, why did you never love me?" (p. 232). Mother and daughter are incapable of being together for a moment without wounding each other. Mrs. Quest's words are like daggers to Martha.

In the presence of her mother, Martha's identity dissolves and she walks around in shock. She remembers herself as a violent, aggressive adolescent who would use any weapon in the fight for survival against an intrusive and overbearing mother. Filled with self-loathing which she projects onto everyone, Mrs. Quest has always belittled her daughter's sexuality and gender identity, as Martha relates to Dr. Lamb. "My mother was a woman who hated her own sexuality and she hated mine too. She wanted me to be a boy always—before I was born" (p. 241). Mrs. Quest's grim marriage is a repetition of the parental union Anna fictionalizes in *The Shadow of the Third.* Husband and wife remain lonely, brooding, embittered. Born and trained as a nurse in England, she marries Martha's father and is then uprooted and taken to the African veld, which remains her prison for the rest of her life. Mrs. Quest is herself a victim of social and historical forces; her own mother had died in childbirth, perhaps linking procreation with death in the daughter's imagination. Mrs. Quest's husband is later crippled during World War I, which deepens her rage against life. The mother's domination of her family causes them to resent bitterly their dependency on her. The only way Martha can free herself is to repudiate her mother's destructive values and, like Anna Wulf, attempt to block off her rage.

Paralleling Mrs. Marks's anecdote in *The Golden Notebook* about the patient who brings his mother with him into analysis only to discover that the mother is the sick one in the family, Martha arranges for an interview between Mrs. Quest and Dr. Lamb. Lessing invests the scene with pathos and humor. Mrs. Quest arranges to see Dr. Lamb in the belief he will treat her arthritis. She cowers in bed before the cab arrives, holding her clothes to her chin like a shield. She departs alone to the psychiatrist and returns in the afternoon with the announcement that she has decided to leave for Africa. Martha's telephone call to Dr. Lamb provides her with the details of her mother's first and last visit to a psychiatrist. She learns that her mother has spent the entire session verbally abusing her daughter to Dr. Lamb and pouring out years of resentment. He asks one question: "If you two don't get on, perhaps it would be better if you weren't in the same house." Mrs. Quest haughtily agrees and before racing out thanks him in a "schizophrenic" way. "It was nice talking to you—it's not often Martha lets me meet one of her friends" (p. 286). The structure of the session corresponds to her letters to Martha, filled with reproaches framed with sweet words. After Mrs. Quest's departure, Martha begins to recover from her breakdown, and her own sessions with Dr. Lamb end. Less than a year later Mrs. Quest dies.

The death of Mrs. Quest does not release Martha from a lifetime of suffering, though. If Dr. Lamb were a more sensitive therapist, he would have encouraged Martha to focus on the tangled mother-daughter relationship and her responses to a pathological parent. How can Martha, or anyone, grow up normally in a family where the mother bitterly despises herself and her offspring? How does a helpless child defend herself against years of reproaches? How does one become loving in defiance to an unloving environment? These are only the more obvious questions that must be thrashed out in therapy. The more subtle questions involve the link between Mrs. Quest's schizophrenia (a clinical diagnosis Lessing apparently accepts here) and Martha's "Self-Watcher," a mysterious schizoidlike detachment from reality characterized by apathy, loss of feeling, withdrawal. Martha's defense against an intrusive mother is passive resistance, beneath which lies rage, her buried "self-hater." Toward the end of *The Four-Gated City,* Martha "plugs into" the violent self-hater without recognizing its link to her maternal identification. Anna Wulf also experiences rage without tracing it back to feelings engendered by maternal abandonment and paternal rejection.

Motherhood is an immensely problematic subject to Martha, and Mrs. Quest's failure as a mother prompts Martha to give up her own daughter, Caroline, in an earlier novel in the series, *A Proper Marriage,* in the hope that the girl will be set free from the nightmare of repetition. But in *The Four-Gated City,* Martha painfully knows that a child is never set free by this illusory independence, especially since her daughter has been left with a woman, Elaine Talbot, who has been utterly dominated by another intrusive mother—a woman who is, ironically, friendly with Mrs. Quest.[70] None of these issues is revealed in Martha's therapy, just as Anna Wulf cannot discuss her family to Mrs. Marks. In fact, the family is a much more intractable problem to the Lessing protagonist than other seemingly more explosive issues, such as sexuality. Nor does Martha explore her ambivalent friendship with Lynda Coldridge, in whose house and with whose family Martha lives for most of the novel. To what extent are Lynda's mental illness, sexual frigidity, and inability to live with her family a repetition of Mrs. Quest's tragic life? Is Martha's participation in Lynda's breakdown, in which both women become "switched in to Hating," a reenactment of the pathological merging that may have characterized Martha's early childhood? And how does Martha's ability to replace Lynda in the Coldridge family reflect the adaptive behavior that enabled her to break away from Mrs. Quest's destructive grasp?

The dialectical tension between patient and analyst in *The Golden Notebook* is singularly absent from *The Four-Gated City.* Mrs. Marks's talking cure has been replaced by Dr. Lamb's "Explosion" therapy, a cruel parody of the early cathartic treatment of Breuer and Freud. Producing catharsis without insight or relief, psychiatric treatment crushes Martha's spirit. After each session she collapses into lethargy, depleted of energy. Her decision to terminate therapy is based on "economics, psychic economics." In Lessing's judgment, it is the best decision Martha makes in her life, sparing her from the fate awaiting Lynda and the other victimized patients in the novel. Dr. Lamb's failure to provide empathy and insight reflects Lessing's conviction that psychiatry has become the instrument of oppression. Before beginning therapy, Martha has disagreed with Lynda's conclusion that psychiatrists are "all the same." Events justify Lynda's cynicism.

Lynda's story is Lessing's exemplum of the antipsychiatry movement. As a child she is treated by a less sophisticated version of Dr. Lamb. She is taken to an expensive mental home where she receives electroshock treatments and insulin therapy. Gifted by visionary powers, which her doctors dismiss as hallucinations, she submits to the psychiatric establishment to avoid further punishment. Despite the doctors' reassurances, she knows she is getting worse. She marries Mark Coldridge precipitously in the hope he will rescue her from despair. No one can save her—electroshock therapy has permanently altered her brain. She finds an ambiguous haven with Dr. Lamb and his mind-numbing drugs. Failing to break the addiction, she remains at the end a psychological cripple, Lessing's warning against the power of the therapeutic state.

Through Lynda's story, Martha discovers that the rejection of psychotherapy is the first step toward health. Madness can be overcome, she believes, by riding it out or voyaging through it. Lessing rejects the twentieth-century model of psychopathology based on disease-object intrusion in favor of an older model of demonological madness based on spirit intrusion—the transference of a foreign spirit into the human object.[21] This is implicit in Mark Coldridge's description of his wife's illness. "It's as if . . . not that *she* is mad, but there's madness. A kind of wavelength of madness—and she hooks into it and out, when she wants. I could hook into it just as easily. Or it could hook into me—it's in the air" (p. 398). Martha's quiet response, "Or into me," becomes terrifyingly prophetic a hundred pages later when she too breaks down. It is not a question of an individual mind falling ill, Lessing implies, but the mind discovering a mad wavelength, a channel that remains outside normal receptivity. The guide for the voyage through inner space is not a psychotherapist, anxious to impose a reductive clinical framework upon a patient, but a knowing friend who has also been mad and who has journeyed back from the unknown shore. In the words of the only psychoanalyst Lessing endorses, "Instead of the *degradation* ceremonial of psychiatric examination, diagnosis and prognostication, we need, for those who are ready for it (in psychiatric terminology, often those who are about to go into a schizophrenic breakdown), an *initiation* ceremonial, through which the person will be guided with full social encouragement and sanction into inner space and time, by people who have been there and back again. Psychiatrically, this would appear as ex-patients helping future patients to go mad."[22]

This is, of course, R. D. Laing speaking. *The Four-Gated City* affirms the Laingian belief that psychological breakdown represents a charting of new psychic territory, a painful but potentially curative self-discovery that radically shocks normative consciousness into higher functioning. Critics have documented Laing's influence on Lessing's fiction, though curiously, she has denied the connection.[23] How successful is she in evoking the wavelength of madness? Readers will probably disagree. During Martha's breakdown she becomes a radio, television set, camera. Aural and visual imagery flood her consciousness. Lessing shatters normal syntax and uses metaphors to an oppressive degree to convey Martha's word salads. The novelist also juxtaposes cryptic songs and allusions with jiggling rhymes and Dali landscapes to suggest that madness may lead not only to breakdown but breakthrough. For some readers, however, the effect of the hypnotic rhetorical flourishes during Martha's mad scenes recalls Dr. Lamb's "explosion" therapy, resulting in a sensory overload.

Predictably, there are ambiguities and contradictions in Lessing's vision of madness. She hints at a static rather than dynamic model of consciousness, like a computer in its functions and malfunctions. Despite her rejection of the Freudian unconscious, her own model of the mind seems less complex and less accessible to illumination. She fails to explain how one successfully rides out the mad journey or the precise experience of the psychotic's hyper-sanity. She offers one of the most stylized views of madness in literature. Notwithstanding Lynda's threats to harm herself or others, she is incapable of real violence, just as both Martha and Anna Wulf are too sensitive to injure anyone. Indeed, Martha's madness is remarkably controlled. She always remains sensible and considerate, never so far removed from reality that she cannot pull herself together to converse with a stranger who, upon hearing that she is "on a trip," has come to inquire about her health. Martha and Lynda have little difficulty in managing each other's illness. Each woman displays a selflessness and generosity suggestive of a perfect marriage—or an idealized relationship with the analyst. Like her controlled regressions, Martha's "self-hater" is extraordinarily well-behaved, lacking the destructive and irrational power often accompanying mental illness.

The criticisms above may be too harsh for a novelist who has given us an epical journey into madness and beyond. The anguished intensity of *The Golden Notebook* and *The Four-Gated City* elevates them above nearly all other novels dealing with psychological breakdown and recovery. No psychological system, psychoanalysis or otherwise, is free from glaring contradictions, and we cannot criticize a novelist for failing to resolve ambiguities other thinkers have been unable to solve. If our sympathy for *The Four-Gated City* diminishes, it is because of Martha Quest's uncharacteristically elitist belief that those who have not lived through a severe breakdown lack the imagination and authenticity achieved by the initiate. Matching the stridency of R. D. Laing, Lessing now maintains that madness demonstrates creative rebellion against repressive civilization, while normalcy betrays mindless acquiescence. Her characters therefore have only two choices—madness or conformity. "Better mad, if the price for not being mad is to be a lump of lethargy that will use any kind of stratagem so as to remain a lump, remain nonperceptive and heavy" (p. 510). Along with the condemnation of psychiatry is the belief that characters like Lynda need never have been ill, that their illnesses were in fact *caused* by psychiatry and modern science. The marriage of madness and mysticism has led to the expulsion of all psychotherapists, who are now cast into the role of scapegoats. Lessing spells this out in capital letters:

> FINALLY: THE CENTRAL FACT, IF AT ANY TIME AT ALL I HAD GONE TO A DOCTOR OR TO A PSYCHIATRIST, THAT WOULD HAVE BEEN THAT. I'M OVER THE EDGE. BUT EVEN IF I STAY HERE I CAN MANAGE (LIKE LYNDA). WHY? BECAUSE I KNOW JUST THAT SMALL AMOUNT ABOUT IT NOT TO LET MYSELF BE STAMPEDED. IF AT ANY MOMENT I'D GIVEN IN DURING THIS SESSION I'D HAVE BEEN SWEPT AWAY. WITHOUT KNOWING WHAT I KNOW, THROUGH LYNDA, I'D NOT HAVE BEEN ABLE TO HOLD ON. THROUGH HINTS AND SUGGESTIONS IN ALL THE BOOKS, THROUGH MY OWN EXPERIENCE, THROUGH LYNDA—BUT WITHOUT THESE, A DOCTOR OR A PSYCHIATRIST WOULD HAVE NEEDED ONLY TO USE THE LANGUAGE OF THE SELF-HATER AND THAT WOULD HAVE BEEN THAT. FINIS, MARTHA! BRING OUT YOUR MACHINES. BRING OUT YOUR DRUGS! YES, YES, YOU KNOW BEST DOCTOR, I'LL DO WHAT YOU SAY: I'M TOO SCARED NOT TO (p. 553).

Many of Lessing's readers, like those of T. S. Eliot's, have implicitly shared her condemnation of psychotherapy. But as we have seen, neither the polite Jungian debates between Anna Wulf and Mrs. Marks nor the hostile confrontations between Martha Quest and Dr. Lamb exhaust the rich promise of psychotherapy, which can be more rigorously analytical than the former and more empathic than the latter. Indeed, while Lessing's seriousness as a novelist is above reproach, her treatment of psychoanalysis hardly does justice to the talking cure. The issue is not whether there are transcendent realities "beyond psychiatry" but whether the novelist has fully imagined a psychoanalytic interpretation of her fictional reality. An empathic woman whose consolation sweetens Anna's life, Mrs. Marks reveals a startling indifference to the fundamental questions that most therapists would raise, questions involving her patient's origins and family interactions. Nor is Dr. Lamb, who has actually witnessed Mrs. Quest's madness, even vaguely interested in Martha's background. He remains more preoccupied with his own self-importance than with reconstructions of Martha's past history or present reality.

Ironically, Lessing's equation of the family with illness and despair lends itself to psychoanalytic scrutiny. Although the novelist is sympathetic to Laing's radical psychiatry and his celebration of madness, her fictional therapists ignore one of his most profound insights. "Our impression, comparing the families of schizophrenics with other families, is that they are relatively closed systems, and that the future patient is particularly enclosed within the family system."[24] Lessing's rejection of psychotherapy would have been more persuasive had she created a fictional therapist who properly focused on the protagonist's family conflicts and whose questions probed into history, biography, and sociology. Only then could the novelist legitimately have dismissed psychotherapy as destructive to the arrival of a transcendent reality. Whether viewed from a traditional Freudian point of view, a Laingian existentialist and phenomenological perspective, or a Kohutian self-psychological vantage point, the conflicts of Anna Wulf and Martha Quest lead inescapably to severe disruptions in the parent-child bond and the absence of love and empathy. Any psychotherapy that conspicuously avoids this crucial subject must necessarily remain inadequate and incomplete.

Nor must a psychoanalytic approach emphasize pathology at the expense of creativity. There are intriguing clinical implications which Dr. Lamb fails to explore between Martha's aberrant family background and the development of her extrasensory perception and communication. Is there a link between Mrs. Quest's intrusiveness and pathological merging, on the one hand, and Martha's belief, which Lessing objectively validates, in her power to read thoughts and merge with other minds, on the other hand? If so, Martha's telepathic merging may be an outgrowth of her mother's pathological symbiosis. This interpretation would suggest not simply the presence of illness in Martha's family but, more importantly, her ability to devise constructive solutions to external and intrapsychic conflicts, a creative malady not unlike the examples we have seen created by earlier writers. For readers who reject Lessing's increasing preoccupation with telepathic phenomena, Martha's extrasensory perception may be viewed as a metaphor of the artist's imagination which, by its very nature, affirms the power of sympathy or empathy.

The Golden Notebook and *The Four-Gated City* represent Lessing's major statements on the talking cure. Dr. Lamb assures Martha that when her analysis is finished she will see it in "proportion." The word recalls Virginia Woolf's psychiatrist in *Mrs. Dalloway,* Sir William Bradshaw, whose divine omniscience similarly protects England from lunacy.[25] As *The Four-Gated City* moves toward its apocalyptic conclusion, the massive destruction of the earth gives rise to the hope of repopulation by an extraordinary race of half-completed creatures endowed with visionary powers deemed "hallucinations" by uncomprehending psychiatrists. In her more recent fiction, Lessing continues to rely upon psychiatric case studies to subvert widespread assumptions about mental illness, but one senses a hardening of her position. In *Briefing for a Descent Into Hell,* Professor Charles Watkins embarks upon a voyage through inner space paralleling the introspective journeys of Anna Wulf and Martha Quest. But gone is the warmly ironic portrait of Mrs. Marks. Gone also is Dr. Lamb. Instead we see two psychiatrists, Doctor X and Doctor Y, who betray the nameless faces of the therapeutic state. The insecure Doctor X argues for medication and electroshock therapy, while the more compassionate Doctor Y urges restraint and a renewed effort to discover the meaning of Watkins' amnesia. The patient remains dubious of all therapy, voicing Lessing's warning against treating inner voyages as medical illnesses. In despair, Watkins rejects the little light of Doctor Y (Doctor Why) and submits to Doctor X's punishing shockiatry. At the end of the novel, Professor Watkins regains his memory but loses the significance of his magical trip into the extraterrestrial Crystal that has come to save humanity from self-destruction. Thanks to the help of psychiatry, he is now ready for a real descent into hell.

EIGHT

Nabokov and
the Viennese Witch Doctor

. . . all my books should be stamped Freudians, Keep Out.
(Introduction, *Bend Sinister,* p. xii) [1]

. . . my books are not only blessed by a total lack of social significance, but
are also mythproof: Freudians flutter around them avidly, approach with itching
oviducts, stop, sniff, and recoil.

("Foreword," *The Eye*)

NO NOVELIST has waged a more relentless campaign against the
talking cure than Vladimir Nabokov. In novel after novel he has
attacked the "Viennese witch doctor," as he sardonically calls Freud. Of
the many types of people Nabokov satirizes, none evokes the foolishness
and evil of the psychoanalyst, who embodies the qualities of sham and
shaman, satan and charlatan, simpleton and stereotyper. In his tireless battle
with Freud, Nabokov has created a new art form, psychiatry baiting, and
elevated the parody of the psychiatric case study to new heights in his
masterpiece, *Lolita.* Tormenting and heckling Nabokov's best characters,
sadistic psychotherapists (a redundancy) conjure up ludicrous Oedipal
complexes and primal scenes in the cruel attempt to explain away the in-
consolable suffering Adam Krug, Pnin, Humbert, and the other solitary
heroes must quietly endure.

In almost every foreword to the English-language editions of his works,
Nabokov has continued his long-standing assault on Freud, an unprecedented war against psychoanalysis. The "Foreword" to *The Defense* reveals his typically sarcastic tone and the comic exaggeration of Freudianism:

> In the Prefaces I have been writing of late for the English-language
> editions of my Russian novels (and there are more to come) I have
> made it a rule to address a few words of encouragement to the Vi-
> ennese delegation. The present Foreword shall not be an exception.
> Analysts and analyzed will enjoy, I hope, certain details of the treat-
> ment Luzhin is subjected to after his breakdown (such as the cura-
> tive insinuation that a chess player sees Mom in his Queen and Pop
> in his opponent's King), and the little Freudian who mistakes a Pix-
> lok set for the key to a novel will no doubt continue to identify my
> characters with his comic-book notion of my parents, sweethearts and
> serial selves (pp. 10–11).

Nabokov's strategy is always the same. First, he belittles the little
Freudians (or their paid agents in American university departments of
English), then he challenges them to analyze or anal-ize his works, warning them, however, of the dangerous traps he has set. Thus the "Foreword" to *The Waltz Invention:* "After the dreadful frustrations Freudians
have experienced with my other books, I am sure they will refrain from
inflicting upon Waltz a sublimation of the push-button power-feeling such
as the manipulation of an elevator, up (erection!) and down (revenge suicide!)." [no page number] And *Despair:* "The attractively shaped object
or Wiener-schnitzel dream that the eager Freudian may think he distinguishes in the remoteness of my wastes will turn out to be on closer in-
spection a derisive mirage organized by my agents" (p. 8). The "Foreword" to *King, Queen, Knave* is different only in the rare concession that
not all his friends share his feelings toward Freud. "As usual, I wish to
observe that, as usual (and as usual several sensitive people I like will look
huffy), the Viennese delegation has not been invited. If, however, a res-
olute Freudian manages to slip in, he or she should be warned that a
number of cruel traps have been set here and there in the novel" (p. x).
The evocation of a departed psychoanalytic ghost appears in the "Introduction" to the uncompleted novel "Ultima Thule." "Freudians are no
longer around, I understand, so I do not need to warn them not to touch
my circles with their symbols" (*A Russian Beauty and Other Stories,* p. 148).
    Even when Nabokov believes Freud is safely dead and buried, he can-
not resist a parting shot, as he does in the "Foreword" to *Glory.* Only
through overkill will the enemy vanish forever. "Nowadays, when Freudism is discredited, the author recalls with a whistle of wonder that not so
long ago—say before 1959 (*i.e.,* before the publication of the first of the
seven forewords to his Englished novels)—a child's personality was sup-

posed to split automatically in sympathetic consequence of parental divorce" (p. xiii). To seal tightly the Freudian coffin, Nabokov writes a letter in 1967 to the editor of *Encounter* to welcome Freud's book on Woodrow Wilson "not only because of its comic appeal, which is great, but because that surely must be the last rusty nail in the Viennese Quack's coffin" (*Strong Opinions*, p. 215). And to make sure that naïve undergraduates do not resurrect the ghost of Freud, Nabokov condemns psychoanalytic literary criticism in *Lectures on Literature.* Rejecting the belief that *The Metamorphosis* reveals Kafka's ambivalent relationship to his father, and that the image of Gregor as an insect symbolizes the son's feelings of worthlessness to his parents, Nabokov sternly warns his students: "I am interested here in bugs, not in humbugs, and I reject this nonsense" (p. 256).

Nabokov's virulence is astonishing and unsoftened by time. The invective is bitter, mirthless, and unprecedented. It is as if Freud is the central figure in Nabokov's life, always shadowing the novelist. Freud's name appears as early as the third paragraph in the autobiographical *Speak, Memory.* In discussing his lifelong rebellion against darkness, Nabokov singles out the most sinister threat to the imagination. "I have ransacked my oldest dreams for keys and clues—and let me say at once that I reject completely the vulgar, shabby, fundamentally medieval world of Freud, with its crankish quest for sexual symbols (something like searching for Baconian acrostics in Shakespeare's works) and its bitter little embryos spying, from their natural nooks, upon the love life of their parents" (p. 20). In addition to associating Freud with antiquated medievalism, Nabokov links him to literary and political repression. At the end of *Speak, Memory,* he bids an unfond farewell to Freud, leaving him and his fellow travelers "to jog on, in their third-class carriage of thought, through the police state of sexual myth (incidentally, what a great mistake on the part of dictators to ignore psychoanalysis—a whole generation might be so easily corrupted that way!)" (pp. 300–301).

It could be argued, of course, that by insisting in his prefaces that Freudians must keep out, Nabokov is actually inviting them to enter and that, if Freud had not existed, Nabokov would have had to invent him. Indeed, one senses that Freud is Nabokov's alter ego, a hated part of the self that the novelist had to defeat again and again. To borrow Richard Curle's vivid description of Joseph Conrad's equally well-known detestation of Dostoevsky, "He did not despise him as one despises a nonentity, he hated him as one might hate Lucifer and the forces of darkness."[2]

Although critics have long recognized Nabokov's animosity, few have been disturbed by it. In fact, most of Nabokov's critics have appeared to share his assumption that Freudians adhere to monolithic dogma, that psychoanalysis has never developed beyond the stage of id psychology, and that Freud never revised his theories nor admitted to intellectual skepticism. "Nabokov appears to object to Freudianism as a kind of internal Marxism proceeding upon the assumption that the common is of greater import than the individual," Andrew Field notes, adding that "in the late 1960's one can already clearly see that the corner has been turned regarding Freudianism in literature, and there are fewer and fewer important writers and critics who slavishly accept and practice the Freudian prescription. . . ."[3] At no time have important writers and critics "slavishly" accepted the Freudian "prescription." Even when Field tries to be more dispassionate than Nabokov, his language gives him away. Alfred Appel, Jr., the editor of the indispensable *The Annotated Lolita,* does not try to be impartial. He accepts all of Nabokov's judgments of psychoanalysis, including disdain of the "clinical-minded." Arguing that the analyst's reductive interpretation of *Lolita* justifies Nabokov's parody (not surprisingly, there have been very few psychoanalytic studies of the novel), Appel assumes there can be only one Freudian approach—unenlightened. "By creating a surface that is rich in 'psychological' clues, but which finally resists and then openly mocks the interpretations of depth psychology, Nabokov is able to dispatch any Freudians who choose to 'play' in the blitzkrieg game that is the novel's first sixty-or-so pages."[4]

A more thoughtful discussion of Nabokov's quarrel with Freud comes from Page Stegner in *The Portable Nabokov.* "Psychotherapy is constantly under attack in Nabokov's fiction, and it becomes a kind of outstanding symbol for the clinical, sterile, stereotyping mind that perceives its surroundings in hackneyed and rigid terms."[5] Yet, in *Escape into Aesthetics,* Stegner concludes his discussion of Nabokov's anti-Freudianism with a statement that is more generous than the truth allows. ". . . his satire of depth psychology, intended or not, emerges really as criticism of the debasement of Freud's work by a passively adaptive, unimaginative, leisured society—most emphatically, though not exclusively, American."[6] It is not the debasement of Freud's work but Freud's debasing vision that Nabokov continually returns to in his writings. Freud is, quite simply, evil incarnate to him. There are bad artists in Nabokov's world but no good psychotherapists.

In his interviews, Nabokov has given many reasons for his rejection of the talking cure. He objects both to the absurdity of Freudian theory and to the gullibility of people who succumb to therapy. Psychoanalysis strikes him as farcical, especially the Oedipus complex. "Let the credulous and the vulgar continue to believe that all mental woes can be cured by a daily application of old Greek myths to their private parts" (*Strong Opinions*, p. 66). A more serious objection to psychoanalysis is the threat it poses to morality and individual freedom. Like Lessing, Nabokov believes that society is moving toward what one critic has called a "psychiatrocracy," a "state in which psychiatry has expanded to fill the roles of police, judges, educators, social workers, and eventually politicians."[7] In Nabokov's words, "The Freudian faith leads to dangerous ethical consequences, such as when a filthy murderer with the brain of a tapeworm is given a lighter sentence because his mother spanked him too much or too little—it works both ways" (*Strong Opinions*, p. 116). Yet, unlike Lessing, he rejects the social or utilitarian view of art, and he would dismiss the idea that his novels are intended directly or indirectly to illuminate the dangers of totalitarianism or the therapeutic state. He has also dismissed the possibility that his contempt for psychoanalysis arises from personal experience with therapy. When asked by an interviewer whether he has ever been in analysis, he expresses horror, indignant at the idea. "Bookish familiarity only," he dryly answers. He ritualistically proceeds to bury his adversary. "The ordeal itself is much too silly and disgusting to be contemplated even as a joke. Freudism and all it has tainted with its grotesque implications and methods appears to me to be one of the vilest deceits practiced by people on themselves and on others. I reject it utterly, along with a few other medieval items still adored by the ignorant, the conventional, or the very sick" (*Strong Opinions*, pp. 23–24). In another interview in *Strong Opinions* he expands upon his aversion to psychiatry, revealing the extent to which Freud occupies his everyday life:

> I cannot conceive how anybody in his right mind should go to a psychoanalyst, but of course if one's mind is deranged one might try anything; after all, quacks and cranks, shamans and holy men, kings and hypnotists have cured people—especially hysterical people. Our grandsons no doubt will regard today's psychoanalysts with the same amused contempt as we do astrology and phrenology. One of the greatest pieces of charlatanic, and satanic, nonsense imposed on a gullible public is the Freudian interpretation of dreams. I take gleeful pleasure every morning in refuting the Viennese quack by recalling and explaining the details of my dreams without using one single

reference to sexual symbols or mythical complexes. I urge my potential patients to do likewise (p. 47).

Freud's name is likely to appear anywhere in Nabokov's universe, sometimes in the least flattering places. In *Bend Sinister,* Adam Krug, who lives in a repressive Marxist kind of state, gazes down into the bottom of a toilet bowl. What does he see? "At the bottom of the bowl a safety razor blade envelope with Dr. S. Freud's face and signature floated" (p. 85). The image is appropriately anal. In *Speak, Memory* Nabokov recalls how underneath the windows of his Biarritz apartment a "huge custard-colored balloon was being inflated by Sigismond Lejoyeux, a local aeronaut" (p. 156). (Freud's name in German means "joy.") In *Ada,* there is a "Dr. Sig Heiler" and a "Dr. Froid . . . who may have been an émigré brother with a passport-changed name of the Dr. Froit of Signy-Mondieu-Mondieu" (p. 27). Although Van is a psychiatrist, he comes to realize that the "mistake—the lewd, ludicrous and vulgar mistake of the Signy-Mondieu analysts consists in their regarding a real object, a pompon, say, or a pumpkin (actually seen in a dream by the patient) as a significant abstraction of the real object, as a bumpkin's bonbon or one-half of the bust . . ." (p. 363). Often, Nabokov does not mention Freud by name, referring to him instead by the city in which he resided: "Viennese quack," "Viennese witch doctor," "Viennese wizard."

Nabokov's quarrel with Freud dates back to the beginning of his career as a writer. His earliest parody of Freud appears in a 1931 Paris weekly. Entitled "What Everybody Must Know," the article—written under the pseudonym Sirin—contains a naïve first-person narrator, obviously a convert to the Freudian faith, who delivers a sales pitch for his newly patented product *Freudism for All.*[8] Nabokov employs his favorite weapon against psychoanalysis, *reductio ad absurdum,* to undermine the Freudian stages of psychosexual development. There is the "Tantalus complex," the "penal servitude complex," the "happy marriage complex." *Freudism for All* contains all the familiar psychoanalytic themes Nabokov satirizes for the remaining 45 years of his writing career: the Oedipus complex, unconscious motivation, dream interpretation, biological drives. Nabokov's antipsychiatry predates Lessing's, though it lacks her introspective analysis in *The Golden Notebook.* Long before most writers began warning of the therapeutic state, Nabokov was ridiculing the cult of psychotherapy and progressive education. The gentle Pnin is embarrassed by the "psihooslinie ('psychoasinine')" interests of his former wife, a psychiatrist. Her husband, also a psychiatrist, evolves the ingenious idea of applying the theories of group therapy to marriage counseling. The procedure involves a "tension-releasing" circle modeled along the lines of a quilting bee, where young women share "with absolute frankness" their marital problems with each other. Later the husbands are similarly interviewed by doctors, and cigars as well as "anatomic charts" are passed around. Nabokov condemns the goal of tension reduction in group psychotherapy because it represents to him a contemptible effort to eliminate the inevitable suffering every sensitive person must endure. Pnin affirms his creator's views when he calls psychotherapy "nothing but a kind of microcosmos of communism—all that psychiatry. . . . Why not leave their private sorrows to people? Is sorrow not, one asks, the only thing in the world people really possess?" (p. 52).

Implicit in Nabokov's rejection of Freud is the link between psychoanalysis and Marxism. Viewing "cure" as a form of manipulation, mind-control, and enslavement, Nabokov cannot imagine therapy that is not collusive and conspiratorial. *Bend Sinister* (1947), Nabokov's first novel in English, is a parable of the therapeutic state in which psychiatry promotes adaptation to an insane political system. Professor Adam Krug, a philosopher, refuses to submit to the party line of Paduk, dictator (and Krug's former classmate) of the young Soviet type of state. Pervading the country is the Marxist-sounding ideology of Ekwilism, a "violent and virulent political doctrine." Allied to Ekwilism is the grim Institute for Abnormal Children where, through a mixup of identities characteristic of the collectivist state, Krug's young son David is sent. Operating according to the tension-reduction principle of group psychotherapy as practiced in *Pnin,* the Institute serves as a euphemistic "release instrument" for hardened criminals. The psychological theory combines cathartic release with orgiastic violence: ". . . if once a week the really difficult patients could enjoy the possibility of venting in full their repressed yearnings (the exaggerated urge to hurt, destroy, etc.) upon some little human creature of no value to the community, then, by degrees, the evil in them would be allowed to escape, would be, so to say, 'effundated,' and eventually they would become good citizens" (p. 218). Mistaken for one of these unfortunate victims, David is fatally beaten up in one of the most gruesome scenes found anywhere in Nabokov's blood-bespattered universe. Invoking the language of the psychotherapist and sociologist, Nabokov mimics the detached objectivity of the social scientist. The brutes at first keep their distance from the little person, but then a transformation begins as the "community spirit (positive) was conquering the individual whims (negative)." They become *organized.* The female psychiatrist Doktor Amalia von Wytwyl refers to the "wonderful moment" in which, to use her technical language, " 'the ego,' he goes 'out' (out) and the pure 'egg' (common extract of egos) 'remains' " (p. 219). Less clinically, the helpless victim is literally torn apart by the blood-thirsty group.

Why does Nabokov place psychoanalysis among the ranks of communism, fascism, and other forms of totalitarian control? One critic has argued that "Ultimately, we have to understand Nabokov's anti-Freudianism in the context of a hatred for allegory and symbolism in general."[9] It is certainly true that he disapproved of allegory and symbolism, believing they impinged upon the artist's freedom, but this hardly seems sufficient to explain the virulence of his attack against Freud. It seems more probable that biographical reasons still unknown to us influenced his thinking. Nabokov's contempt for Freud was part of a larger reaction against despised elements of Russian and German autocracy, which he blamed for the destruction of his family and his exile to Europe and the United States. Most of his fictional psychiatrists have German names: Doktor Frau Amalia von Wytwyl née Bachofen and Dr. Hammecke in *Bend Sinister;* Dr. Eric Wind (a German) and his Russian psychiatrist wife Liza Bogolepov Wind in *Pnin;* Dr. Blanche Schwartzmann and Melanie Weiss in *Lolita,* whose names mean "White Blackman" and "Black White," respectively (because, as Appel notes in *The Annotated Lolita,* "to Nabokov, Freudians figuratively see no colors other than black and white" [p. 326]); Dr. Sig Heiler and Dr. Froit of Signy-Mondieu-Mondieu in *Ada;* and so on. These psychiatrists conform to the stereotype of the vicious German. There are, it is true, non-German psychiatrists. There is an Italian named Dr. Bonomini in "Ultima Thule" and the Anglo-Saxon clinical psychologist John Ray in *Lolita,* both of whom are typically inane but not malevolent. Hovering over all these therapists is their spiritual father, the "Viennese witch doctor," whose German background always remains felt. As Douglas Fowler has observed, "Germany is always a part of the Nabokovian code for evil, and psychiatrists are its high priests."[10]

Yet why does Nabokov endorse these ugly stereotypes, especially when the object of his scorn was also victimized by the same forces the novelist detested? If anything, one might expect Nabokov to feel a degree of sympathy for Freud. Nowhere among Nabokov's savage criticisms of Freud is there the recognition that the psychoanalyst was a member of a minority group that remained outside of German and Viennese society. The Nazis' persecution of the Freud family was as severe as the Bolshevists' persecution of the Nabokov family. Nabokov's brother died in a German concentration camp in 1945, and his father was shot and killed at a political meeting in 1922 while shielding a speaker from two Russian assassins.[11] Although Freud and his immediate family were allowed to flee Vienna, his four elderly sisters were less fortunate; they perished in a German concentration camp. Freud cherished freedom of expression and thought as much as Nabokov did. Both men were repelled by the brutality they witnessed and did everything they could to oppose cruelty and injustice.

Moreover, in viewing Freud as a German victimizer instead of as a Jewish victim, Nabokov contradicts the impassioned discussion of racial prejudice that appears in *Pale Fire*. Kinbote tells us that more than anything on earth John Shade loathed vulgarity and brutality, particularly when they were united in racial prejudice. As a man of letters, Shade "could not help preferring 'is a Jew' to 'is Jewish' and 'is a Negro' to 'is colored'; but immediately added that this way of alluding to two kinds of bias in one breath was a good example of careless, or demagogic, lumping (much exploited by Left-Wingers) since it erased the distinction between two historical hells: diabolical persecution and the barbarous traditions of slavery" (p. 217). Nabokov married a Jewish woman, and he was always sensitive to anti-Semitism.[12] Yet, in rendering Freudianism into Nazism, he seems guilty of his own diabolical persecution.

Nabokov's blind spot to psychoanalysis, then, amounts to an obsession, as a few critics have acknowledged.[13] At what point does a master parodist begin unconsciously to parody himself? Jack Cockerell's heartless impersonations of the eccentric hero of *Pnin* compel the narrator to observe that "the whole thing grew to be such a bore that I fell wondering if by some poetical vengeance this Pnin business had not become with Cockerell the kind of fatal obsession which substitutes its own victim for that of the initial ridicule" (p. 189). Has Nabokov similarly fallen victim to a fatal obsession? Since there is no evidence that Nabokov suffered from psychological illness or entered psychotherapy, his aversion to Freud becomes more mysterious.[14] Indeed, we know very little about Nabokov the man and, as Phyllis A. Roth has concluded in a recent essay, many questions about Nabokov the artist will remain unanswered "until we constitute Nabokov the man behind the mystification."[15]

Until then, we can try to demystify his curious attitude towards Freud from the scattered clues in his fiction and his references to historical psychoanalysts. We may be surprised, in fact, by the degree to which Nabokov's writings reflect psychological theory, apart from the numerous traps he sets to ambush the Freudian critic. Despite his contempt for psychology as a discipline, Nabokov was a psychological novelist, whether or not he was parodying the subject. And he was well acquainted with books on abnormal psychology and case-study material. Andrew Field points out that the library of Nabokov's father contained such titles as *The Sexual Instinct and Its Morbid Manifestations* and a good collection of the works of Havelock Ellis.[16] We also know that Nabokov's fictional characters have been reading actual psychoanalytic studies. In *Pale Fire,* Kinbote recalls how he once tried to read certain tidbits from a learned book on psychoanalysis he had filched from a classroom, a book widely used in American colleges. (Professors of English in American universities, he says, are soaked in Freudian fancies.) Kinbote cites two psychoanalytic texts and gives appropriate quotations from each book. He also helpfully provides us with precise bibliographical information to locate both books:

> By picking the nose in spite of all commands to the contrary, or when a youth is all the time sticking his finger through his buttonhole . . . the analytic teacher knows that the appetite of the lustful one knows no limit in his phantasies.
> (Quoted by Prof. C. from Dr. Oskar Pfister,
> *The Psychoanalytical Method,* 1917, N. Y., p. 79)

> The little cap of red velvet in the German version of Little Red Riding Hood is a symbol of menstruation.
> (Quoted by Prof. C. from Erich Fromm,
> *The Forgotten Language,* 1951, N. Y., p. 240)

Kinbote allows the quotations to speak for themselves, though he cannot resist one caustic rhetorical question: "Do these clowns really *believe* what they teach?" (*Pale Fire,* p. 271).[17]

Kinbote has no difficulty in demolishing Prof. C.'s Freudian approach to literature, and few critics, literary or psychoanalytic, would probably care to defend the quoted passages. Alfred Appel, for example, endorses Kinbote's attack, agreeing that "no parodist could improve on" Fromm's realization or Pfister's "felicitously expressed thought" (*The Annotated Lolita,* p. 327). If one takes the trouble to read *The Psychoanalytic Method* and *The Forgotten Language,* however, the quoted passages appear less ludi-

crous.[18] Pfister, for instance, who was a pastor and seminary teacher in
Zurich, discusses the dynamics of symptomatology in the quoted passage. In the cited case study, he shows how an apparently meaningless
gesture may reveal a complicated symbolism. He talks about a 15-year-old
pupil who was accustomed to make a peculiar and offensive grimace with
his nose and finger. The analyst traces back the obsession to an internal
conflict involving the youth's ambivalence toward masturbation, which
both attracted and repelled him. Since symptoms are always overdeter-
mined, there may be additional meanings to the teenager's compulsive
act that Pfister perhaps missed. However, his interpretation is at least
plausible. And his major thesis is essentially sound: "He who engages for
a long time in the analysis of apparently meaningless gestures, which
constantly recur, gradually becomes able to read intimate secrets with
certainty from these stereotyped habits" (*The Psychoanalytic Method*, p. 78).
Incidentally, one of Nabokov's most celebrated characters, lost in his own
masturbatory reverie, would agree with the "analytic teacher" that "the
appetite of the lustful one knows no limit in his phantasies."

Kinbote's allusion to Erich Fromm's *The Forgotten Language* also has
interest to Nabokov's readers. Fromm's interpretation of Little Red Riding Hood (more precisely, Little Red-Cap, the Brothers Grimm version
of the story) offers several insights into the famous children's fairy tale
and, as we shall see, a famous twentieth-century novel that is in its own
way a supreme fairy tale. In his discussion of the tale, Fromm makes the
sound observation that the command not to stray into the menacing for-
est hints at a warning against the loss of innocence. The little girl is approaching womanhood and is now confronted with the problem of sex.
There is nothing outlandish about Fromm's interpretation of the color
red as suggestive of passion and menstruation. Indeed, Nabokov is notorious for his complete rejection of symbolism, sexual and otherwise. The
wolf in the fairy tale symbolizes a ruthless and cunning man eager to devour the little girl, an act filled with sexual implications. Fromm argues
that the wolf's attempt to usurp the grandmother's role becomes an ironic
commentary on the male's inability to bear children, an interpretation that
is only slightly more difficult to accept. At the end of the story the wolf,
who has swallowed the little girl, is made ridiculous by the attempt to
play the role of a pregnant woman with a living being in his belly. The
girl puts stones into his stomach and he dies. "His deed, according to the
primitive law of retaliation, is punished according to his crime: he is killed
by the stones, the symbol of sterility, which mock his usurpation of the

pregnant woman's role." In Fromm's view, the fairy tale dramatizes the male-female conflict. "It is a story of triumph by man-hating women, ending with their victory, exactly the opposite of the Oedipus myth, which lets the male emerge victorious from this battle."[19] Paradoxically, Little Red Riding Hood's rites of passage experience has intriguing relevance to Nabokov's parodic masterpiece, the novel about a poetical wolf man who, in ravishing the little girl, grows heavy with child and eventually gives birth to one of the great literary creations of the century.

*　　*　　*

With its false scents, clever ambushes, and multiedged ironies, *Lolita* (1955) is the supreme parody of the psychiatric case study. The novel brilliantly puts into practice the strategy Nabokov uses in the forewords to his other stories: It lures in the unsuspecting Freudian and then springs the trap upon him. *Lolita* mocks the psychopathological approach to literature and taunts the reader to solve the mystery of Humbert's obsession with his nymphet. As Elizabeth Phillips remarks, "Nabokov's ironic version of the 'psychopathological' case history ridicules both the method and the content of the formula by which the inspiration of art has been Freudianized."[20] The intensity of the novel's attack on the talking cure is unrivaled in literature. Calling himself "King Sigmund the Second," Humbert belittles Freud at every opportunity, daring anyone to tell him something about himself he does not already know. At times it seems that Freud, not Quilty, is the secret antagonist in *Lolita*. In this novel, the Viennese witch doctor is revealed for what he really is, less a mad doctor than Nabokov's white whale, a shadowy symbol of satanic proportions who must be killed again and again lest the universe go awry. Nothing less than the purity of literature and the survival of the imagination are at stake in *Lolita* and, if both Humbert and his maker become monomaniacal in their pursuit of evil, that is incidental to the outcome. The battle lines are drawn.

The irony begins with the mock "Foreword" to *Lolita* by John Ray, Jr., Ph.D., whose training in clinical psychology qualifies him as a Fraudian. In his role as editor of Humbert's confessional manuscript, Ray confirms Nabokov's belief that the difference between the rapist and therapist is but a matter of spacing. Ray's introduction to Humbert's story lends the appearance of clinical authenticity, which is precisely what Nabokov parodies. Ray asserts that literature should elevate and inculcate, that human nature can be improved, that art functions as a warning of the dangers of abnormalcy and perversion. ". . . for in this poignant

personal study there lurks a general lesson; the wayward child, the ego-
tistic mother, the panting maniac—these are not only vivid characters in
a unique story: they warn us of dangerous trends; they point out potent
evils" (*The Annotated Lolita*, pp. 7–8). Ray assumes, furthermore, that
Humbert is a pervert, that his case study should alert us to future Hum-
berts lusting for our daughters, that the chief value of literature lies not
in aesthetic beauty but in social and ethical import, and that psychopathology menaces us to the same extent that communism does. (His language at the end of the introduction evokes the breathless rhetoric of
McCarthyism.)

The irony, then, is that Ray is editing a story whose literary meaning
remains beyond his understanding. Nabokov introduces the novel to us
through an unreliable narrator and then proceeds to wrest *Lolita* out of
Ray's clinical grasp. Oddly enough, Ray is not without a degree of insight into Humbert's story. He wisely refrains from editing or altering
the manuscript apart from the correction of "obvious solecisms." He preserves the anonymity of the author by telling us that "its author's bizarre
cognomen is his own invention." The psychologist surprisingly rejects the
charge of pornography, arguing that what is "offensive" in a story is frequently a synonym for "unusual." A great work of art, he realizes, is always original and shocking. Although he remains horrified by the author, he can appreciate the power of the manuscript. "But how magically
his singing violin can conjure up a tendresse, a compassion for Lolita that
makes us entranced with the book while abhorring its author!" (Which
author is Ray referring to here—Humbert or Nabokov? If the latter, then
Nabokov is poking fun at Ray even as the psychologist is disparaging the
novelist!) Ray also concedes a point that Nabokov's other therapists would
have missed: "that had our demented diarist gone, in the fatal summer
of 1947, to a competent psycho-pathologist, there would have been no
disaster; but then, neither would there have been this book" (p. 7). In
short, there is a ray of truth in the psychologist's introduction, although
Nabokov would remind us that a "competent psychopathologist" is a
contradiction in terms.

One must wonder, however, whether Dr. Ray is aware of Humbert's
sadistic delight in foiling his psychiatrists. Given Nabokov's delight in
deception, Humbert maintains a poker face in analyzing his "symptomatology" and bouts of insanity. In his contempt of Freud, Humbert is
Nabokov's faithful son. "At first, I planned to take a degree in psychiatry
as many *manqué* talents do; but I was even more *manqué* than that . . ."

(p. 17). Wooed by psychoanalysts with their "pseudoliberations of pseu-
dolibidoes," Humbert claims to have suffered several major psychological
breakdowns which have caused him to be hospitalized in expensive san-
atoriums where he perfects his maker's art: psychiatry-baiting:

> I discovered there was an endless source of robust enjoyment in tri-
> fling with psychiatrists: cunningly leading them on; never letting them
> see that you know all the tricks of the trade; inventing for them elab-
> orate dreams, pure classics in style (which make *them,* the dream-ex-
> tortionists, dream and wake up shrieking); teasing them with fake
> "primal scenes"; and never allowing them the slightest glimpse of one's
> real sexual predicament. By bribing a nurse I won access to some files
> and discovered, with glee, cards calling me "potentially homosexual"
> and "totally impotent." The sport was so excellent, its results—in *my*
> case—so ruddy that I stayed on for a whole month after I was quite
> well (sleeping admirably and eating like a schoolgirl). And then I added
> another week just for the pleasure of taking on a powerful new-
> comer, a displaced (and, surely, deranged) celebrity, known for his
> knack of making patients believe they had witnessed their own con-
> ception (pp. 36–37).

Not for a moment does Nabokov consider Humbert's anti-Freudianism an example of clinical resistance to therapy. Questions of transference
and countertransference seem as alien to Nabokov as they would to B. F.
Skinner. Humbert's criticisms of psychoanalysis coincide exactly with
Nabokov's position, and both use the identical parodic attack to demol-
ish the foe. The reader cannot take seriously Humbert's declarations of
past insanity, and there is nothing that ever threatens his lucidity or verbal power. The psychiatrists fail to uncover his deception. "I love to fool
doctors," he confides merrily. In his role of "Jean-Jacques Humbert," he
fabricates the most histrionic confession. He can play the role of analyst
or patient. "The child therapist in me (a fake, as most of them are—but
no matter) regurgitated neo-Freudian hash and conjured up a dreaming
and exaggerating Dolly in the 'latency' period of girlhood" (p. 126). Never
deviating from his anti-Freudianism, he expects the reader to share his
point of view. "Mid-twentieth century ideas concerning child-parent relationship have been considerably tainted by the scholastic rigmarole and
standardized symbols of the psychoanalytic racket, but I hope I am ad-
dressing myself to unbiased readers" (p. 287).

How much psychoanalytic theory does Humbert—and Nabokov—actually know? The question is difficult to answer, if only because the nov-

elist may be assimilating more Freudian theory than he cares to parody. Humbert's mocking allusion to the "dream-extortionists," and Van's equally contemptuous reference in *Ada* to "Sig's epoch-making confession," suggest that *The Interpretation of Dreams* (1900) forms the cornerstone of Nabokov's understanding or misunderstanding of psychoanalytic theory. Nearly all of the parodist's comments focus on id psychology, which represents historically the beginning of psychoanalysis, the emphasis upon biological drives. Nabokov strongly objects to the biologizing of psychology, especially the Oedipus complex. He also attacks the "theatrical" side of psychoanalysis: the primal scene, the death wish, the birth trauma. Nabokov's fictional psychiatrists undertake the most preposterous research, with predictable conclusions. In "Ultima Thule," Dr. Bonomini is studying the "dynamics of the psyche," seeking to demonstrate that "all psychic disorders could be explained by subliminal memories of calamities that befell the patient's forbears . . ." (*A Russian Beauty and Other Stories*, p. 161). If a patient were suffering from megalomania, for example, it would be necessary to determine which of his great-grandfathers was a power-hungry failure. In *Pale Fire,* an old psychiatrist warns the Prince of Zembla that his vices had subconsciously killed his mother and would continue to kill the mother in him until he renounced sodomy. Otto Rank's theory of birth trauma also comes under attack. The narrator of *Pnin* refers to a "phenomenon of suffocation that a veteran psychoanalyst, whose name escapes me, has explained as being the subconsciously evoked shock of one's baptism which causes an explosion of intervening recollections between the first immersion and the last" (p. 21). Pnin refers disapprovingly to Dr. Halp's "theory of birth being an act of suicide on the part of the infant."

A list of the books written by Nabokov's psychiatric researchers reveals a world gone mad over the mind-curing industry. Psychiatry, progressive education, the self-help business, how-to books, and psychobabble are exposed as the shams of shamans. Once again, Nabokov attacks the biologizing of psychology and the comic nature of psychoanalytic theory. Betty Bliss, one of Pnin's former graduate students, writes a paper on "Dostoevski and Gestalt Psychology," which nicely expresses Nabokov's deprecation of his nineteenth-century Russian predecessor. Before her marriage to Eric Wind, Liza Bogolepov works at the Meudon sanatorium directed by a destructive psychiatrist called Dr. Rosetta Stone. Psychotherapy, implies Nabokov, generates arcane hieroglyphics. The Winds' delightful son Victor proves to be a "problem" child because of his disturbing lack of pathology. The boy contradicts his parents' deeply held belief that "every male child had an ardent desire to castrate his father and a nostalgic urge to re-enter his mother's body." The father is so alarmed by his son's normalcy that he has him tested by the leading prognosticators of psychological health: the Gudunov Drawing-of-an-Animal Test, the Fairview Adult Test, the Kent-Rosanoff Absolutely Free Association Test, and the Augusta Angst Abstract Test. Unfortunately, Victor's interpretation of Rorschach ink blots proves of little interest to the psychologists, and the poor boy is finally left to struggle through life on his own. His parents, though, remain committed to their professional training and collaborate to write an essay on "Group Psychotherapy Applied to Marriage Counseling" for a psychiatric journal. In "Ultima Thule," Dr. Bonomini writes a book called *The Heroics of Insanity*. In *Lolita,* John Ray receives the Poling Prize for a modest work entitled "Do the Senses Make Sense?" in which certain morbid states and perversions are discussed. Nabokov has the last word, however, to this proliferating psychological literature. Near the end of *Ada,* Van grows disgusted with the "Sig" school of psychiatry and writes a paper entitled *The Farce of Group Therapy in Sexual Maladjustment.* The epigraph to the study contains a passage from Sig's epoch-making confession: "In my student days I became a *deflowerer* because I failed to pass my botany examination" (p. 577). This is a reference to a letter Freud wrote to Wilhelm Fliess in 1899.[21] Van's paper proves to be devastating to the psychiatric establishment. "The Union of Marital Counselors and Catharticians at first wanted to sue but then preferred to detumify."

Nabokov demonstrates that he can out-psychologize the most orthodox Freudian, and Humbert is less interested in proving the psychoanalyst incorrect than in casting him into Hell. Both novelist and narrator ransack the psychoanalytic canon and then load their own cannon or torpedoes with enough explosives to sink the deepest depth reading. Humbert would have us believe that his tragic passion for Lolita springs from an unhappy love affair with Annabel Leigh, a lovely child of 13 who is only a few months younger than he. Humbert falls madly in love with her, and they meet surreptitiously to carry on their youthful romance. Fate intervenes and within a few months she dies of typhus, their love unconsummated. Humbert remains convinced that "in a certain magic and fateful way Lolita began with Annabel." The physical similarities between the two girl-children seem to support his statement. He emphasizes the Poesque quality of the doomed love, and he is highly conscious—self-conscious—of the parallels between Annabel Leigh and Poe's Annabel Lee. Humbert marries Charlotte Haze to be near her daughter, just as Poe marries his child-cousin to be near his beloved aunt. But the parallel to Poe is misleading, as Andrew Field points out. "The historian of literature knows, however, that Poe married his child bride primarily to tighten his rather strange and neurotic ties to her guardian aunt. If *Lolita* were indeed modeled on the life of Poe (as at least one article has tried to maintain), Humbert would marry Lolita in order to be closer to her mother Charlotte!"[22] The possibility that Humbert's love for Lolita is a repetition of his thwarted love for another nymphet, Annabel Leigh, thus turns out to be a dead end.

Another psychiatric dead end is the "Daddy's Girl" theme. Just as Humbert never tires of referring to Lolita as his daughter, so does Nabokov exploit all the ironies implicit in the apparently incestuous relationship. "Be a father to my little girl" (p. 70) Charlotte writes to Humbert, and he proceeds to carry out her wish. He marries the detestable mother only to be near her desirable daughter whom he is happy to help raise. "Lolita, with an incestuous thrill, I had grown to regard as *my* child" (p. 82), he adds parenthetically. After Charlotte's death, he informs Lolita that "For all practical purposes I am your father" (p. 121). This is the relationship he announces to others, particularly to motel owners. His lecture on the history of incest is truly impressive: No one can question his devotion to research. When he finally catches up with Quilty, he introduces himself as Lolita's father and insists that the playwright stole his child. Quilty denies the kidnapping and maintains that he rescued the girl from a "beastly pervert."[23] The reader's response to this Oedipal play is that Humbert protests too much. There are simply too many Freudian "clues" for us to take seriously and, like Roth's Portnoy, Humbert is too comfortable in his posture of lying on the analytic couch. It is possible, of course, that there are Oedipal implications of Humbert's relationship to Lolita, but not the interpretation he deceptively offers.

Similarly, Nabokov parodies the subjects of homosexuality and impotence. Humbert refers gleefully to the psychiatrist's diagnosis of him as "potentially homosexual" and "totally impotent." He recalls a dream that seems to be culled from *The Interpretation of Dreams*. "Sometimes I attempt to kill in my dreams. But do you know what happens? For instance I hold a gun. For instance I aim at a bland, quietly interested enemy. Oh, I press the trigger all right, but one bullet after another feebly drops on the floor from the sheepish muzzle. In those dreams, my only thought is to conceal the fiasco from my foe, who is slowly growing annoyed" (p. 49). The limpness of the unmanly bullets foreshadows the comic killing of Claire Quilty, Humbert's "evil double." Lest we miss the deep symbolism of the shooting, Humbert pointedly tells us that "we must remember that a pistol is the Freudian symbol of the Ur-father's central forelimb" (p. 218). Fingering his gun in the presence of the man who has married Lolita, Dick Schiller, Humbert imagines shooting his sexual rival. But one wonders whether murder or detumescence is Humbert's goal. He conjures up a scene in which he "pulled the pistol's foreskin back, and then enjoyed the orgasm of the crushed trigger: I was always a good little follower of the Viennese medicine man" (p. 276). On another occasion, Humbert psychoanalyzes the symbolism of the fountain pen, the anatomical relative of the pistol. The fact that Quilty does not use a fountain pen clearly indicates, "as any psychoanalyst will tell you," that the patient was a "repressed undinist" (p. 252). Quilty obligingly admits that he had no fun with Dolly because he is "practically impotent," and he then implores Humbert to postpone the killing so that he can nurse his impotence. The actual shooting of Quilty parodies the ineffectuality of Humbert's bullets and the incomplete sexual gratification of the act. As the phallic bullets penetrate Quilty, his face twitches in an absurd clownish manner and he emits a "feminine 'ah!' " as if the bullets were tickling him.

Nabokov parodies the Daddy's Girl theme in *Lolita* and the impotence motif, but he remains more serious about traumatic loss. In the beginning, Humbert discloses cryptically that his mother died in a freak accident—"picnic, lightning"—when he was three years old. He returns to the theme of maternal loss near the end of the story, telling us that "in retrospect no yearnings of the accepted kind could I ever graft upon any moment of my youth, no matter how savagely psychotherapists heckled me in my later periods of depression" (p. 289). Apart from the question why sadistic therapists would want to heckle him, Humbert fears a similarly tragic death awaiting Lolita. Nabokov teases us with the names of Quilty's plays, such as *The Lady Who Loved Lightning*. Lolita dies not from lightning but during childbirth, as does Humbert's first wife, Valeria. Is there a link between pregnancy and death? Is there a significance in the premature deaths of Humbert's women: his mother, Annabel Leigh, Valeria, Lolita? Is Nabokov parodying the theme of traumatic loss, or is he using parody to conceal the overwhelming pain of death?

In other words, to what extent does Nabokov's use of parody invalidate a psychological interpretation of *Lolita*? If parody is viewed as a protective shield, against what is the novelist defending? No writer poses a greater threat or challenge to psychoanalytic criticism than Nabokov, who is not only the most virulently anti-Freudian artist of the century but one of the greatest literary figures of our time, unquestionably a genius—and a genius at deception. His duplicity, James R. Rambeau has observed, places his readers in a defensive position: "they must first prove they understand what Nabokov is *doing* before they can judge the final effects of his fiction."[24] Most readers have concluded that Nabokov's fiction is psychoanalytically impenetrable. Curiously, Nabokov's condemnation of psychoanalysis derives from his belief that it perpetrates a cruel hoax or deception on an unsuspecting public. "Freudism and all it has tainted with its grotesque implications and methods appears to me to be one of the vilest deceits practiced by people on themselves and on others" (*Strong Opinions*, pp. 23–24). One would assume that Nabokov is irrevocably opposed to deception and that everything deceptive is evil. Not true. He consistently affirms the quality of deception within art and nature. "I discovered in nature the nonutilitarian delights that I sought in art. Both were a form of magic, both were a game of intricate enchantment and deception" (*Speak, Memory*, p. 125). And in *Strong Opinions* he reveals that "all art is deception and so is nature; all is deception in that good cheat, from the insect that mimics a leaf to the popular enticements of procreation" (p. 11). How, then, does the deception of the psychoanalyst differ from the artist's duplicity? Cannot the analyst be a good cheat, as the insect and artist are, inventing strategies that unlock hidden truths?

Obviously not, for Nabokov. He praises the artist as an encoder of fictional reality, while he condemns the analyst as a false decoder of psychic reality. The issue for Nabokov is not the question of deep reality—his novels are as multilayered as onions and as difficult to peel—but the principle of freedom and control. Anything that impinges upon the artist's ability to create a self-enclosed and self-determined world becomes a threat to his autonomy. And the major threat lies in the Freudian assertion that man is neither fully aware nor in control of his fears and desires. Nabokov's reality is generated and sustained by the artist, not the reality unlocked by the analyst. Nothing could be further from Nabokov's assumptions than a world in which dreams follow psychic, as opposed to artistic, laws and which contain meanings discoverable through the tools of psychoanalysis. Nabokov insists that only the artist can create magical reality; only the artist can lie truthfully. In *Pale Fire*, Kinbote mentions that

" 'reality' is neither the subject nor the object of true art which creates its own special reality having nothing to do with the average 'reality' perceived by the communal eye" (p. 130). The artist's deceptions lead to freedom and independence; the psychoanalyst's deceptions lead to slavery. For Nabokov, the artist is married to creation, the analyst wedded to destruction.

Behind Nabokov's explicit rejection of psychology lies an implicit psychology of art: the belief that art and psychoanalysis exist at opposite poles of the imagination; the conviction that art, not analysis, is the last defense against suffering and injustice; the affirmation of the artist's autonomy amidst deterministic forces. Art and psychoanalysis represent good and evil, respectively, in Nabokov's world. Thus, Humbert begins his story in a psychopathic ward and drives his doctors crazy. One of Nabokov's earliest and most perceptive critics, Vladislav Khodasevich, wrote in 1937 that the basic theme to which the novelist returns is the "life of the artist and the life of a device in the consciousness of the artist." The artist or writer is never shown directly, however, but always behind a mask.[25] Art becomes a refuge or sanctuary, with the artist, not the therapist, as the real healer.

Contrary to Humbert's assertions, there is an implicit psychology underlying *Lolita,* and it involves Humbert, a lyrical writer, whose theme is the creation and preservation of his beloved nymphet as a delicately wrought object of art. Critics have noted the two Lolitas in the novel: the real Dolores Haze, whose coarse mannerisms and speech betray a satirical and often unflattering portrait of innocence and experience; and the symbolic or mythic Lolita, the creation of Humbert's imagination. There is an almost Platonic need to subordinate the real Dolly Haze to the alluring manmade fantasy of Lolita, to transmute fleshy reality into artistic purity. "What I had madly possessed was not she, but my own creation, another, fanciful Lolita—perhaps, more real than Lolita; overlapping, encasing her; floating between me and her, and having no will, no consciousness—indeed, no life of her own" (p. 64). Humbert loves the gum-chewing, comic-book-reading, hardened bobby-soxer, juvenile clichés and all; but he is more enchanted with his own autoerotic creation, the product of his febrile imagination. He cannot help rendering her into an object of art, a fictional love object in his own image. His imagination animates Lolita; without him, she cannot exist. Insofar as Lolita is created by Humbert, a diarist whose heroic faith in the power of language endows her with immortality, he becomes, like his own creator—Vladimir Nabokov—a rescuer and redeemer of beauty and truth.

It is Humbert's imagination, not his phallus, that is the vital energizing spirit behind his artistic creativity. "It is not the artistic aptitudes that are secondary sexual characters as some shams and shamans have said; it is the other way around: sex is but the ancilla of art" (p. 261). Yet, whichever theory of creativity one accepts, the psychoanalyst's or novelist's, Humbert's devotion to Lolita resides less in her body or sex than in his imaginative recreation of her. "I am not concerned with so-called 'sex' at all. Anybody can imagine those elements of animality. A greater endeavor lures me on: to fix once for all the perilous magic of nymphets" (p. 136). Whether or not we take seriously his self-proclaimed nympholepsy, his fascination for girl-children arises from a paradoxical union of "tender dreamy childishness and a kind of eerie vulgarity," a fusion of chaste and profane love. For all its eroticism, *Lolita* remains curiously suspicious of the biological components of sexuality. Like Pygmalion, Humbert demonstrates that the artist can rival God as the creator of life; but unlike the Greek sculptor, Humbert remains more infatuated with the inner artistic vision, the ravished bride of stillness whose flight and pursuit are forever frozen into marble immobility. Humbert inevitably loses Lolita, as all people must lose their loved ones; but through the creation of the manuscript, the writer preserves a merged relationship with her, a union that will never dissolve, not even after the deaths of Dolly Haze and Humbert Humbert. Artistic creation unites artist and subject in an ecstatic oneness suggestive of the mother-child relationship. Humbert's devotion to art may be seen as an attempt to master the inevitability of death and to recreate a new reality that will defy the ravages of time. The artist thus pursues a rescue fantasy in which the nymphet's unformed beauty is given shape and preserved from change.

At the risk of succumbing to clinical black magic, we may invoke briefly the voodooism of the Viennese witch doctor to explain Humbert's rescue fantasy. In "A Special Type of Choice of Object Made by Men" (1910), part of Freud's contributions to the psychology of love, the analyst discusses the phenomenon of rescue fantasies and the family romance. He lists four necessary preconditions for this type of object choice. First, there must be an injured third party, such as a husband, fiancé, or friend, who claims possession of the girl or woman in question. Second, the woman's fidelity or reliability must be open to question—either the faint hint of scandal attached to a married woman or the implication of an openly promiscuous way of life. This is often termed "love for a prostitute." This precondition is necessary, Freud says, because the man experiences jealousy toward the third party. "What is strange is that it is not the lawful possessor of the loved one who becomes the target for this jealousy, but strangers, making their appearance for the first time, in relation to whom the loved one can be brought under suspicion."[26] Third, instead of the woman's value being measured by her sexual integrity and correspondingly reduced by promiscuous behavior, as it is in "normal" love, the situation is reversed. A woman becomes more desirable as she approaches the behavior of a prostitute. The final precondition is that a man of this type expresses the need to rescue the woman he desires from ruin. "The man is convinced that she is in need of him, that without him she would lose all moral control and rapidly sink to a lamentable level" (p. 168).

The psychical origins of this type of love derive from the infantile fixation of tender feelings on the mother, Freud claims, and represent a consequence of that fixation. The love objects usually turn out to be mother surrogates, and the object from which he is rescuing the mother surrogate usually is the father. "It is at once clear that for the child who is growing up in the family circle the fact of the mother belonging to the father becomes an inseparable part of the mother's essence, and that the injured third party is none other than the father himself" (p. 169). To defend himself against the realization of incestuous attachment to the mother, the son divorces spiritual from sensual love. The split reveals the antithetical image of woman: the madonna and the prostitute. Freud links the rescue motif to the Oedipus complex (he uses the term for the first time in this essay) and relates it to the idea of the family romance he had discussed in the preface to Otto Rank's well-known book, *The Myth of the Birth of the Hero*. In the family romance the son exalts one or both of his parents in an effort to recreate the happy, vanished days of his childhood when his parents seemed to be the noblest and dearest of all people. In one of his most daring imaginative leaps in "A Special Type of Choice of Object Made by Men," Freud asserts that the son's need to rescue his mother acquires the significance of giving her a child in his own image:

> His mother gave him a life—his own life—and in exchange he gives her another life, that of a child which has the greatest resemblance to himself. The son shows his gratitude by wishing to have by his mother a son who is like himself: in other words, in the rescue-phantasy he is completely identifying himself with his father. All his instincts, those of tenderness, gratitude, lustfulness, defiance and independence, find satisfaction in the single wish *to be his own father*. Even the element of danger has not been lost in the change of mean-

ing; for the act of birth itself is the danger from which he was saved
by his mother's efforts (p. 173).

Without presuming to illuminate the mystery of *Lolita,* we may suggest that Humbert's rescue fantasy affirms the refuge of art, the only immortality he can bequeath upon his beloved Dolly. Just as the rescue fantasy implies a splitting of the mother image into the sacred and profane,
so does Humbert see Lolita and all nymphets as a paradoxical fusion of
tender dreamy childishness and eerie vulgarity. From a legal point of view,
he kidnaps and corrupts an innocent adolescent; yet from the novelist's
point of view, he attempts to rescue her from sordid reality and to worship her to the point of Mariolatry. There are several ironies surrounding
Lolita's identity and Humbert's treatment of her. The innocent girl turns
out to be far more sexually experienced than Humbert ever imagined, and
it is she who seduces him. Although Humbert does not know this in advance, her desirability to him only increases when she is stolen by Quilty,
the "injured third party" and the object of Humbert's rage. Humbert is
less guilty of sexually violating Lolita than of attempting to control omnipotently her life and smothering her independence. Gladys M. Clifton
is certainly correct when she argues that readers have tended to overvalue
Humbert's perspective and to undervalue Lolita's.[27]

Ironically, although Humbert brutally thwarts Lolita's natural wishes
for separation and independence, thus depriving her not only of her
childhood but her right to choose her own adult life, he also unconsciously attempts to save her from the life experiences, particularly marriage and motherhood, that will eventually destroy her. The world of reality
proves deadly to the doomed Lolita, not because Humbert is trying to
extinguish her autonomy, but because the novel insists upon her premature crucifixion by time and the biological trap. Risking life and liberty
for the pursuit of a cruel mistress, Humbert is the classic unrequited lover,
betrayed by a woman who is unaware of his heroic sacrifice. This too is
one of the preconditions Freud talks about in his analysis of the rescue
fantasy. "By her propensity to be fickle and unfaithful the loved one brings
herself into dangerous situations, and thus it is understandable that the
lover should be at pains to protect her from these dangers by watching
over her virtue and counteracting her bad inclinations" (p. 172). This is
what Humbert does: He is an all-controlling father.

The little we learn about his own father is inconclusive evidence on
which to speculate Humbert's relationship to the family romance. Be-

sides, Nabokov is probably setting another trap for the psychoanalytic reader who is seeking a connection between the father and son. Humbert insists he adored his father, a strong, virile man. It may be that Humbert's attraction to the tomboyish quality of nymphets contains a bisexual element related to his identification with the father. "The specific psychological character of Humbert's perversion is very close to homosexuality," Andrew Field writes, emphasizing, however, that Humbert is not in fact homosexual.[28] By contrast, Quilty is homosexual and represents Humbert's perverse alter ego. Nabokov's parody of the double has been extensively explored.[29] Psychoanalytically, the phenomenon of the double affirms the ability to split off part of the self to maintain a cohesive identity. Quilty may be interpreted in several ways: a narcissistic extension of the self, a mirror image of Humbert's bad self, the human tendency toward duplication. Otto Rank's conclusion in his pioneering study, *The Double,* has interesting relevance to the Humbert-Quilty relationship. "So it happens that the double, who personifies narcissistic self-love, becomes an unequivocal rival in sexual love; or else, originally created as a wish-defense against a dreaded eternal destruction, he reappears in superstition as the messenger of death."[30] Compared to perverted Quilty, Humbert seems wondrously normal. Humbert refers to him as his brother, but he may also be the bad father in his unloving treatment of Lolita. Hence Humbert's need to murder him. Both men are artists, one an enormously prolific playwright, the other a lyrical-confessional novelist. Significantly, neither Quilty nor Humbert is procreative.

Lolita is a novel of passion but not procreation. The distinction is worth pursuing. The link among love, pregnancy, and death identifies the novel with fatal passion, destructive to the childbearing mother and aborted offspring. Lolita's death seems to be a punishment for her illicit love, illicit not from society's point of view but from Humbert's, the brokenhearted lover. The deaths of his first wife, Valeria, and eternal wife, Lolita, reveal a sterility associated with reality that sharply contrasts the fecundity of the artist's imagination. Lolita's creativity turns out to be literally a figment of Humbert's imagination. Feeling her warm weight in his lap, he remarks that he was "always 'with Lolita,' as a woman is 'with child' " (p. 109). As man and artist, Humbert embodies all the roles in the Freudian family romance. He is the loyal son devoted to the muse of invention; the mature lover or enchanted hunter in quest of his Mission Dolores; the spiritual father hovering over his child in an effort to protect her from inartistic lovers and from the mortal enemy of the nymphet, time; and the mother creator, always pregnant with Lolita, begetting and immortalizing her through the novelist's act of labor, the creation of art.

The Freudian interpretation of Humbert's rescue fantasy suggests an underlying Oedipal level of meaning, but, in light of more recent psychoanalytic research in the areas of ego psychology, identity formation, and separation and individuation, other meanings emerge from *Lolita*. Although, in his attack on psychoanalysis, Nabokov does not seem to be aware of ego psychology, the shift in emphasis away from instinctual drives to the defensive and adaptive functions of the autonomous ego, Humbert's commitment to art reveals an attempt to master fears of death and to preserve forever Lolita's beauty. This agrees with Phyllis Roth's conclusion that "despite his asseverations to the contrary, Nabokov, like others, employed his art to master fears, anxieties, and unacceptable desires, transforming them into a transcendent fiction which is acceptably 'aesthetic.'"[31] Paradoxically, the fear of death leads to the strongest affirmation of immortality, thus demonstrating Nabokov's triumphant assertion of individuality and free will. One of the mysteries of the novel is how Humbert can continue to idealize Lolita even after she repeatedly rejects him. But Nabokov also shows how the creative process resolves the dualistic tension between unity and separation. Before Humbert writes the manuscript, he is separated from Lolita; yet he fuses with her during the creative act to achieve a new union. And insofar as his story is intended for others to read and participate in, Nabokov affirms once again the paradox of separation and oneness that defines all interactions. Humbert's merging with a higher ideal that will outlive him has an undeniably therapeutic effect on him. "I see nothing for the treatment of my misery but the melancholy and very local palliative of articulate art" (p. 285). Humbert is the only therapist Nabokov celebrates, the creative artist, who rescues life from death, form from chaos, triumph from defeat.

Lolita also has interesting implications for Kohut's emerging self-psychology. Although Humbert sees Lolita with painful clarity, he also idealizes her and mirrors her self-love.[32] The act of writing resembles the mirroring and idealizing transference relationship that Kohut speaks about in the treatment of narcissistic personality disorders, though it is not necessary to label Humbert in pathological terms. Kohut's psychology, in fact, can be extended to normal personality development.[33] Viewed from this perspective, the creation of the manuscript allows Humbert to restore his damaged self by transmuting the object (or in Kohutian terms the self-object) of his autoerotic love, Lolita, into new internalizations. Through art he achieves a restoration of the self.

Lolita, then, is not exempt from its own unique subterranean mythic system and psychology. Curiously, Nabokov's story is a reversal of the fairy tale of the wolf and Little Red Riding Hood that Kinbote dismisses in *Pale Fire.* Fromm's interpretation, we recall, suggests that the wolf is made ridiculous in the attempt to imitate a pregnant woman by having a living being in its belly. Humbert does not eat Lolita, though he would like to. "My only grudge against nature was that I could not turn my Lolita inside out and apply voracious lips to her young matrix, her unknown heart, her nacreous liver, the sea-grapes of her lungs, her comely twin kidneys" (p. 167). Humbert first incorporates her into his imagination and then into the body of his art. Interestingly, in Nabokov's fairy tale the roles of the huntsman and wolf are reversed. Instead of rescuing the innocent teenager, the huntsman marries her, impregnates her, and fills her belly with the living thing that will eventually destroy her. As lover and husband, Dick Schiller is the unenchanted hunter. Life without art is sterile and meaningless. By contrast, the poetical wolf is the good father in his attempt to rescue his beloved daughter from Quilty's maltreatment and Schiller's artificial insemination. Despite the wolf's tyrannical control over her, neither his voracious appetite nor his deceptive identity has harmed the little girl. Fromm's interpretation of the classic fairy tale emphasizes the man's defeat in the Oedipal battle, but in Nabokov's transformation the wolf has the last word. He has swallowed the delicious girl and then given birth to a new Lolita who will outlive all the participants in the magical drama.

Given their differences over sex, love, psychoanalysis, and art, it is impossible to believe that Freud and Nabokov could ever agree on anything; yet, in the final analysis, there are surprising similarities between the two. The voodooism or black magic of the Viennese witch doctor parallels the marvelous spells and wiles of the novelist, who remains a trickster. In Nabokov's view, Freud is more of an artist (albeit a bad one) than a social scientist, and the Russian is always attempting to prove that his magic is more potent than the Viennese's. Indeed, Nabokov's sorcery may be viewed as an elaborate "disappearing act" to cast the psychoanalyst into the void, yet in a curious way he needed to keep Freud alive, if only to make him appear upon command in his forewords and fictions. Nabokov's criticisms of Freud may also be turned against the novelist.

Rejecting Freud's labyrinthine symbolism and mythology ("something like searching for Baconian acrostics in Shakespeare's works"), Nabokov himself became, next to Joyce, the supreme fabulous artificer of twentieth-century literature. He has devised a fictional system of Baconian acrostics that has confounded a generation of literary critics eager to decipher hidden patterns and wicked word puzzles in his writings. Moreover, both men adapted their obsessional personalities to creative purposes. Freud's quest for knowledge and faith in his intellectual powers were matched by Nabokov's complete mastery and omnipotent control of his fictional universe. Freud's case studies probably contain no greater assortment of mad and eccentric characters than those found in Nabokov's stories, which present a dazzling array of psychopaths, sadists, perverts, paranoids, and suicides. Freud wrote like a novelist (when his name was mentioned for the Nobel Prize, it was more often for literature than for medicine), and Nabokov had the insight of a shrewd clinician. Both geniuses changed their professions in ways we are only beginning to understand. Each was fascinated by the other's field but also deeply ambivalent toward it. Although Freud's admiration for the artist is well known, he also disparaged him, reducing the man of letters to a neurotic[34] or a narcissist[35] and claiming that unlike the scientist, which he considered himself to be, the artist is incapable of abstinence[36] or renunciation.[37] Nabokov reciprocated these feelings with a vengeance.

Finally, both men had strong prejudices and, in affirming the autonomy of their separate disciplines, erred in ways that are not dissimilar. Not only does Freud equate art with the pleasure principle and science with the reality principle, he makes the astonishing statement that "We may lay it down that a happy person never phantasies, only an unsatisfied one."[38] The psychoanalyst can be guilty of the most outrageous pronouncements: "The 'creative' imagination, indeed, is quite incapable of *inventing* anything; it can only combine components that are strange to one another."[39] The assertion is no less startling than Nabokov's insistence that the artist's fictional universe remains fiercely independent of reality. "Literature was born not the day when a boy crying wolf, wolf came running out of the Neanderthal valley with a big gray wolf at his heels: literature was born on the day when a boy came crying wolf, wolf and there was no wolf behind him" (*Lectures on Literature*, p. 5). Future scholars will no doubt explore the extent to which Nabokov's celebrated Wolf Man, Humbert Humbert, echoes the unheard cries of the young artist. Nor should this distress Nabokov's faithful readers. It is inconceivable that biographical knowledge will diminish the greatness of his achievement or the mystery of his art. As Freud prudently wrote, "Before the problem of the creative artist analysis must, alas, lay down its arms"— a truth and truce not even Nabokov would fail to heed.[40]

NINE
Philip Roth's Psychoanalysts

W HEN A PHILIP ROTH character finds himself lying on a couch, more than likely he is engaged not in sex but in psychoanalysis. Therapy becomes the most intimate and imaginative event in life for the beleaguered hero, the one love affair he cannot live without. Of all novelists, Roth is the most familiar with the theory and practice of psychoanalysis, and from the beginning of his career he has demonstrated a keen interest in the therapeutic process. His characters are the most thoroughly psychoanalyzed in literature. Beginning with Libby Herz's dramatic encounter with Dr. Lumin in *Letting Go*, Roth has repeatedly returned to the psychoanalytic setting.[1] Through Alex Portnoy's stylized confession to the mute Dr. Otto Spielvogel in *Portnoy's Complaint*, Peter Tarnopol's troubled relationship to the greatly expanded Spielvogel in *My Life as a Man*, and David Kepesh's analysis with Dr. Klinger in *The Breast* and *The Professor of Desire*, Roth offers lively and fascinating accounts of the talking cure.

To his credit, Roth avoids stereotyping his analysts, and they remain conspicuously apart from and superior to other fictional therapists. Their uniqueness derives from their professional authenticity, sensitivity to language, and their refusal to subvert the therapeutic process. Indeed, Roth's analysts become more impressive when compared to other fictional healers who either misunderstand psychotherapy or exploit their patients' illnesses. Roth's therapists do not marry their patients or have incestuous affairs with them, as do Dick Diver in *Tender Is the Night*, Palmer Anderson in Iris Murdoch's *A Severed Head*, and Erica Jong's lustful Adrian Goodlove in *Fear of Flying*. They do not perform lobotomies or administer drugs, as Kesey describes in his psychiatric horror story, *One Flew Over the Cuckoo's Nest*, nor do they use electroshock therapy, as in Plath's *The Bell Jar*. Dr. Lamb's "Explosion" therapy in Lessing's *The Four-Gated*

City and the behavioral modification found in Anthony Burgess' *A Clock-work Orange* are both alien to Roth's world. His analysts are neither priests in disguise, as is Sir Harcourt-Reilly in Eliot's *The Cocktail Party*, nor therapeutic con artists, like Dr. Tamkin in Bellow's *Seize the Day*. And they are certainly unlike the sadistic caricatures posing as therapists in Nabokov's stories.

In short, Roth pays tribute to psychoanalysis by demystifying the patient-analyst relationship and by refusing to render therapists into caricatures or mythic figures. Even when Roth has been wildly inventive in his patients' confessions or symptoms, the novelist is scrupulously realistic in his portrayal of psychoanalysts. They are men of good will, expertise, and integrity. They maintain a proper distance from their patients, follow the rules of their profession, and avoid subverting their position into an instrument of evil power. They are orthodox Freudians in their theoretical orientation but pragmatic in their world view. They affirm the consolations of the reality principle, urging reconciliation and reintegration. They are scholarly, dignified, mildly ironic in speech, and even tempered. They are not charmed by their patients' praise, bullied by their threats, or horrified by their revelations. Above all, they are excellent listeners.

In *Reading Myself and Others* Roth has perceptively commented upon the importance of psychoanalysis in his fiction, but he has been characteristically reluctant to discuss the autobiographical sources of his artistic preoccupation with therapy or the exact parallels between his own life and those of his fictional creations. Referring to the varied therapeutic experiences of Libby, Portnoy, Tarnopol, and Kepesh, Roth notes that "All of these characters, in pain and in trouble, turn to doctors because they believe psychoanalysis may help them from going under completely. *Why* they believe this is a subject I haven't the space to go into here, nor is it what I've given most thought to in these books" (pp. 93–94). His main interest, he adds, is "in the extent to which unhappy people *do* define themselves as 'ill' or agree to view themselves as 'patients,' and in what each then makes of the treatment prescribed." Roth leaves unanswered, however, many important questions regarding the relationship between the creative and therapeutic process. Despite the profound similarities between the artist's and psychoanalyst's vision of reality, there are no less profound differences, chief of which is, perhaps, the assumptions of understanding reality.[2] Roth's patients, who are generally writers or professors of literature, maintain the belief that reality is intractable: Human passions are unruly, suffering cannot be explained or alleviated, and reality seems impervious to understanding. Roth's analysts, by contrast, believe that psychological illness derives from childhood experiences, that conflict can be understood psychodynamically, and that guilt and rage can be worked through.

Toward which paradigm of reality, the artist's or psychoanalyst's, is the reader more sympathetic? And what effect does psychoanalysis have on Roth's protagonists? It is clear that they continually brood over the subject of psychological illness, often becoming depressed or paralyzed. Yet why does "illness" liberate Portnoy's spirit while it only depresses Tarnopol's? In reading the analytic confessions of Roth's characters, where does one draw the line between healthy or humorous fantasies and pathological needs? And what is the relationship between art and aggression, creativity and psychopathology? In particular, can a novelist write about his own psychoanalysis and sharply disagree with his analyst's interpretation without engaging in "resistance" or "narcissistic melodramas"?

The 11-page segment of Libby Herz's stormy interview with Dr. Lumin in *Letting Go* represents one of the most brilliant fictional depictions of a patient's first analytic session. Although Libby summons all her strength to make the dreaded appointment, she still shows up 20 minutes late. To arrive on time, she fears, would be symptomatic of weakness. Upon seeing Lumin she is disheartened, for he fulfills none of the reassuring European stereotypes she has imagined. A short, wide man with oversized head and hands, he has the beefy appearance of a butcher, which intensifies Libby's terror. Roth invests the scene with a wonderful scriocomic tone, handling the problem of narrative distance with equal expertise. Everything is filtered through Libby's consciousness as the novelist records her small shocks, such as her indecision over whether to sit or lie down on the analytic couch and, if to lie down, whether to take off her shoes. Alarmed at having her preconceptions of therapy shattered, she fears she is boring or angering the analyst. She remains a prisoner of her nervousness, victimized by a frantic heart and perspiring body. "It was like living with an idiot whose behavior was unpredictable from one moment to the next: what would this body of hers do ten seconds from now?" (p. 344).

Like all of Roth's psychoanalysts, Lumin maintains a passive demeanor throughout the session, allowing Libby to direct the flow of talk. Midway through the hour, however, he grows impatient with her chatter and, during a bantering exchange, he almost springs out of the chair to demand: "Come on, Libby . . . What's the trouble?" The unexpected question devastates her and for a full five minutes she breaks down and sobs, just as Tarnopol does when he begins his analysis with Spielvogel in *My Life as a Man*. When she finally looks up, Lumin is still there, "a thick, fleshy reality, nothing to be charmed, wheedled, begged, tempted, or flirted with" (p. 347). Neither a father surrogate nor an alter ego, Lumin remains Lumin. His name suggests his function in the novel: He helps Libby to illuminate her confused thoughts and to focus on her contradictory emotions. She reveals more to him in a few minutes than she has admitted to anyone in her life, including herself. She expresses anger toward her husband for not making love to her more than once a month. ("Well," says Lumin with authority, "everybody's entitled to get laid more than that.") She confesses to her self-preoccupation and self-pity, discovers that she does not love the rootless Gabe Wallach but only the freedom she imagines him to have, and admits to behaving badly. These are not great insights, but they do represent a beginning.

In a novel filled with endless small talk and self-absorption, Lumin's silence becomes paradoxically eloquent. His attentive listening jolts Libby into a more rigorous self-examination than she has ever undertaken. The analyst offers no psychological formulas or medical truisms. He simply listens to her and occasionally asks pointed questions. When Libby demands to know what is wrong with her, he restates the question; when she begins to play the role of the mental patient, claiming she is "cracked as the day is long," he abruptly stops her. In a gruff but compassionate voice, he reproaches her for exaggerating her problems. He is not exactly a mirroring or empathic analyst, but his no-nonsense approach works.

Letting Go has received harsh criticism for its sprawling structure, desultory plotting, and self-indulgence, yet the scene between Libby and Lumin demonstrates Roth's writing at its best. The compressed descriptions, dramatic pacing, expansion and contraction of Libby's point of view, and sparkling dialogue suggest that psychoanalysis has enlivened Roth's art. Lumin's speech has the desired effect on Libby, and she suddenly feels an awakening warmth for the analyst who has given her a new perspective to her problems. Interestingly, Libby brings to therapy an uncommon knowledge of the intricacies of the patient-analyst relationship. "She had, of course, heard of transference, and she wondered if it could be beginning so soon" (p. 350). It is questionable whether an inexperienced patient, in analysis for less than an hour, would be so aware of transference. Yet Roth's characters bring to psychoanalysis an extraordinary awareness of the mind, as if they had grown up on Dr. Freud instead of Dr. Spock. Libby's positive transference toward Lumin soon gives way to rage, however, upon learning at the end of the hour the expense of psychoanalysis. When Lumin informs her that the fee is 25 dollars an hour—a figure that surely dates the novel!—she nearly faints. The scene is both funny and sad and ends with Libby storming out of his office, convinced the analyst has betrayed her. Thus ends her only experience with therapy. It is significant that Roth reserves this psychoanalytic initiation for a woman, not a man: Gabe, not Libby, seems the more likely candidate for analysis, and in future stories psychoanalysis remains a distinctly male activity.

Portnoy's Complaint (1969) is not only Roth's most celebrated psychoanalytic monologue but the novel which brought the analytic couch into the living rooms of millions of American families. Alex's attitude toward the talking cure may be gleaned from his reading habits, both by what and how he reads. Describing the set of Freud's *Collected Papers* he has bought, he remarks: "since my return from Europe, [I] have been putting myself to sleep each night in the solitary confinement of my womanless bed with a volume of Freud in my hand. Sometimes Freud in hand, sometimes Alex in hand, frequently both" (p. 185). Freud as a soporific? Or as an aphrodisiac? Portnoy reads Freud's writings for the usual reasons—intellectual curiosity, historical awareness, personal self-discovery—yet, he embraces psychoanalytic theory primarily for self-justification. The analyst becomes for Portnoy an erotic plaything, a masturbatory sex object, a handy "how-to" book. As Spielvogel's name suggests in German, he is a "playbird" to be stroked, serenaded, seduced.

Portnoy thus transmutes Freudian ideas into imaginative self-play, the first of many instances in which Roth transforms clinical case studies into the stuff of art. Portnoy's preference for orthodox Freudian psychoanalysis, uncorrupted by revisionist doctrine, reveals the same purist impulse that allows him to quote freely from other great classical writers—Shakespeare, Dostoevsky, Kafka. Portnoy reads Freud's seminal essay, "The Most Prevalent Form of Degradation in Erotic Life," and then confides to us erotic fantasies and past exploits that would make the Viennese physician blush. In holding up the Freudian mirror to life, Roth's hero is bedazzled by what he sees and by the tantalizing possibilities of life imitating the psychiatric case study. Contemporary analysts speak of fusion with the lost object, but Portnoy's story is an example of a character in search of the author of the *Standard Edition* (or the less epical *Collected Papers*), from which he quotes with Mosaic authority. The promised land for Portnoy is not Israel, toward which he ambivalently moves, but the rich landscape of textbook Oedipal fantasies. Rendered impotent in his mother country, he suffers no loss of verbal potency or bravado when journeying through virgin psychoanalytic territory.

It is obvious from the manic comic tone of the novel that Portnoy hungers not for redemption, as he mistakenly asserts, but for applause and validation. Humor aside, Portnoy does not exist. To question his "illness" seems to be in bad taste, as if to perform an autopsy on a good joke or to translate a pun from another language. "*Traduttore—traditore*," as Freud remarked in his own Joke Book.[3] Nevertheless, we may wonder whether Portnoy's reading of Freudian theory allows him to chart new imaginative territory or merely to restrict his vision. The question is not how much psychoanalytic theory Portnoy has studied but the uses and misuses of his knowledge. Accordingly, we may analyze one of the most intriguing aspects of the novel, Portnoy's transference relationship to Spielvogel. The inexperienced Libby knows enough about transference in *Letting Go* to call it by its proper name. Portnoy, however, seems indifferent to the transactional nature of psychoanalysis. Indeed, he refuses to allow Spielvogel to speak until the last line of the novel. The patient monopolizes the session in a dizzying display of Freudian virtuosity. He allows nothing to interrupt his monologue, neither doubts about psychoanalytic theory nor queries addressed to Spielvogel. All of Portnoy's questions are rhetorical.

Portnoy's transference relationship to Spielvogel suggests the desire to match his Freudian expertise against the analyst's, to compete with him, secure his approval, and ultimately to replace him as an authority. The intense identification with Spielvogel reveals the urge to incorporate him, as if Portnoy were digesting a book. Although he addresses him as "Your Honor" and "Your Holiness," the patient usually regards him as an intellectual equal. "Surely, Doctor, we can figure this thing out, two smart Jewish boys like ourselves." Portnoy never relinquishes his superiority. Identifying himself with Freud's famous case studies, he cites an illustrious artist whose fantasies coincide with his own. "I have read Freud on Leonardo, Doctor, and pardon the hubris, but my fantasies exactly: this big smothering bird beating frantic wings about my face and mouth *so that I cannot even get my breath*" (p. 121). Later Portnoy challenges Spielvogel (his own "playbird") to another competition, singing the songs of the service academies. "Go ahead, name your branch of service, Spielvogel, I'll sing you your song! Please, allow me—it's my money" (p. 235). *Portnoy's Complaint* is itself a raucous anthem to the psychoanalytic process, with the patient paying homage to His Majesty Spielvogel while at the same time making plans for his own succession to the throne.

What does all this mean? To the extent that Portnoy attempts to win his analyst's love and to usurp his magical potency, he recreates Spielvogel into an idealized father figure—a judge, lawgiver, king—the antithesis of his constipated and passive real father, Jack Portnoy. But insofar as Portnoy refuses to surrender verbal control to Spielvogel, thus enforcing silence and passivity upon the analyst, he attempts to manipulate him into his father's submissive position. The transference relationship is consequently an accurate reflection of his life. Portnoy's cocky attitude toward Spielvogel is a disguised attempt to usurp the Oedipal father, to castrate him. Roth's hero never sees the irony. Nor does he comment upon the hidden meaning behind the exhibitionistic impulse to perform or spill forth to the analyst. In his nonstop verbal pyrotechnics, his quest for perfectionism and omnipotent self-control, his unceasing self-mythologizing, and his need to instruct Spielvogel with years of inherited wisdom, Portnoy becomes his own Jewish mother. The irony is crucial. Portnoy criticizes his seductive overprotective mother for overwhelming her docile son; but the son, now a grown man, has internalized his mother's values to the extent that even while rebelling against her, he cannot prevent himself from similarly overwhelming the analyst-father. The mother uses food to overnourish her son; Alex uses a more symbolic form of orality, language, to satiate his analyst. The words never cease. In its unrelenting intensity, Alex's language suggests love and hate, nourishment and suffocation.

And so despite his impressive reading of psychoanalytic theory, Portnoy misses the significance of his ejaculative performance to Spielvogel. "I lose touch instantaneously with that ass-licking little boy who runs home after school with his A's in his hand, the little over-earnest innocent endlessly in search of the key to that unfathomable mystery, his mother's approbation . . ." (p. 49). Portnoy's colorful language offers the hope of rigorous self-examination and increased narrative perspective; yet, he still does not recognize that, instead of rejecting the mama's-boy values he professes to despise, he has unconsciously transferred these values to Spielvogel, whose approbation he is now demanding. Only now it is an "A" in psychoanalysis he is pursuing in his independent study.

How should Dr. Spielvogel react to Portnoy's artful monologue? In a satirical article entitled "Portnoy Psychoanalyzed," Bruno Bettelheim offers his interpretation of Spielvogel's responses. Portnoy's "diarrhea" of talk, observes Bettelheim's analyst, represents a reaction formation to his father's constipation of character. The patient's problem is reflected in his indiscriminate sexual and verbal discharge, a frantic defense against the threat of being unmanned. Accompanying Portnoy's castration fear is the contradictory wish to *have* a castrating father to restore his wounded image of male power. Portnoy's confession is self-indulgent, claims Bettelheim's Spielvogel, because he regards psychoanalysis as a quick and easy catharsis rather than as a difficult process of self-healing through self-discovery. The analyst suggests additionally that although Portnoy believes his psychic impotence arises from an Oedipal attachment, the oral attachments to the mother determine his wish to remain a child forever. Bettelheim's most provocative insight is that Portnoy's complaint of an overprotective mother disguises the disappointment that she was not more exclusively preoccupied with him. "While consciously he experienced everything she did as destructive, behind it is an incredible wish for more, more, more; an insatiable orality which is denied and turned into the opposite by his continuous scream of its being much too much."[4]

Ironically, Bettelheim's Spielvogel is as perceptive in analyzing Portnoy's transference relationship as he is imperceptive in admitting to his own negative countertransference. Unable to concede any sympathy for his "troublesome—aren't they all?—new patient," the analyst is filled with anger, contempt, and intolerance, as if the patient's narcissistic defenses have triggered off his own. He fails to acknowledge anything worthwhile about Portnoy's character. Reading "Portnoy Psychoanalyzed," one is unable to explain the vitality and wit of the Rothian hero, not to mention the novel's linguistic brilliance. Angered by his inability to break through Portnoy's monologue, and worried (rightly, as it turns out) that he will be unable to establish a minimal transference necessary for analysis to succeed, Bettelheim's Spielvogel never admits that countertransference is the key problem. Not even Eliot's Sir Harcourt-Reilly is as belligerent as Bettelheim's Spielvogel. He is offended by Portnoy's vulgar language, ingratitude toward his parents, inferiority complex, narcissistic rage, and failure in interpersonal relationships. Why, then, is the patient in analysis if he is not to work through these conflicts? In his narrow clinical judgments, threatening tactics, and European condescension, Bettelheim's Spielvogel becomes an unconscious parody of a self-righteous, withholding parent. Indeed, Roth could not have imagined a more unflattering portrait of an analyst. And the absence of authorial distance between the eminent psychoanalyst and his fictional creation makes "Portnoy Psychoanalyzed" more disturbing.

Bettelheim's hostility toward *Portnoy's Complaint* may derive in part from the psychoanalytic community's defensiveness of its image in literature. The angry denunciations of *Equus* suggest this, though certainly the play's flaws justify criticism. A more serious problem of "Portnoy Psychoanalyzed" is its unawareness of the satirical art of *Portnoy's Complaint* and Bettelheim's reduction of Roth's novel to a psychiatric case study. Only at the end of the essay does the author consider the possibility that *Portnoy's Complaint* is a literary production, not a clinical confession. He concedes that at best it is "not more than an effort to tell a good story." But he places no value on a good story. He also wishes to tell Portnoy—and his creator—that "it is time to stop being a man of letters so that, through analyzing himself, he might finally become a man" (p. 10). Behind Spielvogel's hostility toward Portnoy lies, of course, Bettelheim's rejection of Roth. Roth's own Spielvogel in *My Life as a Man* demonstrates greater compassion and understanding than the Spielvogel of "Portnoy Psychoanalyzed," which is to say that Roth is a better psychoanalyst than Bettelheim is a literary critic.[5]

Despite its appearance as a psychiatric case study, *Portnoy's Complaint* retains its allegiance to the interior monologue developed by Joyce, Faulkner, and Virginia Woolf. Beginning with *Portnoy's Complaint* and proceeding through *The Breast, My Life as a Man,* and *The Professor of Desire,* Roth has evolved his own narrative form in which the interior monologue is wedded to a contemporary psychoanalytic setting. The analyst, heard or unheard, becomes the recipient of the comic or anguished utterances of a patient searching for psychic relief and moral redemption. The free-association technique, the recurrent phallic-and-castration imagery, the Oedipal triangles, the idealization of the analyst, and the multilayered texture of Portnoy's consciousness help to create the psychoanalytic authenticity. "The style of *Portnoy's Complaint*," Sheldon Grebstein observes, "is the rhetoric of hysteria, or perhaps the rhetoric of neurosis."[6]

Roth's prose style also captures perfectly the nuances of psychoanalysis. His language is analytic, restlessly interrogative, self-mocking. The prose is always capable of anticipating the objections of an implied listener who usually turns out to be, of course, an analyst. The language is attuned to the nuances of spiritual imprisonment and moral ambiguity, capable of distorting small humiliations into traumatic injustices, and straining for a release that never quite comes. The voice bespeaks a romantic disillusionment that rarely frees itself from the suspicion that, contrary to what an analyst might say, an unruly personal life is good for a novelist's art. There is a self-lacerating quality about Roth's prose that has remained constant over the years. David Kepesh's observation in *The Professor of Desire* holds true for all of Roth's heroes. "I am an absolutist—a *young* absolutist—and know no way to shed a skin other than by inserting the scalpel and lacerating myself from end to end" (p. 12). Roth's stories dramatize the struggle between the impulse for sensual abandon, on the one hand, and the capacity for pain-filled renunciation, on the other. And the novelist is always willing to incriminate himself in the service of art, preoccupied as he is in novel after novel with illicit and ungovernable passions at war with a rigid conscience.

Does Portnoy discover anything about himself in the course of the novel? The circular form of *Portnoy's Complaint* undercuts the illusion of self-discovery. Roth's comments in *Reading Myself and Others* indicate the contradiction between the realistic and satirical elements of the story. "It is a highly stylized confession that this imaginary Spielvogel gets to hear, and I would guess that it bears about as much resemblance to the drift and tone of what a real psychopathologist hears in his everyday life as a love sonnet does to the iambs and dactyls that lovers whisper into one another's ears in motel rooms and over the phone" (p. 94). The simile reveals Roth's own spirited love affair with psychoanalysis, at least during the creation of *Portnoy's Complaint*. In *My Life as a Man,* he will strive for and achieve stark realism in the treatment of the patient-analyst relationship, but, in *Portnoy's Complaint,* he uses a psychoanalytic setting mainly as the context for his protagonist's lyrical confessions. Never has confession sounded as poetic as this, as free and spontaneous and inventive as these artful outpourings. Portnoy has acquired his psychoanalytic armor before the novel opens, and he seems disinclined to lay down his defenses as the story closes. Consequently, he reaches few if any real insights, nothing comparable to a Joycean epiphany.

Patricia Meyer Spacks has pointed out the affinities of *Portnoy's Complaint* to the picaresque novel, but Roth's story also recalls the dramatic monologue.[7] Robert Langbaum has called the dramatic monologue "the poetry of experience," the doctrine that the "imaginative apprehension gained through immediate experience is primary and certain, whereas the

analytic reflection that follows is secondary and problematical."[8] Nearly
all of Langbaum's observations in *The Poetry of Experience* apply to *Portnoy's Complaint,* including the tension between our sympathy and moral
judgment for a speaker who is outrageous or reprehensible. They apply
to the circular rather than linear direction of the narrative. ("The speaker
of the dramatic monologue starts out with an established point of view,
and is not concerned with its truth but with trying to impress it on the
outside world.") Also, they apply to the gratuitous but lyrical nature of
the speaker's utterance. "The result is that the dramatic situation, incomplete in itself, serves an ultimately self-expressive or lyrical purpose which
gives it its resolution" (p. 182). And so it is with Portnoy's complaint.
Interpreted as a Browningesque dramatic monologue, the novel ceases to
be a psychiatric case study. The self-indulgent confession gives way to an
internally structured monologue, the psychomoral complexity shifts away
from Portnoy as character or object onto the reader's problematic relationship to him, the patient's self-analysis becomes linked to self-decep-
tion, and Portnoy's failure to achieve a therapeutic cure is offset by his
refusal to have acknowledged any illness.

Nowhere is the reader's troubled relationship to Portnoy better demonstrated than by the enormous controversy the novel has generated.
Portnoy shrewdly anticipates the accusations of his critics. "I hear myself
indulging in the kind of ritualized bellyaching that is just what gives psychoanalytic patients such a bad name with the general public" (p. 94).
Do we praise his candor or criticize his rationalization? Or both? How
do we respond to his next set of questions? "Is this truth I'm delivering
up, or is it just plain *kvetching?* Or is *kvetching* for people like me a *form*
of truth?" The answer depends upon the reader's sympathy for Portnoy,
but of course this evades the prior questions of how and why the reader's
sympathy for Portnoy is or is not engaged. Irving Howe's influential indictment of *Portnoy's Complaint* in *Commentary* remains the most caustic
evaluation. "There usually follows in such first-person narratives a spilling-out of the narrator which it becomes hard to suppose is not also the
spilling-out of the author. Such literary narcissism is especially notable
among minor satirists, with whom it frequently takes the form of self-
exemptive attacks on the shamefulness of humanity."[9] This remains an
extreme position, however, and amidst the claims and counterclaims of
Roth's critics, a reader is likely to become confused. As Mark Shechner
has noted in an admirable essay, one's enthusiasm for Roth's fiction is

complicated though not necessarily diminished by the discovery that one's loyalty to *Portnoy's Complaint* as a version of the truth is not widely shared by other readers.[10]

Paradoxically, despite Portnoy's incessant complaints, it is hard to take seriously his demand for therapeutic relief. He may gripe that his parents have psychically crippled him, but they have also been responsible for shaping an imagination that never wavers in its comic inventiveness and vitality. The novel is less a complaint than a celebration. Why should Portnoy be cured of fantasies that are so entertaining? The exuberance of his language works against his claims for deliverance. The voice never assumes the flatness, fatigue, or disconnectedness that is symptomatic of depression. Narcissism notwithstanding, Portnoy realizes that he is not the center of the universe, and Roth's ability to conjure up a rogue's gallery of minor characters testifies to his escape from solipsism. Portnoy's voice never falters in its curiosity and delight in commentary. "The true center of Portnoy's heroism is his speech," Patricia Meyer Spacks has observed.[11] It is true that Portnoy has not figured out all the psychoanalytic dynamics of his situation. He prefers to discuss Oedipal fixations rather than pre-Oedipal narcissistic injuries. However, if he is consumed by guilt, he seems to be thriving on his imaginative disorders.

The delight in reading *Portnoy's Complaint* lies not in the analysis of a diseased mind but in the appreciation of one of the most fertile imaginations found in contemporary literature. Unlike *The Catcher in the Rye,* which ends with Holden Caulfield's psychotic breakdown, institutionalization, and uncertain return to society, *Portnoy's Complaint* concludes with the protagonist as an outpatient. Spielvogel's punch line, "So. . . . Now vee may perhaps to begin. Yes?", perfectly satirizes Portnoy's bookish self-analysis. Through Spielvogel's one-liner, Roth tells us that Portnoy's psychoanalytic (or pre-psychoanalytic) monologue is both inadequate and incomplete. The analyst has the last word and the last laugh. Yet, Portnoy has discovered one crucial truth that will prepare him for psychoanalysis or any other introspective activity. He has casually dropped upon us (in a parenthesis, no less) the moral of his story: "Nothing is never ironic, there's always a laugh lurking somewhere" (p. 93). *Portnoy's Complaint* appropriately ends with a Joycean "yes." And in the spirit of *Ulysses,* which also climaxes with Molly Bloom's final affirmation as she drifts off to sleep dreaming autoerotic visions of past and present lovers, so does Roth's self-reliant hero, far from being drained or limp from his imaginative foreplay, return to Freud, on the one hand, and himself, on the other, ready to play with his Spielvogelian truths.

*   *   *

Unfortunately, psychoanalysis proves less inspiring to Roth's next protagonist-patient. Portnoy's masturbatory fantasies pale in comparison to the endocrinopathic catastrophe befalling the unfortunate hero of *The Breast*. Worse still, David Kepesh's metamorphosis into a giant breast remains inexplicable to his psychoanalyst, Dr. Frederick Klinger, who insists upon, oddly enough, a physiological etiology. To accept Klinger's judgment is to reject all efforts to interpret Roth's story. Devoid of psychological interest, *The Breast* wanders in a no-man's land between *Portnoy's Complaint* and *My Life as a Man,* without the great comic exuberance of the former or the intriguing involutions of the latter.[12] Unlike Portnoy, Kepesh's complaints seem joyless and unimaginative; unlike Tarnopol, his life as a man seems unworthy of extended critical attention. *The Breast* strays between realism and fantasy, unable to commit itself to either outlook. For whatever reason, Roth restrains the farcical implications of the story. The problem with *The Breast* is that it is not fantastic enough. The premise of the story would seem to indicate an abandonment of the reality principle and a leap into pure fantasy; yet, Kepesh always sounds like Kepesh—before, during, and after the metamorphosis. The story remains exclusively preoccupied with the trivial facts of the transformation, thus neglecting the narrator's dislocation of consciousness. The metamorphosis into a breast fails to alter the dreary consistency of Kepesh's perceptions and speech, perhaps necessitating a more radical surgical procedure for Roth's curious novella.

In retrospect, *The Breast* occupies a transitional position in Roth's career. David Kepesh's life embodies most of the characteristics, external and internal, of the archetypal Roth protagonist. Kepesh and Tarnopol are similar in age, profession, parental and marital problems, and temperament. Both men have been in psychoanalysis for five years and teach English literature in colleges or universities where Roth himself has studied or taught. Interestingly, the age of the Roth narrator can be determined by subtracting the year of Roth's birth, 1933, from the publication date of the novel. The Roth hero ages from novel to novel at the same speed as the novelist himself. Gabe Wallach is 28, Roth's age when he finished writing *Letting Go.* Alex Portnoy is born in 1933. Kepesh says that he is 38 and that he turned into a breast in 1971 (the novella was published in 1972), thus placing his birth in 1933. Both Nathan Zuckerman and Tarnopol, in *My Life as a Man,* also were born in 1933. Similarly, the titles of Roth's stories reveal an allegorical pattern. They narrate the complaint of a professor of desire, whose struggle for manhood is undercut by the difficulty of letting go of a literal or metaphorical breast. Roth has always been striving to write *The Great American Novel,* though the title of *Goodbye, Columbus* may suggest the increasing remoteness of the quest. The titles *Goodbye, Columbus, Letting Go, When She Was Good,* and *The Ghost Writer* also hint at an element of nostalgia and perhaps elegy, as if the past is more romantic than the present. Yet there is a depressing fear that, to echo Roth's contemporary, Joseph Heller, something happened.

The Klinger-Kepesh relationship in *The Breast* dramatizes the tension between rationality and irrationality, restraint and hysteria, the reality principle and the pleasure principle. Like all of Roth's analysts, Klinger is concerned with normal rather than abnormal psychology. He never claims omniscience or omnipotence. Roth continues to demystify the analyst, making him eminently human and sensible. To his credit, Klinger avoids threatening clinical tactics, obscurantist theories, and professional jargon. "You are not mad," he tells Kepesh, "You are not in the grip of a delusion, or haven't been till now. You have not suffered what you call 'a schizophrenic collapse' " (p. 55). Klinger mercifully abstains from Laingian metaphors of "journeying through inner space" and other fashionable psychiatric theories.

Yet, if Kepesh's illness originates from a hormonal imbalance, what is Klinger doing in *The Breast?* The analyst insists that Kepesh's metamorphosis cannot be explained in psychoanalytic terms, such as wish fulfillment or regression to infancy. Does Roth need an analyst to tell us this? Better an endocrinologist. Klinger's vocabulary is not psychological but moralistic; he uses expressions like "strength of character" and "will to live" to help his patient adapt to the bizarre illness. Both the analyst and novelist take Kepesh's story too seriously. Perhaps one can excuse Kepesh's hypochondria and self-dramatizing; he is, after all, the patient and therefore entitled to his rightful suffering. "Alas, what has happened to me is like nothing anyone has ever known; beyond understanding, beyond compassion, beyond comedy . . . ." (p. 11). Klinger encourages Kepesh's self-inflation, and even the analyst's dialogue sounds wooden at times. "You have been heroic in your efforts to accommodate yourself to

this mysterious misfortune" (p. 55). Roth's great gift for dialogue fails him
here, suggesting that the novelist cannot believe in Kepesh's "heroic" plight.
Nevertheless, Roth continues to insist upon his patient's heroic stature,
arguing, in *Reading Myself and Others,* that Kepesh's predicament is far
more poignant and harrowing than Lucy Nelson's, the heroine of *When
She Was Good,* or Portnoy's. "Kepesh strikes me as far more heroic than
either of these two: perhaps a man who turns into a breast is the first
heroic character I've ever been able to portray" (p. 66). Despite Roth's
intentions, his hero seems neither sick nor imaginative enough to justify
his fantastic situation. Why the metamorphosis into a breast instead of a
penis, mouth, anus, brain? Why Kepesh's five years of therapy prior to
the opening of the story, only to be told that psychoanalytic reality does
not apply to a biochemical disorder? Why attempt to remain a "citadel
of sanity" when real madness seems more appropriate? Far from being
the uplifting story Roth intended, *The Breast* remains pointless, a joke
gone sour.

✳   ✳   ✳

My Life as a Man is Roth's most profound investigation of the relationship between literature and psychoanalysis. The full complexity of the
novel becomes apparent only upon subsequent rereadings and an examination of its biographical sources. No novelist has given us a more authentic account of psychoanalysis in its intellectual and emotional vaga-
ries than Roth does in *My Life as a Man.* The novel is unrivaled in its
narration of the problems that arise when the novelist and psychoanalyst
clash over different interpretations of reality. In this story, Roth develops
a psychoanalyst for the first time and explores the impact of therapy upon
the artist's life and work, the connection between art and neurosis, and
the often-problematic distinction between acting out and working through
psychic conflict. As with *I Never Promised You a Rose Garden,* we see a
novel originating from an actual psychiatric case study and the problems
arising from the issue of medical confidentiality. Although Roth has written
about therapy prior to *Portnoy's Complaint* and subsequent to *My Life as
a Man,* these two novels complete a major cycle in the writer's career.

My Life as a Man is composed of the story of three novelists. The first
novelist is Nathan Zuckerman, the fictional hero of two useful fictions,
"Salad Days" and "Courting Disaster (Or, Serious in the Fifties)." Zuckerman's promising literary career is cut short by a catastrophic, loveless
marriage to a self-abnegating divorcée and then, after her suicide, a joy-

less union with a daughter much like Lolita. The second novelist is Peter Tarnopol, the author of these two "Useful Fictions" and the narrator of an autobiographical novella called *My True Story,* which chronicles a myriad of personal problems ranging from a nightmarish marriage to a "psychopath," to another entangling alliance with a self-destructive woman. The third novelist is Philip Roth, whose relationship to *My Life as a Man* contradicts the Joycean injunction of the impersonal Godlike artist who "remains within or behind or beyond or above his handiwork, invisible, refined out of existence." The two structural divisions of the novel, "Useful Fictions" and *My True Story,* emphasize Roth's deliberate blurring of literature and life, fiction and autobiography. The story falls into the category of the self-reflexive, Post-Modernist novel. It is highly self-conscious in narration, yielding little authorial distance. Filled with long passages of literary criticism and expository material, *My Life as a Man* also comments directly upon Roth's previous novels, including a summary of the writer's fortunes and misfortunes. Tarnopol occupies an ambiguous middle position between his fictional son Nathan Zuckerman and his autobiographical father, Philip Roth. Like all the father-son relationships in Roth's world, it is deeply troubled.

To meet Peter Tarnopol is to remember Alex Portnoy. Tarnopol opens his section of the novel by asking: "Has anything changed?" A reader may ask the same question. Portnoy is an assistant commissioner on human opportunity, Tarnopol an assistant professor of literature. It is clear that they come not only from similar backgrounds but from the same imagination. They are exclamatory in their speech and ejaculatory in their sex. Mistrustful of women, they split females into spiritual and sexual antinomies and find happiness with neither type. Portnoy has his Monkey, Tarnopol his Maureen. Both men are highly competitive and temperamentally incapable of silence. Emotionally nourished by Jewish mothers and intellectually nurtured on Jewish mentors, Freud and Kafka, they are sensitive to the charge of narcissism which their behavior seems to invite. Filled with guilt and pent-up rage, they commit themselves to the same eminent psychoanalyst, Dr. Otto Spielvogel. And, as further proof of similarity, their names are anagrams: six of the seven letters of "Portnoy" appear in "Tarnopol."

But whereas Portnoy calls Spielvogel "Your Honor" and "Your Holiness," Tarnopol refers to him, with double-edged irony, as "Warden Spielvogel." The title hints at Roth's shift of attitude toward psychoanalysis. In *Portnoy's Complaint,* Spielvogel has the last word, but in *My Life as a Man* the analyst's role is less privileged. "The doctor he reminded me of most," Tarnopol tells us, "was Dr. Roger Chillingworth in Hawthorne's *Scarlet Letter*. Appropriate enough, because I sat facing him as full of shameful secrets as the Reverend Arthur Dimmesdale" (p. 203). But it is Dr. Freud whom Spielvogel resembles. Apart from his German-Jewish name and accent, Spielvogel is battling cancer. Yet he refuses to give up his work. Like Freud, he has a framed photograph of the Acropolis on his desk, and he demonstrates a keen interest in the application of psychoanalytic theory to art criticism. His specialty is treating "creative" people. The analyst's professional judgment of his patient is summarized in one wry sentence. "Mr. Tarnopol is considered by Dr. Spielvogel to be among the nation's top young narcissists in the arts." Tarnopol's judgment of Spielvogel is considerably more complicated.

Although Tarnopol's relationship to Spielvogel echoes previous encounters between patients and analysts in Roth's fiction, *My Life as a Man* is more than a variation on an old theme. From the memorable description of Tarnopol's first session with Spielvogel to their last farewell, we realize we are in the presence of an extraordinary event in the novelist's life. Roth invests Tarnopol's psychoanalysis with drama, humor, and pathos. The juxtaposition of interior monologue and dialogue is superb, and the tone sparkles with ironic wit and literary allusiveness. Entering Spielvogel's office for the first time, Tarnopol feels an impulse to "get up and leave, my shame and humiliation (and my disaster) still my own—and simultaneously to crawl into his lap." Tarnopol breaks down and weeps for several minutes, as Libby has done in *Letting Go*. "Are you finished?" Spielvogel finally asks. Years later Tarnopol still reflects upon these classic words. "There are lines from my five years of psychoanalysis as memorable to me as the opening sentence of *Anna Karenina*—'Are you finished?' is one of them. The perfect tone, the perfect tactic. I turned myself over to him, then and there, for good or bad" (pp. 203–204).

Spielvogel is one of the most formidable psychoanalysts in literature, a *tour de force*. Roth does not allow anything, including the falling out between Tarnopol and Spielvogel, to undercut the analyst's toughness of character, European dignity, and unswerving commitment. From beginning to end he remains the repository of Tarnopol's intimate history, the instrument of his psychic, even spiritual, recovery. Although a darker side to Spielvogel's character emerges during his dispute with Tarnopol, Roth does not allow the portrait of the analyst to deteriorate into caricature. Spielvogel displays an immunity to criticism that both dismays and impresses his patient; although the analyst's refusal to concede responsibility for the apparent breach of confidentiality that later arises, or at least the unfortunate accident of publication, strikes Tarnopol as unforgivable, the patient is emphatic about one point. Without the years of psychoanalytic treatment, Tarnopol would not have survived, at least not as a reasonably integrated and functional person. Bereft of the will to live, unable to write, dependent upon a wife he despised, Tarnopol had given up all hope. "On the June afternoon that I first stepped into Dr. Spielvogel's office, I don't think a minute elapsed before I had given up all pretense of being an 'integrated' personality and begun to weep into my hands, grieving for the loss of my strength, my confidence, and my future" (p. 101). The Fitzgerald mood suggests Roth's preoccupation with *The Crack-Up,* the hope of discovering a pattern to the broken pieces of his life. Roth's psychoanalysts are more toughminded than Fitzgerald's Dr. Dick Diver, however, and more effective.

Curiously, the therapeutic relief Roth's male characters receive from treatment does not extend to the females, although they are also in extensive analysis. Lydia Ketterer, Zuckerman's wife, commits suicide; Susan McCall, Tarnopol's girl friend, attempts suicide; and Maureen Tarnopol dies violently in a suspicious automobile accident. All three women have been in analysis or group therapy. Perhaps Roth's male analysts cannot figure out, like Freud, what women really want; or perhaps the fatal or near-fatal endings of these women betray the novelist's wishful thinking. Whatever, psychoanalysis seems to be a male therapy in Roth's world.

As *My Life as a Man* progresses, though, Roth takes an increasingly skeptical view of psychoanalytic theory. Zuckerman is frustrated in his efforts to discover the significance of his crippling migraines and, despite his literary training, which predisposes him to see the migraines as *"standing for something,* as a disclosure or 'epiphany,' " he rules out therapy. The headaches inexplicably disappear. Reality proves impenetrable both to Zuckerman and to David Kepesh in *The Breast.* The two men, in fact, are in a similar situation: Kepesh turns into a breast, Zuckerman succumbs to headaches. Both professors of literature search futilely for a meaning to their disastrous lives, finally acknowledging defeat. Ruling out psychoanalysis, literary interpretation, or other treatments of choice, they fall back upon obscure physiological explanations. Both men spend a good deal of the time flat on their backs, infantilized. It is as if they are punished for the desire to understand or control their lives, to achieve meaning in an absurd society. Both men deny, perhaps too strenuously, the link between their incapacitating illnesses and the wish to escape responsibility for their actions. Zuckerman concludes despairingly that literature, with its assumptions of unity, coherency, and design, has influenced too strongly his attitudes toward life. Unable to make a clear connection between the order of art and the disorder of life, he mindlessly accepts and/or rejects all explanations of his self-imprisonment. He is certain about only one fact, that instead of fulfilling his high ambitions, he has irrevocably squandered his manhood.

What does Zuckerman's story reveal about Tarnopol? About Roth? Do "Salad Days" and "Courting Disaster" prophesy the direction of Tarnopol's life or his fate had he not entered psychoanalysis? It is ironic that Zuckerman and Tarnopol, both sympathetic toward Freudian orientations, should finally repudiate the psychoanalytic model of reality. Or perhaps it is not ironic at all. A psychiatrist diagnoses Zuckerman's migraines as signifying "pent-up rage," raising the obvious question whether his escape into philosophical theorizing is a subtle rationalization. But to interpret Tarnopol's two stories from a psychoanalytic viewpoint is to risk the dangers one encounters in reading Nabokov's fiction. The novel deviously lures in the Freudian critic, baits him with Oedipal morsels, and then springs the trap. Tarnopol is admittedly aware of the Oedipal implications of Zuckerman's dependency on Lydia Ketterer and her daughter Moonie. Part of Zuckerman's attraction to Lydia derives from the fact that she has been raped by her father and apparently ennobled through suffering. Zuckerman's marriage only deepens her anguish. His dependency upon women parallels the incestuous regression implicit in Dick Diver's attraction to Nicole Warren. Tarnopol is very self-conscious in his use of the Daddy's Girl theme for his own fiction. After Lydia's suicide, Zuckerman engages in another loveless relationship with her daughter. Tarnopol's literature contains a rescue theme in which he attempts to save both Lydia, raped by her father and brutalized by her former husband, and Moonie, abandoned by her father. But instead of liberating mother and daughter, Zuckerman adds to their misery and his own.

From the psychoanalytic perspective which Tarnopol steadfastly rejects, Zuckerman's masochistic attachment to Lydia and Moonie represents an acting out of his own loveless childhood, an unsuccessful attempt to compensate for his underprotectiveness as a child. The problem with this interpretation is that Zuckerman's parents (and Tarnopol's) seem loving and supportive, his childhood happy and halcyon—in short, the "Salad Days" the novelist has described. The counterargument is that

Zuckerman and Tarnopol both idealize their childhood, with Roth's concurrence, to conceal the narcissistic injuries of all three figures. The argument cannot be resolved, at least not on the basis of the evidence offered in *My Life as a Man*.

This brings us to the clash between Tarnopol and Spielvogel over their conflicting interpretations of the novelist's dependency on his hateful wife Maureen. This section of *My Life as a Man* reads like a psychiatric case study, and indeed it is. In explaining how Tarnopol has been reduced by his wife to a bewildered, defenseless little boy, Dr. Spielvogel argues that his patient's vulnerability derives from a lack of love as a child. The analyst sees Tarnopol's mother as "phallic castrating" in her emotional coldness toward him. To protect himself from the profound anxiety engendered by the rejection, separation, and helplessness he experienced in his mother's presence, Tarnopol adopts narcissistic defenses. He continues to idealize his mother and childhood, denying his disappointment toward an effectual father.[13] The need to reduce women to "masturbatory sexual objects," as Spielvogel puts it, is both a derivative of the narcissism and a symptom of repressed rage toward the mother. The analyst devises a therapeutic strategy to deplete the fund of Tarnopol's maternal veneration on which Maureen has drawn.

Tarnopol's version of his analysis differs from that of Spielvogel. He sharply disagrees with Spielvogel's characterization of the phallic castrating mother and ineffectual father. If his mother is responsible for her son's slavish dependency, he says, it is because of her adoration of him. Tarnopol concedes that his father may have been supernumerary but only because he was struggling successfully to make a living for his family. Tarnopol rejects Spielvogel's theory that the novelist's relationship to Maureen is a repetition of an ancient trauma. Tarnopol maintains, by contrast, that the uniqueness of the horror has rendered him powerless to deal with it because his childhood consisted only of parental love. "Wasn't it possible that in my 'case,' as I willingly called it, triumph *and* failure, conquest *and* defeat derives from an indestructible boyish devotion to a woman as benefactress and celebrant, protectress and guide? Could we not conjecture that what had made me so available to the Bad Older Woman was the reawakening in me of that habit of obedience that had stood me in such good stead with the Good Older Woman of my childhood" (p. 216).

Which of these two interpretations, the psychoanalyst's or novelist's, is more plausible? Roth's sympathy is clearly for Tarnopol, who consis-

tently outargues Spielvogel. Never has a fictional patient seemed as articulate and psychoanalytically informed. He invokes not only psychoanalysis but other systems of reality, including literature and mythology, to
argue his case. Simply on the basis of language, he wins the argument.
Unlike Spielvogel's reductive prose style, which flattens out ambiguity and
nuance, Tarnopol's language is precise, eloquent, and richly suggestive.
Spielvogel has an annoying tendency to label all of Tarnopol's actions
"narcissistic," and gradually the word loses precise meaning. Moreover,
despite the analyst's claim that he uses the word nonjudgmentally, the
label justifiably provokes Tarnopol's anger. (Spielvogel is apparently closer
to Otto Kernberg's theoretical position regarding narcissism than Heinz
Kohut's.) Tarnopol is also able to anticipate and summarize Spielvogel's
argument, which gives him an advantage, as does his first-person narration. And Tarnopol's awareness of transference strengthens his point of
view. Indeed, there is little, if anything, about psychoanalysis that escapes
Tarnopol's attention. He is the better writer of the two and, it almost
seems, the better analyst. In addition, Spielvogel errs on a couple of related issues. He interprets Tarnopol's fear that Susan McCall might commit suicide as "narcissistic self-dramatization," but after she does attempt
to kill herself, the analyst acknowledges he is not a fortuneteller. He also
dismisses the gesture as only an "attempted" suicide, a statement that
provokes Tarnopol's disbelief.

However, Tarnopol may be winning the battle but losing the war. Despite the fact that he is a better debater, he still cannot figure out his humiliating relationship to his wife. At times, he uses the analytic setting
more as an intellectual or philosophical forum than as a testing ground
for emotional truth. And it is difficult to know when Tarnopol's objectivity ends and his special pleading begins: He is a man of many obsessions and few certainties.

Before the combatants are able to resolve their conflicting interpretations of reality, a serious dispute arises over Spielvogel's publication of
an article in a special issue of the *American Forum for Psychoanalytic Studies* focusing on "The Riddle of Creativity." At the time of the article's
publication, Tarnopol has been in analysis for three years. He sees the
journal lying on Spielvogel's desk, receives permission to read it, and grows
incensed with the analyst's biographically transparent discussion of his own
case study. Spielvogel's article is called "Creativity: The Narcissism of the
Artist." Although only two pages of the essay pertain to Tarnopol, he is
horrified by the rhetorical and substantive crudities. In his attempt to dis-

guise his patient's identity, Spielvogel writes about a "successful Italian-American poet in his late forties" instead of a troubled Jewish-American novelist in his late twenties. After reading the article, Tarnopol bitterly accuses Spielvogel of creating narrow fictions to pursue a simplistic psychoanalytic thesis. He also condemns the analyst for blurring important genetic differences between the poet's sensibility and the novelist's. Tarnopol angrily dismisses the entire thesis of the article. Whereas Spielvogel maintains, along with Freud, that the artist is narcissistic, Tarnopol insists that the artist's success depends on his powers of detachment, on *de*narcissizing himself. Reading Spielvogel's case study, Tarnopol can hardly believe the analyst's caricature of his life. Spielvogel has distorted his age, accomplishment, background, and vocation. Tarnopol cannot read a sentence without discovering significant factual errors, incorrect inferences, or distorted characterizations. He accuses Spielvogel, in short, of being a poor psychoanalyst and a poorer fiction writer, and of embracing a narrow thesis at the expense of an ambiguous and perplexing actuality.

What most infuriates Tarnopol, however, is that Spielvogel's essay has seriously compromised his identity. Anyone who reads Spielvogel's publication, Tarnopol charges, will realize that he is the analyst's patient. The situation is aggravated by the fact that Spielvogel has related a highly personal incident about his patient's life, which Tarnopol has also written about in an autobiographical story published in the *New Yorker*. The incident involves a traumatic childhood incident during World War II when Tarnopol's family is forced to move from one apartment to another. The day after the move, the nine-year-old boy returns to his old apartment after school, only to find several men standing inside. Instead of realizing they are housepainters, Tarnopol imagines them as Nazis who have taken away his mother. The hysterical child instinctively runs to the new apartment, whereupon he sees his mother and in tears collapses into her arms. Spielvogel's interpretation emphasizes the patient's guilt over the aggressive fantasies directed toward the mother. Tarnopol's interpretation of the incident, which appears in a short story in journal form called "The Diary of Anne Frank," emphasizes the relief at finding the new apartment transformed into a perfect replica of the old one, thus reassuring the boy that he is living in safe America rather than war-ravaged, Jew-hating Europe. By the time Spielvogel learns about Tarnopol's story in the *New Yorker,* his own essay containing the identical incident is already at the printer.

Spielvogel's defense—though he does not use the word—is that he did nothing wrong in publishing the article. Since both men were writing simultaneously, he had no way of knowing about the unfortunate coincidence. The analyst insists that Tarnopol's rage is both unjustified and illogical in that the patient accuses him of excessive yet finally insufficient distortions. Spielvogel also denies that he was ethically required to secure Tarnopol's permission to publish the essay. "None of us could write such papers, none of us could share our findings with one another, if we had to rely upon the permission or the approval of our patients in order to publish." In Spielvogel's judgment, Tarnopol is disturbed not by the disclosure of his identity but by the fact that the analyst has "plagiarized and abused" the writer's material. The argument rages back and forth with neither man altering his position. Spielvogel finally gives Tarnopol an ultimatum—either to forget about his anger or break off therapy. Despite the analyst's inflexible position, Tarnopol decides reluctantly to continue treatment. He remains convinced that he has been helped by analysis and that without Spielvogel's therapy, he would not have survived the marital crisis. Nevertheless, his faith in Spielvogel's art is permanently shaken.

The controversy between Tarnopol and Spielvogel raises intriguing questions about the link between *Portnoy's Complaint* and *My Life as a Man*. However questionable Spielvogel's diagnosis is of Tarnopol, it does seem to illuminate Alex Portnoy's dilemma: the use of narcissistic defenses against the anxiety engendered by separation from the mother, the reduction of women to masturbatory sexual objects, the acting out or libidinizing of aggression, the phallic castrating mother and ineffectual father, and so on. Has the Spielvogel of *My Life as a Man* been using *Portnoy's Complaint* as a psychiatric case study from which to base his judgment of Tarnopol? Or has Roth created *My Life as a Man* to refute Spielvogel's silent condemnation of the narcissistic hero of the earlier novel? Do we approach these two novels as separate, autonomous literary creations having little thematic relationship to each other apart from the dramatization of a hero's misadventures in manhood. Or do we read *My Life as a Man* as Roth's revisionist interpretation of *Portnoy's Complaint,* narrated by a disillusioned patient who is now ready to repudiate the virtuoso Freudianism of the earlier story? Where is Roth in relation to Tarnopol? Does the lack of narrative distance in *My Life as a Man* reinforce Spielvogel's thesis of the self-preoccupied artist who is unable to prevent himself from narrating narcissistic melodramas?

Tarnopol's psychoanalysis leads us inevitably to the biographical elements of *My Life as a Man*. "Roth's own driving compulsions are, at best, only thinly disguised in the robes of Tarnopol," Sanford Pinsker observes.[14] To that Tarnopol might reply, as he does to Spielvogel: "I do not write 'about' people in a strict factual or historical sense." But Roth's dismissal of the autobiographical nature of his fiction is too easy, and he goes out of his way to invite public scrutiny of his private life. Even a cursory glance at Tarnopol's biography reveals twinship with his maker.[15] Both the real and fictional novelists were born near New York City in 1933; graduated *magna cum laude* or *summa cum laude* in 1954; served briefly in the U.S. Army and were discharged because of injuries; enrolled for a year and a half in the Ph.D. program at the University of Chicago "before falling by the wayside, a casualty of 'Bibliography' and 'Anglo-Saxon' "; published first novels in 1959 for which they received major literary awards in 1960; resided at a writer's colony (Tarnopol's "Quahsay" is based on Roth's Yaddo); and entered into a catastrophic marriage to a woman later killed in an automobile accident (Tarnopol's marriage to Maureen Johnson in 1959 ended in her violent death in 1966; Roth's marriage to Margaret Martinson Williams in 1959 ended in her violent death in 1968). Both novelists write parallel autobiographical narratives about characters who cannot give up their self-destructive obsessions.

Roth's critics have also noticed the lack of authorial distance in his fiction, and several have complained about the resulting solipsism. Remarking on the similarities between Tarnopol and Roth, John McDaniel tentatively concluded in a 1974 booklength study that "These parallels merely invite us to consider certain *proximities,* however, and I am not suggesting that Roth's fiction is to be read as thinly-disguised autobiography."[16] But other critics have gone further in their attack on the autobiographical element of Roth's fiction. Pierre Michel complains that "Roth betrays a turn of mind that exhibits a capacity for endless variations on similar themes that are limited to near-pathological behavior. We may wonder indeed if all those obsessions are not simply Philip Roth's. . . ."[17] A more severe indictment appears in a *Newsweek* review of *The Professor of Desire.* With the "cumulative failure" of Roth's inability to create objective characters, "it becomes increasingly difficult to credit the traditional distinction between narrator and author—the convention that asks us to believe that no matter what self-serving foolishness the narrator serves up, the author sees him clearly and has presented him that way for specific strategic (or artistic, if you like) reasons."[18] Without endorsing this harsh judgment, which neglects the strategic mirroring techniques of a novel like *My Life as a Man* and the deliberate juxtaposition of illusion and reality, we may still ask to what extent Roth's novel reads like thinly disguised autobiography, especially the long account of Tarnopol's psychoanalysis.

There can be no doubt anymore. This is confirmed by the discovery of the actual 30-page essay published in a psychoanalytic journal which serves as the major source of the controversy between Tarnopol and Spielvogel. And in light of Roth's retaliatory response, nothing could be more ironic than the title of Dr. Hans J. Kleinschmidt's essay appearing in the 1967 spring-summer issue of *American Imago:* "The Angry Act: The Role of Aggression in Creativity."[19]

Along with six other essays devoted to the theme of creativity and psychopathology, "The Angry Act" seeks to establish a wider framework for the understanding of the creative process than traditional psychoanalytic theory has allowed. The author argues in the beginning of the essay that concepts such as sublimation of libido, neutralization of energy, and regression in the service of the ego are reductive because they do not affirm the adaptive, integrative aspects of the creative process. In rejecting these classical formulations, however, he proposes a theory of the artistic temperament that is based on several questionable assertions: The childhood of the artist is burdened by his awareness of being special or different; the artist is forced to rely on narcissism as a primary defense against overdependency on his mother, whom he idealizes; and, as a consequence of his narcissism, the artist is filled with anger and remains indifferent to the needs of others. Based on the evidence offered in "The Angry Act," one cannot generalize, as the analyst does, that all artists are narcissistic or that they all perceive their mothers as unobtainable and their fathers as inadequate. Nor does he distinguish healthy narcissism from pathological narcissism, as Otto Kernberg and other theoreticians have insisted upon. (Why is the artist necessarily more narcissistic than other people, including psychoanalysts?) Nevertheless, there is truth in the thesis that for some writers, art may reflect sublimated aggression. Arguing that the "artist is the uncommitted criminal who remains passive and is ambivalent about his passivity," Dr. Kleinschmidt maintains that, in contrast to the criminal, the artist does not act on his destructive fantasies. Instead, his artistic achievement allows him to confront reality without involving himself in it. "To have established the unique identity and accomplished the near-perfect artistic object means to have committed the crime, the angry act . . ." (p. 116).

Most of "The Angry Act" is devoted to a discussion of Kandinsky and

Thomas Mann, but, toward the end of the article, the analyst introduces case-study material based upon two of his own patients, a painter and a Southern playwright. The analyst disguises (or "fictionalizes") their identity to preserve medical confidentiality, but Roth unmasks the identity of the writer by basing the fictional Spielvogel's essay, "Creativity: The Narcissism of the Artist," closely upon "The Angry Act." A comparison of the medical case study and *My Life as a Man* clearly demonstrates that Roth based the clinical interpretations of Tarnopol's illness on the material Dr. Kleinschmidt discusses in the 1967 article. First comes the real analyst's discussion in "The Angry Act." "A successful Southern playwright in his early forties illustrates the interplay of narcissism and aggression while his points of fixation are later [than those of the painter] and his conflicts oedipal rather than pre-oedipal. He came into therapy because of anxiety states experienced as a result of his tremendous ambivalence about leaving his wife, three years his senior" (p. 123). Roth's fictional analyst, Dr. Spielvogel, puts it this way in *My Life as a Man*. "A successful Italian-American poet in his forties entered into therapy because of anxiety states experienced as a result of his enormous ambivalence about leaving his wife" (p. 239). Castration anxiety is important in the interpretations of both the real and fictional analyst. "It soon became apparent that his main problem was his castration anxiety vis-à-vis a phallic mother figure," writes the analyst in "The Angry Act" (p. 124). "It soon became clear that the poet's central problem here as elsewhere was his castration anxiety vis-à-vis a phallic mother figure," writes the analyst in *My Life as a Man* (pp. 240–241). The characterization of the father is identical. "His father was ineffectual and submissive to the mother" ("The Angry Act," p. 124); "His father was a harassed man, ineffectual and submissive to his mother" (*My Life as a Man,* p. 241). Both analysts view their patients as acting out repressed sexual anger. "His way of avoiding a confrontation with his feelings of anger and his dependency needs toward his wife was to act out sexually with other women. He had been doing this almost from the beginning of his marriage" ("The Angry Act," p. 125). Dr. Spielvogel echoes this interpretation. "In order to avoid a confrontation with his dependency needs toward his wife the poet acted out sexually with other women almost from the beginning of his marriage" (*My Life as a Man,* p. 242). Finally, the psychoanalysts offer the identical interpretation of their patients' hostility toward women. "The playwright acted out his anger in his relationships with women, reducing all of them to masturbatory sexual objects and by using his hostile masturbatory fantasies in his literary output" ("The Angry Act," p. 125). "The poet acted out his anger in his relationships with women, reducing all women to masturbatory sexual objects" (*My Life as a Man*, p. 242).

The ironies are astonishing and extend everywhere. Roth never expected anyone to make the connection between "The Angry Act" and *My Life as a Man*. Or did he? It is now clear that Roth's fiction is more autobiographical than anyone has suggested and that Dr. Spielvogel owes his existence to a real psychoanalyst. In *My Life as a Man* Spielvogel argues that, in Tarnopol's opinion, the analyst "plagiarized and abused" his words. If so, Roth has stolen back the analyst's words, as if to authenticate, however unbeknown to the reader, Spielvogel's character.

More importantly, "The Angry Act" serves as an invaluable bridge between *Portnoy's Complaint* and *My Life as a Man*. We can now appreciate for the first time the continuity between both novels. It is clear, for example, that Tarnopol's psychoanalysis recapitulates Portnoy's adventures and misadventures in therapy. Indeed, *Portnoy's Complaint* unexpectedly owes a great deal to "The Angry Act." Roth playfully attributes "Portnoy's Complaint" syndrome to Spielvogel's learned essay, "The Puzzled Penis," published in an authentic-sounding and properly Germanic journal, *Internationale Zeitschrift für Psychoanalyse*. "The Puzzled Penis" is none other than "The Angry Act" in disguise. Spielvogel's sentence (which Roth uses as the frontispiece of *Portnoy's Complaint*)—"Acts of exhibitionism, voyeurism, fetishism, auto-eroticism, and oral coitus are plentiful"—parodies the real psychoanalyst's language: "Practices of voyeurism, exhibitionism and fetishism abound" ("The Angry Act," p. 125). Every incident described by Spielvogel in *My Life as a Man* corresponds to a similar incident in the analyst's discussion of the Southern playwright in "The Angry Act." And "The Angry Act" remains an indispensable commentary upon *Portnoy's Complaint*. In fact, the two novels and the psychoanalytic essay represent an unparalleled example of the symbiotic relationship between literature and therapy. The major difference between *Portnoy's Complaint* and *My Life as a Man* is that, whereas the earlier novel apparently confirms the analyst's clinical interpretation in "The Angry Act," the later novel ingeniously attempts to refute the charge of the artist's narcissistic personality. It is as if *Portnoy's Complaint* and *My Life as a Man* represent, transferentially, the loving idealization and harsh devaluation of the analyst, respectively. This does not imply that Tarnopol's dispute with

Spielvogel over the publication of the analyst's essay can be dismissed simply as negative transference. Nothing is simple about Roth's extraordinarily complex relationship to psychoanalysis.

Interestingly, the proliferation of psychiatric case studies arising from Roth's life and art has led to a lively public forum in which several analysts, real and fictional, have reached remarkably similar conclusions about the Roth hero. There is no evidence to indicate that Bruno Bettelheim was aware of "The Angry Act" when he published his satirical essay, but his own Spielvogel confirms many of Dr. Kleinschmidt's observations, namely, that the patient's complaint of an overprotective mother disguises the deep disappointment that she was not more exclusively devoted to her son, that the complaint of an ineffectual father disguises the wish for a castrating father to restore the son's faith in male power, and that the writer's incessant barrage of words is a reaction against the withholding father. The belief that the Roth hero reduces women into masturbatory sexual objects—a charge Tarnopol emphatically denies—has been echoed by many other critics. In a thoughtful review of *The Professor of Desire,* Patricia Meyer Spacks complains about Roth's inability to imagine women as full-fledged human beings who are not hopelessly dependent upon men. "The women in *The Professor of Desire,* like those in *Portnoy* and *My Life as a Man,* objectify male fantasies, infinitely ingenious in lust or endlessly cooperative with masculine demands or totally bitchy, devoid of identity apart from their central relationships."[20]

The discovery of "The Angry Act" allows us to see the process in which a novelist transforms a psychiatric case study into a work of fiction and how the artist's conscious intentions are often shaped by unconscious forces. It is a psychological truism that observation and interpretation inevitably change the phenomena under scrutiny; Heisenberg's principle of uncertainty applies to psychoanalysis as well as to physics. Accordingly, the analyst's observations in "The Angry Act" have coincided with conspicuous changes in Roth's subsequent fiction. The castrating Jewish mother and ineffectual father no longer appear in Roth's novels, and the parents cease to be objects of the son's attack. Whether this is due to the novelist's conscious repudiation of the psychoanalyst's interpretation or the writer's interest in imagining other relationships is impossible to say. Significantly, the one major change Roth makes in incorporating "The Angry Act" into *My Life as a Man* lacks aesthetic conviction. In the psychiatric case study, the analyst discloses the patient's overinvolvement with his wife's 14-year-old son from another marriage. "He was emotionally quite involved with the stepson and used the boy's dependency on him and his feelings of guilt if he abandoned him, as an excuse for his inability to make a decision concerning the divorce" ("The Angry Act," p. 123). Roth transforms this into Zuckerman's Humbertlike dependency upon Lydia Ketterer's crass teenage daughter Moonie in "Courting Disaster." The incestuous relationship reinforces the Daddy's Girl theme and thus suggests an Oedipal component in Tarnopol's need to rescue Maureen from her brutal past. Nevertheless, the Zuckerman-Moonie relationship remains improbable, and one can only imagine how Tarnopol—and Roth—would have handled the writer's devotion to a teenage stepson. Elsewhere, Roth has convincingly described the hero's quest for an idealized father figure. In *The Ghost Writer*, Zuckerman warmly admires the distinguished Jewish-American writer E. I. Lonoff. Zuckerman's unexpected affirmation of the patriarchal father represents one of the major postanalytic developments in Roth's fiction.

How do we finally evaluate Roth's relationship to "The Angry Act"? To say the least, the novelist shrewdly exploited the self-fulfilling ironies of the title. Psychoanalysis liberated the artist's imagination in *Portnoy's Complaint* and then provoked his sharp counterattack in *My Life as a Man*. Although "The Angry Act" does not persuasively demonstrate the relationship between narcissism and art in the works of Kandinsky and Mann, it does accurately describe the centrality of narcissism and aggression in Roth's fictional world. Appropriately, in *Reading Myself and Others*, Roth confirms the thesis of art or satire as aggression. "What begins as the desire to murder your enemy with blows, and is converted (largely out of fear of the consequences) into the attempt to murder him with invective and insult, is most thoroughly sublimated, or socialized, in the art of satire. It's the imaginative flowering of the primitive urge to knock somebody's block off" (p. 53). Roth's colorful language and imagery, which are far closer to Spielvogel's paradigm of reality in *My Life as a Man* than to Tarnopol's insistence upon the inscrutability of reality, may be interpreted both as a tribute to his analyst's insight and as a wry acknowledgment of the novelist's urge to "murder" him in his art. However, there is also a more positive interpretation of the creative process, in which the artist seeks reparation from an earlier psychic injury. Behind Tarnopol's fiction lies a strong counterphobic motive suggestive of the mysterious relationship between neurotic suffering and artistic creativity. There can be little doubt about the adaptive and integrative implications of the artist's decision to write about his own illness in the attempt to gain mastery over it. This does not imply, of course, that every work of art is successful therapeutically, or that it is always possible to distinguish between the neurotic repetition of an illness (acting out) or the successful resolution of conflict (working through).

From one point of view, the nearly simultaneous publication of *Portnoy's Complaint* and "The Angry Act" was an unfortunate accident. One can appreciate Roth's anger when he discovered that an embarrassing incident appearing in an early chapter of *Portnoy's Complaint*—"The Jewish Blues," published in the first issue of *New American Review* in September 1967—contained material that his analyst used in "The Angry Act" published at about the same time.[21] Roth rightly feared that anyone reading "The Jewish Blues" and "The Angry Act" would be able to identify him as the source of the analyst's "Southern playwright." From another point of view, however, the accident gave birth to one of Roth's most impressive literary creations, *My Life as a Man,* in which the novelist painstakingly explores the relationship between the creative and therapeutic process. Although Tarnopol bitterly accuses Spielvogel of opening up his life to biographical scrutiny through the untimely and insufficiently disguised psychiatric case study, it is on the basis of *My Life as a Man,* not *Portnoy's Complaint,* that a reader is more likely to connect Roth to "The Angry Act." This observation, admittedly, does not free the critic from the dilemma of pursuing literary scholarship without calling attention to the accidental exposure of the patient-analyst relationship.[22] Nevertheless, by using the analyst's own language and by supplying the necessary biographical and bibliographical clues in *My Life as a Man* to locate the existence of the analyst's medical case study, Roth ambivalently invites the reading public to participate vicariously in his own psychoanalysis. To write about one's life in this way by using a published psychiatric case study as a major text of a purportedly fictional work seems both brave and risky, enlightening and self-justifying. Readers will doubtlessly come to different conclusions about whose version of reality is closer to the truth, the novelist's or psychoanalyst's.

Tarnopol's amiable departure from Spielvogel in *My Life as a Man* signals Roth's movement away from psychoanalysis. Maureen Tarnopol's violent death "releases" but does not "free" her husband at the end of the novel, a distinction upon which Spielvogel insists. The last sentence of the story—"This me who is me being me and none other!"—evokes the protagonist's thwarted movement, the maddening circularity of a broken record. "If there is an ironic acceptance of anything at the conclusion of

My Life as a Man," Roth remarks in *Reading Myself and Others,* "it is of the *determined* self. And angry frustration, a deeply vexing sense of characterological enslavement, is strongly infused in that ironic acceptance. Thus the exclamation mark" (p. 108). Despite all the problems of Tarnopol's psychoanalysis and the unprecedented controversy over the issue of patient-analyst confidentiality, the talking cure has helped to untangle or at least clarify the writer's determined self. Nor is Dr. Spielvogel the last of Roth's fictional psychoanalysts. In *The Professor of Desire,* we read about David Kepesh's analyst, Dr. Klinger, a "solid, reasonable man" who is a generalist in common sense. A key figure in psychoanalytic circles, as modern in dress as Spielvogel is old-fashioned European, Klinger is a "snazzy energetic conquistador." Klinger demythologizes Kepesh's unstable wife, Helen, and offers him the practical advice and ironic humor that restore the young man's sanity. Although the analytic sessions in *The Professor of Desire* seem anticlimactic in comparison to Tarnopol's tempestuous relations with Spielvogel, Roth succeeds in dramatizing the affection, humor, and goodwill implicit in the Kepesh-Klinger relationship. Klinger sounds less like an analyst than a warm-hearted father—a transference Roth is content not to analyze. If we read Roth's fiction as a continuing drama of a protagonist's arduous self-analysis, then Kepesh's warm farewell to Dr. Klinger in *The Professor of Desire* represents a moving valediction to Philip Roth's psychoanalysts. Leaving Klinger for the last time, Kepesh shakes the analyst's hand and, in response to the invitation to "Stay in touch," the patient declares: "Let's hope I don't have to." Filled with elation and gratitude, which he dares not express out of fear of an outburst of tears, Kepesh leaves Klinger's office and thinks: "I've come through!" (pp. 158–159).

TEN

Freud Revisited:
The White Hotel

Long may poetry and psychoanalysis continue to highlight, from their different perspectives, the human face in all its nobility and sorrow.
"Sigmund Freud," *The White Hotel*[1]

READING D. M. THOMAS' *The White Hotel* (1981) is like discovering a lost Shakespeare play: It is as if "Frau Anna G.," the
fictional Freudian case study that serves as the centerpiece of the novel,
has existed since the turn of the century, no less real or vivid than *Dora*,
the *Rat Man*, or the *Wolf Man*—stories whose enduring literary interest
transcends the narrow confines of psychiatric literature. The reader is
stunned by the authenticity and power of Thomas' novel. Within its
structure lies an exquisitely complex and elegantly written case study that
comes eerily close to a study that the historical Freud might have written
had he created a sixth major case history. Thomas' fictional Freud is,
without question, the most majestic portrait of the analyst that has yet
appeared in imaginative literature. Never before, not even in Roth's *My
Life as a Man*, has a novelist so brilliantly captured the psychoanalytic
process, including Freud's audacious exploration of the psyche, the relentless tracing back of symptoms to their distant childhood aetiology,
and the magical nature of the talking cure. Yet, "Frau Anna G." is only
one section of *The White Hotel*. The neurotic illness that besets Lisa Erdman reflects a larger force assaulting modern civilization. Thomas ambi-
tiously presents us with a case history of the twentieth century—an analysis of hysteria and World War, a biography of a self-tormented young
woman and a war-ravaged century, a story of the age-old battle between
love and death.

The White Hotel consists of seven parts, including a prologue. Each part is tightly connected to the others and must be analyzed in depth. The reader must decipher the bewildering chronology of events and compare the ways in which Lisa transforms external events—including apocalyptic fires, sexual violations, and catastrophic falls—into her poetry and prose. Thomas' heroine begins psychoanalysis with Freud in the fall of 1919 at about the time when the historical analyst is working on the manuscript of his controversial *Beyond the Pleasure Principle*. Lisa has been suffering for years from what appear to be hysterical symptoms—breathlessness that has been mistakenly diagnosed as asthma, pains in her left breast and ovary, and morbid hallucinations of fire. A few months into treatment, Freud's daughter unexpectedly dies, and he temporarily suspends the analysis. With her aunt, Lisa travels to a health resort in the Austrian Alps, Bad Gastein, where she writes a long erotic poem based upon a transference fantasy of making love to Freud's son Martin, whose photograph she has seen in the analyst's office. She later writes a longer prose narrative in the form of a journal based on the same fantasy. Freud analyzes the two remarkable documents and succeeds in tracing back Lisa's hysterical symptoms to several traumatic events in her early childhood, including the death of her mother and uncle in a hotel fire. Lisa's analysis with Freud ends in 1920 with the remission of her symptoms. But *The White Hotel* does not end here. Remarrying late in life after a disastrous early marriage, Lisa experiences happiness for the first time, but the joy is cut short when she and her husband are separated by the turbulent events of World War II. Along with tens of thousands of other Jews, she and her stepson are murdered at the infamous ravine in Babi Yar. In a breath-taking coda to the novel, she is resurrected and reunited with her dead friends and relatives in an other-worldly Palestinian refugee camp after the war.

The prologue of *The White Hotel* opens with an exchange of letters among Freud, Sandor Ferenczi, and Hanns Sachs. Although these letters, along with all case studies in the novel, are fictional, Thomas' Freud abides by the generally known facts of his historical counterpart's life. We overhear Ferenczi writing in 1909 to his future wife Gisela about the whirlwind tour of America he, Freud, and Jung have embarked upon. One detail in the letter stands out, a dream Ferenczi recalls concerning Gisela's anxiety over divorcing her first husband to marry the Hungarian psychoanalyst. Later, in "Frau Anna G.," Lisa narrates a dream to Freud in which she telepathically intuits the death of Gisela's husband. Like so many of the details in *The White Hotel*, this is based upon historical fact. Gisela's first husband committed suicide on the day she married Ferenczi; the suicide was hushed up by the psychoanalytic community.[2] This is one of the numerous uncanny premonitions and telepathic experiences that come true in the novel.

The other letters of the prologue heighten the reader's interest in Freud's patient. In a letter to Ferenczi on February 9, 1920, Freud grieves over the tragic death of his daughter, Sophie Halberstadt, who died on January 25 at the age of 26. She left behind two young children, one of whom, Heinz, was to die three years later—an event Lisa also predicts. Quoting from Schiller and Goethe, Thomas' Freud refers to the "deep narcissistic hurt" that is not to be healed. The letter has the ring of authenticity to it, and no wonder. The novelist has used one of the actual letters written by the historical Freud.[3] Thomas' analyst then refers to his new manuscript, *Beyond the Pleasure Principle,* wherein he posits a "death instinct, as powerful in its own way (though more hidden) as the libido." In the same paragraph, he mentions for the first time a young female patient who has just "given birth" to some writings which lend support to his new theory. The prologue concludes with three other brief letters, one in which Freud tells Sachs about his patient's remarkable writings, a "genuine pseudocyesis"; a postcard from Sachs to Freud in which he interprets the patient's fantasy as "like Eden before the Fall"; and a third in which Freud forwards "Frau Anna G." along with the patient's own writings to the Goethe Centenary Committee in 1931 for publication in a special volume honoring the psychoanalyst's contributions to literature.

Part I of *The White Hotel,* entitled "Don Giovanni," is a 375-line poem consisting of irregularly rhyming couplets. An erotic fantasy written in the first person, the poem celebrates the terrible beauty of sensual love. The imagery dramatizes the clash between Eros and Thanatos. The poem, we learn later, is written in a three-day period at the end of January and beginning of February 1920 while Lisa is awaiting resumption of her analysis with Freud. In the poem, which is written between the staves of a score of *Don Giovanni,* she imagines Martin Freud as a Don Juan who makes love to her on a train and then takes her to a white lakeside hotel where they spend a week of shameless passion. Their orgiastic lovemaking is shattered by catastrophes befalling the white hotel. The roof of a summer-house pagoda comes crashing down in a storm. Several people drown on the lake. Engaged in frenzied intercourse while sailing on the lake, Lisa witnesses a blaze coming from the hotel. She screams in delight from being sexually impaled by Martin, but no one hears her cries, for they are lost in the horrified wailings of people plunging to their death from the upper stories of the hotel. She dreams of a whale moaning a lullaby to her corset, a breast sheared away, the birth of a wooden embryo. She awakens in relief to discover her body still intact. Like the spirit of the white hotel, her body has a restorative effect on the other guests. Her breasts supply endless milk for the men who gratefully drink from them, including a kindly old priest and the hotel's chef. Despite the disasters occurring to the guests, "no one was selfish in the white hotel" (p. 28). The endless penetration of Lisa's body only intensifies her desire; nothing seems out of place in the white hotel, not even the marriage of Eros and Thanatos. In its Chagall-like surrealism and Lawrentian eroticism, Lisa's poem leaves the reader confused but transfixed.

How do we judge Lisa's wildly original verse? Are her writings an example of psychopathological ruminations or visionary art? Are her "brain storms" symptomatic of a neurotic disorder or a manifestation of a singular poetic sensibility able to intuit a hidden reality glimpsed only by the mystic poet? In short, are we dealing with hysteria or history? The nightmarish quality of her experience points to a bad dream or private horror, but the historical events that frame the poet's life lend objectivity to her vision. The wild storm battering the hotel is not simply one woman's mental agony but an entire century's monstrous upheaval, just as the hotel fire prefigures the conflagration of world war. Not even the idyllic seclusion of the hotel can protect it from menacing reality. Although Freud elaborates upon the rich symbolism of the white hotel in his case study, it is apparent from the beginning of the novel that it represents the maternal body, a garden of earthly delights miraculously able to survive the harshest environment. The fantasied lover who ravishes the poet's body symbolizes not only the Oedipal father but the boundless reservoir of libidinal instinct and autoeroticism Lisa draws upon in pleasure and solace. For Thomas, "narcissism" is as affirmative as life itself.

Yet not even the pleasure principle can deflect the dreamer's compulsion to repeat terrifying reality. The disasters to which the poet bears witness testify to the dualistic power of nature to create and to destroy. In its ability to conjure up the child's image of prelapsarian Eden, the inevitable movement toward darkness and death, and the incantatory rhythms and hallucinatory imagery, "Don Giovanni" evokes Dylan Thomas' poetry. Surprisingly, there is little mention of human cruelty in Lisa's poem. The embattled guests are united in their communal resolve to withstand the harsh elements. Only later in the novel does violence take on a recognizably human form. Yet there are disturbing hints of sadism in the poem, along with the most vexing question in *The White Hotel:* the meaning of Lisa's psychic powers. The description of sexual impalement amidst the screams of the falling bodies from the fiery hotel foreshadows the Russian soldier's bayonet at Babi Yar, which is used to rape and murder Lisa. And the line of mourners in the gloom anticipates the image of thousands of Jewish victims cast into the deep pits by the conscripted Russians. This too is described in gruesome detail in a later section of the story.

We gain a deeper insight into the writer's mind in the next chapter of the novel, "The Gastein Journal," a 55-page prose narrative that elaborates upon the erotic fantasy of "Don Giovanni." The lyrical first person poem gives way to the evocative journal in which Lisa creates a host of characters residing in the white hotel. Both the poem and journal open with a similar dream in which the young woman finds herself running through a woods. In the poem she is running to escape a wild storm, while in the journal she is fleeing from soldiers. Unable to disappear through a trap door or to make herself invisible by merging into the trees, she prepares for her death. She looks into the frightened face of a small boy who reassures her: "Don't be frightened, lady . . . I'm alive too" (p. 32). As she crawls through the woods with the boy trailing her, she feels bullets "pumping into her right shoulder, quite gently" (p. 32). With that, she awakens to find herself on a train traveling to Bad Gastein. Her premonition of death is not averted, only postponed.

In "The Gastein Journal" Lisa meets a Viennese soldier, Martin Freud, who is returning home from the Great War. The two engage in shameless lovemaking, oblivious to the startled ticket collector who gazes at them. A train carries them to a remote hotel in the mountains where they spend a passionate interlude. Once again Eros leads to Thanatos as the plot repeats the catastrophic events described in "Don Giovanni." It is as if the soldier's frenzied assault on the young woman's body leads to the devastation of the white hotel. At once violent and tender, selfish and generous, the sexual storm never abates. Inexplicable events astound the guests: falling stars large as maple leaves, a livid stroke of lightning, a school of whales. A mysterious force animates the world of the white hotel, a force that is at once ominous and magical. The guests testify to weird sightings and phantasmagoric happenings. A statesman conjectures that the presence of the whales may be explained by the appearance of Madame Cottin, a corsetière whose corset, made of dead whale, has "called" the whales.

A flying breast, petrified embryo, and gliding womb elicit statements from various female guests who have undergone surgery for removal of parts of their bodies.

Despite these and other tragic events, life returns to normal, and the two lovers deepen their relationship to each other and to the guests. "My father says there are four people present whenever lovemaking takes place," Martin tells Lisa. "They are here now, of course. My parents" (p. 62). The allusion is to a letter the historical Freud writes to Fliess in 1899 affirming the role of bisexuality.[4] In a curious transubstantiation, Lisa's breasts begin to give out milk. Her ample body and generosity of spirit revive the passion of the ailing guests, especially a kindly old Catholic priest whose religious certainties symbolize her feelings toward Freud, who holds out the promise of psychoanalytic healing. "The Gastein Journal" ends with a celebration of the beauty and generosity of the white hotel, its miraculous regenerative power, and its ability to withstand the most devastating assaults on the human spirit.

No plot summary of Lisa's writings can reproduce their startling eroticism and incandescent glow. The artist conveys a sensitivity that never becomes solipsistic or sentimental. She strikes us as neither sick nor self-absorbed. She remains the antithesis of the hypochondriacal patient: She is always aware of the suffering of others. Just as the white hotel symbolizes the fecundity of the maternal body, so does it evoke the creative mystery of art. Despite Freud's successful reconstruction of his patient's childhood in the next section of *The White Hotel*, "Frau Anna G.," Lisa's art remains, in the final analysis, a miracle. The themes of her art may arise from her neurotic obsessions, but the form and technique affirm artistic control. She succeeds in suspending our disbelief, in making us see the wondrous world of the white hotel, with all its logical improbabilities. On nearly every page of the journal a delight awaits us, as in this description of the sky: "And every few moments a star would slide diagonally through the black sky, like a maple leaf drifting from the branch or the way lovers rearrange themselves with gentle movements while they sleep" (p. 43). The comparison of a shooting star to a drifting leaf and sleeping lovers suggests a literary sensibility of the first order, able to unify contradictions and intuit new truths. Nothing in Lisa's biography accounts for the vision of lovers rearranging themselves with gentle movement while they sleep; terms such as sublimation cannot explain her gift for language or her reverence for life.

Readers of *The White Hotel* may feel torn between two contradictory approaches to the novel, the desire to analyze (and psychoanalyze) the patient's multilayered accounts of reality, decoding her symbolism and unpacking her language, versus the equally strong inclination to accept the mystery of her art, to remain content with half-knowledge, to affirm in Keats's words the *"Negative Capability"* of art: "That is when man is capable of being in uncertainties, Mysteries, doubts, without any irritable reaching after fact & reason."[5] Lisa's mastery of lyrical poetry and prose fiction, haunting aural and visual imagery, and evocation of the Woolfian "moment" *(The White Hotel* points in the direction of *To the Lighthouse)* identify her as a major artist, able to transmute personal suffering into enduring literature. The only unbelievable detail about her writings is that they could have been created so quickly and effortlessly, without the laborious revision that usually accompanies serious art. "The Gastein Journal" ends with an image of swans soaring between mountain peaks, an image less sexual than transcendent.

Like his historical counterpart, one of the supreme rationalists of his age, Thomas' Freud is relentlessly analytical. Devoid of the lyricism and mysticism of "Don Giovanni" and "The Gastein Journal," "Frau Anna G." reflects the psychoanalyst's herculean efforts to discover the root causes of his patient's suffering and to reconstruct her shadowy past. Thomas' Freud embodies the diverse roles of the analyst: historian, lawyer, detective, biographer, novelist, therapist, confessor. He exists as a real person to Lisa, listening to her complaints, eliciting her fantasies and fears, offering sympathy and understanding. He also exists as a projection figure of her imagination, which transforms him through the phenomenon of transference into a multitude of roles: insatiable Don Juan, father confessor, trusted friend.

In the "Author's Note" to *The White Hotel,* Thomas refers readers to the historical Freud's case studies, which the novelist calls "masterly works of literature, apart from everything else." It is equally clear that he has created his own masterly work of literature in "Frau Anna G." Following Thomas' clue, we may turn to Freud's actual case studies to discover the novelist's indebtedness to the psychoanalyst. It is no disparagement of Thomas' achievement to learn that he has taken many passages from *Studies on Hysteria* (1893–1895), the starting point of psychoanalysis. Lisa's reluctance to reveal the "storms in her head" (p. 90) echoes "Frau Emmy von R."[6] In fact, the opening paragraphs of "Frau Anna G." repeat, at times word for word, the opening descriptions of Freud's "Fräulein Elisabeth von R." in *Studies on Hysteria.*[7] In particular, they describe how Freud

came to treat his patient, her symptomatology, the details of the first interview, and the theoretical discussion of hysteria. Many of the sentences
in Thomas' fictional psychiatric case study come straight from *Studies on
Hysteria:* "What she had in her consciousness was only a secret and not a
foreign body" (*The White Hotel*, p. 99).[8] A long description near the end
of "Frau Anna G." pertaining to the patient's resistance is taken almost
verbatim from "Fräulein Elisabeth von R." In both the fictional and historical case study, the analyst offers identical consolation. "The degree of
suffering, and the intensity of her struggle, did not slacken until I offered
her my two pieces of consolation—that we are not responsible for our
feelings; and that her behaviour, the fact that she had fallen ill in these
circumstances, was sufficient evidence of her moral character" (*The White
Hotel*, pp. 135–136).[9] The fictional Freud's reassurance to Lisa—"much will
be gained if we succeed in turning your hysterical misery into common
unhappiness" (p. 127)—echoes Freud's famous conclusion to *Studies on
Hysteria*.[10] In the same way, the ending of "Frau Anna G." recalls the
conclusion of "Miss Lucy R." in which Freud talks about meeting his
former patient by chance in a summer resort.[11]

Nor does Thomas limit his borrowings to Freud's celebrated case studies; the novelist has also been reading the analyst's less well known technical papers. The fictional Freud's discussion of the limits of memory—
"I have my doubts if we ever deal with a memory *from* childhood; memories *relating* to childhood may be all that we possess" (*The White Hotel*,
p. 109)—comes verbatim from Freud's essay "Screen Memories" (1899).[12]
And the fictional analyst's discussion of the breast as the first love object
(*The White Hotel*, p. 116) comes directly from the *Three Essays on the Theory of Sexuality* (1905).[13] Quite literally, then, the illnesses of Freud's patients have served as a major inspiration for *The White Hotel*.

Thomas also captures the historical analyst's instinctive gift for narration. Freud could not recite a case history without transforming it into a
story. In *Studies on Hysteria*, he apologized for the fact that although he
was trained as a neuropathologist, his case histories "read like short stories" and, he was afraid, lack the "serious stamp of science."[14] He disin-
genuously suggests that it is the nature of the subject rather than his own
artistry that is responsible for his affinity to imaginative writers. The truth
is, of course, that Freud was a consummate storyteller whose case histories read like novels.[15] Thomas' Freud begins "Frau Anna G." by sum-
marizing his patient's symptoms, recording the opening interviews, and
evoking her character in a few strokes of dialogue. Like a novelist, he

remains interested in character for its own sake, and he reveals an extraordinary ability to enter into another point of view. Quoting Charcot, he remarks that "Theory is good but it doesn't prevent the facts from existing." Thomas captures the one-step-forward-two-steps-backward rhythm of psychoanalysis in which insight produces resistance and retreat. The analyst's method of narration anticipates the impressionistic novelist. Because Lisa is always retracting or modifying her story, we are continually thrown off balance, as her doctor is, and forced to read backwards as well as forwards.

The veils are constantly lifted and dropped. As in a detective story, the reader must circle back to recover the clues necessary for forward movement. In the actual case histories, Freud invents a new type of narration to imitate the general rule of inverse chronological order that is characteristic of psychoanalysis. The patient begins with the most recent and least important impressions; only at the end does he usually reach the primary impression which has the greatest causal significance.[16] The longer analysis proceeds, the farther back into time the patient travels until he has overcome infantile amnesia. This is Freud's narrative strategy in the case studies and the fictional analyst's technique in "Frau Anna G." The doctor's narrative power never falters in *The White Hotel*. He deciphers a confusing and contradictory story, imposing order to his patient's disjointed statements. When he is wrong, it is because of a brilliant inference based upon misleading evidence the patient has conveyed to him.

It would be hard to imagine a better listener than Thomas' Freud. Like his historical counterpart, he has a photographic memory and nothing escapes his attention. He subtly encodes clues into the early pages of the narrative and decodes them at the end. He tells us, for example, that Lisa was forced to abandon her dancing career because "she was becoming a woman, and gaining flesh which she could not lose, even though she was eating next to nothing" (p. 95). Only later does he reveal that his normally anorexic patient had become secretly pregnant and that the pregnancy was aborted in a fall. In recounting the improbable events of her life, he apologizes for imposing upon the reader's belief. "Were I a writer of novellas instead of a man of science," he says, echoing Freud's prefatory remarks in *Dora*, "I should hesitate to offend against my readers' artistic sensibilities . . ." (pp. 111–112). And like a good storyteller, he is always aware of his audience.

Thomas presents us with an immensely appealing portrait of Freud. He is a Promethean figure, unwilling to allow anything, including his own personal suffering, to interfere with his efforts to uncover the mysteries of the psyche. We see courage amidst adversity, the refusal to indulge in self-pity even when he suffers the devastating loss of his daughter in 1920 and his grandson in 1923. Thomas captures Freud's imagery and irony, stoicism and compassion. Invoking literature, mythology, and philosophy, the narrator of "Frau Anna G." compares his patient to Medusa, Cassandra, Ceres. Like the master prose stylist who received the Goethe Award for Literature, Thomas' Freud enriches his case study with allusions to *A Midsummer Night's Dream, The Possessed,* Goethe's "Wanderer's Song at Night," and G. von Strassburg's *Tristan.* The allusions are made effortlessly, reflecting Freud's vast humanistic learning.

Significantly, Thomas' Freud is not guilty of the serious technical and empathic failures the real analyst committed in his only major case study of a woman, *Fragment of an Analysis of a Case of Hysteria.* Freud's treatment of Dora has been justifiably criticized by psychoanalysts and feminists alike for his surprising belligerence toward the troubled adolescent, and his premature and intrusive interpretations. The story of Dora betrays an aggressive and vindictive Freud who seems offended by his patient's vanity and annoyed by her resistance.[17] By contrast, Thomas' Freud coaxes and guides his patient toward difficult truths without becoming overly confrontive. He does become impatient with her on occasion, but Thomas softens these moments by the candor of the analyst's admissions. He remains deeply human throughout "Frau Anna G." He has no trouble in maintaining a proper distance from her, neither encouraging nor discouraging her Oedipal fantasies. There is remarkably little countertransference, apart from the curious decision to name his patient after his last daughter who, in 1931 (when the fictional analyst completes the manuscript of "Frau Anna G."), was serving as his nurse during the painful years he was suffering from cancer of the jaw.

Lisa is very aware of Freud's greatness, and, perhaps because of her premonitions of the lurking tragedies in his life, she is extraordinarily sensitive to his feelings and apparently free of any unconscious hostility toward him.[18] The actual case studies, however, are filled with aggressive statements directed toward the analyst. Anna O. was abusive to Breuer. Frau Emmy von N. shouted at Freud, "Keep still! Don't say anything!— Don't touch me!"[19] The Rat Man hurled violent anal execrations at the analyst. In his first interview, the Wolf Man offered to defecate on Freud's head and engage in anal intercourse with him.[20] Thomas omits these stormy negative transference elements from "Frau Anna G.," presenting us instead with an admiring account of the patient-analyst relationship. Psychoanalysis proves to be a noble humanistic endeavor, with the patient and analyst collaborating in a single-minded pursuit of truth. Anyone who underestimates the complexity of psychoanalysis will appreciate the enormity of the analyst's task in "Frau Anna G.," and Thomas compels the reader to follow in Freud's footsteps as he investigates the sources of Lisa's hysteria. Yet "Frau Anna G." occupies only about a fifth of *The White Hotel,* and Freud's point of view is not omniscient.

Freud first meets Lisa in 1919. Her presenting symptoms are severe pains in the left breast and pelvic region, and a chronic respiratory condition. She is 29-years old, married but separated from her husband and living with her aunt. Illness has cut short a promising musical career. Freud interviews her and is alarmed by the extent of her physical suffering and her extreme thinness. She seems to be literally starving herself to death and, like Anna O., subsisting entirely on oranges.[21] Unlike most hysterics she describes her pains precisely, betraying no erotic pleasure when Freud examines her.[22] Convinced her symptoms are organic, she confesses to suffering from frightful visual hallucinations for which she fears she will be locked away. After reassuring her that she is not mad, Freud begins a summary of her life to us. The second child and only daughter of moderately wealthy parents, she is born in the Ukraine in 1890. She has an older brother who never figures into the story. Her father is a Russian Jew and her mother a Polish Catholic. In marrying across racial and religious barriers, the parents incur the opposition of other family members. Only one relative, the mother's identical twin, remains close to them. The mother's sister is married to a Viennese teacher of languages. Shortly after her birth, Lisa and her family move to Odessa where her father is able to indulge his only relaxation, sailing on his splendid yacht.

The central loss in Lisa's life occurs at the age of five when her mother dies in a Budapest hotel fire. In analysis, she recalls a storm raging outside when she is told the news of the death. Freud links the storm to the tempest raging in her head. He connects two of her recurrent hallucinations in later life, a storm at sea and a fire in a hotel, to the tragic events surrounding maternal loss. Toward the end of analysis, Lisa retrieves another crucial memory with Freud's help. She discovers that her uncle had not died of a heart attack, as she was told, but had perished in the same hotel fire as her mother. Lisa's mother and uncle, it turns out, had been engaging in an illicit love affair. The revelation brings to the surface two other long-repressed incidents from early childhood. In 1893 she had wandered on to her father's yacht and witnessed a dreadful sight—her mother, aunt, and uncle performing intercourse *a tergo*. One or two years later, she sees her mother and uncle making love while her aunt lies asleep on the beach.

Freud reconstructs these dim childhood events on the basis of the symbolism of the white hotel in Lisa's writings. The white hotel, he observes, is the body of the mother, a place without sin or remorse. Interpreting the hotel as the wholehearted commitment to orality—"sucking, biting, eating, gorging, taking in, with all the blissful narcissism of a baby at the breast" (p. 116)—he views her art as evidence of a profound identification with the mother, preceding the Oedipus stage. Her writings indicate the attempt to be reunited with the long-dead mother, "to return to the time when oral erotism reigned supreme, and the bond between mother and child was unbroken." The good side of the white hotel represents the mother's nourishment and warmth, the lifelong pleasure she lovingly bequeathed to her child. The bad side of the hotel, the shadow of death, reflects the other side of the mother's character, the lust, deception, and selfishness surrounding the clandestine relationship to her sister's husband. Lisa cannot integrate the good and bad mother. Only at the end of therapy does she acknowledge for the first time her rage toward the mother. She admits that as a child she had wished her mother would die, a wish that comes true, to her horror. Through the omnipotence of thought, she comes to believe she has actually killed her. For her entire life, Lisa has remained oppressed by guilt and grief.

She recalls other distressing events in her life through free association. Imperfectly remembered details assume new clarity as she penetrates more deeply into her unconscious self. In the beginning of treatment, she relates a terrible incident that occurred to her when she was 15 years old. She and two other girls had improvidently ventured into the docks area of the city, only to be threatened by a group of insurgents. By the end of analysis she remembers, incorrectly, as it turns out, that the sailors had also made obscene remarks about her mother, saying that they knew she had died with a lover. Only several years after analysis does Lisa confide in a letter to Freud that the dock episode had been more terrifying than she previously admitted. A group of sailors from a merchant-marine ship carrying grain for her father had seized her, reviled her for being Jewish, and then forced her to perform oral sex with them. Her lifelong symptom of breathlessness originates from the act of fellatio. She never tells Freud about another event from which arises an additional symptom, her seduction on a train by a young officer (the "Martin Freud" of her poem and journal). The 17-year-old young woman's first act of sexual intercourse coincides with her first experience of hallucination. Soon after, she forms an attachment with a young student, "A" ("Alexei"). She tells Freud it was a "white" relationship, but he correctly deduces over her energetic protests that she had had an affair with him. Her use of the English word "fall" allows the analyst to reach one of his most intuitive insights, that she had become pregnant by Alexei and lost the baby in a fall. Freud does not pursue another suspicion, that she had unconsciously sought to abort the unwanted fetus.

Around this time, Lisa becomes friendly with a woman destined to play a major role in her life and art. Called "Madame R." in Freud's case study and "Madame Cottin" in Lisa's journal, Ludmila Kedrova is her ballet teacher and friend. A widow, she invites Lisa to live with her. The two women remain close friends even after Ludmila decides to marry a retired naval officer. Freud asks Lisa why she has transformed her friend into a corsetière in her writings. "Because she always stressed discipline, if we wanted to succeed in the ballet. Self-discipline to the point of pain" (p. 122). On the basis of Lisa's writings, Freud suspects a latent homosexual relationship between the women. He argues that, in Ludmila's home, Lisa's self-esteem is restored; Lisa transforms the older woman into an idealized mother with whom she fantasizes sexual intercourse in the poem and journal. This is the only part of Freud's interpretation that Lisa rejects.

Lisa's marriage to an Austrian lawyer proves to be painful when he turns out to be violently anti-Semitic. She is forced to conceal her half-Jewishness from him, just as she withholds from Freud her resentment and guilt over her Jewish heritage. In analysis, she reveals the details of her disastrous marriage, including the hallucinations that inevitably accompany her sexual life. The pretense of being transported into ecstasies of happiness disguises the terrifying hallucinations she later describes in her art: the hotel fire, flood, fall, and burial. Freud suggests that her hysterical illness originates as a pretense to justify separation from her dreaded husband. She neither confirms nor denies this interpretation, but, in a letter to the analyst in 1931, she confesses that she ended the marriage to her husband during the Great War because his anti-Semitism was literally making her ill. "He said he loved me; but if he had known I had Jewish blood he would have hated me. Whenever he said 'I love you' I understood it as 'I hate you'" (p. 190).

These are only the highlights of "Frau Anna G." Just as a summary of "Don Giovanni" and "The Gastein Journal" fails to capture their power to startle and delight the reader, so does a synopsis of Freud's psychiatric case study omit the unfolding intellectual drama. The analyst approaches his patient's symptoms as a literary critic approaches symbolism, as a revelation of inner reality. There is nothing reductive or farfetched in Freud's elucidation; he warns against rigid classification of sexual symbolism, preferring suggestive or evocative meanings. He wisely disobeys Lisa's request to destroy her manuscripts, which she has come to despise. He encourages her to analyze each passage of her art for clues into her past. He even enlists the help of his published case study, *From the History of an Infantile Neurosis* (1918), which he has given Lisa to read. It is one of the many fascinating intersections of history and fiction in *The White Hotel*. She eagerly questions Freud on the meaning of the Wolf Man's obsession with coitus *more ferarum,* and the analyst cannot help being reminded of a similar incident in her journal. He succeeds in deciphering an argument with Alexei during a weekend cruising holiday as a screen memory of the earlier yachting incident when the three-year-old child had witnessed her mother, aunt, and uncle performing intercourse *a tergo*.

Freud's analysis of Lisa's art is also impressive. Although he approaches her writings from a psychopathological point of view, with all the limitations of the theory that art is a substitute gratification, he admires her work and accords it the seriousness it deserves. He does not respond, admittedly, to the aesthetic quality of her writings, viewing her art instead as a revelation of the artist's unconscious mind. To this extent Thomas has accurately reproduced the historical Freud's approach to art. Moreover, the fictional analyst is at first shocked by the explicitness of his patient's sexual descriptions. Nevertheless, Freud's analysis illuminates the ways in which his patient weaves autobiography into art, including the hotel fire, the two yachting incidents in 1903 and 1910, the summer-house experience, the dock episode, and so on. He sees in her art the workings of both the pleasure principle and the repetition-compulsion principle. The lover in "Don Giovanni" and "The Gastein Journal" is a product of the transference fantasy toward Freud, the idealized father. The fantasy of marrying Freud's son suggests the need to heal the terrible loss created by the premature death of the analyst's daughter. In Kohutian terms, the merger with Martin Freud allows Lisa to create an idealized self-object who will heal the profound wound engendered by the neglect from her actual father. Through the creative process, she discovers the healthy mirroring and idealizing responses which strengthen her fragmented self. Art serves multiple needs: insight into reality, escape from an intolerable environment, and a new recreation of life in which the artist achieves reparation from a narcissistic injury and restitution for the loss of an object. Lisa's writings move toward catastrophe and rebirth, loss and recovery. Although Lisa's art repeats itself, it never becomes repetitive. Like the soaring swans at the end of "The Gastein Journal," the artist's imagination expands in ever-widening circles.

Before proceeding to the next section of *The White Hotel*, we may inquire into the authenticity of Thomas' psychiatric case study. As students of Freud know, he was constantly revising his theories. He was not averse to repudiate an earlier thesis or to contradict himself on a major point, as he did with the dual instinct theory and the theory of narcissism. In reading the 23 volumes of writings in the *Standard Edition*, one must know the date of a particular work—the early years of the libido theory (*The Interpretation of Dreams*, 1900, or the *Three Essays on the Theory of Sexuality*, 1905), the middle years of ego psychology (*The Ego and the Id*, 1923), or the final years of his most far-reaching speculative writings (*Civilization and Its Discontents*, 1930). It would be anachronistic to come across the structural theory of the mind prior to 1923, or the death instinct before 1920. Insofar as the "Frau Anna G." section of *The White Hotel* aims to be mimetic, we may reasonably expect that Thomas' fictional analyst should have the same theoretical understanding of hysteria that the historical Freud had in the autumn of 1919, when the fictional Elisabeth Erdman begins treatment. Freud began working on a first draft of *Beyond the Pleasure Principle* in March 1919, completing the manuscript in May 1920. Thomas once again perfectly intersects the fictional and historical analysts. Freud connects his patient's illness to the two major ideas he is advancing in his book, the repetition-compulsion principle, in which Lisa relives the night of the storm when she learns of her mother's death in a hotel fire, and the death instinct, the tendency of all living organisms to return to an inorganic state.

Ironically, in constructing "Frau Anna G." on *Beyond the Pleasure Principle*, Thomas grounds his fictional case study on one of Freud's shakiest foundations. With the exception of the supporters of Melanie Klein, the English school of psychoanalysis, nearly all contemporary analysts have abandoned Freud's death instinct.[23] The importance of *Beyond the Pleasure Principle* lies not in the highly speculative death instinct, lacking as it does biological or psychological inevitability, but in the repetition-compulsion principle, which has empirical foundation. Freud used this idea to explain the tendency to repeat traumatic situations for the purpose of mastery, thus making possible the adaptive and integrative functions of the ego. Art serves a counterphobic purpose by allowing the artist to re-create distressing experiences to gain control over them. The artist converts a passive situation into an active one, transforming defeat into victory. Artistic control, Lionel Trilling has pointed out, is antithetical to neurosis.[24] There is no reason to assert, as Freud does in *Beyond the Pleasure Principle,* that the repetition-compulsion principle is grounded in a previously undiscovered human instinct or that aggression arises from a tendency of all living organisms to return to an inorganic state. Freud's profound exploration of the dynamics of aggression—the relationship between masochism and sadism, the destructive consequences of repression, and the ego's failure to mediate between the claims of the id and superego—does not require the metaphysical postulation of a death instinct.

Consequently, in analyzing Lisa Erdman's life as a struggle between Eros and Thanatos, Thomas' Freud remains faithful to the author of *Beyond the Pleasure Principle* but unaware of the potentially more significant social and cultural implications of her dilemma. Her brother is conspicuously not mentioned in the case study, nor is her father, who is mentioned only briefly despite the fact that his daughter lived with him until the age of 17. Freud never questions Lisa's saddened acceptance of her brother's privileged position in the male-dominated family. Given her anger toward the cold rejecting father, and her troubled relations with the other men in her life, including Alexei and her husband, it is surprising that she does not experience a turbulent transference relationship with her analyst. After all, it is likely that she would attempt to reject Freud just as she has rejected the other men in her life. Curiously, the opposite is true. She remains solicitous of Freud, as if afraid that her inner rage (in the form of premonitions of death) will destroy him. It is also puzzling that the analyst does not explore in depth the castration imagery in his patient's art. In "The Gastein Journal" a young woman has her womb surgically removed, a prostitute has undergone a mastectomy, and the lawyer's wife has received an abortion. One is struck by Lisa's fear of bodily mutilation. During a stressful period of analysis, her symptoms worsen as she pleads with Freud to arrange for an operation to remove her breast and ovary. She also wishes him to destroy her writings, which for the artist may symbolize castration or death. These are all crucial issues for analysis and touch upon areas of greater consequence than a biological death wish, such as female sexuality, masochism, repression, and narcissism.[25]

In the next section of *The White Hotel*, "The Health Resort," Thomas continues his account of Lisa's story from 1929, when we see her traveling by train between Vienna and Milan, to 1936. Within this 70-page section, narrated in the third person, are several letters exchanged between Lisa and Freud, who writes to her requesting permission to publish "Frau Anna G." "The Health Resort" opens with Lisa, a professional opera singer, traveling to La Scala to replace one of the world's leading sopranos, Vera Serebryakova, who has injured herself in a fall. She meets Vera's companion and leading man, Victor Berenstein, a white-haired gentleman in his fifties who is singing the role of Eugene Onegin. She mistakes Vera and Victor for secret lovers, not realizing until later that they are married. Lisa experiences an attack of breathlessness upon learning of her friend's pregnancy, and at night she dreams of standing over a deep trench filled with many coffins and the naked body of Vera. Is the breathlessness an hysterical symptom, perhaps suggestive of her tangled feelings toward Vera? Lisa is horrified to discover several months later that Vera has died in childbirth, presumably the result of the earlier fall. Vera's death recalls Lisa's fall several years before, resulting in the aborted fetus. History does not precisely repeat itself, however, since Vera dies giving birth to her son Kolya. At about this time, there is an exchange of letters between Lisa and Freud. She fills in the missing details of her case study and reconfirms his analytic interpretation. The correspondence concludes with their warm feelings for each other. The remaining pages of "The Health Resort" document Victor's marriage to Lisa in 1934 and their passionate honeymoon. For the first time in her life, Lisa experiences no hallucinations during sexual intercourse. They return to the city of her youth where she places flowers on the grave of her mother and visits the crematorium housing the ashes of her father.

Crematorium imagery gives way to the Holocaust in the penultimate section of *The White Hotel*, "The Sleeping Carriage." Along with millions of other Jews, Lisa travels inexorably to her death as the Nazis execute their perverse death wish upon the victims. Separated from her husband, who has been put to death earlier by Stalinist terrorists, Lisa and Kolya are rounded up by the Nazi invaders of Kiev and deluded into thinking they are being sent to Palestine. Instead, they are marched to Babi Yar. She has the opportunity to save herself when she flashes an out-of-date identity card, claiming she is not Jewish, to a Cossack soldier, but when she realizes she cannot save Kolya from extermination, she affirms her Jewishness to the bemused guard. Forced to strip, she watches in speechless horror as person after person is shot or clubbed to death and then thrown into a steep ravine. She hears a Ukrainian officer tell a former actress at the Kiev puppet theatre, Dina Pronicheva, that they will shoot the Jews first and then let her out. Lisa and Kolya are among the last of the group to be shot; but as she plunges into the pit, she is horrified by the discovery she is not yet dead. Climbing into the pit to retrieve the valuables of the slain victims, an SS guard notices Lisa is still alive. "He drew his leg back and sent his jackboot crashing into her left breast. She moved position from the force of the blow, but uttered no sound. Still not satisfied, he swung his boot again and sent it cracking into her pelvis" (p. 248). It is as if Lisa has endured a lifetime of "hysterical" symptoms—pains in her left breast and ovary—in anticipation of appalling reality. A soldier tries futilely to rape the almost cold body, then inserts his bayonet into her genital opening. She is impaled, her screams drowned out by the other lingering screams from the bodies plunging into the ravine. The description uncannily recalls the poem Lisa had written more than two decades earlier in which she had fantasized the sensation of being impaled by Martin Freud (pp. 19–20). "The Sleeping Carriage" concludes with Lisa's merciful death and the account of Dina Pronicheva's miraculous escape from Babi Yar. Scrambling up the ravine, she confronts a little boy who whispers to her: "Don't be scared, lady! I'm alive too" (p. 250)—the identical words Lisa had once dreamed and used for the beginning of "The Gastein Journal" (p. 32).

This raises the most troubling question in *The White Hotel*, the meaning of Lisa's premonitions and telepathic gifts. How do we interpret the heroine's occult powers in a novel that faithfully captures the spirit of psychoanalysis, with its fiercely antireligious and antisupernatural assumptions? Mysticism, telepathy, and the occult are often present in imaginative literature, but do they have a legitimate place in a psychiatric case study? Would the rationalistic Freud, arch foe of illusions, assent to the existence of his patient's psychic powers, as Thomas' analyst does? Freud tells Lisa that not only have her dreams convinced him of her telepathic powers, but that his own clinical experience has demonstrated to him the presence of these inexplicable forces. Would the real Freud actually assert that "If I had my life to go over again, I should devote it to the study of this factor [telepathy]" (p. 196)?

Surprisingly, yes. Freud was unpredictably fascinated by occult phenomena. "If I had my life to live over again I should devote myself to psychical research rather than to psychoanalysis," he wrote to the editor of a periodical specializing in occultism.[26] His belief in the occult perplexed his students and biographers. Ernest Jones offers a lively discussion of Freud's interest in telepathy, a subject D. M. Thomas has carefully researched. Although Freud did not believe in the "less respectable" areas of the occult such as levitation, palmistry, or astrology, he displayed surprising interest in areas that few psychoanalysts take seriously. Jones relates Freud's longstanding belief in premonitions and superstitions: the magical actions he enacted to ward off disaster, the fear that his engagement ring he had accidentally broken presaged marital disaster, and the idea (originating from 1900) that he was destined to die at the age of 61 or 62. Jones reports how in the years prior to World War I he had several talks with Freud on the subject of occultism and related topics:

> He was fond, especially after midnight, of regaling me with strange or uncanny experiences with patients, characteristically about misfortunes or deaths supervening many years after a wish or prediction. He had a particular relish for such stories and was evidently impressed by their more mysterious aspects. When I would protest at some of the taller stories Freud was wont to reply with his favorite quotation: "There are more things in heaven and earth than are dreamed of in your philosophy" (Jones, Vol. III, p. 381).

Reading this statement in light of *The White Hotel,* we wonder whether Lisa, with her telepathic powers, was one of the patients Freud was talking about to the incredulous Jones.

Freud's interest in the occult spanned three decades of writings. His attitude, Jones remarks, always seemed to be wavering between skepticism and open belief. As early as *The Psychopathology of Everyday Life* (1901), Freud denied he was a superstitious person or that he had ever experienced anything of a remotely superstitious nature, such as presentiments that later came true. Yet in a sentence added in 1924 to the same work, he enigmatically admits to having had in the last few years "a few remarkable experiences which might easily have been explained on the hypothesis of telepathic thought-transference."[27] In "The Occult Significance of Dreams" (1925), originally intended for a late edition of *The Interpretation of Dreams* but published elsewhere so that its dubious subject matter would not weaken the credibility of his most famous work,

Freud discusses two categories of dreams which claim to be reckoned as occult phenomena: prophetic and telepathic dreams. He rejects the former but remains more receptive to the latter. "One arrives at a provisional opinion that it may well be that telepathy really exists and that it provides the kernel of truth in many other hypotheses that would otherwise be incredible."[28] In Lecture 30 of *New Introductory Lectures on Psycho-Analysis* (1933), "Dreams and Occultism," he returns to the subject. After expressing the fear that interest in occultism may be motivated by the belief in religion and thus, to him, alien to the spirit of scientific inquiry, Freud once again suggests the probability of telepathy and speculates that it was the original archaic method of human communication.[29]

Thomas has unerringly recreated the historical Freud's abiding interest in the occult, his fascination with the bizarre, irrational, and unknown. In his fictional portrait of Freud, Thomas reveals an intriguing aspect of the analyst's personality that has not been apparent from the actual case studies, once again affirming, paradoxically, the truth of fiction. In fact, the portrait of Freud in "Frau Anna G." is so faithful to the details of its subject's life that we are hardly surprised to learn that the historical Freud wrote the first of several short essays on occult phenomena, "Psycho-Analysis and Telepathy," in August 1921 at Bad Gastein, the health resort he loved to visit. The essay is written only a few months after Lisa Erdman has terminated therapy, implying that Thomas' fictional character has influenced the history of psychoanalysis. Although Freud acknowledges in "Psycho-Analysis and Telepathy" that his attitude toward the subject remains "unenthusiastic and ambivalent," he attempts to reconcile the analyst's allegiance to exact science with the mysterious and perhaps occult workings of the unconscious mind. He claims an uneasy alliance between the analyst and occultist in their investigation of the material and spiritual worlds, respectively, since the unconscious may consist of both realities.[30] In his next paper, "Dreams and Telepathy" (1922), he displays the same ambivalence. The essay poses a minor problem to readers of *The White Hotel*. "During some twenty-seven years of work as an analyst I have never been in a position to observe a truly telepathic dream in any of my patients."[31] He does not rule out the existence of telepathic dreams, however, and he continues to hope that psychoanalysis may one day contribute to an understanding of the mystery.

The question confronting us in *The White Hotel* is not whether the historical Freud would have accepted or rejected his patient's telepathic powers—his attitude was contradictory enough to befuddle any researcher—but whether Thomas maintains the delicate balance between psychiatric realism and imaginative belief. The inconclusive findings of psychic research suggest that it might have been better for the novelist to leave the question unresolved rather than to strip away the ambiguities of telepathic and prophetic dreams. Since the occult and supernatural are enveloped in ambiguity, there is no compelling aesthetic reason to resolve these issues, one way or the other. We have no trouble accepting the metaphorical truth of Lisa's art; it does not strain credibility that her 1920 poem could have predicted the impending catastrophe of World War II. But it does strain credibility to suggest that "Don Giovanni" could have predicted the exact details of her murder at Babi Yar. Similarly, although there is a possible explanation of Lisa's premonition of the death of Freud's daughter, there is no rational interpretation of the premonitory dream opening "The Gastein Journal," in which Lisa's flight from the soldiers foreshadows the events surrounding Dina Pronicheva's escape from Babi Yar. We are now in the realm of the supernatural, as Thomas authorially confirms. "Lisa had once dreamt those words, when she was taking the thermal springs at Gastein with Aunt Magda. But it is not really surprising, for she had clairvoyant gifts and naturally a part of her went on living with these survivors . . ." (p. 250). *The White Hotel* leaves us with the feeling of being transported to another world, a universe populated with the spirits of the living and dead. It is a place where the laws of time and space have given way to animistic belief and where the bizarre and uncanny reign supreme.

Freud has explored the feelings described above in "The 'Uncanny'" (1919), and it is worth reading the essay because of its relevance to *The White Hotel*. Indeed, Thomas has surely read Freud's paper. Discussing the resemblance between the white hotel and the maternal body, the fictional analyst writes in "Frau Anna G.": "There is a joke saying that 'Love is a homesickness'; and whenever a man dreams of a place or a country and says to himself, while he is still dreaming: 'This place is familiar to me, I've been here before,' we may interpret the place as being his mother's genitals or her body" (*The White Hotel*, p. 115). The statement comes verbatim from "The 'Uncanny.'"[32] Freud discusses in the essay the aesthetic and psychological implications of the uncanny and relates it to that which is frightening. He defines the uncanny as that class of the frightening which leads back to what is known of old and long familiar. Freud associates the uncanny with two psychoanalytic ideas, the repetition-compulsion principle and the omnipotence of thought. After discussing several writers, including E. T. A. Hoffmann, Freud inquires into the distinctions between the depiction of the uncanny in literature and in life. He argues that, although the imaginative writer is not constrained by the need to test reality, the creative artist can evoke the uncanny only if he pretends to move in the world of common reality. The uncanny does not exist in fairy tales because the reader knows that the world of reality is left behind. Anything is possible in an animistic world. By contrast, the uncanny can exist only in a world in which the laws of reality are mysteriously and temporarily suspended. The artist has the freedom to contrive a story in such a way as to create a sense of the uncanny that cannot possibly occur within life. However, there is a danger here, Freud says:

> In doing this he is in a sense betraying us to the superstitiousness which we have ostensibly surmounted; he deceives us by promising to give us the sober truth, and then after all overstepping it. We react to his inventions as we would have reacted to real experiences; by the time we have seen through his trick it is already too late and the author has achieved his object. But it must be added that his success is not unalloyed. We retain a feeling of dissatisfaction, a kind of grudge against the attempted deceit (*Standard Edition*, Vol. XVII, pp. 250–251).

These are stern words coming from a man who elsewhere embarrassed his students by speculating in print on the probability of psychic phenomena. Yet, readers of *The White Hotel* may also feel that the novelist has overstepped the boundary of the probable.

There is, however, a more serious objection to the heavy reliance upon telepathic and premonitory dreams in *The White Hotel*. The existence of psychic phenomena calls into question the validity of the psychoanalytic approach to symptomatology Thomas has reproduced in "Frau Anna G." Is he suggesting that Lisa Erdman's hysterical symptoms ultimately have an organic basis, originating from the gruesome rape and murder at Babi Yar? But if so, how can the future influence the past? The only way in which one can argue that Lisa's lifelong pains in her left breast and ovary determine the precise details of her death is through a self-fulfilling prophecy, which does not apply here. If we accept Thomas' premise, any therapeutic treatment, psychoanalytic or otherwise, would have been futile. Why go to a therapist for treatment of a neurosis when the patient is suffering from the nightmare of history? Individual neurosis and social history are undoubtedly interrelated and, like the proverbial chicken-egg argument, it may not be possible to determine which comes first. Nevertheless, to view Lisa's hysterical symptoms as inseparable from a worldwide illness is to embrace a more deterministic and fatalistic position than the historical Freud would ever allow. It is ironic, then, that, while the fictional Freud attempts to demystify his patient's illness in "Frau Anna G.," Thomas undercuts the analyst's rationalism elsewhere in the novel. Like Doris Lessing (though without her shrillness), Thomas finally affirms not psychoanalysis but spiritual transcendence.

This is what occurs in the final section of *The White Hotel*, "The Camp," where the novelist magically returns all the dead characters to life. The setting shifts from the Babi Yar ravine to a Palestinian refugee camp after the war. Unlike the problematic emphasis upon the occult, we are not troubled by Thomas' bold coda, for it is an imaginary universe, a metaphor of the mind's capacity for regenerative illusions. Here, Lisa is reunited with her relatives and friends. The past is reborn into the present: the transit camp is another version of the white hotel. Even Freud shows up in the camp, ailing but alive. Lisa desires to comfort him, but she rejects the idea because she would have to cast doubts on the accuracy of his diagnosis. Yet, when she hears her mother's confessions, we realize that Freud has accurately reconstructed her past. Nothing is permanently lost in the final section of *The White Hotel*. The funereal tone of the wintry Holocaust yields to the joyous return of spring. Suffering and death are exposed as illusions, and the imagination proves stronger than history. Lisa's crucifixion and resurrection incarnate her half-Jewish, half-Christian identity. Victimized for being a Jew and martyred like Christ for affirming religious faith, she is reborn into the refugee camp where she plays the same restorative role she had created in the white hotel. Although Thomas steers clear of any single religious point of view, a current of mysticism and Messianism flows through *The White Hotel*. The coda affirms the eternal spirit of human nature and the power of the imagination to overcome the forces of death.

Whether viewed in religious, supernatural, or mythic terms, the impulse toward transcendence points to a major distinction between the psychiatric case study and imaginative literature. True to *Studies on Hysteria* and the other historical case studies, Thomas' "Frau Anna G." backs off from visionary metaphors. Both the historical and fictional Freud limit their aspirations to the modest goals of psychological insight and therapeutic relief. The goal Freud announced in *Studies on Hysteria* remained his credo for 45 years. "One works to the best of one's power, as an elucidator (where ignorance has given rise to fear), as a teacher, as the representative of a freer or superior view of the world, as a father confessor who gives absolution, as it were, by a continuance of his sympathy and respect after the confession has been made" (*Standard Edition*, II, p. 282). There is, admittedly, more than a hint of religious imagery in this testament, and it is true that Freud never overcame the Promethean elements of his character. His belief in knowledge as power remained an act of faith. Yet his focus was on this world, not the next, and the antireligious spirit of psychoanalysis has changed little in 80 years.[33] By contrast, Thomas' allegiance at the close of *The White Hotel* is to the visionary imagination. Using emigration as a metaphor of resurrection, the novelist affirms through his heroine's life that wherever there is love in the heart, there is hope of salvation.

With *The White Hotel*, we have come full circle to *Studies on Hysteria* and Anna O.'s celebrated talking cure. The symbiotic relationship between literature and psychoanalysis remains healthy despite the inevitable antagonisms the artist and psychoanalyst bring to each other's field. As long as artists explore the intricacies of the psyche and analysts encourage the gift of verbal expression, the talking cure will remain the unique intersection of these two parallel paths to human enlightenment. *The White Hotel* will certainly not be the last novel to employ the medium of psychiatric case studies to probe the mystery of human life—Judith Rossner's *August* (1983) is the latest example—but it is difficult to conceive of a more powerful and authentic work of art. And it is astonishing to believe that Thomas' knowledge of psychoanalysis is merely that of the "interested layperson," as reported in an interview.[34] Yet, this is precisely how Freud would have evaluated his own novelistic powers.

How would the historical Freud have reacted to his fictional *Doppelgänger* in *The White Hotel*? Actually, we have a clue in an intriguing footnote buried in his essay "The 'Uncanny.'" Wondering aloud about one's reaction to meeting up with a mirror image, Freud narrates an amusing story that appropriately serves as a "premonition" of *The White Hotel*. One day, the analyst writes, he was sitting alone in his wagon-lit compartment when a sudden jolt of the train threw open the door of the adjourning washing cabinet. In walked an elderly gentleman in a dressing gown and traveling cap. Assuming the man had wandered into the wrong bathroom, Freud jumped up with the intention of scolding him. To his dismay he realized he was confronting his own reflection in the mirror. "I can still recollect that I thoroughly disliked his appearance" (*Standard*

Edition, XVII, 248n). With the creation of Elisabeth Erdman's case history, Thomas' novel has miraculously caught up to Sigmund Freud's speeding train. Though the psychoanalyst might be jolted by the uncanny reflection greeting his eyes in "Frau Anna G.," a reflection highlighting the human face in all its nobility and sorrow, grateful readers need not look beyond the pleasure principle to appreciate *The White Hotel.*

Appendix

Chronology of Events in *The White Hotel*

The following chronology is based on the fictional Freud's "Frau Anna G.," Lisa Erdman's subsequent account of her life as narrated in her letters to the analyst and the final sections of the novel. Information on the historical Freud not found in *The White Hotel* is bracketed.

1890   Birth of Elisabeth Morozova (Freud's "Frau Anna G."), the second child and only daughter of moderately wealthy parents, in the Ukraine. Her father is a Russian Jew, her mother a Polish Catholic. Shortly after birth she and her family move to Odessa.
1893   Lisa wanders on to her father's yacht and sees her mother, Aunt Magda (the mother's identical twin), and Uncle Franz performing intercourse *a tergo*.
1894 or 1895   The summer-house incident in which Lisa sees her mother and uncle making love while her aunt lies on the beach.
1895   Death of Lisa's mother and uncle in a Budapest hotel fire. In Lisa's mind, fire symbolizes illicit passion and death.
1905   Incident on the dock. Lisa is threatened by a group of sailors, reviled for being a Jew, and made to perform oral sex. Origin of her symptom of breathlessness.
1907   Lisa leaves Odessa for St. Petersburg. On the train she is seduced by a young officer. Her first experience with sexual intercourse coincides with her first hallucination. In St. Petersburg she has a ballet audition.
1907–1910   Affair with Alexei. They spend a weekend cruising on the Gulf of Finland, during which a bitter argument ensues. Lisa becomes pregnant but loses the fetus in a fall. Beginning of hallucination of falling through the air to her death. Friendship with Ludmila Kedrova. After Ludmila's marriage, Lisa is invited to live with her Aunt Magda in Vienna. She becomes a devout Roman Catholic at this time.
1913–1917   Lisa's new career as an opera singer. Marriage to Herr Erdman, an anti-Semitic Austrian barrister. Lisa conceals her half-Jewishness from him. Honeymoon in Switzerland. Recurrence of breathlessness in 1915 when her husband returns on his first home leave from army service. She also develops inca-

pacitating pains in her left breast and ovary. Separation from husband and annulment of marriage. Lisa returns to live with her aunt.

Autumn 1919   Lisa begins analysis with Freud in Vienna. She has a telepathic dream of the suicide of the first husband of the woman who married Freud's colleague, Sandor Ferenczi, earlier that year [in March 1919]. Lisa dreams of the deaths of Freud's daughter and grandson. [Publication of Freud's essay, "The 'Uncanny.' "]

25 January 1920   Death of Freud's second daughter, Sophie Halberstadt, aged 26. The fictional Freud temporarily suspends treatment with Lisa, resuming therapy a couple of weeks later. She writes the poem "Don Giovanni" during a three-day period from the end of January to the beginning of February while vacationing at Bad Gastein, awaiting resumption of analysis with Freud. Immediately afterwards, she writes "The Gastein Journal" at the request of Freud.

9 February 1920   Freud's letter to Ferenczi, thanking him for his condolences. [This letter is modeled on the actual letter Freud wrote to Ferenczi on 4 February 1920. See Ernst Freud, ed., *The Letters of Sigmund Freud* (New York: Basic Books, 1975), p. 328.] First mention of an hysterical patient whose writings lend support to Freud's new manuscript, *Beyond the Pleasure Principle* [which the analyst started working on in March 1919 and completed in May 1920].

4 March 1920   Freud's letter to Hanns Sachs, to whom he sends a copy of "The Gastein Journal" along with his patient's poem. Freud's analysis of Lisa presumably ends during this year, although he does not complete the manuscript of the case study until 1931.

[August 1921   Freud writes "Psycho-Analysis and Telepathy" at Bad Gastein, the first of several essays on the subject. The essay is published posthumously in 1941.]

[19 June 1923   Death of Freud's beloved grandson Heinz (second child of the late Sophie Halberstadt), aged four and a half, of military tuberculosis. The loss of his favorite grandson has a devastating effect on Freud. Ernest Jones reports that Heinz's death was the only occasion in Freud's life when he was known to shed tears. "He told me afterward that this loss had affected him in a different way from any of the others he had suffered. They had brought about sheer pain, but this one had killed something in him for good." See Jones, *The Life and Work of Sigmund Freud,* Vol. III, p. 92.]

Spring 1929   Lisa travels by train between Vienna and Milan, where she is to perform in *Eugene Onegin* at La Scala. She meets Vera Serebryakova and Victor Berenstein. In the winter Vera dies while giving birth to her son, Kolya.

1930   Freud is awarded the Goethe Prize for Literature [given by the city of Frankfurt to a "personality of established achievement whose creative work is worthy of an honour dedicated to Goethe's memory." The ailing Freud is unable to accept the award in person. His daughter Anna reads his "Address Delivered in the Goethe House at Frankfurt." See *Standard Edition,* Vol. XXI, pp. 206–212.]. The fictional Freud is invited by the Frankfurt City Council to write a psychoanalytic paper to be published in a limited edition in honor of the centenary of Goethe's death in 1932, and the fortieth anniversary of *Studies on Hysteria* (Breuer and Freud). The publication of "Frau Anna G." is delayed indefinitely when the centenary committee refuses to publish the patient's "pornographic" writings in an appendix to the case study. In the winter of 1930, Ludmila Kedrova dies of cancer at the age of 50.

March? 1931   Freud writes to Lisa, informing her that he has completed his case study of her, "Frau Anna G." He encloses the manuscript along with her writings. At the end of March, Lisa writes back a long letter in which she grants him permission to publish the case study and fills in missing details of the story. She inquires about his grandsons, expressing the premonition she had during analysis that "one of them would not long survive his mother." Freud writes back in May to confirm that his grandson had died. "With him, my affectional life came to an end." In the next letter Freud acknowledges that he has known about her telepathic powers.

1932   Freud and Lisa accidentally meet at Bad Gastein, where he is on vacation with his sister-in-law, Minna Bernays.

1934   Marriage of Lisa and Victor Berenstein. Her hysterical symptoms disappear.

[23 September 1939   Death of Sigmund Freud at the age of 83.]

September 1941   Murder of Lisa Berenstein and her adopted-son Kolya at Babi Yar. (Her husband has already been murdered.) Their bodies are thrown into a ravine. One person escapes, Dina Pronicheva.

1945?   Resurrection and reunion of Lisa, friends, relatives, and Freud in a refugee camp in Palestine.

NOTES

1: Introduction: The Talking Cure

[1] Breuer and Freud, *Studies on Hysteria, Standard Edition of the Complete Psychological Works of Sigmund Freud* (London: The Hogarth Press, 1955), Vol. II, p. 41.

[2] Ernest Jones, *The Life and Work of Sigmund Freud* (New York: Basic Books, 1953), Vol. I, p. 223n.

[3] This quotation comes from Freud's letter to Stefan Zweig, 2 June 1932. Ernst L. Freud, ed., *The Letters of Sigmund Freud* (New York: Basic Books, 1960), p 413. All references are to this edition. "At this moment he held in his hand the key that would have opened the 'doors to the Mothers,' but he let it drop," Freud continues in the next paragraph. "With all his great intellectual gifts there was nothing Faustian in his nature. Seized by conventional horror he took flight and abandoned the patient to a colleague. For months afterwards she struggled to regain her health in a sanatorium." For Freud's additional commentary on "Fräulein Anna O." see *Five Lectures on Psycho-Analysis*, (1910), *Standard Edition* (London: The Hogarth Press, 1957), Vol. XI, pp. 9–15, 17–22; *On the History of the Psycho-Analytic Movement* (1914), *Standard Edition* (London: The Hogarth Press, 1957), Vol. XIV, pp. 11–12; and *An Autobiographical Study* (1925), *Standard Edition* (London: The Hogarth Press, 1959), Vol. XX, pp. 20–21.

[4] Jones's account of "Fräulein Anna O.," it should be pointed out, is not only one sided but factually inaccurate. For a more balanced account, see Henri Ellenberger, *The Discovery of the Unconscious* (New York: Basic Books, 1970), pp. 480–484.

[5] Jones, op. cit., p. 225.

[6] For a biographical sketch of Bertha Pappenheim, see Ellen M. Jensen, "Anna O—A Study of Her Later Life," *Psychoanalytic Quarterly*, Vol. 39, No. 2 (1970), pp. 269–293. Despite her lack of sympathy toward psychoanalytic interpretations of Bertha Pappenheim's life, Jensen concludes on the basis of a careful study of her letters that "there is at times something manic in her writings and actions although without the flight of thought and the lack of basic reality met with in real mania" (p. 285). Jensen also quotes a letter from Pappenheim's second cousin, saying that her famous relative was a "clear case of a manic-depressive." Lucy Freeman has written a lively fictionalized biography of Bertha Pappenheim, *The Story of Anna O.* (New York: Walker and Company, 1972).

[7] Robert Langs, *The Psychotherapeutic Conspiracy* (New York: Jason Aronson, 1982).

[8] Erik H. Erikson, *Insight and Responsibility* (New York: Norton, 1964), p. 36.

[9] Sigmund Freud: *The Origins of Psychoanalysis: Letters to Wilhelm Fliess* (New York: Basic Books, 1954), p. 325. All references are to this edition.

[10] Jules Glenn, "Freud's Adolescent Patients," in Mark Kanzer and Jules Glenn, eds., *Freud and His Patients* (New York: Jason Aronson, 1980), p. 32. Anyone wishing to learn more about Freud's case studies will find a wealth of information in this volume.

[11] Erikson, op. cit., p. 168.

[12] Mark Kanzer, "The Transference Neurosis of the Rat Man," in Mark Kanzer and Jules Glenn, eds., *Freud and His Patients* (New York: Jason Aronson, 1980), p. 139.

[13] See Norman N. Holland, "An Identity for the Rat Man," *International Review of Psycho-Analysis,* Vol. 2 (1975), pp. 157–169. *"To control the reversals in the self caused by things going out and coming in*—that would be one possible summary statement of an identity theme for Lorenz which would interrelate the many, many details we know about him" (p. 164).

[14] Leonard Sheingold, "More on Rats and Rat People," in Mark Kanzer and Jules Glenn, eds., *Freud and His Patients,* (New York: Jason Aronson, 1980), pp. 180–202.

[15] Muriel Gardiner, ed., *The Wolf-Man,* by the Wolf-Man (New York: Basic Books, 1971). All references are to this edition. This fascinating volume contains Freud's original case study, the Wolf Man's memoirs, and Ruth Mack Brunswick's supplementary case study. Of Freud's five major case studies, the Wolf Man is the only patient whose identity has not been publicly revealed. Born in 1887, he was still alive in 1971 when the book bearing his name was published. Interestingly, the Wolf Man declined Muriel Gardiner's invitation to write an article evaluating his analysis with Freud. The Wolf Man's memoir is curiously lacking in psychological penetration; indeed, he goes out of his way to maintain a surface narrative of the events of his life.

[16] For an extended critique of Freud's misalliance with the Wolf Man, Brunswick's countertransference problems, and other background information on the Wolf Man's life, see Mark Kanzer and Jules Glenn, eds., *Freud and His Patients* (New York: Jason Aronson, 1980), pp. 341–405.

[17] See in particular Alexander Grinstein, *On Sigmund Freud's Dreams* (Detroit: Wayne State University Press, 1968).

[18] Erik H. Erikson, *Young Man Luther* (New York: Norton, 1958), p. 151.

[19] For contemporary views of countertransference, see Lawrence Epstein and Arthur H. Feiner, eds., *Countertransference* (New York: Jason Aronson, 1979); Albert J. Rose, "Fusion States," in Peter Giovacchini, ed., *Tactics and Techniques in Psychoanalytic Therapy* (New York: Jason Aronson, 1975), Vol. 2, pp. 170–187; Ernest S. Woolf, "Transferences and Countertransferences in the Analysis of Disorders of the Self," *Contemporary Psychoanalysis,* Vol. 15 (1979), pp. 577–594; Lea Goldberg, "Remarks on Transference-Countertransference in Psychotic States," *International Journal of Psycho-Analysis,* Vol. 60 (1979), pp. 347–356; Ted Zaretsky,

"The Analyst's Narcissistic Vulnerability," *Contemporary Psychoanalysis,* Vol. 16, No. 1 (January 1980), pp. 82–89.

[20] D. W. Winnicott, "Hate in the Counter-Transference," *International Journal of Psychoanalysis,* Vol. 30, Part 2 (1949), pp. 69–74.

[21] H. Searles, "The Effort to Drive the Other Person Crazy—An Element in the Aetiology and Psychotherapy of Schizophrenia," in *Collected Papers on Schizophrenia and Related Subjects* (New York: International Universities Press, 1965), p. 278.

[22] Tilmann Moser, *Years of Apprenticeship on the Couch* (New York: Urizen Books, 1977).

[23] See Arnold A. Rogow, *The Psychiatrists* (New York: Putnam, 1970), for a discussion of the high suicide rate among psychiatrists. Citing obituary notices in the *Journal of the American Medical Association* and official death certificates, Rogow reports that 203 psychiatrists commited suicide between 1895 and 1967, 54 of them between 1962 and 1967, "more than had done so in any previous decade" (*The Psychiatrists,* p. 51n). Rogow notes further that while there is evidence to suggest that there is less aggression in psychiatrists than in other physicians, "there is also evidence that many physicians who become psychiatrists do so, at least in part, because of personal troubles for which, hopefully, their psychiatric training and practice will offer a solution. Indeed, the possibility that 'some who take up psychiatry probably do so for morbid reasons' has been advanced as an explanation for the disproportionate number of suicides among psychiatrists, even taking account of the fact that 'Doctors of Medicine are more prone to suicide than men in other occupations' " (*The Psychiatrists,* pp. 50–51).

Counterphobic measures, however, are not always successful against morbid fears, either for the artist or the analyst. "On the contrary," writes Bernard C. Meyer, in his psychobiographical study, *Houdini: A Mind in Chains* (New York: Dutton, 1976), "it is characteristic of such psychological defenses that they demand constant renewal, for the original forbidden childhood impulses, as well as the reactions erected against them that have resulted in the phobia, press repeatedly for discharge. The physician who hopes to discover in the letters MD attached to his name an amulet guaranteed to ward off the threat of illness and death may continue to be harassed by hypochondriacal anxiety for the rest of his life, or at least as long as the emotional matrix of his childhood brush with illness and death remains untouched" (p. 117).

In *Freud and His Followers* (New York: New York University Press, 1985), Paul Roazen lists the names of the early analysts who committed suicide, including Paul Federn, Wilhelm Stekel, Victor Tausk, Herbert Silberer, and Karen Stephen (who was Clive Bell's sister-in-law).

[24] Richard Karpe, "The Rescue Complex in Anna O's Final Identity," *Psychoanalytic Quarterly,* Vol. 30 (1961), p. 9. See also Frederick M. Bram, "The Gift of Anna O.," *British Journal of Medical Psychology,* Vol. 38 (1965), pp. 53–58.

[25] For a candid discussion of the misuse of resistance, see Richard C. Robertiello, " 'Acting Out' or 'Working Through?' " in Lawrence Edwin Abt and Stuart L. Weissman, eds., *Acting Out: Theoretical and Clinical Aspects* (New York: Grune & Stratton, 1965), pp. 40–45. Robertiello points out how easily analysts abuse the

concept of acting out by applying it to any behavior (in a patient or friend) of which they morally disapprove.

[26] Erik H. Erikson, *Gandhi's Truth* (New York: Norton, 1969), pp. 65–66.

[27] Norman N. Holland is the leading American psychoanalytic literary theoretician; see *5 Readers Reading* (New Haven: Yale University Press, 1975) and Holland's "UNITY IDENTITY TEXT SELF," *PMLA*, Vol. 90 (1975), pp. 813–822.

[28] Arthur Marotti, "Countertransference, the Communication Process, and the Dimensions of Psychoanalytic Criticism," *Critical Inquiry*, Vol. 4, No. 3 (Spring 1978), p. 474. See also James E. Gorney, "The Field of Illusion in Literature and the Psychoanalytic Situation," *Psychoanalysis and Contemporary Thought*, Vol. 2, No. 4 (1979), pp. 527–550.

[29] Two important works worth mentioning here are Frederick J. Hoffman, *Freudianism and the Literary Mind*, 2nd ed. (Baton Rouge: Louisiana State University Press, 1967), and W. David Sievers, *Freud on Broadway* (New York: Cooper Square Publishers, 1970). Neither book, however, discusses the role of transference and countertransference in fictional representations of the patient-analyst relationship. For an analysis of Freud's influence on popular culture, see Frederick C. Redlich, "The Psychiatrist in Caricature: An Analysis of Unconscious Attitudes toward Psychiatry," *American Journal of Orthopsychiatry*, Vol. 20 (1950), pp. 558–571; Irving Schneider, "Images of the Mind: Psychiatry in the Commercial Film," *The American Journal of Psychiatry*, Vol. 134, No. 6 (June 1977), pp. 613–620; Leslie Y. Rabkin, "The Celluloid Couch: Psychiatrists in American Films," *Psychocultural Review*, Vol. 3, No. 2 (Spring 1979), pp. 73–90.

[30] Jay Ehrenwald, *The History of Psychotherapy* (New York: Jason Aronson, 1976), p. 17.

[31] Donald Meltzer, "Routine and Inspired Interpretations," Lawrence Epstein and Arthur H. Feiner, eds., *Countertransference* (New York: Jason Aronson, 1979), p. 138.

[32] See Harry Slochower, *Mythopoesis* (Detroit: Wayne State University Press, 1970).

[33] Virginia Woolf, *Mrs. Dalloway* (London: Chatto & Windus, 1925, rpt. 1968), p. 110.

[34] Lillian Feder, *Madness in Literature* (Princeton: Princeton University Press, 1980), p. 9.

[35] Freud's most revealing characterization of the artist appears in *Introductory Lectures on Psycho-Analysis:*

> An artist is once more in rudiments an introvert, not far removed from neurosis. He is oppressed by excessively powerful instinctual needs. He desires to win honour, power, wealth, fame and the love of women; but he lacks the means for achieving these satisfactions. Consequently, like any other unsatisfied man, he turns away from reality and transfers all his interest, and his libido too, to the wishful constructions of his life of phantasy, whence the path might lead to neurosis (*Standard Edition* [London: The Hogarth Press, 1963], Vol. XVI, p. 376).

In comparing the artist to the neurotic, Freud comes dangerously close to reducing literature to psychopathology. He also equates art with the "pleasure principle" and science with the "reality principle," thus dichotomizing the artistic and scientific temperament. Though he often paid homage to the artist, it was the scientist who embodied for him heroic discipline. "Science is, after all, the most complete renunciation of the pleasure principle of which our mental activity is capable" (*Standard Edition*, Vol. XI, p. 165). Nowhere does he offer proof, however, that "artists in particular suffer from a partial inhibition of their efficiency owing to neurosis," as he claims in the *Introductory Lectures*. In short, Freud's theory of the neurotic artist reveals less about the psychology of the artist than about Freud's ambivalence toward art. The contrast he saw between the artist and scientist—intuition versus empiricism, gratification versus renunciation, neurotic suffering versus classical health—no doubt reflected a profound split in his own character.

The early psychoanalytic theoreticians tended to echo Freud's pronouncements of the neurotic artist. At times, their language reveals unconscious self-parody, as the following statement demonstrates. "The release of quantities of affective energy through the work of art is brought about through this fluctuating mixture of delusion and admission that 'it is only play' which creates an atmosphere enabling various cathexes to escape to some extent the control of the censor, just as in dreams our conscience consoles us when we say to ourselves: 'It is only a dream' " (Richard Sterba, "The Problem of Art in Freud's Writings," *Psychoanalytic Quarterly*, Vol. 9 [1940], p. 266). Later critics, such as Ernst Kris (*Psychoanalytic Explorations in Art* [New York: International Universities Press, 1952]), attempted to avoid mechanistic approaches by stressing the adaptive and integrative role of the ego. Kris refers to the "regression in the service of the ego." In *The Psychoanalyst and the Artist* (New York: Farrar, Straus, 1950) Daniel Schneider affirms the healthy implications of art, but his book remains too vague to be useful. In *Neurotic Distortions of the Creative Process* (Lawrence, Kansas: University of Kansas Press, 1958), Lawrence Kubie discusses the role of the preconscious in the creative process.

One of the best books on the subject is Simon O. Lesser's *Fiction and the Unconscious* (New York: Vintage, 1957). "Art, including fiction, is neither a means of avoiding pain nor of dulling oneself to it: neither a renunciation nor a narcotic. Like play, fantasy and wit, which are its close relations, it represents an attempt to augment the meager satisfactions offered by experience through the creation of a more harmonious world to which one can repair, however briefly, for refuge, solace and pleasure" (p. 21). The most recent major psychoanalytic study of the creative process is Albert Rothenberg's *The Emerging Goddess* (Chicago: University of Chicago Press, 1979).

[36] George Pickering, *Creative Malady* (New York: Delta, 1976), p. 19. In *The Discovery of the Unconscious*, Ellenberger (see n. 4) makes a similar point about Freud's creative illness (p. 535).

[37] Max Schur, Freud's personal physician during the last years of his life, provides a full discussion of the analyst's neurotic suffering, including extensive cardiac symptoms. See *Freud: Living and Dying* (New York: International Universities Press, 1972), pp. 63–92.

[38] Joseph Wortis, *Fragments of an Analysis with Freud* (New York: McGraw-Hill, 1975), p. 154.

[39] Freud was able to admit privately that psychoanalysts were often neurotic. In *Diary of My Analysis with Sigmund Freud* (New York: Hawthorn, 1971), Smiley Blanton reports the following statement Freud made during Blanton's training analysis:

> "Of course," said Freud, "A man may be a surgeon through accident, but a really good surgeon is one who has made this fundamental sublimation.
>
> "Do you know why psychiatrists go into their specialty?" he continued. "It is because they do not feel that they are normal, and they go into this work because it is a means of sublimation for this feeling—a means of assuring themselves that they are really normal. Society puts them in charge of the mentally abnormal, and so they feel reassured. Also, they are so much more normal than their patients. . . . Of course, some psychiatrists go into this work through accident" (pp. 46–47).

[40] In his famous essay "Freud and Literature," in *The Liberal Imagination* (Garden City: Anchor Books, 1953), Lionel Trilling writes: "When, on the occasion of the celebration of his seventieth birthday, Freud was greeted as the 'discoverer of the unconscious,' he corrected the speaker and disclaimed the title. 'The poets and philosophers before me discovered the unconscious,' he said. 'What I discovered was the scientific method by which the unconscious can be studied' " (p. 32).

Virtually every psychoanalytic literary critic, including myself, has dutifully cited Trilling's words but, since he does not footnote the quotation, it has been hitherto impossible to track down the source. Even after I systematically read all of Freud's writings and correspondence, I still could not locate the quote. Nor were the other psychoanalytic critics with whom I spoke able to solve the mystery. Did Trilling fabricate the saying? Just when I began to think so, I located the source of the quotation. A physician named Philip R. Lehrman, Professor of Neurology and Psychiatry at Columbia University, wrote an essay called "Freud's Contributions to Science" appearing in the Hebrew journal *Harofé Haivri*, Vol. 1 (1940), pp. 161–176. Trilling apparently took the quotation from this article. ("Freud and Literature" first appeared in 1940, so that he might have come across Lehrman's article at about the same time he was writing his own.) According to Lehrman, Freud made the remark in Berlin in 1928 to a Professor Becker, the Prussian Minister of Art, Science and Education.

[41] Thomas Mann, "The Making of *the Magic Mountain*," *The Magic Mountain*, H. T. Lowe-Porter, trans. (New York: Vintage, 1969), pp. 724–725.

[42] Edmund Wilson, *The Wound and the Bow* (New York: Oxford University Press, 1965), p. 240. Wilson's interpretation has been challenged by another depth critic, Louis Fraiberg, who argues in *Psychoanalysis and American Literary Criticism* (Detroit: Wayne State University Press, 1960) that the "fatal defect of this theory is that it does not explain what connection there is, if any, between artistic talent and emotional maladjustment" (p. 163).

[43] Thomas Mann, "Freud's Position in the History of Modern Thought," *The Criterion*, Vol. 12 (July 1933), p. 565. The essay is reprinted in T. S. Eliot, ed., *Collected Edition of the Criterion* (Faber and Faber/Barnes and Noble, 1967).

[44] Heinz Kohut, "Reflections on *Advances in Self Psychology*," in Arnold Goldberg, ed., *Advances in Self Psychology* (New York: International Universities Press, 1980), p. 516.

2: The Unrestful Cure: Charlotte Perkins Gilman and "The Yellow Wallpaper"

[1] Aileen S. Kraditor, *The Ideas of the Woman Suffrage Movement, 1890–1920* (New York: Columbia University Press, 1965), p. 97.

[2] William L. O'Neill, "Introduction" to Charlotte Perkins Gilman, *The Home: Its Work and Influence* (1903; rpt. Urbana: University of Illinois Press, 1972), p. vii.

[3] Andrew Sinclair, *The Better Half: The Emancipation of the American Woman* (New York: Harper & Row, 1965), p. 272.

[4] Carl N. Degler, "Charlotte Perkins Gilman on the Theory and Practice of Feminism," *American Quarterly*, Vol. 8, No. 1 (Spring 1956), p. 22.

[5] *The Nation*, June 8, 1899, p. 443. Quoted by Degler, op. cit., p. 21.

[6] Mary Gray Peck, *Carrie Chapman Catt: A Biography* (New York: H. W. Wilson, 1944), p. 434.

[7] Ibid., p. 455.

[8] Charlotte Perkins Gilman, *The Living of Charlotte Perkins Gilman: An Autobiography* (1935; rpt. New York: Harper and Row, 1975), p. 8. All references are to this edition. Born Charlotte Perkins in 1860, she married Walter Stetson in 1884, gave birth to her daughter Katherine in 1885, and immediately suffered a breakdown. She divorced Stetson a few years later. In 1900 she married her cousin, Houghton Gilman. Curiously, in the 335-page autobiography she devotes only two sentences to her second husband. This is only one of many conspicuous omissions in her autobiography. The reader interested in learning more about Gilman's life should consult Mary A. Hill, *Charlotte Perkins Gilman: The Making of a Radical Feminist 1860–1896* (Philadelphia: Temple University Press, 1980). Although not psychoanalytic, the biography confirms Gilman's intense ambivalence toward her parents and also discusses her marital difficulties with Stetson and her tension toward her daughter Katherine.

[9] Charlotte Perkins Gilman, "Parasitism and Civilised Vice," in Samuel D. Schmalhausen and V. F. Calverton, eds., *Woman's Coming of Age* (New York: Liveright, 1931), p. 123. Many of the feminists who have written on Gilman share her feelings toward Freud. Witness this judgment by her friend Zona Gale in the "Foreword" to *The Living*: ". . . after all her prophetic thinking, it comes about that to-day Mrs. Gilman is regarded by many of the new generation as reactionary, because of her impatience at the useful bunglings of Freud, that husky bull in the Venetian-glass shop of certain still veiled equilibriums" (p. xxv).

[10] Hill, op. cit., p. 130.

[11] Charlotte Perkins [Stetson] Gilman, *Concerning Children* (Boston: Small, Maynard and Company, 1901), pp. 193–194.

[12] Patricia Meyer Spacks, *The Female Imagination* (New York: Avon, 1976), p. 270.

[13] Gilman, *The Home,* op. cit., p. 60.

[14] Charlotte Perkins Stetson, *Women and Economics* (Boston: Small, Maynard and Company, 1899), p. 181.

[15] Degler, op. cit., p. 36.

[16] Not surprisingly, Gilman's biographer provides abundant evidence of the daughter's severe criticisms of her feminist mother. In interviewing Katherine Beecher Stetson Chamberlin in 1975, when Charlotte's daughter was 90-years-old, Mary Hill concluded that "Katherine's recollections of Charlotte suggest a repetition of themes of mother-daughter history Charlotte described with Mary. So often, as mothers, both Mary and Charlotte had been exhausted by economic and emotional responsibilities, and both Katherine and Charlotte criticized their mothers for being churlish and mean." (Hill, op. cit., p. 232.)

[17] Ernest Earnest, *S. Weir Mitchell: Novelist and Physician* (Philadelphia: University of Pennsylvania Press, 1950), p. v.

[18] Walter Freeman, *The Psychiatrist: Personalities and Patterns* (New York: Grune and Stratton, 1968), p. 6.

[19] S. Weir Mitchell, *Fat and Blood* (Philadelphia: Lippincott, 1884), pp. 57–58.

[20] Ibid., pp. 60–61.

[21] Interestingly, Freud was well aware of Mitchell's work and surprisingly sympathetic toward it. He wrote a review of *Fat and Blood* in 1887 in which he praised Mitchell as the "highly original nerve specialist in Philadelphia" and endorsed the rest cure as a means to overcome severe and long established states of nervous exhaustion. See Freud, "Review of Weir Mitchell's *The Treatment of Certain Forms of Neurasthenia and Hysteria [Fat and Blood],*" *Standard Edition* (London: The Hogarth Press, 1966), Vol. I, p. 36. In the short essay "Hysteria" (1888), Freud elaborates on his praise for Mitchell:

> In recent years the so-called "rest-cure" of Weir Mitchell (also known as Plairfair's treatment) has gained a high reputation as a method of treating hysteria in institutions, and deservedly so. . . . This treatment is of extraordinary value for hysteria, as a happy combination of *"traitement moral"* with an improvement in the patient's general nutritional state. It is not to be regarded, however, as something systematically complete in itself; the isolation, rather, and the physician's influence remain the principal agents, and, along with massage and electricity, the other therapeutic methods are not to be neglected (*Standard Edition,* Vol. I, p. 55).

In *Studies on Hysteria* (1895), Freud again praises Mitchell and observes that the rest cure in combination with cathartic psychotherapy yields excellent results, better results indeed than either method alone. Curiously, Freud makes a statement that a few years later he would have repudiated—that a danger of the rest cure is that patients "not infrequently fall into the habit of harmful day-dreaming" (*Standard Edition* [London: The Hogarth Press, 1955] Vol. II, p. 267). Freud later constructed a psychology that would make accessible for the first time the inner world of daydreaming which, when deciphered, offers clues into the causes of mental illness.

Incidentally, Freud's praise of Mitchell was never reciprocated. Like most of his colleagues, Mitchell was shocked and horrified by Freud's emphasis on sex. (This is one of the few sources of agreement between Mitchell and Gilman.) David Rein points out that "There are few references to sex in his books and articles on nervous diseases in women, nor is there much appreciation of the role of sex in normal behavior." See David M. Rein, *S. Weir Mitchell as a Psychiatric Novelist* (New York: International Universities Press, 1952), p. 44. Earnest comments that late in life Mitchell "attacked the psychoanalytic theories on the basis that they held 'that neurasthenia is always a disease of the mind alone—a psychogenesis.' His own belief was that 'a goodly proportion of neurasthenia . . . has no more psychic origin than has a colic.'" Mitchell's biographer adds that "Today, of course, even the source of a colic would be sought in the mind." See Earnest, op. cit., pp. 228–229. According to Earnest, Mitchell was so incensed with psychoanalytic theory that when he began to read a book on Freud that he had borrowed from the medical library, he sputtered: "Where did this filthy thing come from?" and threw the book in the fire.

[22] S. Weir Mitchell, *Doctor and Patient* (New York: Arno Press, 1972 [Reprint of 1888 edition]), p. 48.

[23] Ibid., p. 49.

[24] S. Weir Mitchell, *Wear and Tear* (New York: Arno Press, 1973 [Reprint of 1887 edition]), p. 32.

[25] Ibid., p. 57.

[26] Rein, op. cit., p. 46.

[27] Ibid., p. 50.

[28] Mitchell, *Doctor and Patient,* op. cit., p. 10.

[29] Ibid., p. 12.

[30] Ibid., p. 72.

[31] Ibid., p. 73.

[32] The preceding account comes from Gilman, *The Living,* op. cit., pp. 95–96, and Gilman, "Why I Wrote the Yellow Wallpaper," *The Forerunner,* Vol. 4 (1913), p. 271.

[33] Charlotte Perkins Gilman, *The Yellow Wallpaper* (1899; rpt. New York: The Feminist Press, 1973), p. 18. All references are to this edition.

[34] Freud, *Standard Edition,* (London: The Hogarth Press, 1953), Vol. IV, p. 225.

[35] William O'Neill has observed that "Mrs. Gilman's personal difficulties, and her distrust of sexual relations, prevented her from seeing that while popular Freudianism and the new sex ethic were certainly masculine in character, their purpose was not to divert women from marriage and motherhood but to repopularize these institutions, to make them intellectually respectable, as it were." See *Everyone Was Brave* (Chicago: Quadrangle Books, 1971), p. 319.

[36] "Why I Wrote The Yellow Wallpaper," p. 271.

[37] For a discussion of Howells' relationship to Mitchell, see Edwin H. Cady, *The Realist at War* (New York: Syracuse University Press, 1958), pp. 97–98. When Winifred Howells suffered what appeared to be a nervous breakdown in 1888, Howells called in Mitchell, an old friend and correspondent, to care for his daughter. In the words of Howells' biographer, "Mitchell agreed that Winifred's case was psycho-neurotic; he proposed to disregard her delusions of pain and force-

feed her from her shocking state of starvation back to the place where he could safely treat her for hysteria." After the daughter's unexpected death, an autopsy was performed and revealed that her terminal illness was organic, not psychological. Howells was flooded with guilt and remorse, though he did not blame Mitchell for the incorrect diagnosis.

[38] Mitchell seems to have played a more positive therapeutic role with another woman of letters, Edith Wharton. Edmund Wilson reports that Mitchell was instrumental in encouraging Wharton to write fiction during her nervous breakdown. See Wilson, *The Wound and the Bow* (New York: Oxford University Press, 1965), p. 160. Cynthia Wolff confirms the story in her biography, *A Feast of Words: The Triumph of Edith Wharton* (New York: Oxford University Press, 1977), p. 89. Joseph Lovering remarks, however, in *S. Weir Mitchell* (New York: Twayne, 1971), p. 26, that he is unable to corroborate this idea in any of the sources he has seen. There is no mention of Mitchell's relationship to Edith Wharton in another biographical study, Richard Walter, *S. Weir Mitchell, M.D.—Neurologist: A Medical Biography* (Springfield, Illinois: Charles C. Thomas, 1970).

[39] Gilman, "Why I Wrote The Yellow Wallpaper," op. cit., p. 271.

[40] Ibid., p. 271.

3: *Tender Is the Night:* Fitzgerald's *A Psychology for Psychiatrists*

[1] The Notes to *Tender Is the Night* quoted here and elsewhere may be found in "Appendix B" of Arthur Mizener's biography of Fitzgerald, *The Far Side of Paradise* (Boston: Houghton Mifflin, Sentry Edition, 1965), pp. 345–352.

[2] Matthew J. Bruccoli, *The Composition of Tender Is the Night* (Pittsburgh: University of Pittsburgh Press, 1963), p. 82.

[3] In addition to Mizener's biography, see Andrew Turnbull, *Scott Fitzgerald* (New York: Scribner's, 1962) and Matthew J. Bruccoli, *Some Sort of Epic Grandeur* (New York: Harcourt Brace Jovanovich, 1981). See also Nancy Milford, *Zelda* (New York: Harper and Row, 1970, Avon, 1971).

[4] For collections of Fitzgerald's correspondence, see Andrew Turnbull, ed., *The Letters of F. Scott Fitzgerald* (New York: Scribner's, 1963); John Kuehl and Jackson R. Bryer, eds., *Dear Scott/Dear Max* (New York: Scribner's, 1971); Matthew J. Bruccoli and Jennifer M. Atkinson, eds., *As Ever, Scott Fitz—* (New York: Lippincott, 1972); Matthew J. Bruccoli and Margaret M. Duggan, eds., *Correspondence of F. Scott Fitzgerald* (New York: Random House, 1980).

[5] Nancy Milford notes in *Zelda* (pp. 199–200) that Prangins Clinic, which opened in 1930, quickly became established as the foremost European clinic for the treatment of mental illness. James Joyce's daughter was diagnosed as schizophrenic by Dr. Oscar Forel, the director of Prangins, and twice institutionalized there.

[6] Bruccoli and Duggan, eds., *Correspondence of F. Scott Fitzgerald,* op. cit., p. 253.

[7] Ibid., p. 254. In the same letter Fitzgerald seems troubled by the vagueness of the expression "rest and 're-education' " that constituted Zelda's treatment at Prangins.

[8] Milford, op. cit., p. 220.

[9] Bruccoli and Duggan, eds., *Correspondence of F. Scott Fitzgerald,* op. cit., p. 284.

[10] Zelda Fitzgerald, *Save Me the Waltz* (New York: Scribner's, 1932, Signet, 1968).

[11] Matthew J. Bruccoli, "Afterword," Zelda Fitzgerald, *Save Me the Waltz,* op. cit., p. 205.

[12] Bruccoli, *Some Sort of Epic Grandeur,* op. cit., p. 347. The following quotations from the psychiatric transcript come from Bruccoli's biography, pp. 349–350.

[13] Bruccoli and Duggan, eds., *Correspondence of F. Scott Fitzgerald,* op. cit., p. 363. I have not corrected Fitzgerald's spelling in the quoted passage.

[14] To cite one example, in late summer/early fall of 1930 Zelda wrote Fitzgerald a long rambling letter from Prangins in which she accuses him of hurting her. "You gave me a flower and said it was 'plus petite et moins entendue'—We were friends—Then you took it away and I grew sicker, and there was nobody to teach me, so here I am, after five months of misery and agony and desperation" (Bruccoli and Duggan, eds., *Correspondence of F. Scott Fitzgerald,* op. cit., p. 249). In one of the letters Nicole Warren writes from her Swiss sanitarium to Dr. Dick Diver, she says: "One man was nice—he has a French officer and he understood. He gave me a flower and said it was 'plus petite et moins entendue.' We were friends. Then he took it away. I grew sicker and there was no one to explain to me." See F. Scott Fitzgerald, *Tender Is the Night* (New York: Scribner's, 1934, 1962 rpt.), p. 122. All subsequent references to the novel come from the 1962 edition.

[15] Bruccoli, *Some Sort of Epic Grandeur,* op. cit., p. 346. For a psychiatrist's report on Fitzgerald's alcoholism, see pp. 186–187.

[16] Bruccoli and Duggan, eds., *Correspondence of F. Scott Fitzgerald,* op. cit., p. 301.

[17] Turnbull, ed., *The Letters of F. Scott Fitzgerald,* op. cit., p. 238.

[18] Bruccoli and Duggan, eds., *Correspondence of F. Scott Fitzgerald,* op. cit., p. 372.

[19] *The Journal of Nervous and Mental Disease,* Vol. 82 (July–December, 1935), pp. 115–117.

[20] Jackson R. Bryer, "A Psychiatrist Reviews 'Tender Is the Night,' " *Literature and Psychology,* Vol. 16, Nos. 3–4 (1966), pp. 198–199.

[21] Frederick J. Hoffman, *Freudianism and the Literary Mind,* 2nd ed. (Baton Rouge: Louisiana State University Press, 1967), p. 271.

[22] After the original publication of this chapter in *Literature and Psychology,* I came across Mary E. Burton's interesting essay, "The Countertransference of Dr. Diver," *English Literary History,* Vol. 38, No. 3 (1971), pp. 459–471. Although Burton does not relate Fitzgerald's treatment of psychiatry in *Tender Is the Night* to Zelda's mental illness, she does briefly touch upon the significance of transference and countertransference in the novel. She does not explore, however, the dynamics of transference love in the story. For a psychiatrist's medical objections to certain aspects of *Tender Is the Night,* see the summary in Henry Dan Piper, *F. Scott Fitzgerald: A Critical Portrait* (New York: Holt, Rinehart and Winston, 1965). Interestingly, in *Some Sort of Epic Grandeur* (p. 414) Bruccoli quotes a memo Fitzgerald drafted to his daughter in 1936 on "How Would I grade my Knowledge

at 40." He gave himself a B+ in literature and attendant arts but only a C in his knowledge of psychiatry—a judgment that reflects Dr. Dick Diver's barely passing competency in his field.

[23] For a study of the various stages and revisions through which Fitzgerald's story evolved, see Bruccoli, *The Composition of Tender Is the Night,* op. cit.

[24] Turnbull, ed., *The Letters of F. Scott Fitzgerald,* op. cit., p. 346.

[25] Sigmund Freud, *An Autobiographical Study* (1925), *Standard Edition* (London: The Hogarth Press, 1959), Vol. XX, p. 42.

[26] Sigmund Freud, "Observations on Transference-Love" (1915), *Standard Edition* (London: The Hogarth Press, 1958), Vol. XII, p. 159. The following quotations come from this essay.

[27] Sigmund Freud, "Lines of Advance in Psycho-Analytic Therapy" (1919), *Standard Edition* (London: The Hogarth Press, 1955), Vol. XVII, p. 163.

[28] Bruccoli, *The Composition of Tender Is the Night,* op. cit., p. 206.

[29] D. S. Savage, "The Significance of F. Scott Fitzgerald," in Arthur Mizener, ed., *F. Scott Fitzgerald: A Collection of Critical Essays* (Englewood Cliffs, New Jersey: Prentice-Hall, 1963), pp. 152–153.

[30] Robert Stanton, " 'Daddy's Girl': Symbol and Theme in 'Tender Is the Night,' " *Modern Fiction Studies,* Vol. 4, No. 2 (Summer 1958), p. 136.

[31] Ibid., p. 142.

[32] For an early mention of incestuous love in *Tender Is the Night,* see Maxwell Geismar, "A Cycle of Fiction," in Robert E. Spiller, *et al.,* eds., *Literary History of the United States* (New York: Macmillan, 1949). Geismar writes: "Fitzgerald's work, like Poe's, is colored by the imagery of incest. *Tender Is the Night,* psychologically perhaps the most interesting of all Fitzgerald's novels, deals directly with this theme, but, as the later Fitzgerald said about his friend Ring Lardner, 'he had agreed with himself to speak only a small portion of his mind' " (p. 1299). Of the many later critics writing on this theme, see Richard Lehan, *"Tender Is the Night,"* in Marvin J. LaHood, ed., *Tender Is the Night: Essays in Criticism* (Bloomington: Indiana University Press, 1969): "When Nicole falls in love with Dick, he takes the place of her father. The fact that she falls out of love with him and that Dick commits symbolic incest with Rosemary, an act which leagues him with Devereux Warren, reveals Dick's failure to become a responsible 'father,' a position which, in this novel, Fitzgerald seems to equate with maturity" (p. 68).

[33] Savage, op. cit., p. 153.

[34] Mizener, *The Far Side of Paradise,* op. cit., p. 3.

[35] F. Scott Fitzgerald, "Babylon Revisited," in Arthur Mizener, ed., *The Fitzgerald Reader* (New York: Scribner's, 1963), p. 316. Charlie Wales's insight here eloquently illuminates the pattern of incestuous fixation in *Tender Is the Night.*

[36] See Turnbull, ed., *The Letters of F. Scott Fitzgerald,* op. cit., p. 64 and 78.

[37] Bruccoli, *Some Sort of Epic Grandeur,* op. cit., p. 79.

[38] For a discussion of Fitzgerald's fear of homosexuality, see ibid., pp. 278–279; 289. See also Ernest Hemingway's notorious account of Fitzgerald's fear of a small penis in "A Matter of Measurements," *A Moveable Feast* (New York: Scribner's, 1964), pp. 189–193.

[39] Leslie Fiedler, "Some Notes on F. Scott Fitzgerald," in Mizener, ed., *F. Scott Fitzgerald: A Collection of Critical Essays,* op. cit., p. 74.

[40] For examples of Fitzgerald's vituperative attack on women, see the following interviews published in Matthew J. Bruccoli and Jackson R. Bryer, eds., *In Our Own Time: A Miscellany* (New York: Popular Library, 1971): "Our American Women are Leeches," pp. 255–258, and "All Women Over Thiry-Five Should Be Murdered," pp. 263–266. Although there is a great deal of posturing in these early interviews as well as deliberate outrageousness, they do reveal in overstated language the misogyny that subtly appears in *Tender Is the Night*. For example, compare the following statement to any of the descriptions of the parasitic Baby Warren in *Tender Is the Night*. "Our American women are leeches. They're an utterly useless fourth generation trading on the accomplishment of their pioneer great-grandmothers. They simply dominate the American man" (p. 256).

[41] See Sigmund Freud, *The Origins of Psycho-Analysis: Letters to Wilhelm Fliess* (New York: Basic Books, 1954), pp. 215–218; 221–225, for Freud's account of the reasons for his abandonment of the seduction theory and his discovery of the importance of psychical wishes in the creation of seduction fantasies. In these letters Freud articulates for the first time the Oedipus complex and offers his interpretation of *Hamlet*.

[42] Matthew J. Bruccoli, ed., *The Notebooks of F. Scott Fitzgerald* (New York and London: Harcourt Brace Jovanovich, 1978), p. 204.

[43] It is interesting to see how Bruccoli, the foremost Fitzgerald scholar, has reluctantly reached this position. In *The Composition of Tender Is the Night,* op. cit., he criticizes the "Psychoanalytic branch of criticism" for establishing a close relationship between the Fitzgeralds and the Divers. He also dismisses the element of wishful thinking behind Nicole's recovery. "On this interpretation, Mrs. Fitzgerald's impossible recovery is achieved through Nicole; Fitzgerald is seen to be punishing himself for his complicity in his wife's breakdown by means of Dick's ignoble end. But it is not really necessary to plunge into the author's subconscious mind, for in the case of Fitzgerald the obvious parallels are sufficiently remarkable" (p. 82). In *Some Sort of Epic Grandeur,* op. cit., however, he implicitly endorses the psychoanalytic position. "In achieving Zelda's impossible cure in fiction Fitzgerald may have been trying to absolve himself of whatever guilt he felt for his wife's madness—as well as to punish himself for his self-indulgence and self-betrayal" (p. 341).

[44] One of Fitzgerald's most justly celebrated statements in *The Crack-Up* (New York: New Directions, 1945) eloquently describes Bleuler's idea of ambivalence: ". . . the test of a first-rate intelligence is the ability to hold two opposed ideas in the mind at the same time, and still retain the ability to function" (p. 69).

4: Religious Conversion or Therapy: The Priestly Psychiatrist in T. S. Eliot's *The Cocktail Party*

[1] T. S. Eliot, *The Cocktail Party,* in *The Complete Poems and Plays: 1909–1950* (New York: Harcourt, Brace & World, 1952), p. 342. All subsequent references are to this edition.

[2] T. S. Eliot, "The Search for Moral Sanction," *The Listener,* Vol. 7, No. 168 (30 March 1932), p. 445.

³T. S. Eliot, "The Future of an Illusion," *The Criterion,* Vol. 8, No. 31 (December 1928), p. 350.

⁴T. S. Eliot, "Thoughts After Lambeth," *Selected Essays* (London: Faber and Faber, 1932, Reprinted 1966), p. 370. All subsequent references are to the reprinted edition.

⁵T. S. Eliot, "Baudelaire in Our Time," *Essays Ancient and Modern* (New York: Harcourt, Brace and Company, 1936), p. 65.

⁶T. S. Eliot, "The Frontiers of Criticism," *On Poetry and Poets* (New York: Farrar, Straus, 1957), p. 123.

⁷Eliot, *Essays Ancient and Modern,* op. cit., p. 69.

⁸Eliot, *On Poetry and Poets,* op. cit., p. 107.

⁹The psychoanalyst, Freud writes in "On Beginning the Treatment: Further Recommendations on the Technique of Psycho-Analysis," *Standard Edition* (London: The Hogarth Press, 1958), Vol. XII, p. 130, "sets in motion a process, that of the resolving of existing repressions. He can supervise this process, further it, remove obstacles in its way, and he can undoubtedly vitiate much of it. But on the whole, once begun, it goes its own way and does not allow either the direction it takes or the order in which it picks up its points to be prescribed for it."

¹⁰Valerie Eliot, ed., *The Waste Land: A Facsimile and Transcript of the Original Drafts* (New York: Harcourt Brace Jovanovich, 1971), p. 129. All subsequent references are to this edition.

¹¹A. Alvarez, *The Savage God* (New York: Bantam, 1973).

¹²Bertrand Russell, *The Autobiography of Bertrand Russell: 1914–1944* (Boston: Little, Brown, 1968), p. 64.

¹³Stephen Spender, *T. S. Eliot* (New York: Viking, 1975), p. 134. Bertrand Russell quotes a letter he received from Eliot in 1925, emphasizing the responsibility he felt for his wife's illness. "I will tell you now that everything has turned out as you predicted 10 years ago. You are a great psychologist. Living with me has done her so much damage" *(The Autobiography of Bertrand Russell,* op. cit., p. 255). In *Great Tom* (New York: Harper and Row, 1974), T. S. Matthews cites a psychiatrist's comments after reading Vivienne's diaries. "The young girl is neurotic, feels insecure, particularly about her femininity. She suffers from psychosomatic illnesses. . . . In the end there is a picture of a full-blown paranoia with delusions. Absurd and pathetic as her delusions may appear, they are her reality. Her suffering is real . . . most likely a gifted person, at the same time vivacious and morose and 'complex'—a combination which can be very attractive if difficult to live with" (p. 104n.).

¹⁴Lyndall Gordon, *Eliot's Early Years* (Oxford: Oxford University Press, 1977), p. 75. Gordon suggests an intriguing link between Eliot's inhibition and his father's view of sex as "nastiness" that future biographers may wish to investigate further. "Henry Ware Sr. considered public [sex] instruction tantamount to giving children a letter of introduction to the Devil. Syphilis was God's punishment and he hoped a cure would never be found. Otherwise, he said, it might be necessary 'to emasculate our children to keep them clean' " (p. 27).

¹⁵Bernard Bergonzi, in *T. S. Eliot* (New York: Macmillan, 1972), has connected

Eliot's psychiatric treatment in Lausanne with these lines from *The Waste Land:* "By the waters of Leman I sat down and wept," and "On Margate sands/ I can connect/ Nothing with nothing" (p. 77).

[16] Harry Trosman, M.D., "T. S. Eliot and *The Waste Land:* Psychopathological Antecedents and Transformations," *Archives of General Psychiatry,* Vol. 30 (May 1974). All page numbers refer to this article. Also see Dr. Trosman's other article on Eliot, "After *The Waste Land:* Psychological Factors in the Religious Conversion of T. S. Eliot," *International Review of Psycho-Analysis,* Vol. 4 (1977), pp. 295–304.

[17] John Peter, "A New Interpretation of *The Waste Land*," *Essays in Criticism,* Vol. 2 (July 1952), pp. 242–266. Peter's controversial interpretation, linking Jean Verdenal to Phlebas the Phoenician in *The Waste Land,* infuriated Eliot. His solicitors succeeded in confiscating and destroying most of the copies of the issue.

[18] James E. Miller, Jr., *T. S. Eliot's Personal Waste Land* (University Park: Pennsylvania State University Press, 1977).

[19] Eliot, Valerie, ed., *The Waste Land: A Facsimile. . . ,* op. cit., p. xxiv.

[20] In *T. S. Eliot: A Memoir* (New York: Dodd, Mead, 1971) Robert Sencourt describes meeting Eliot and his wife in a spa near Geneva, where they all received hydrotherapy. "The treatment at Divonne which the Eliots and I took and from which Tom profited more than Vivienne, was a variant of the *douche écossaise* in which strong gushes of hot, alternating with icy cold, water were played on the naked body. The doctors on the whole deprecated drugs and avoided psychoanalysis. Their idea was that once they had gained a patient's confidence, he would soon divulge the reasons for his strain. It was evident that the strain from which my new friends were suffering was that they no longer lived together in deepest unity" (pp. 124–125).

[21] Eliot, *On Poetry and Poets,* op. cit., p. 116.

[22] For the earliest and best discussion of the psychiatric authenticity of Reilly, see Richard B. Hovey, "Psychiatrist and Saint in *The Cocktail Party,*" *Literature and Psychology,* Vol. 9, Nos. 3–4 (Summer and Fall 1959), pp. 51–55. Hovey argues that Eliot's "Inadequate understanding of depth psychology points up a limitation of his insight into Christianity" (p. 51). For Eliot's comments on Reilly, see "An Interview with T. S. Eliot," *The New York Times,* 16 April 1950, Section 2, p. 1. Eliot also discusses Reilly in "Reflections on *The Cocktail Party,*" *World Review,* New Series 9 (November 1949), pp. 19–22. To the question whether the psychiatrist is a *deus ex machina,* Eliot observes: "The doctor could not be a god *from* the machine, since he appears throughout, and not merely at the end. He might, however, be a god *in* the machine, and he certainly bears some slight resemblance to Heracles in Euripides' *Alcestis.* He is also an exceptional doctor who uses somewhat original methods" (p. 21).

[23] Robert B. Heilman, "Alcestis and *The Cocktail Party,*" *Comparative Literature,* Vol. 5 (1953), pp. 105–116.

[24] Abraham Kaplan, "Poetry, Medicine and Metaphysics," *Journal of the American Academy of Psychoanalysis,* Vol. 9, No. 1 (January 1981), pp. 106–107.

[25] Sigmund Freud, *The Ego and the Id* (1923), *Standard Edition* (London: The Hogarth Press, 1961), Vol. XIX, p. 50n.

²⁶ For a good discussion of the psychoanalytic meaning of emptiness, see Melvin Singer, "The Experience of Emptiness in Narcissistic and Borderline States, Parts I and II, *International Review of Psychoanalysis,* Vol. 4, Part 4 (1977), pp. 460–479.

²⁷ Leonard Unger, "T.S. Eliot's Images of Awareness," in Allen Tate, ed., *T.S. Eliot: The Man and His Work* (London: Chatto & Windus, 1967), p. 206.

²⁸ Grover Smith, *T.S. Eliot's Poetry and Plays* (Chicago: University of Chicago Press, 1956), p. 223.

²⁹ Lionel Trilling, *The Opposing Self* (New York: Viking, 1968), p. 146.

³⁰ Heinz Kohut, *The Analysis of the Self* (New York: International Universities Press, 1977), p. 20. For a different view of narcissism, see Otto Kernberg, *Borderline Conditions and Pathological Narcissism* (New York: Jason Aronson, 1980).

³¹ Kohut, op. cit., p. 85.

³² Sigmund Freud, "Mourning and Melancholia" (1917), *Standard Edition* (London: The Hogarth Press, 1957), Vol. XIV, p. 248.

³³ See Robert Langs, *Psychotherapy: A Basic Text* (New York: Jason Aronson, 1982). Langs defines misalliance as "A quality of the basic relationship between patient and therapist, or of a sector of that relationship, that is consciously or unconsciously designed to bypass adaptive insight in favor of either some other maladaptive form of symptom alleviation or the destruction of effective therapeutic work" (p. 733).

³⁴ Sigmund Freud, "The Loss of Reality in Neurosis and Psychosis" (1924), *Standard Edition* (London: The Hogarth Press, 1961), Vol. XIX, p. 185.

³⁵ Jacob A. Arlow and Charles Brenner, *Psychoanalytic Concepts and the Structural Theory* (New York: International Universities Press, 1964), p. 168.

³⁶ E. Martin Browne, *The Making of a Play: T. S. Eliot's The Cocktail Party* (Cambridge: Cambridge University Press, 1966), p. 22.

³⁷ The critics who approve of Celia's martyrdom include Helen Gardner, "The Comedies of T. S. Eliot," in Allen Tate, ed., *T. S. Eliot: The Man and His Work,* op. cit. She writes: "In Celia, the romantic quest for union is directed to its true object and consummated in death. *Causa diligendi Deum Deus est; modus est sine modo.* It is a happy ending for her, for we see the alternative in her first savage reaction to Edward's cowardice and rejection of her" (p. 171). Joseph Chiari, in *T. S. Eliot: Poet and Dramatist* (London: Vision Press, 1972), uses euphemistic language and intoxicated rhythms to describe the martyrdom. "Although the death of Celia could have been less colourful, the religious theme of the play emerges steadily and ripples out, embracing all the aspects of the social life to which the characters belong, and carrying with it an aura of greater and greater light, which lifts the 'Comedy' to a high level of dramatic achievement" (p. 135). Raymond Williams, in *Drama from Ibsen to Eliot* (Oxford: Oxford University Press, 1953), expresses similar approval.

Of the many critics who are disturbed by Eliot's treatment of Celia's death, Rossell Hope Robbins offers the most outspoken point of view in *The T. S. Eliot Myth* (New York: Henry Schuman, 1951). "The drama turns on Reilly's work as psychiatrist missionary in reconciling the Chamberlaynes to their hopeless inferiorities and to living with them and with themselves in dreary resignation; and in dispatching Celia, who has nobler stuff, into a convent and later on a mission where she will be privileged with the martyrdom of being eaten alive by ants nailed to a crucifix. This 'martyrdom' is the outstanding example in the play of Eliot's callous disregard for people" (pp. 21–22). Other critics who disapprove of the crucifixion include Philip Rahv, "T. S. Eliot: the Poet as Playwright," *Literature and the Sixth Sense* (Boston: Houghton Mifflin, 1969), p. 350; Trilling, *The Opposing Self,* p. 147; W. K. Wimsatt, Jr., "Eliot's Comedy," *Sewanee Review,* Vol. 58 (Autumn 1950), p. 667; Denis Donoghue, *"The Cocktail Party,"* in Hugh Kenner, ed., *T. S. Eliot: A Collection of Critical Essays* (Englewood Cliffs, N.J.: Prentice-Hall, 1962), pp. 183–184.

[38] For a discussion of the rigid determinism in *The Cocktail Party* and the failure of Celia's attempted salvation, see William Lynch, S. J., "Theology and the Imagination," *Thought* (Spring 1954), pp. 66–67. Walter Stein argues in "After the Cocktails," *Essays in Criticism,* Vol. 3, No. 1 (January 1953) that Eliot's vision of the play is "not that of a humane . . . Christianity" but of a disturbing Manichean world. For an analysis of Eliot's tendency toward determinism, see Yvor Winter's essay in Leonard Unger, ed., *T. S. Eliot: A Selected Critique* (New York: Holt Rinehart & Winston, 1948), pp. 97–113.

[39] Stephen Spender, *T. S. Eliot,* op. cit., p. 218. Other critics concur. Subhas Sarkar, in *T. S. Eliot the Dramatist* (Calcutta: Minerva Associates, 1972), remarks: "No one can escape the feeling that the playwright has, rather, forced upon Celia a cruel fate she does not deserve" (pp. 180–181). He quotes another critic's observation of Celia's martyrdom: "She was bullied into sainthood—Shanghaied" (p. 181).

[40] If Vivienne lived on a "knife-edge," as Russell suggested, Eliot must have wondered at whom the blade was pointed. His biographers have acknowledged his unconscious aggressive impulses toward women, a conclusion that is consistent with the misogyny in *The Cocktail Party.* Matthews notes: "Eliot's sense of guilt seems not only to have been built into him but to have centered on two peculiar obsessions which he stated as general truths: that every man wants to murder a girl; that sex is sin is death" (*Great Tom,* op. cit., p. 98). In "After *The Waste Land,*" op. cit., Dr. Trosman writes that "there are indications of increasing preoccupations with unconscious aggression directed towards his wife in the years prior to his conversion" (p. 302). Given Eliot's aggression toward women, it is difficult to avoid the conclusion that both the playwright and Dr. Reilly are projecting the identical death wish in the form of glorious martyrdom upon Celia. See also George Whiteside, "T. S. Eliot: The Psychobiographical Approach," *The Southern Review* (University of Adelaide, Australia), Vol. 6 (March 1973), pp. 3–26. Curiously, even so excellent a psychological literary critic as C. L. Barber has defended the belief that Reilly's actions are only slightly unusual. "But if his conduct is sometimes unprofessional—or para-professional—his attitude towards himself and his powers is more human, more humble, than that of many an actual professional man on whom we force the role of medicine man." See "The Power of Development" in F. O. Matthiessen, *The Achievement of T.S. Eliot* (Oxford: Oxford University Press, 1959, pp. 235–236). The distinguished literary critic and biographer Leon Edel makes the same mistake when he observes that "The

interpersonal strategy used by the psychoanalyst in *The Cocktail Party* springs also out of a familiarity with modern psychoanalytic theory." See "Psychoanalysis and the 'Creative' Arts" in Judd Marmor, ed., *Modern Psychoanalysis: New Directions and Perspectives* (New York: Basic Books, 1968, p. 636). The truth is not that Eliot goes "beyond psychiatry," as too many readers have assumed, but that he never comes close to imagining the art of psychiatry, with its limitations and therapeutic possibilities.

[41] T. S. Eliot, "Introduction" to G. Wilson Knight, *The Wheel of Fire* (London: Methuen and Company, 1962), p. xx.

[42] Eliot's fear of self-exposure may explain his reluctance to speak about the "meaning" of his art and the extreme defensiveness of his remarks when he does offer commentary. An example is his often-quoted dismissal of the meaning of *The Waste Land*. "Various critics have done me the honor to interpret the poem in terms of the contemporary world, have considered it, indeed, as an important bit of social criticism. To me it was only the relief of a personal and wholly insignificant grouse against life; it is just a piece of rhythmical grumbling" (*The Waste Land: A Facsimile*, p. 1). By contrast, recall D. H. Lawrence's shrewd observation: never trust the teller, only the tale.

[43] See D. W. Winnicott, "Transitional Objects and Transitional Phenomena" (1953) and "The Location of Cultural Experience" (1967), both reprinted in *Playing and Reality* (London: Tavistock Publications, 1971).

[44] Robert Waelder, "The Principle of Multiple Function," *Psychoanalytic Quarterly*, Vol. 5 (1936), pp. 45–62.

[45] Erik H. Erikson, *Young Man Luther* (New York: Norton, 1958), p. 36.

5: "If Writing Is Not an Outlet, What Is?": Sylvia Plath and *The Bell Jar*

[1] Frances McCullough, ed., *The Journals of Sylvia Plath,* (New York: Dial, 1982), pp. 113–114. Hereafter referred to as *Journals*. All references are to this edition.

[2] See A. Alvarez, *The Savage God* (New York: Bantam, 1973), pp. 3–39.

[3] Aurelia Schober Plath, ed., *Letters Home* (New York: Harper and Row, 1975), p. 3. All references are to this edition.

[4] Ted Hughes, ed., *The Collected Poems,* (New York: Harper and Row, 1981), p. 245. All references are to this edition.

[5] See Plath's *Journals,* p. 269, for her own account of this marriage note.

[6] For a brief characterization of Otto Plath, see Edward Butscher, *Sylvia Plath: Method and Madness* (New York: Seabury, 1976). "All those who knew Otto Plath intimately," Butscher writes, "agreed that he was nothing like the Prussian tyrant later projected by his daughter's writing; but in varying degrees they also felt that there was a certain rigidity about him, a stiffness in his behavior and attitudes, which became more pronounced as he grew older" (p. 7). Nancy Hunter Steiner, Plath's roommate at Smith, reports in *A Closer Look at Ariel* (New York: Popular Library, 1973) that she talked freely about her father's death and her reactions to it. " 'He was an autocrat,' she recalled. 'I adored and despised him, and I proba-

bly wished many times that he were dead. When he obliged me and died, I imagined that I had killed him' " (pp. 62–63).

[7] In her *Journals* Plath discusses the psychological origin of ulcers, and she implicitly has her mother in mind. "Ulcers: desire for dependency & feeling it is wrong to be dependent: you reject food (mother's milk), dependency, and yet get dependency by being sick: it's the ulcer to blame, not you" (p. 291).

[8] Butscher, op. cit., p. 7. Given the closeness of age between Plath's father and maternal grandfather, and the fact that after Otto Plath's death Sylvia's grandparents moved in to live with the Plath family, Frank Schober must have played an important role in the formation of Sylvia's image of men; yet we know very little about him and his influence on her.

[9] See Margaret S. Mahler, *On Human Symbiosis and the Vicissitudes of Individuation* (New York: International Universities Press, 1968), *Volume 1, Infantile Psychosis,* and Margaret S. Mahler, Fred Pine, and Anni Bergman, *The Psychological Birth of the Human Infant* (New York: Basic Books, 1975). Mahler defines the separation and individuation process as the "establishment of a sense of separateness from, and relation to, a world of reality, particularly with regard to the experience of *one's own body* and to the principal representative of the world as the infant experiences it, the *primary love object*" (*The Psychological Birth of The Human Infant,* p. 3).

[10] In the "Foreword" to *The Journals* Ted Hughes remarks that the published journals constitute perhaps a third of the entire content. Two other notebooks survived for a time, continuing Plath's autobiographical account from late 1959 to within three days of her death. Hughes destroyed one of the notebooks because he did not want the children to read their mother's writings. The other notebook, Hughes says, disappeared.

[11] The "omissions" are not only present in Plath's journals but, we suspect, in her correspondence as well. In *Letters Home* there is a gap between August 1, 1958 and July 29, 1959— a turbulent period for Plath in that it was during this time that she began to acknowledge inner rage, directed mainly toward her parents. The liberation of these feelings also coincided with or was released by the resumption of psychotherapy. There is no indication in *Letters Home* that she was beginning to work through her volatile emotions toward her mother. Indeed, it is remarkable how Plath avoids revealing anything of a disturbing nature to her mother. *Letters Home* remains Plath's greatest fiction, an elaborate mask which expresses only sweetness and loyalty. It is impossible for us to know whether she did indeed write letters filled with accusation and bitterness, which Mrs. Plath understandably withheld from publication, or whether Sylvia was simply unable to acknowledge these feelings in a letter.

[12] Hughes, ed., op. cit., p. 117. Actually, "Electra on Azalea Path" is less about the daughter's love for her father than it is about her hate for him. Although the poem ends with the line, "It was my love that did us both to death," the implication is that the daughter's murderous thoughts were responsible for his death (as Plath said in her comments to Nancy Hunter Steiner). Azalea Path, incidentally, was the name of the cemetery path beside which Otto Plath's grave lies in Winthrop, Mass. For a discussion of the various ways in which instincts undergo

transformations, see Freud's important essay, "Instincts and Their Vicissitudes," (1915), *Standard Edition* (London: The Hogarth Press, 1957), Vol. XIV, pp. 111–140. One of Freud's statements about the ambivalence of love has particular relevance to Plath's convoluted feelings toward her father. "If a love-relation with a given object is broken off, hate not infrequently emerges in its place, so that we get the impression of a transformation of love into hate" (p. 139). Although Freud does not consider the transformation of hate into love, this is what happens during the process of overidealization. In the same volume of the *Standard Edition* appears another important essay, "Mourning and Melancholia" (1917), which Plath read and commented upon in her journals.

[13] There are additional elements in the dream that we have not commented upon, such as the reference to Mrs. Plath's father in the manifest dream content (Frank Schober worked in various capacities at the Brookline Country Club).

[14] Dr. Beuscher's name was first revealed in an editorial comment in *The Collected Poems* (p. 288), though oddly enough the name is misspelled on both occasions. (The name appears as "Beutscher," a cross between Beuscher and Butscher, Plath's biographer. Given Ted Hughes's displeasure with the biography—in *The Journals* there is a reference to the "absence of a good biography" on Plath—his misspelling of the psychiatrist's name may be a "Freudian slip.")

[15] *American Psychiatric Association: Biographical Directory of the Fellows and Members* (New York: Bowker, 1977), p. 70.

[16] Readers interested in Dr. Barnhouse's publications should begin with Ruth Tiffany Barnhouse and Urban T. Holmes, III, eds., *Male and Female: Christian Approaches to Sexuality,* (New York: Seabury, 1976), and Ruth Tiffany Barnhouse, *Homosexuality: A Symbolic Confusion* (New York: Seabury, 1977). Among her articles are "Sex in Counseling: Some Theoretical Aspects," *Counseling and Values,* Vol. 19, No. 3 (April 1975), pp. 147–154; "The Spiritual Exercises of St. Ignatius and Psychoanalytic Therapy: A Comparison," *The Way* (Spring 1975), pp. 74–82; "The Religious Identity of Women," *NICM Journal* (Fall 1976), pp. 7–19; and "Sex Between Patient and Therapist," *Journal of the American Academy of Psychoanalysis,* Vol. 6, No. 4 (1978), pp. 533–546.

[17] Anyone who sees an irresolvable antagonism between religion and psychotherapy—as T. S. Eliot obviously did—should read Dr. Barnhouse's publications. She gracefully puts to rest many of the arguments that continue to be expressed by partisans of one camp or another. Stating that the Christian doctrine of original sin is compatible with the psychoanalytic concept of illness, she makes a statement that Eliot's psychiatrist, Sir Harcourt-Reilly, would do well to heed:

> "The concept of illness in the psychological and emotional fields should
> have been used to illuminate the concept of sin, not to replace it. It
> should have been used to assist us in understanding the dynamics of
> particular failures, to illuminate the virtue of mercy, to bring wisdom
> to the delicate processes involved both in penitence and in absolu-
> tion. But just as the concept of sin was often abused by those who,
> lost in personal power and pride, wished to dominate and control
> others while hiding behind a cynical pretense of saving their souls,

so the concept of illness is now being abused in parallel ways, and for the same sinful reasons" (Barnhouse, *Homosexuality: A Symbolic Confusion*, p. 150).

[18] Edward Butscher argues that as a result of Plath's psychiatric treatment in 1953 there were changes, often startling, in her feelings and behavior, but that these changes were "the result of Freudian additions to the mask and did not represent any basic alteration in character" (Butscher, *Sylvia Plath: Method and Madness*, p. 125). This may have been true, but it is clear from her journals that not only were there startling changes in her feelings as a consequence of her second treatment with Dr. Beuscher (which the biographer was not aware of), she was analyzing her masks as well. Whether the half-year analysis was sufficiently long to effect major changes in her life is impossible to say; the fact that she committed suicide five years later does not invalidate the emotional and intellectual gains she made during treatment.

[19] On more than one occasion in the journals, Plath expresses a strong aversion to her body and a wish to have been born a man. "Being born a woman is my awful tragedy. From the moment I was conceived I was doomed to sprout breasts and ovaries rather than penis and scrotum; to have my whole circle of action, thought and feeling rigidly circumscribed by my inescapable femininity" (*The Journals*, p. 30). There are several interpretations of this wish, and it is unclear whether Freud's controversial theory of penis envy applies here and, if so, whether we are talking about cultural, biological, or psychological factors. Dr. Barnhouse, who sharply disputes Freud's understanding of female psychology, takes an equivocal position on the subject of penis envy. "More than once in my professional career I have toyed with the idea of giving up that concept altogether only to have some woman come into my office and in the very first interview tell me that as a child she desperately wanted to be a boy and the worst frustration of her life was when she finally had to accept the fact that she could not urinate standing up!" (Barnhouse, *Homosexuality: A Symbolic Confusion*, p. 69). The psychiatrist concludes that until we live in a culture which values women as much as it values men, it will be impossible to sort out cultural from psychological factors in the formation of female sexuality.

[20] ". . . no patient ever gets well because the doctor has figured out what is wrong," Dr. Barnhouse writes. "Patients must learn to *feel differently* about themselves and this can only come about through a corrective emotional experience which is based on the interpersonal transaction between the patient and the therapist" (Barnhouse, *Homosexuality: A Symbolic Confusion*, p. 98).

[21] For a detailed discussion of the *Doppelgänger* relationship between Esther Greenwood and Joan Gilling, see Jeffrey Berman, "Sylvia Plath and the Art of Dying" in Leonard F. Manheim, M. D. Faber, and Harvey L.P. Resnik, eds., *A New Anatomy of Melancholy: Patterns of Self-Aggression Among Authors, University of Hartford Studies in Literature,* Vol. 10, Nos. 1, 2, 3 (Fall 1978), pp. 137–155.

[22] Butscher asserts, though without citing evidence, that, toward the end of Plath's treatment with Dr. Beuscher in the fall of 1954, their "friendship had developed to the point where they spent most of the hour gossiping about college af-

fairs"(*Sylvia Plath: Method and Madness,* op. cit., p. 137). There is certainly no evidence in *The Journals* that the psychiatrist had violated the ground rules of therapy in the 1958–1959 treatment.

[23] The human quality of Plath's psychiatrist is apparent to anyone who reads her publications. In acknowledging the potentially destructive effect of the analyst's countertransference upon the patient, Dr. Barnhouse candidly speaks about the difficulty of maintaining analytic neutrality in certain situations. "For instance, I myself am not able to treat patients who batter their children. I know intellectually that these people need help, and even what their general problems are likely to be. But the anger and outrage I feel toward anyone who abuses children is so great that I am completely unable to form a therapeutic alliance with them" (Barnhouse, *Homosexuality: A Symbolic Confusion,* pp. 98–99).

[24] Sigmund Freud, "Dostoevsky and Parricide" (1928), *Standard Edition* (London: The Hogarth Press, 1961), Vol. XXI, p. 177.

[25] Quoted by Lois Ames, "Sylvia Plath: A Biographical Note," in *The Bell Jar* (1963; rpt. New York: Harper and Row, 1971), p. 293. All references to *The Bell Jar* come from the reprinted edition.

[26] Judith Kroll, to cite but one critic, insists in *Chapters in a Mythology* (New York: Harper and Row, 1976) on a rigorous separation between Plath's art and life. Kroll is certainly correct to separate Plath the serious poet from the writer who has become the unfortunate object of cult popularity. Additionally, Kroll's sensitive literary readings have demonstrated Plath's artistry and unity of vision. Kroll urges an aesthetic detachment, however, that is not only impossible for most readers but also highly questionable in its moral and psychological implications. Art, like life, always involves value judgments, and the suspension of these judgments exacts a human price. To approach Plath mainly as a mythic poet and to minimize the confessional aspects of her work is to see her art as less disturbing than it really is. Such an approach represents, psychoanalytically, the attempt to insulate art from life and thus deny the terrifying reality of Plath's vision. Her art cannot be reduced to a psychiatric case study, as Kroll rightly notes, nor can it be divorced from Plath's inner conflicts, defenses, and adaptive strategies. Plath was a mythic poet, to be sure, but her self-created mythic system was also a product of unconscious fears and fantasies. Childhood experiences give rise to myths which in turn shape adult behavior. The question is not whether the literary critic uses "psychology" but the accuracy of the critic's psychologizings. Kroll observes, for example, that the tension between Plath's false and true selves was "initially determined by her relation to her father" (*Chapters in a Mythology,* op. cit., p. 10); but this contradicts everything we know about developmental psychology, which offers overwhelming proof of the primary influence of the mother in the formation of the child's identity. And when Kroll suggests that "in the case of her mother, the need to exorcise may reflect not a lack but an excess of gratitude" (p. 253), she is contradicting Plath's explicit analysis of her feelings in the journals. There can never be an excess of genuine love; Plath was struggling against love that was contingent upon success and perfection. The publication of her journals gives us a deeper insight into the formative influences on her art and life, and many of

the biographical and literary statements that have been made about Plath will need to be revised, including the mythic assumptions.

[27] Edward Butscher refers to Plath's "schizophrenic depression," but there is no evidence that she was schizophrenic in the precise meaning of the term. There apparently were no schizophrenic symptoms, such as delusions or hallucinations, and no evidence that she broke completely with reality. Nor was she psychotic. For a different psychoanalytic view from the one I am proposing here, see David Holbrook, *Sylvia Plath: Poetry and Existence* (London: Athlone Press, 1976). Relying upon the British school of psychoanalysis (Melanie Klein, D. W. Winnicott, W. R. D. Fairbairn), Holbrook argues that Plath reveals a schizoid vision of reality. One of the limitations of his approach, however, is that he assumes that Plath had an untroubled relationship with her mother and father, and that consequently her rage toward them had no biographical justification.

[28] The two leading theoreticians in the area of narcissism, Heinz Kohut and Otto Kernberg, both agree on the clinical description of narcissism and on the existence of the "grandiose self," but they disagree on the origins and treatment of the disorder. Kohut maintains that the grandiose self reflects a fixation (or developmental arrest) of an archaic, normal primitive self. Kernberg argues that the grandiose self is a pathological structure, clearly different from normal infantile narcissism. Whereas Kohut believes that the analyst must accept the patient's narcissistic transference to complete a normal process that has been arrested, Kernberg maintains that the analyst must interpret the rage behind the patient's overidealization. Of the two approaches to narcissism, Kohut's is the more original, Kernberg's the more classical. Despite their sharp disagreements on narcissism, the basic agreement of Kohut and Kernberg on the existence of the grandiose self is what most concerns us here.

[29] Otto Kernberg, *Borderline Conditions and Pathological Narcissism* (New York: Jason Aronson, 1975), p. 227. All references come from this edition.

[30] See Edith Jacobson, *The Self and the Object World* (New York: International Universities Press, 1964).

[31] Others have noticed the theme of identity diffusion in Plath's life and art. In *A Closer Look at Ariel*, Nancy Hunter Steiner remarks on how she had to distance herself from Plath to maintain her own separate identity. "She referred to me in letters to her mother as her alter ego," Steiner writes, "and often remarked that we presented a mirror image or represented opposite sides of the same coin" (p. 58). David Holbrook quotes Ted Hughes affirming the lack of distance between wife and husband. "There was no rivalry between us . . . in these circumstances you begin to write out of one brain . . . we were like two feet of one body . . . A working partnership, all absorbing" (*Sylvia Plath: Poetry and Existence,* [London: Athlone Press, 1976], p. 119). As Holbrook notes, Plath came to reject this intense identification. Biographical evidence suggests that the symbiotic relationship between mother and daughter was repeated in all her later friendships, and that she both desired and feared this excessive closeness.

[32] One of the main differences between the journals and the novel is that in the former we see a more complete portrait of Plath's craving for academic and artis-

tic success, while in the latter Esther implies that she never really believed in the perfectionism she was pursuing. Esther's jaded view of success does not accurately reflect the complexity of Plath's feelings on the subject.

[33] In one of her journal entries, Plath chillingly plots a future attack on one of her best friends. "Given time . . . I'll attack her next year and get at her good innards. Innocence my mask" (*The Journals*, p. 186).

[34] In *The Journals* Plath describes her visit to her father's grave in 1959, while she is deep in therapy; in *The Bell Jar* Esther's visit to the cemetery immediately precedes her suicide attempt in 1953. The effect of the chronological change is to strengthen the connection between Esther's suicide attempt and the fusion with the father, whereas Plath's suicide attempt in 1953 may have more directly involved pre-Oedipal issues of separation from the mother.

[35] Worm imagery in Plath's poetry often contains phallic symbolism. In "Daddy" the speaker defiantly rejects both her father and husband, proclaiming: "The black telephone's off at the root,/ The voices just can't worm through"; in "Lady Lazarus" she compares her suicide attempt to a withdrawal into a seashell: "They had to call and call/ And pick the worms off me like sticky pearls."

[36] See *The Journals* (p. 312) for Plath's fear of infertility. "If I could not have children—and if I do not ovulate how can I?—How can they make me?—I would be dead. Dead to my woman's body. Intercourse would be dead, a dead end."

[37] See Frederick Crews, *Out of My System* (Oxford: Oxford University Press, 1975), for a useful distinction between reductive and reductionistic approaches to literature. A reductive approach, he suggests, may divert "attention from the text to something that purportedly lies behind the text and helps to explain it"; a reductive interpretation may be "possibly quite justifiable and helpful" (p. 169). In general, however, Crews—who has been sympathetic to psychoanalytic literary criticism in the past—now takes a dim view of it, dismissing most of it as reductionistic.

[38] H. D., *Tribute to Freud* (New York: McGraw-Hill, 1974). Although there is no evidence that Plath read this book, there are interesting similarities between *Tribute to Freud* and *The Bell Jar*, including the central metaphor. "There was . . . a second globe or bell-jar rising as if it were from my feet. I was enclosed. I felt I was safe but seeing things as through water" (H. D., *Tribute to Freud*, p. 130). Compare this to Esther's statement in *The Bell Jar*: "To the person in the bell jar, blank and stopped as a dead baby, the world itself is the bad dream" (p. 267). H. D.'s psychoanalysis with Freud freed her from writer's block and made possible a burst of literary productivity. There are other similarities which, however coincidental, are worth noting. A character named Hilda (H. D.'s first name) appears in *The Bell Jar*, and in *Tribute to Freud* a figure called Joan seizes H. D.'s personal belongings in a way that anticipates Joan Gilling's symbolic appropriation of Esther Greenwood's personality.

[39] David Holbrook argues that Dr. Nolan "is even more sinister than Dr. Gordon: she coerces in such a *nice* way" (*Sylvia Plath: Poetry and Existence,* op. cit., p. 102), but this is a misreading. Far from being a "petrifier," the female psychiatrist befriends Esther and helps to restore her trust in others.

[40] Quoted by Butscher, op. cit., p. 159.

[41] Murray M. Schwartz and Christopher Bollas, "The Absence at the Center: Sylvia Plath and Suicide," *Criticism*, Vol. 18, No. 2 (Spring 1976), pp. 147–172. Reprinted in Gary Lane, ed., *Sylvia Plath: New Views on the Poetry* (Baltimore: Johns Hopkins University Press, 1979), pp. 179–202.

[42] Butscher, op. cit., p. 308.

[43] Kroll, op. cit., p. 148.

[44] In *The Savage God* Alvarez gives the impression that Plath was doomed by the intensity of her art, and that she was resigned to suicide. Nothing could be further from the truth. Although Alvarez is correct when he says that artistic creation is not always therapeutic (he maintains, in fact, the opposite view: that art increases the vulnerability of certain writers to suicide), he fails to acknowledge the extent to which Plath's writing contributed to her psychic health. So too does he fail to appreciate Plath's indebtedness to her psychiatrist. "Having been bitten once by American psychiatry," he writes, "she hesitated for some time before writing for an appointment" with another psychotherapist in England (p. 32). As *The Journals* eloquently makes clear, she was not "bitten" by psychiatry but helped in ways that we are only now beginning to appreciate.

6: *I Never Promised You a Rose Garden:* The Limits of the Fictional Psychiatric Case Study

[1] Sigmund Freud, *Fragment of an Analysis of a Case of Hysteria* (1905), *Standard Edition* (London: The Hogarth Press, 1953), Vol. VII, p. 9.

[2] Hannah Green, "In Praise of My Doctor—Frieda Fromm-Reichmann," *Contemporary Psychoanalysis*, Vol. 4, No. 1 (Fall 1967), pp. 73–77. In presenting the Frieda Fromm-Reichmann Award in 1967, the Awards Committee, consisting of members of the American Academy of Psychoanalysis, characterized the impact of *Rose Garden* in the following way. "The book has made an enormous impact upon large sections of the general population and has exerted particularly strong appeal to medical students and residents. At the University of Pennsylvania I would estimate that one half of the medical students have read this book, and that it has done as much for their understanding of psychiatry in general, and schizophrenia, particularly, as any other single aspect of our teaching program. . . ." I am grateful to Joanne Greenberg for sending me a copy of this talk and for her responses to my inquiries.

[3] For Joanne Greenberg's lively discussion of the reasons for using a pseudonym in *Rose Garden* and the decision to use her real name, see Stephen E. Rubin, "Conversations with the Author of '*I Never Promised You a Rose Garden*,'" *The Psychoanalytic Review*, Vol. 59, No. 2 (1972), pp. 201–215.

[4] Frieda Fromm-Reichmann, *Psychoanalysis and Psychotherapy*, Dexter M. Bullard, ed., "Foreword" by Edith V. Weigert (Chicago: University of Chicago Press, 1959). Frieda Fromm-Reichmann also wrote *Principles of Intensive Psychotherapy* (Chicago: University of Chicago Press, 1950). All references come from these editions. For a discussion of the uniqueness of Chestnut Lodge Sanitarium, see Helm Stierlin, *Conflict and Reconciliation: A Study in Human Relation and Schizophrenia* (Garden City: Anchor, 1969), pp. 231–235.

[5] Joanne Greenberg, *I Never Promised You a Rose Garden* (New York: Signet, 1964), p. 18. All references come from this edition.

[6] Peter Shaffer, *Equus* (New York: Avon, 1974), p. 124. Also see Jeffrey Berman, *"Equus:* 'After Such Little Forgiveness, What Knowledge?' " *The Psychoanalytic Review,* Vol. 66 (Fall 1979), pp. 407–422.

[7] Anthony Burgess, *A Clockwork Orange* (New York: Norton, 1963), p. 129.

[8] Kary K. and Gary K. Wolfe, "Metaphors of Madness: Popular Psychological Narratives," *Journal of Popular Culture,* Vol. IX, No. 4 (Spring 1976), p. 905. For a social scientist's approach to *Rose Garden,* replete with statistical tables and reliability scales, see Philip Lichtenberg and Dolores G. Norton, "Honesty, Trust, Equality in the Treatment of Schizophrenia: An Analysis of *I Never Promised You a Rose Garden,*" *Pennsylvania Psychiatric Quarterly,* Vol. 10 (1970), pp. 33–40.

[9] According to Joanne Greenberg, she and Frieda Fromm-Reichmann planned to coauthor a book on schizophrenia. The psychiatrist's death in 1957 made this impossible. See "Conversations with the Author of '*I Never Promised You a Rose Garden,*' " p. 206.

[10] Sigmund Freud, *An Outline of Psycho-Analysis, Standard Edition* (London: The Hogarth Press, 1964), Vol. XXIII, p. 174.

[11] In accepting the Frieda Fromm-Reichmann Award, Greenberg expressed a quality of the psychiatrist not found in *Rose Garden:*

> Frieda was one of the great natural actresses. This skill permitted her to show subtle gradations of approval or disapproval without committing herself to the force of a word. She liked to use her face and voice to mimic—sometimes to satirize parts of both the sick and the reasonable worlds. Her satire was balanced and never used in malice. The acting was from herself but she never seemed to *act herself* as a role. She had less need for this protection than any one I know. Frieda's hallmark was an artist's—a light touch. Her genius was to bring it to her work whole and as naturally as breathing" (Green, "In Praise of My Doctor—Frieda Fromm-Reichmann," p. 75).

For a humorous portrait of Frieda Fromm-Reichmann by a patient who is now a distinguished analyst, see Leslie H. Farber, "Lying on the Couch," *Lying, Despair, Jealousy, Envy, Sex, Suicide, Drugs, and the Good Life* (New York: Basic Books, 1976), pp. 215–218. Also see "Sincerity and Authenticity: A Symposium with Lionel Trilling, Irving Howe, Leslie H. Farber and William Hamilton," *Salmagundi,* Vol. 41 (Spring 1978), pp. 102–104.

[12] In *Principles of Intensive Psychotherapy,* Frieda Fromm-Reichmann warns against the abandonment of strict analytic neutrality. "Deep down in his mind, no patient wants a nonprofessional relationship with his therapist, regardless of the fact that he may express himself to the contrary. Something in him senses, as a rule in spite of himself, that an extra-professional relationship with his psychiatrist will interfere with a patient's tendency toward change and improvement in his mental condition" (p. 46).

[13] The effort to preserve the analyst's confidentiality led Tilmann Moser to avoid disclosing the name or any biographical details of his own analyst. Moser's book,

Years of Apprenticeship on the Couch (New York: Urizen Books, 1977), is a remarkable narration of the author's training analysis. For a delightful account of how
an analyst can become entrapped in his patient's fabrications, see Robert Lindner,
The Fifty-Minute Hour: A Collection of True Psychoanalytic Tales (New York: Holt,
Rinehart and Winston, 1955).

[14] See Jeffrey Berman, "The Multiple Faces of *Eve* and *Sybil:* 'E Pluribus Unum,' "
Psychocultural Review, Vol. 2, No. 1 (Winter 1978), pp. 1–25.

[15] The ambiguities of "Full weight" are lost to the reader of *Rose Garden* unless
he knows that the words "wet" and "weight" derive from a traumatic childhood
incident at camp, during which the youth expressed in symbolic form her resentment of her father and defiance of her mother, respectively. Frieda Fromm-
Reichmann narrates the story in considerable detail in *Psychoanalysis and
Psychotherapy,* op. cit., pp. 182–183, to demonstrate that a psychotic patient can
untangle a knotty linguistic pattern, with the analyst's help. There can be no doubt
about the identity of the anonymous patient. In a preceding paragraph the doctor
alludes to an operation performed on the five-year-old-girl, who had been punished and humiliated by her parents for bed-and-pants-wetting:

> . . . she came from a family in which the women were disposed to
> become overweight, and avoidance of overweight was made a reli-
> gion. In defiance, the patient developed into an obese, compulsive
> eater. "Pants-wetting and overweight belong together," she volun-
> teered one day during a psychoanalytic interview, "and not only be-
> cause both are connected with defiance and resentment against my
> parents and with the anxiety connected with these feelings." There
> followed a pause. Then she went on, *"Wet* and *weight* belong to-
> gether, but I don't know how." Eventually a childhood memory fol-
> lowed: the patient was in the dressing cabin at the swimming pool
> of a camp which she attended upon parental dictum and against her
> own wishes. She shared this cabin with another girl. While alone there
> in the nude, she had to urinate, and she wet her large turkish towel.
> When the patient heard the other girl coming into the cabin, she tried
> to wring the wet towel, and she remembered how hard it was to do
> this when she was only a little girl. "It was 'the *weight*' of the '*wet*'
> towel which made it so hard," she stated. "There you are, 'weight
> and wet.' 'Wet' has to do with my resentment against my father,
> 'weight' with my defiance against mother, and I hated them both for
> forcing me to go to that camp. So they might not love me any more.
> . . . So I was frightened. . . . There you have my whole hostility
> and meanness, and my whole anxiety. 'Wet' and 'weight' are father
> and mother, and the camp stands for both of them."

In *Rose Garden* we learn about Deborah's overeating, and her embarrassment
and humiliation at summer camp, but not about the relationship between "wet"
and "weight." Surely the novelist did not expect us to make this connection, but
are we to infer from the psychiatric case study that Deborah's assertion of "full
weight" at the end of *Rose Garden* has unexpected meaning, her healthy defiance
of and independence from her parents? In any event, the creation of *Rose Garden*

was a cathartic act, a lifting of an intolerable weight or burden from the artist. Like *The Bell Jar, Rose Garden* ends on a note of resolution and health but, unlike Plath's biography, Greenberg's life has remained free from mental illness. Her continued literary production—she has written three other novels and two collections of short stories—affirms the truth of Frieda Fromm-Reichmann's statement in *Psychoanalysis and Psychotherapy:* "A person can emerge from a severe mental disorder as an artist of rank. His previous liabilities in terms of his pathogenic history, the expression of his subsequent mental disorder—that is, symptomatology—or his inner responses to either of them can be converted into assets" (p. 5). Occasionally, fairy-tale endings to troubled beginnings do come true, both in life and art; and we can learn as much from these stories as from the tragic ones.

7: Doris Lessing's Antipsychiatry

[1] Philip Rieff, *The Triumph of the Therapeutic* (New York: Harper and Row, 1966).

[2] Jonas Robitscher, *The Powers of Psychiatry* (Boston: Houghton Mifflin, 1980), p. 8. The author, a psychiatrist and lawyer, impressively details the ways in which the almost unchecked power of psychiatry infringes upon a free society.

[3] Doris Lessing, *Briefing for a Descent Into Hell* (1971; rpt. New York: Bantam, 1977), pp. 277–278. Other Lessing novels referred to include, in order of publication, *Martha Quest* [*Children of Violence*, Vol. 1] (1952; rpt. New York: Simon and Schuster, 1964); *A Proper Marriage* [*Children of Violence*, Vol. 2] (1954; rpt. New York: Simon and Schuster, 1964); *A Ripple from the Storm* [*Children of Violence*, Vol. 3] (1958; rpt. New York: Simon and Schuster, 1966); *The Golden Notebook* (1962; rpt. New York: Bantam, 1979); *Landlocked* [*Children of Violence*, Vol. 4] (1965; rpt. New York: Simon and Schuster, 1966); *The Four-Gated City* [*Children of Violence*, Vol. 5] (1969; rpt. New York: Bantam, 1979). All references come from these editions. For a bibliography see Dee Seligman, ed., *Doris Lessing: An Annotated Bibliography of Criticism* (Westport, Conn.: Greenwood Press, 1981).

[4] Doris Lessing, *A Small Personal Voice*, Paul Schlueter, ed. (New York: Vintage, 1975), p. 68. All references come from this edition.

[5] Letter from Doris Lessing to Roberta Rubenstein, 28 March 1977. In Roberta Rubenstein, *The Novelistic Vision of Doris Lessing* (Urbana: University of Illinois Press, 1979), pp. 110–111, n.4. Rubenstein's book is indispensable for Lessing scholars.

[6] No biographical study of Lessing has yet appeared, and the little information we have about her life comes from *A Small Personal Voice*. She begins the essay "My Father" by saying that "We use our parents like recurring dreams, to be entered into when needed; they are always there for love or for hate; but it occurs to me that I was not always there for my father" (p. 83). The salient detail she reveals about her father was the amputation of his leg in a battle during World War I and its effect on his life:

> His leg was cut off at mid-thigh, he was shell-shocked, he was very
> ill for many months, with a prolonged depression afterwards. "You
> should always remember that sometimes people are all seething un-

derneath. You don't know what terrible things people have to fight
against. You should look at a person's eyes, that's how you tell. . . .
When I was like that, after I lost my leg, I went to a nice doctor man
and said I was going mad, but he said, don't worry, everyone locks
up things like that. You don't know—horrible, horrible, awful things.
I was afraid of myself, of what I used to dream. I wasn't myself at
all" (pp. 88–89).

Marrying his nurse in 1919, he left England with her and traveled to Persia, where
Doris was born in the same year. In 1925, they moved to Southern Rhodesia where
they eked out a difficult living. The mother apparently suffered most of all. "After
a period of neurotic illness, which was a protest against her situation, she became
brave and resourceful. But she never saw that her husband was not living in a
real world, that he had made a captive of her common sense" (p. 91). Lessing has
not spoken very much about her own life. "I married in my teens, when I was
far too young, and had two children. That marriage was a failure and I married
again" (p. 46). When her second marriage failed, she left Rhodesia with her third
child, a son, and settled in England where she has lived ever since.

[7] Between the early 1940s and the 1950s, when it ceased to be popular, there
were an estimated 40,000 to 50,000 lobotomies performed in the United States.
See *Robitscher,* op. cit., p. 88.

[8] See Lessing's essay on Sufism in *A Small Personal Voice,* pp. 129–137. "Sufism
believes itself to be the substance of that current which can develop man to a
higher stage in his evolution. It is not contemptuous of the world. 'Be in the
world, but not of it,' is the aim" (p. 133).

[9] Frederick R. Karl, "Doris Lessing in the Sixties: The New Anatomy of Melancholy," *Contemporary Literature,* Vol. 13 (Winter 1972), p. 1.

[10] Carl G. Jung, "On the Psychology of the Unconscious." Quoted in Liliane
Frey-Rohn, *From Freud to Jung,* Fred E. Engreen and Evelyn K. Engreen, trans.
(New York: Delta, 1976), p. 59.

[11] Quoted by Rubenstein, op. cit., p. 111, n. 14. Rubenstein also notes that Lessing's therapist was a Jungian Roman Catholic who converted from Judaism.

[12] John Barth, *The End of the Road* (New York: Bantam, 1969). Jacob Horner's
devilish psychiatrist defines *mythotherapy* as follows: "Mythotherapy is based on
two assumptions: that human existence precedes human essence, if either of the
two terms really signifies anything; and that a man is free not only to choose his
own essence but to change it at will" (p. 88). He advises Jake to change roles or
masks at will, lest the patient become immobilized. Jake's mythotherapy fails,
however, because of his fatal commitment to life.

[13] Esther Menaker, "Some Inner Conflicts of Women in a Changing Society,"
in Alan Roland and Barbara Harris, eds., *Career and Motherhood,* (New York:
Human Science Press, 1979), p. 89.

[14] See Phyllis Sternberg-Perrakis, *"The Golden Notebook:* Separation and Symbiosis," in *American Imago,* Vol. 38, No. 4 (Winter 1981), pp. 407–428. "Although Anna's mother herself plays a very small role in Anna's conscious life, she
is visible everywhere in *The Golden Notebook* in the many mother figures in the
novel" (p. 410). Apart from this suggestive article (which does not explore Anna's

relationship to her parents), there is no mention of the obvious gap in Anna's psychoanalysis. Critics have commented on the mother-daughter relationship in the *Children of Violence* series, however. See Linnea Aycock, "The Mother-Daughter Relationship in the *Children of Violence* Series," *Anonymous: A Journal for the Woman Writer,* Vol. 1 (Spring 1974), pp. 48–55. For an Eriksonian approach to *Children of Violence* see Ellen Cronan Rose, "The Eriksonian *Bildungsroman:* An Approach Through Doris Lessing," *Hartford Studies in Literature,* Vol. 7, No. 1 (1975), pp. 1–15, and also her *The Tree Outside the Window: Doris Lessing's Children of Violence* (Hanover, N.H.: University Press of New England, 1976).

[15] Heinz Kohut, *The Restoration of the Self* (New York: International Universities Press, 1977), p. 130.

[16] For an excellent critical discussion of Anna Wulf's integration, see Rubenstein's chapter on *The Golden Notebook,* pp. 71–112. Also see her essay, "Doris Lessing's *The Golden Notebook:* The Meaning of its Shape," *American Imago,* Vol. 32, No. 1 (Spring 1975), pp. 40–58.

[17] Lessing's future biographers must inevitably confront the question of her relationship to her parents and their objective resemblance to the fictionalized parents in her novels. For example, Lessing's father's leg was amputated during World War I; Ella's father "got unfit for the army and was in the administration for a time" (p. 190); and the cruel old man in Anna's recurrent dream has a wooden leg, a crutch, a hump, or a similar deformity. Just as the spiteful old man in Ella's dream embodies joy and vitality, so does Lessing's brief biographical sketch of her father call attention to his vigor before the terrible disfigurement. "I think the best of my father died in that war, that his spirit was crippled by it. The people I've met, particularly the women, who knew him young, speak of his high spirits, his energy, his enjoyment of life. . . . I do not think these people would have easily recognised the ill, irritable, abstracted, hypochondriac man I knew" (*A Small Personal Voice,* p. 86).

[18] Karl, op. cit., pp. 20–26.

[19] Esther Menaker, "Self-Psychology Illustrated on the Issue of Moral Masochism: Clinical Implications," *American Journal Of Psychoanalysis,* Vol. 41, No. 4 (1981), p. 305.

[20] Aycock, op. cit., pp. 51–54. "Caroline can not escape from her mother any more than Martha herself can. Later Martha sees the sad irony of the situation. Caroline has not escaped the problems associated with Martha. She ultimately becomes more involved with Martha's parents than Martha is. And someday she will have to know that her mother deserted her" (p. 53).

[21] See Henri Ellenberger's *The Discovery of the Unconscious* (New York: Basic Books, 1970), especially pp. 3–52.

[22] R. D. Laing, *The Politics of Experience* (New York: Pantheon, 1967), p. 89.

[23] Several critics have documented the numerous close parallels between Charles Watkins' journey in Lessing's *Briefing for a Descent Into Hell,* op. cit., and Jessie Watkins' similar journey in Laing's case study, "A Ten-Day Voyage," in *The Politics of Experience* (New York: Pantheon, 1967). See Marion Vlastos, "Doris Lessing and R. D. Laing: Psychopolitics and Prophecy," *PMLA,* Vol. 91, No. 2 (March 1976), pp. 245–257; Roberta Rubenstein, "Briefing on Inner Space: Doris Lessing

and R. D. Laing," *The Psychoanalytic Review,* Vol. 63, No. 1 (Spring 1976), pp. 83–93; Douglass Bolling, "Structure and Theme in *Briefing for a Descent Into Hell,*" in Annis Pratt and L. S. Dembo, eds., *Doris Lessing: Critical Studies* (Madison: University of Wisconsin Press, 1974), pp. 133–147. Oddly enough, Lessing denied having read Laing's *The Politics of Experience.* See her letter to Rubenstein, *The Novelistic Vision of Doris Lessing,* op. cit., pp. 196–197, n. 7.

[24] R. D. Laing and A. Esterson, *Sanity, Madness, and the Family* (New York: Basic Books, 1971), p. 213. For a useful discussion of Laing see Robert Boyers, ed., *R. D. Laing & Anti-Psychiatry* (New York: Octagon Books, 1974). In an article generally unsympathetic to Laing's assumptions of reality (namely, the belief that reality is "crazy"), the Yale psychiatrist Theodore Lidz acknowledges that Laing has made an important contribution in establishing a link between family structure and schizophrenia:

> We have seen results of research conducted in many parts of the world, and one thing is clear: there has never been a schizophrenic who came from a stable family—at least we can't find any. The hallmark of the thought disorder we identify as a schizophrenic reaction is that it does not lie simply in the patient. There's something wrong in the communication of one or both parents, a disturbing quality in the pattern of the family's interpersonal relations that one can begin to bet on (p. 166).

[25] Virginia Woolf, *Mrs. Dalloway* (London: Chatto & Windus, 1968). "Worshipping proportion, Sir William not only prospered himself but made England prosper, secluded her lunatics, forbade childbirth, penalised despair, made it impossible for the unfit to propagate their views until they, too, shared his sense of proportion . . ." (p. 110). For a discussion of the relationship between madness and the female condition in four representative female writers, see Barbara Hill Rigney, *Madness and Sexual Politics in the Feminist Novel* (Madison: University of Wisconsin Press, 1978). Two of the writers in Rigney's book are Woolf and Lessing, and she briefly compares their hostility toward psychiatry. "Sir William Bradshaw humiliates his patients by forcing them to drink milk in bed, but Dr. Lamb's medications are far more potent" (p. 81).

The story of Virginia Woolf's experience with psychiatry is depressing and deserves brief mention here. The source of the fictional Sir William Bradshaw was the eminent psychiatrist Sir George Savage (1842–1921), President of the Medico-Psychological Association of Great Britain. An old friend of the illustrious Stephen family, he treated Virginia for many years. An advocate of the Weir Mitchell Rest Cure, he prescribed the same treatment for her as Charlotte Perkins Gilman received: enforced rest, complete isolation, and rich diet. The results were as catastrophic. Like Gilman, Woolf bitterly resented the prohibition from work, and her long history of psychiatric treatment—none of which involved modern depth psychology—contributed to her despair. Her correspondence indicates the extent to which she regarded her psychiatric treatment as punishment. "Think— not one moment's freedom from doctor discipline—perfectly strange—conventional men; 'you shant read this' and 'you shant write a word' and 'you shall lie still and drink milk'—for six months" (Nigel Nicolson and Joanne Trautmann, eds., *The Letters of Virginia Woolf* [New York: Harcourt Brace Jovanovich, 1978], Vol. IV, p. 180). For her husband's account of her mental illness and psychiatric treatment, see Leonard Woolf, *Beginning Again: An Autobiography of the Years 1911 to 1918* (New York: Harcourt, Brace & World, 1964), especially pp. 75–82; 150–165. Also see Jean O. Love, *Virginia Woolf: Sources of Madness and Art* (Berkeley: University of California Press, 1977), and Jan Ellen Goldstein, "The Woolfs' Response to Freud: Water Spiders, Singing Canaries, and the Second Apple," Edith Kurzweil and William Phillips, eds., *Literature and Psychoanalysis* (New York: Columbia University Press, 1983), pp. 232–255.

Ironically, one of the greatest achievements of the Hogarth Press, which Leonard and Virginia Woolf owned and ran, was the publication of Freud's work in English. (The Hogarth Press publishes the *Standard Edition*.) In *Downhill All the Way: An Autobiography of the Years 1919–1939* (New York: Harcourt, Brace & World, 1967), Leonard Woolf recounts their first and only meeting with Freud, in 1939, after the analyst had fled Vienna for London:

> I feel no call to praise the famous men whom I have known. Nearly all famous men are disappointing or bores, or both. Freud was neither; he had an aura, not of fame, but of greatness. The terrible cancer of the mouth which killed him only eight months later had already attacked him. It was not an easy interview. He was extraordinarily courteous in a formal, old-fashioned way—for instance, almost ceremoniously he presented Virginia with a flower. There was something about him as of a half-extinct volcano, something sombre, suppressed, reserved. He gave me the feeling which only a very few people whom I have met gave me, a feeling of great gentleness, but behind the gentleness, great strength (pp. 168–169).

8: Nabokov and the Viennese Witch Doctor

[1] The following editions by Nabokov are cited in the text. All references are to these editions. *Ada or Ardor: A Family Chronicle* (New York: McGraw-Hill, 1969); Alfred Appel, Jr., ed., *The Annotated Lolita* (New York: McGraw-Hill, 1970); *Bend Sinister*, 1947 (New York: McGraw-Hill, paperback ed., 1974); *The Defense*, 1930 English translation by Nabokov and Michael Scammell (New York: Putnam, 1964); *Despair*, 1936 English translation by Nabokov (New York: Putnam, 1966); *The Eye*, 1938 English translation (New York: Phaedra, 1965), *Glory*, 1932 English translation by Dimitri Nabokov and Vladimir Nabokov (New York: McGraw-Hill, 1971); *King, Queen, Knave*, 1928 English translation by Dimitri Nabokov and Vladimir Nabokov (New York: McGraw-Hill, 1968); Fredson Bowers, ed., *Lectures on Literature* (New York: Harcourt Brace Jovanovich, 1980); *Pale Fire* (New York: Putnam, 1962); *Pnin* (New York: Doubleday, 1957); Page Stegner, ed., *The Portable Nabokov* (New York: Viking, 1973); *The Real Life of Sebastian Knight*, 1941 (New York: New Directions, 1959); *A Russian Beauty and Other Stories* (New York: McGraw-Hill, 1973); *Speak, Memory: An Autobiography Revisited*, rev. ed. (New York: Putnam, 1966); *Strong Opinions* (New York: McGraw-Hill, 1973); *The Waltz Invention* 1938 English translation (New York: Phaedra, 1966).

[2] Richard Curle, *The Last Twelve Years of Joseph Conrad* (Garden City: Double-day, 1928), p. 26.

[3] Andrew Field, *Nabokov: His Life in Art* (Boston: Little, Brown, 1967), p. 264.

[4] Appel, ed., *The Annotated Lolita*, op. cit., p. lxi–lxii.

[5] Page Stegner, *The Portable Nabokov*, op. cit., p. xxi.

[6] Page Stegner, *Escape into Aesthetics* (New York: The Dial Press, 1966), p. 43.

[7] James Robitscher, *The Powers of Psychiatry* (Boston: Houghton Mifflin, 1980), p. 473.

[8] Quoted by Field, *Nabokov: His Life in Art*, op. cit., p. 263.

[9] Thomas R. Frosch, "Parody and Authenticity in *Lolita*," in J. E. Rivers and Charles Nicol, eds., *Nabokov's Fifth Arc* (Austin: University of Texas Press, 1982), p. 175.

[10] Douglas Fowler, *Reading Nabokov* (Ithaca: Cornell University Press, 1974), p. 196.

[11] Alfred Appel, Jr., "Nabokov: A Portrait," in J. E. Rivers and Charles Nicol, eds., op. cit., *The Fifth Arc*, p. 5. For Nabokov's attitude toward his father and the details of V. D. Nabokov's murder, see Andrew Field, *Nabokov: His Life in Part* (New York: Viking, 1977), *passim*.

[12] Field, *Nabokov: His Life in Part*, op. cit., p. 275.

[13] See Page Stegner, *Escape into Aesthetics*, op. cit., pp. 35–43, and G. M. Hyde, *Vladimir Nabokov: America's Russian Novelist* (London: Marion Boyars, 1977). Hyde correctly points out that "It would be wrong to assume that Nabokov has *in fact* repudiated Freud just because of his frequent anti-Freudian quips." He also agrees with Stegner that Nabokov's objections to Freud often seem themselves obsessive (pp. 96–97, n. 24).

[14] Although no one has yet commented upon this, *The Nabokov-Wilson Letters*, Simon Karlinsky, ed. (New York: Harper and Row, 1979) contains a veiled reference to Nabokov's "nervous exhaustion" in June 1946, shortly after completing *Bend Sinister*. Nabokov writes in a letter to Wilson:

> With the feeling I had 1. some serious heart trouble, 2. ulcers, 3. cancer in the gullet and 4. stones everywhere, I had myself thoroughly examined at a good hospital. The doctor (a Prof. Siegfried Tannhäuser) found that I was constitutionally in fine shape but was suffering from acute nervous exhaustion due to the entomology-Wellesley-novel combination, and suggested my taking a two months vacation (p. 170).

In the next letter to Wilson, July 18, 1946, Nabokov adds: "I am 'recuperating' (from what was practically a 'nervous breakdown') in New Hampshire." Nabokov's use of quotation marks in the second letter suggests a greater degree of ironic self-detachment than in the first letter where the tone, apart from the contrived Wagnerian name of the doctor, is more serious. If he was indeed approaching a mental breakdown, it seems unlikely that he would have consulted a much-hated psychotherapist. Andrew Field makes no mention of this in *Nabokov: His Life in Part*, though he does say that "throughout his life Nabokov has suffered from recurrent headaches, which no pills have helped enough" (p. 251).

[15] Phyllis A. Roth, "Toward the Man Behind the Mystification," J. E. Rivers and Charles Nicol, eds., *The Fifth Arc*, op. cit., p. 58.

[16] Field, *Nabokov: His Life in Part,* op. cit., p. 96.

[17] Kinbote errs slightly in the spelling of Pfister's book, which is *The Psychoanalytic Method,* Charles Rockwell Payne, trans. (New York: Moffat, Yard and Company, 1917). All references are to this edition.

[18] It is obvious from Appel's misspelling that he has not read Pfister's book.

[19] Erich Fromm, *The Forgotten Language* (New York: Holt, Rinehart and Winston, 1951), p. 241. All references are to this edition. A contemporary psychoananlytic interpretation of Little Red Riding Hood may be seen in Bruno Bettelheim's *The Uses of Enchantment* (New York: Vintage Books, 1977).

[20] Elizabeth Phillips, "The Hocus-Pocus of *Lolita,*" *Literature and Psychology,* Vol. 10, No. 4 (Autumn 1960), p. 101. Phillips argues that in *Lolita* Nabokov is satirizing Marie Bonaparte's psychoanalytic study of Edgar Allan Poe.

[21] Van is referring to Freud's letter to Wilhelm Fliess, 19 February 1899, in which he alludes to an individual with a fantasy of being a "deflowerer" of every person he comes across. See Sigmund Freud, *The Origins of Psycho-Analysis* (New York: Basic Books, 1954), p. 278. After returning home from a trip to the Rockies, Nabokov wrote a letter to Edmund Wilson in August 1956 in which in a bemused tone he quotes from Freud's correspondence. "Incidentally, in one of his letters to Fliess the Viennese Sage mentions a young patient who masturbated in the w. c. of an Interlaken hotel in a special contracted position so as to be able to glimpse (now comes the Viennese Sage's curative explanation) the Jungfrau" (Karlinsky, ed., *The Nabokov-Wilson Letters,* p. 300). Karlinsky misdates Freud's letter to Fliess to which Nabokov alludes. Interestingly, in *Lolita* there is a three-page account of Humbert's ecstatic masturbation in the presence of his "Jungfrau," the maiden Dolly Haze.

[22] Field, *Nabokov: His Life in Art,* op. cit., p. 338.

[23] See L. R. Hiatt, "Nabokov's *Lolita:* A 'Freudian' Cryptic Crossword," *American Imago,* Vol. 24 (1967), pp. 360–370. Hiatt argues that despite Nabokov's antipathy to psychoanalysis, he endows Humbert with the classic symptoms of an Oedipus complex. "Nabokov has given him an Oedipus complex; he has also given him a set of defences against self-understanding. He has, in addition, thrown up a smoke-screen to hide his hero's secret from public gaze. It is a strange game for an author to play. If he wins, the reader loses the point of the book" (p. 370).

[24] James R. Rambeau, "Nabokov's Critical Strategy," J. E. Rivers and Charles Nicol, eds., *The Fifth Arc,* op. cit., p. 30.

[25] Vladislaw Khodasevich, "On Sirin," in Alfred Appel, Jr. and Charles Newman, eds., *Nabokov: Criticism, Reminiscences, Translations, and Tributes* (Evanston: Northwestern University Press, 1970), p. 100.

[26] Sigmund Freud, "A Special Type of Choice of Object Made by Men" (1910), *Standard Edition* (London: The Hogarth Press, 1957), Vol. XI, p. 167. All references are to this edition.

[27] Gladys M. Clifton, "Humbert Humbert and the Limits of Artistic License," J. E. Rivers and Charles Nicol, eds., *The Fifth Arc,* op. cit., p. 164.

[28] Field, *Nabokov: His Life in Art,* op. cit., p. 339. It is appropriate to mention here, as Field does in *Nabokov: His Life in Part,* the "remarkable gallery of homosexual characters in Nabokov's writing" (p. 63). Psychoanalytic biographers may

wish to explore the relationship between Nabokov's artistic preoccupation with homosexuality and his keen distress over his brother Sergei's homosexuality. Nabokov's maternal uncle, Vasily Ivanovich, was also homosexual. Field records Nabokov's inordinate difficulty in speaking about his brother's homosexuality despite the fact, as the biographer observes, that "I know well and with no possibility of error that Sergei's homosexuality was a subject about which his brother himself spoke with the greatest frankness and naturalness, even to his sisters and his mother" (*Nabokov: His Life in Part,* p. 13). Nabokov's father was an expert on the legal and social ramifications of homosexuality. According to Field, Vladimir Nabokov shared his father's belief that homosexuality was an illness transmitted by heredity. By contrast, a contemporary view would suggest that gender identity arises from psychological and interpersonal factors. In *The Nabokov-Wilson Letters,* Karlinsky mentions that Sergei died in a German concentration camp as a consequence of Hitler's campaign to exterminate homosexuals (p. 157, n. 4).

Nabokov's interest in homosexuality almost certainly derives from autobiographical concerns and, given his fascination with identical twins as well as his physical resemblance to Sergei (as suggested by a photograph of the two brothers in *Nabokov: His Life in Part*), it may be that his parody of the homosexual theme in the Humbert-Quilty *Doppelgänger* relationship and elsewhere is a defense against submerged bisexual drives and an effort to transform fears and anxieties into art.

[29] To cite but a few works: Claire Rosenfeld, "The Shadow Within: The Conscious and Unconscious Use of the Double," *Daedalus,* Vol. 92 (1963), pp. 326–344; Robert Rogers, *A Psychoanalytic Study of the Double in Literature* (Detroit: Wayne State University Press, 1970); Phyllis A. Roth, "The Psychology of the Double in Nabokov's *Pale Fire,*" *Essays in Literature,* Vol. 2 (1975), pp. 209–229.

[30] Otto Rank, *The Double,* Harry Tucker, Jr., ed. and trans. New York: Meridian, 1979), p. 86. For an excellent study of Rank's importance as an unacknowledged forerunner of ego psychology and modern developmental theory, see Esther Menaker, *Otto Rank: A Rediscovered Legacy* (New York: Columbia University Press, 1982).

[31] Phyllis A. Roth, *The Fifth Arc,* J. E. Rivers and Charles Nicol, eds., op. cit., p. 44.

[32] Clifton points out in *The Fifth Arc,* J. E. Rivers and Charles Nicol, eds., op. cit., that the most convincingly erotic passage in the novel "is not one in which Humbert actually possesses Lolita but one which involves masturbation" (p. 167).

[33] See, for example, Robert D. Stolorow and Frank M. Lachman, *Psychoanalysis of Developmental Arrests* (New York: International Universities Press, 1980) and Arnold Goldberg, ed., *Advances in Self Psychology* (New York: International Universities Press, 1980).

[34] Sigmund Freud, *Introductory Lectures on Psycho-Analysis,* Part III (1916–1917), *Standard Edition* (London: The Hogarth Press, 1963), Vol. XVI, pp. 375–376.

[35] Stanley A. Leavy, trans., *The Freud Journal of Lou Andreas-Salomé* (New York: Basic Books, 1964), p. 109.

[36] Sigmund Freud, " 'Civilized' Sexual Morality and Modern Nervous Illness" (1908), *Standard Edition* (London: The Hogarth Press, 1959), Vol. IX, p. 197.

[37] Sigmund Freud, "Formulations on the Two Principles of Mental Function-

ing" (1911), *Standard Edition* (London: The Hogarth Press, 1958), Vol. XII, p. 224.

[38] Sigmund Freud, "Creative Writers and Day-Dreaming" (1908), (London: The Hogarth Press, 1959), *Standard Edition,* Vol. IX, p. 146.

[39] Sigmund Freud, *Introductory Lectures on Psycho-Analysis,* Part II (1915–1916), *Standard Edition* (London: The Hogarth Press, 1961), Vol. XV, p. 172.

[40] Sigmund Freud, "Dostoevsky and Parricide," (1928), *Standard Edition* (London: The Hogarth Press, 1961), Vol. XXI, p. 177.

9: Philip Roth's Psychoanalysts

[1] The following editions by Roth are cited in the text. All references are to these editions. *Letting Go* (New York: Random House, 1962); *Portnoy's Complaint* (New York: Random House, 1969); *The Breast* (New York: Holt, Rinehart and Winston, 1972); *My Life as a Man* (New York: Holt, Rinehart and Winston, 1974); *Reading Myself and Others* (New York: Farrar, Straus, 1975); *The Professor of Desire* (New York: Farrar, Straus, 1977); *The Ghost Writer* (New York: Farrar, Straus and Giroux, 1979).

[2] For an extended discussion of the differences between the artist's endeavor and the psychoanalyst's, see Phoebe C. Ellsworth, "Regarding the Author as Patient," *New Literary History,* Vol. 12, No. 1 (Autumn 1980), pp. 187–197. The entire issue of *New Literary History* is devoted to contemporary trends in literature and psychology and contains several valuable essays, including Ernest S. Wolf's article, "Psychoanalytic Psychology of the Self and Literature," an examination of Kohut's contributions.

[3] Sigmund Freud, *Jokes and Their Relation to the Unconscious, Standard Edition* (London: The Hogarth Press, 1960), Vol. VIII, p. 34.

[4] Bruno Bettelheim, "Portnoy Psychoanalyzed," *Midstream,* Vol. 15, No. 6 (June/July, 1969), p. 4. All references are to this edition.

[5] In *Surviving and Other Essays,* (New York: Vintage, 1980), Bettelheim prefaces the republication of "Portnoy Psychoanalyzed" with remarks intended to convey a more positive evaluation of the literary success of Roth's novel than he initially implied. "Asked to write a review of Philip Roth's *Portnoy's Complaint,* I attempted a satire instead. Only an interesting work of fiction permits and deserves to be made the substance of a satire—which suggests my evaluation of this book" (p. 387).

[6] Sheldon Grebstein, "The Comic Anatomy of *Portnoy's Complaint,*" in Sarah Blacher Cohen, ed., *Comic Relief: Humor in Contemporary American Literature* (Urbana: University of Illinois Press, 1978), p. 160.

[7] Patricia Meyer Spacks, "About Portnoy," *The Yale Review,* Vol. 58 (Summer 1969), p. 623.

[8] Robert Langbaum, *The Poetry of Experience* (New York: Norton, 1963), p. 35. All references are to this edition.

[9] Irving Howe, "Philip Roth Reconsidered," *Commentary,* Vol. 54, No. 6 (December 1972), p. 72.

[10] Mark Shechner, "Philip Roth," *Partisan Review,* Vol. 41, No. 3 (1974), pp.

410–427. All references are to this edition. Shechner's essay, which remains the best psychological discussion of Roth's fiction, has been reprinted in Sanford Pinsker, ed., *Critical Essays on Philip Roth* (Boston: G. K. Hall, 1982), pp. 117–132.

[11] Spacks, "About Portnoy," op. cit., p. 630.

[12] For a psychoanalytic interpretation of *The Breast,* see Daniel Dervin, "Breast Fantasy in Barthelme, Swift, and Philip Roth: Creativity and Psychoanalytic Structure," *American Imago,* Vol. 33, No. 1 (Spring 1976), pp. 102–122.

[13] Mark Shechner has observed that the source of terror in Roth's fictional world derives not from the castrating mother but from the ineffectual father. "Paternity is a legal fiction in Roth's books where sons and fathers turn out to be brothers under the skin, locked into generations by an unfortunate biological fate" ("Philip Roth," *Partisan Review,* op. cit., p. 413).

[14] Sanford Pinsker, *The Comedy that 'Hoits'* (Columbia: University of Missouri Press, 1975), p. 115.

[15] For a biographical sketch of Roth see Bernard F. Rodgers, Jr., *Philip Roth* (Boston: Twayne Publishers, 1978). Rodgers has also published *Philip Roth: A Bibliography* (Metuchen, New Jersey: Scarecrow, 1974).

[16] John McDaniel, *The Fiction of Philip Roth* (Haddonfield, New Jersey: Haddonfield House, 1974), p. 218. More recent critical studies of Roth include Judith Paterson Jones and Guinevera A. Nance, *Philip Roth* (New York: Frederick Ungar, 1981) and Hermione Lee, *Philip Roth* (London: Methuen, 1982).

[17] Pierre Michel, "Philip Roth's Reductive Lens: From 'On the Air' to *My Life as a Man.*" *Revue des Langues Vivantes Tijdschrift Voor Levende Talen* (1976/5), p. 518.

[18] R. Boeth, "The Same Old Story," *Newsweek,* 26 (September 1977), p. 83. Review of *The Professor of Desire.*

[19] Hans J. Kleinschmidt, "The Angry Act: The Role of Aggression in Creativity," *American Imago,* Vol. 24, Nos. 1, 2 (Spring–Summer, 1967), pp. 98–128. All references are to this edition.

[20] Patricia Meyer Spacks, "Male Miseries," *Nation* 15 (October 1977), p. 375. Review of *The Professor of Desire.* See also Sarah Blacher Cohen's criticism of Roth's female characters in "Philip Roth's Would-Be Patriarchs and Their *Shikses* and Shrews," in Pinsker, ed., op. cit., pp. 209–216.

[21] In *Portnoy's Complaint* (pp. 50–51), Alex describes a painful incident during his adolescence in which his mother makes a typically castrating remark to him, filling him with humiliation and anger. The incident appears in the chapter of the novel called "The Jewish Blues," first published in *New American Review,* No. 1 (September 1967), p. 145. Dr. Kleinschmidt discusses the identical incident in "The Angry Act" (p. 124).

[22] I must mention here that after I wrote this chapter, containing the discovery of Roth's relationship to "The Angry Act," I sent a copy of the manuscript to Professor Shechner. In a letter he told me that he, too, had made the discovery while engaged in the research for his essay on Roth. Shechner chose not to mention "The Angry Act," although he did inject some of the analyst's language, in disguised form, into his own essay.

10: Freud Revisited: *The White Hotel*

[1] D. M. Thomas, *The White Hotel* (New York: Viking, 1981), 143n. All references come from this edition. For representative reviews see *Commentary,* Vol. 72 (August 1981), pp. 56–60; *Encounter,* Vol. 57 (August 1981), pp. 53–57; *Maclean's,* Vol. 94 (4 May 1981), pp. 56–58; *The Nation,* Vol. 232 (2 May 1981), pp. 537–539; *New Leader,* Vol. 64 (20 April 1981), pp. 13–14; *New Republic,* Vol. 184 (28 March 1981), pp. 35–37; *New Statesman,* Vol. 101 (16 January 1981), p. 21; *Newsweek,* Vol. 97 (16 March 1981), p. 89; *New York,* Vol. 14 (16 March 1981), p. 50; *New York Review of Books,* Vol. 28 (28 May 1981), pp. 20–23; *New York Times Book Review,* Vol. 86 (15 March 1981); *Time,* Vol. 117 (16 March 1981), p. 88. Nearly all the reviews were highly enthusiastic, praising the book for its extraordinary power and beauty. *The Nation* called it "as stunning a work of fiction as has appeared in a long while."

[2] See Paul Roazen, *Freud and His Followers* (New York: New York University Press, 1985), p. 358.

[3] Freud's letter to Ferenczi, 4 February 1920. Ernst L. Freud, ed., *The Letters of Sigmund Freud* (New York: Basic Books, 1960), p. 328.

[4] See Freud's letter of 8 January 1899 to Fliess: "Now for bisexuality! I am sure you are right about it. And I am accustoming myself to the idea of regarding every sexual act as a process in which four persons are involved." Sigmund Freud, *The Origins of Psycho-Analysis* (New York: Basic Books, 1954), p. 289.

[5] Carl Woodring, ed., *Prose of the Romantic Period* (Boston: Houghton Mifflin, 1961), p. 525.

[6] In "Frau Emmy von N." Freud writes: "Her chief complaint was of frequent states of confusion—'storms in her head' as she called them." *Studies on Hysteria, Standard Edition* (London: The Hogarth Press, 1955), Vol. II, p. 78.

[7] To see how closely Thomas' language follows Freud's, compare the first two sentences of "Fräulein Elisabeth von R." with the opening of "Frau Anna G.":

> In the autumn of 1892 I was asked by a doctor I knew to examine a young lady who had been suffering for more than two years from pains in her legs and who had difficulties in walking. When making this request he added that he thought the case was one of hysteria, though there was no trace of the usual indications of that neurosis (*Studies on Hysteria,* p. 135).

> In the autumn of 1919 I was asked by a doctor of my acquaintance to examine a young lady who had been suffering for the past four years from severe pains in her left breast and pelvic region, as well as a chronic respiratory condition. When making this request he added that he thought the case was one of hysteria, though there were certain counter-indications which had caused him to examine her very thoroughly indeed in order to rule out the possibility of some organic affection (*The White Hotel,* p. 89).

[8] Sigmund Freud, "Fräulein Elisabeth von R.," *Studies on Hysteria, Standard Edition* (London: The Hogarth Press, 1955), Vol. II, p. 139. Interestingly, Fräulein

Elisabeth von R. is advised by her doctor to travel to Gastein in the Austrian Alps to receive hydropathic treatment.

[9] Ibid., p. 157.

[10] Sigmund Freud, "the Psychotherapy of Hysteria," *Studies on Hysteria, Standard Edition* (London: The Hogarth Press, 1955), Vol. II, p. 305.

[11] Sigmund Freud, "Miss Lucy R.," *Studies on Hysteria, Standard Edition* (London: The Hogarth Press, 1955), Vol. II, p. 121.

[12] Sigmund Freud, "Screen Memories" (1899), *Standard Edition* (London: The Hogarth Press, 1962), Vol. III, p. 322. "It may indeed be questioned whether we have any memories at all *from* our childhood: memories *relating to* our childhood may be all that we possess."

[13] ". . . a child sucking at his mother's breast has become the prototype of every relation of love. The finding of an object is in fact a refinding of it." Sigmund Freud, *Three Essays on the Theory of Sexuality* (1905), *Standard Edition* (London: The Hogarth Press, 1953), Vol. VII, p. 222.

[14] Sigmund Freud, "Fräulein Elisabeth von R.," *Studies on Hysteria, Standard Edition* (London: The Hogarth Press, 1955), Vol. II, p. 160.

[15] For a discussion of the Freudian psychiatric case study as literary art, see Steven Marcus, "Freud and Dora: Story, History, Case History," in *Representations* (New York: Random House, 1975). Marcus demonstrates that *Dora* "is a great work of literature—that is to say, it is both an outstanding creative and imaginative performance and an intellectual and cognitive achievement of the highest order" (p. 248).

[16] Sigmund Freud, "Frau Emmy von N., *Studies On Hysteria, Standard Edition* (London: The Hogarth Press, 1955), Vol. II, p. 75n.

[17] For a discussion of the technical mistakes and empathic failures in Freud's case of *Dora,* see the essays by Jules Glenn, Robert J. Langs, and Mark Kanzer in Mark Kanzer and Jules Glenn, eds., *Freud and His Patients* (New York: Jason Aronson, 1980).

[18] It is possible, of course, that a patient's premonitions of death may reflect unconscious hostility. Curiously, Freud does not consider the possibility that Lisa's premonitions reveal a death wish toward him.

[19] Sigmund Freud, "Frau Emmy von N., *Studies on Hysteria, Standard Edition* (London: The Hogarth Press, 1955), Vol. II, p. 49.

[20] Ernest Jones, *The Life and Work of Sigmund Freud* (New York: Basic Books, 1955), Vol. II, p. 274.

[21] Josef Breuer, "Fräulein Anna O.," *Studies on Hysteria, Standard Edition* (London: The Hogarth Press, 1955), Vol. II, p. 33.

[22] This is one of the few questionable details in "Frau Anna G." Freud warns against an analyst examining his patient, since the erotic component of a physical examination inevitably makes the transference relationship more troublesome.

[23] Since its publication, *Beyond the Pleasure Principle* has produced strong controversy among psychoanalysts. Otto Fenichel offers a persuasive critique of the death instinct in *The Psychoanalytic Theory of Neurosis* (New York: Norton, 1945). "Of course, the existence and importance of aggressive drives cannot be denied.

However, there is not proof that they always and necessarily came into being by a turning outward of more primary self-destructive drives. It seems rather as if aggressiveness were originally no instinctual aim of its own, characterizing one category of instincts in contradistinction to others, but rather a mode in which instinctual aims sometimes are striven for, in response to frustrations or even spontaneously" (p. 59). Significantly, in *Analysis of a Phobia in a Five-Year-Old Boy* (1909) Freud had earlier ruled out an aggressive instinct. "I cannot bring myself to assume the existence of a special aggressive instinct alongside of the familiar instincts of self-preservation and of sex, and on an equal footing with them" (*Standard Edition* [London: The Hogarth Press, 1955], Vol. X, p. 140). Bruno Bettelheim writes in the *New Yorker* (March 1, 1982, p. 89) that the mistranslation of the German word "Trieb" as "instinct" instead of the more accurate word "drive" or "impulse" has hopelessly obscured the meaning of Freud's theory. "Freud never spoke of a death instinct—only of a mostly unconscious drive or impulse that provokes us to aggressive, destructive, and self-destructive actions."

By contrast, Freud's death instinct has fascinated literary theoreticians. Invoking Jacques Lacan's dialectical readings of Freud, Harold Bloom argues in "Freud and the Poetic Sublime," *Antaeus*, Vol. 30/31 (Spring 1978), that the death instinct leads to a catastrophe theory of creation. "The repressed rhetorical formula of Freud's discourse in *Beyond the Pleasure Principle* can be stated thus: *Literal meaning equals anteriority equals an earlier state of meaning equals an earlier state of things equals death equals literal meaning*. Only one escape is possible from such a formula, and it is a simple formula: *Eros equals figurative meaning*" (p. 368).

[24] Lionel Trilling, "Freud and Literature," *The Liberal Imagination* (Garden City, New York: Anchor Books, 1953).

[25] The absence of any prolonged discussion of female sexuality in "Frau Anna G." may be salutary, since Freud's most notorious statements about women were being formulated not long after Lisa Erdman leaves therapy. In "Some Psychical Consequences of the Anatomic Distinction Between the Sexes" (1925), Freud writes: "I cannot evade the notion (though I hesitate to give it expression) that for women the level of what is ethically normal is different from what it is in men. Their super-ego is never so inexorable, so impersonal, so independent of its emotional origins as we require it to be in men" (*Standard Edition*, Vol. XIX, p. 257). Thomas' Freud is considerably more enlightened. However, Freud's Victorian bias does not invalidate the existence of castration fear and penis envy in personality development, although these processes become reinforced and distorted by social and cultural assumptions.

[26] In Ernest Jones, *The Life and Work of Sigmund Freud* (New York: Basic Books, 1957), Vol. III, p. 392, this sentence is quoted from Freud's letter to Hereward Carrington. The full letter appears in *The Letters of Sigmund Freud*, Ernst L. Freud, ed., op. cit., p. 334: "I am not one of those who dismiss *a priori* the study of so-called occult psychic phenomena as unscientific, discreditable or even as dangerous. If I were at the beginning rather than at the end of a scientific career, as I am today, I might possibly choose just this field of research, in spite of all difficulties." The letter is dated 24 July 1921 from Bad Gastein. Freud later denied making this statement, but Jones located the letter.

[27] Sigmund Freud, *The Psychopathology of Everyday Life* (1901), *Standard Edition* (London: The Hogarth Press, 1960), Vol. VI, pp. 261–262.

[28] Sigmund Freud, "The Occult Significance of Dreams" (1925), *Standard Edition* (London: The Hogarth Press, 1961), Vol. XIX, p. 136.

[29] Sigmund Freud, "Dreams and Occultism," *New Introductory Lectures on Psycho-Analysis* (1933), *Standard Edition* (London: The Hogarth Press, 1964), Vol. XXII, p. 55.

[30] Sigmund Freud, "Psycho-Analysis and Telepathy" (1941 [1921]), *Standard Edition* (London: The Hogarth Press, 1955), Vol. XVIII, pp. 177–193.

[31] Sigmund Freud, "Dreams and Telepathy" (1922), *Standard Edition* (London: The Hogarth Press, 1955), Vol. XVIII, p. 199.

[32] Sigmund Freud, "The 'Uncanny'" (1919), *Standard Edition* (London: The Hogarth Press, 1955), Vol. XVII, p. 245. All references come from this edition.

[33] A definite confirmation of this appears in a statement made by Reuben Fine in *A History of Psychoanalysis* (New York: Columbia University Press, 1979). "No prominent analyst today could be said to believe that religion has any real value for mankind" (p. 449). In a review published in *Bulletin of the Menninger Clinic*, Vol. 45, No. 3 (May 1981), John J. Fitzpatrick takes issue with Fine's generalization. "Religion may have real importance to people as a source of healthy illusion, solace, or affiliation, and the understanding that it may also serve certain neurotic needs does not detract from its positive value" (pp. 271–272).

[34] *Publishers Weekly*, 27 March 1981, p. 6. In another interview (*The Charlotte Observer*, 18 April 1982), Thomas stated that he has never been in psychoanalysis, an observation that startled the analysts who attended his discussion of *The White Hotel* at the Albert Einstein College of Medicine in New York in April 1982. But as one surprised psychiatrist later said, ". . . as I think about it, . . . it makes sense that he [Thomas] was able to do that because Freud himself . . . was able to tap into human imagination through the literary imagination."

BIBLIOGRAPHY

Alvarez, A. *The Savage God*. New York: Bantam, 1973.

Arlow, Jacob A., and Charles Brenner. *Psychoanalytic Concepts and the Structural Theory*. 1964; rpt. New York: International Universities Press, 1979.

Aycock, Linnea. "The Mother-Daughter Relationship in the *Children of Violence* Series." *Anonymous: A Journal for the Woman Writer*, 1 (Spring 1974), pp. 48–55.

Barnhouse, Ruth Tiffany, and Urban T. Holmes, III, eds. *Male and Female: Christian Approaches to Sexuality*. New York: Seabury, 1976.

Barnhouse, Ruth Tiffany. *Homosexuality: A Symbolic Confusion*. New York: Seabury, 1977.

Barth, John. *The End of the Road*. 1967; rpt. New York: Bantam, 1969.

Berman, Jeffrey. "Sylvia Plath and the Art of Dying." *A New Anatomy of Melancholy: Patterns of Self-Aggression Among Authors*. Eds. Leonard F. Manheim, M. D. Faber, and Harvey L. P. Resnick. *University of Hartford Studies in Literature*, 10 (Nos. 1, 2, 3 Fall 1978), pp. 137–155.

———. "The Multiple Faces of *Eve* and *Sybil*: 'E Pluribus Unum.' " *Psychocultural Review*, 2 (Winter 1978), pp. 1–25.

———. "*Equus*: 'After Such Little Forgiveness, What Knowledge?' " *The Psychoanalytic Review*, 66 (Fall 1979), pp. 407–422.

Bettelheim, Bruno. "Portnoy Psychoanalyzed." *Midstream*, 15 (June/July, 1969), pp. 3–10.

Blanton, Smiley. *Diary of My Analysis with Sigmund Freud*. New York: Hawthorn Books, 1971.

Boyers, Robert, ed. *R. D. Laing & Anti-Psychiatry*. New York: Octagon, 1974.

Bram, Frederick M. "The Gift of Anna O." *British Journal of Medical Psychology*, 38 (1965), pp. 53–58.

Browne, E. Martin. *The Making of a Play: T.S. Eliot's The Cocktail Party.* Cambridge: Cambridge University Press, 1966.

Bruccoli, Matthew J. *The Composition of Tender Is the Night.* Pittsburgh: University of Pittsburgh Press, 1963.

————. *Some Sort of Epic Grandeur.* New York: Harcourt Brace Jovanovich, 1981.

Bryer, Jackson R. "A Psychiatrist Reviews 'Tender Is the Night.' " *Literature and Psychology,* 16, 3–4 (1966), pp. 198–199.

Burton, Mary E. "The Countertransference of Dr. Diver." *English Literary History,* 38 (September 1971), pp. 459–471.

Butscher, Edward. *Sylvia Plath: Method and Madness.* New York: Seabury, 1976.

Crews, Frederick. *Out of My System.* Oxford: Oxford University Press, 1975.

Degler, Carl N. "Charlotte Perkins Gilman on the Theory and Practice of Feminism." *American Quarterly,* 8 (Spring 1956), pp. 21–39.

Earnest, Ernest. *S. Weir Mitchell: Novelist and Physician.* Philadelphia: University of Pennsylvania Press, 1950.

Edel, Leon. "Psychoanalysis and the 'Creative' Arts." *Modern Psychoanalysis: New Directions and Perspectives,* ed. Judd Marmor. New York: Basic Books, 1968, pp. 626–641.

Ehrenwald, Jay. *The History of Psychotherapy.* New York: Jason Aronson, 1976.

Eliot, T. S. "The Future of an Illusion." Review of *The Future of an Illusion* by Sigmund Freud. *The Criterion,* 8 (December 1928), pp. 350–353.

————. "Introduction" to *The Wheel of Fire,* by G. Wilson Knight. London: Methuen and Company, 1962, xiii–xx.

————. *Selected Essays.* London: Faber and Faber, 1966.

————. "The Search for Moral Sanction." *The Listener,* 7 (30 March 1932), pp. 445–446; 480.

————. *Essays Ancient and Modern.* New York: Harcourt, Brace and Company, 1936.

————. "Reflections on *The Cocktail Party.*" *World Review,* New Series, 9 (November 1949), pp. 19–22.

————. "An Interview with T. S. Eliot." *The New York Times,* 16 April 1950, Section 2, p. 1.

————. *The Cocktail Party.* In *The Complete Poems and Plays: 1909–1950.* New York: Harcourt, Brace and World, 1952.

————. *On Poetry and Poets.* New York: Farrar, Straus and Cudahy, 1957.

———. *The Waste Land: A Facsimile and Transcript of the Original Drafts,* ed. Valerie Eliot. New York: Harcourt Brace Jovanovich, 1971.

Ellenberger, Henri. *The Discovery of the Unconscious.* New York: Basic Books, 1970.

Epstein, Lawrence, and Arthur Feiner, eds. *Countertransference.* New York: Jason Aronson, 1979.

Erikson, Erik H. *Young Man Luther.* 1958; rpt. New York: Norton, 1962.

———. *Insight and Responsibility.* New York: Norton, 1964.

———. *Gandhi's Truth.* New York: Norton, 1969.

Farber, Leslie H. "Lying on the Couch." *Lying, Despair, Jealousy, Envy, Sex, Suicide, Drugs, and the Good Life.* New York: Basic Books, 1976, pp. 205–220.

Feder, Lillian. *Madness in Literature.* Princeton: Princeton University Press, 1980.

Fiedler, Leslie. "Some Notes on F. Scott Fitzgerald." *F. Scott Fitzgerald: A Collection of Critical Essays,* ed. Arthur Mizener. Englewood Cliffs, New Jersey: Prentice-Hall, 1963, pp. 70–76.

Field, Andrew. *Nabokov: His Life in Art.* Boston: Little, Brown, 1967.

———. *Nabokov: His Life in Part.* New York: Viking, 1977.

Fitzgerald, F. Scott. *Tender Is the Night.* 1934; rpt. New York: Scribner's, 1962.

———. *The Crack-Up,* ed. Edmund Wilson. New York: New Directions, 1956.

———. "Babylon Revisited." *The Fitzgerald Reader,* ed. Arthur Mizener. New York: Scribner's, 1963, pp. 302–322.

———. *The Letters of F. Scott Fitzgerald,* ed. Andrew Turnbull. New York: Scribner's, 1963.

———. *In Our Own Time: A Miscellany,* eds. Matthew J. Bruccoli and Jackson R. Bryer. New York: Popular Press, 1971.

———. *The Notebooks of F. Scott Fitzgerald,* ed. Matthew J. Bruccoli. New York: Harcourt Brace Jovanovich, 1978.

———. *Correspondence of F. Scott Fitzgerald,* eds. Matthew J. Bruccoli and Margaret M. Duggan. New York: Random House, 1980.

Fitzgerald, Zelda. *Save Me the Waltz.* New York: Signet, 1968.

Fraiberg, Louis. *Psychoanalysis and American Literary Criticism.* Detroit: Wayne State University Press, 1960.

Freeman, Lucy. *The Story of Anna O.* New York: Walker, 1972.

Freeman, Walter. *The Psychiatrist: Personalities and Patterns.* New York: Grune and Stratton, 1968.

Freud, Sigmund. *The Origins of Psychoanalysis: Letters to Wilhelm Fliess,*
eds. Marie Bonaparte, Anna Freud, and Ernst Kris; trans. Eric Mos-
bacher and James Strachey. New York: Basic Books, 1977.

————. *The Standard Edition of the Complete Psychological Works of Sigmund Freud,* trans. James Strachey, et al. 24 Volumes. London: The
Hogarth Press, 1958–1974.

————. *The Letters of Sigmund Freud,* ed. Ernst L. Freud; trans. Tania
Stern and James Stern. New York: Basic Books, 1975.

Frey-Rohn, Liliane. *From Freud to Jung,* trans. Fred E. Engreen and Evelyn K. Engreen. New York: Delta, 1976.

Fromm, Erich. *The Forgotten Language.* New York: Holt, Rinehart and
Winston, 1951.

Fromm-Reichmann, Frieda. *Principles of Intensive Psychotherapy.* Chicago:
University of Chicago Press, 1950.

————. *Psychoanalysis and Psychotherapy,* ed. Dexter M. Bullard. Chicago:
University of Chicago Press, 1959.

[Gilman] Charlotte Perkins Stetson. *Women and Economics.* Boston: Small,
Maynard and Company, 1899.

————. *The Yellow Wallpaper.* New York: The Feminist Press, 1973.

————. *Concerning Children.* Boston: Small, Maynard and Company, 1901.

————. *The Home: Its Work and Influence.* 1903; rpt. Urbana: University
of Illinois Press, 1972.

————. "Why I Wrote The Yellow Wallpaper." *The Forerunner,* 4 (1913),
p. 271.

————. "Parasitism and Civilised Vice." *Woman's Coming of Age,* eds.
Samuel D. Schmalhausen and V. F. Calverton. New York: Liveright, 1931, pp. 110–126.

————. *The Living of Charlotte Perkins Gilman: An Autobiography.* 1935;
rpt. New York: Harper and Row, 1975.

Gordon, Lyndall. *Eliot's Early Years.* Oxford: Oxford University Press, 1977.

Greenberg, Joanne. *I Never Promised You a Rose Garden.* 1964; rpt. New
York: Signet, no date.

Greenberg, Joanne [Hannah Green]. "In Praise of My Doctor—Frieda
Fromm-Reichmann." *Contemporary Psychoanalysis,* 4 (Fall 1967), pp.
73–77.

H.D. *Tribute to Freud.* 1956; rpt. New York: McGraw-Hill, 1974.

Heilman, Robert B. "Alcestis and *The Cocktail Party*." *Comparative Literature,* 5 (1953), pp. 105–116.

Hemingway, Ernest. *A Moveable Feast.* New York: Scribner's, 1964.

Hill, Mary A. *Charlotte Perkins Gilman: The Making of a Radical Feminist 1860–1896.* Philadelphia: Temple University Press, 1980.

Hoffman, Frederick J. *Freudianism and the Literary Mind,* 2nd ed. Baton Rouge: Louisiana State University Press, 1967.

Holbrook, David. *Sylvia Plath: Poetry and Existence.* London: Athlone Press, 1976.

Holland, Norman N. "An Identity for the Rat Man." *International Review of Psycho-Analysis,* 2 (1975), pp. 157–169.

———. *5 Readers Reading.* New Haven: Yale University Press, 1975.

———. "UNITY IDENTITY TEXT SELF." *PMLA,* 90 (1975), pp. 813–822.

Hovey, Richard. "Psychiatrist and Saint in *The Cocktail Party.*" *Literature and Psychology,* 9, 3–4 (Summer and Fall 1959), pp. 51–55.

Jacobson, Edith. *The Self and the Object World.* New York: International Universities Press, 1964.

Jensen, Ellen M. "Anna O—A Study of Her Later Life." *Psychoanalytic Quarterly,* 39 (1970), pp. 269–293.

Jones, Ernest. *The Life and Work of Sigmund Freud.* 3 Volumes. New York: Basic Books, 1953–1957.

Kanzer, Mark, and Jules Glenn. *Freud and His Patients.* New York: Jason Aronson, 1980.

Kaplan, Abraham. "Poetry, Medicine and Metaphysics." *Journal of the American Academy of Psychoanalysis,* 9 (January 1981), pp. 101–128.

Karl, Frederick R. "Doris Lessing in the Sixties: The New Anatomy of Melancholy." *Contemporary Literature,* 13 (Winter 1972), pp. 15–33.

Karlinsky, Simon, ed. *The Nabokov-Wilson Letters.* New York: Harper and Row, 1979.

Karpe, Richard. "The Rescue Complex in Anna O's Final Identity." *Psychoanalytic Quarterly,* 30 (1961), pp. 1–27.

Kernberg, Otto. *Borderline Conditions and Pathological Narcissism.* New York: Jason Aronson, 1980.

Kleinschmidt, Hans J. "The Angry Act: The Role of Aggression in Creativity." *American Imago,* 24, 1–2 (Spring–Summer 1967), pp. 98–128.

Kohut, Heinz. *The Analysis of the Self.* 1971; rpt. New York: International Universities Press, 1977.

———. *The Restoration of the Self.* New York: International Universities Press, 1977.

————. "Reflections on *Advances in Self Psychology.*" *Advances in Self Psychology,* ed. Arnold Goldberg. New York: International Universities Press, 1980, pp. 473–554.

Kraditor, Aileen S. *The Ideas of the Woman Suffrage Movement, 1890–1920.* New York: Columbia University Press, 1965.

Kris, Ernst. *Psychoanalytic Explorations in Art.* New York: International Universities Press, 1952.

Kroll, Judith. *Chapters in a Mythology.* New York: Harper and Row, 1976.

Laing, R. D., and A. Esterson. *Sanity, Madness, and the Family.* 1964; rpt. New York: Basic Books, 1971.

Laing, R. D. *The Politics of Experience.* New York: Pantheon, 1967.

Langbaum, Robert. *The Poetry of Experience.* New York: Norton, 1963.

Langs, Robert. *Psychotherapy: A Basic Text.* New York: Jason Aronson, 1982.

————. *The Psychotherapeutic Conspiracy.* New York: Jason Aronson, 1982.

Lehrman, Philip R. "Freud's Contributions to Science." *Harofe Haivri* [*Hebrew Physician*], I (1940), pp. 161–176.

Lesser, Simon O. *Fiction and the Unconscious.* New York: Vintage, 1957.

Lessing, Doris. *Martha Quest* [*Children of Violence,* Vol. 1]. 1952; rpt. New York: Simon and Schuster, 1964.

————. *A Proper Marriage* [*Children of Violence,* Vol. 2]. 1954; rpt. New York: Simon and Schuster, 1964.

————. *A Ripple from the Storm* [*Children of Violence,* Vol. 3]. 1958, rpt. New York: Simon and Schuster, 1966.

————. *The Golden Notebook.* 1962; rpt. New York: Bantam, 1979.

————. *Landlocked* [*Children of Violence,* Vol. 4]. 1965; rpt. New York: Simon and Schuster, 1966.

————. *The Four-Gated City* [*Children of Violence,* Vol. 5]. 1969; rpt. New York: Bantam, 1979.

————. *Briefing for a Descent Into Hell.* 1971; rpt. New York: Bantam, 1977.

————. *A Small Personal Voice,* ed. Paul Schlueter. New York: Vintage, 1975.

Lindner, Robert. *The Fifty-Minute Hour: A Collection of True Psychoanalytic Tales.* New York: Holt, Rinehart and Winston, 1955.

Lovering, Joseph. *S. Weir Mitchell.* New York: Twayne, 1971.

Mahler, Margaret. *On Human Symbiosis and the Vicissitudes of Individuation: Volume I, Infantile Psychosis.* New York: International Universities Press, 1968.

Mahler, Margaret, Fred Pine, and Anni Bergmann. *The Psychological Birth of the Human Infant.* New York: Basic Books, 1975.

Mann, Thomas. "Freud's Position in the History of Modern Thought." *The Criterion,* 12 (July 1933); rpt. *The Collected Edition of The Criterion.* Ed. T. S. Eliot. New York: Faber and Faber/Barnes and Noble, 1967, pp. 549–570.

———. "The Making of *The Magic Mountain.*" *The Magic Mountain,* trans. H. T. Lowe-Porter. New York: Vintage, 1969, pp. 717–727.

Marcus, Steven. *Representations.* New York: Random House, 1975.

Marotti, Arthur. "Countertransference, the Communication Process, and the Dimensions of Psychoanalytic Criticism." *Critical Inquiry,* 4 (Spring 1978), pp. 471–489.

Matthews, T. S. *Great Tom.* New York: Harper and Row, 1974.

Menaker, Esther. "Some Inner Conflicts of Women in a Changing Society." *Career and Motherhood,* eds. Alan Roland and Barbara Harris. New York: Human Science Press, 1979, pp. 87–101.

———. "Self-Psychology Illustrated on the Issue of Moral Masochism: Clinical Implications." *American Journal of Psychoanalysis,* 41 (1981), pp. 297–305.

Meyer, Bernard C. *Houdini: A Mind in Chains.* New York: Dutton, 1976.

Milford, Nancy. *Zelda.* 1970; rpt. New York: Avon, 1971.

Miller, James E., Jr. *T.S. Eliot's Personal Waste Land.* University Park: Pennsylvania State University Press, 1977.

Mitchell, S. Weir. *Fat and Blood.* Philadelphia: Lippincott, 1884.

———. *Wear and Tear.* 1887; rpt. New York: Arno Press, 1973.

———. *Doctor and Patient.* 1888; rpt. New York: Arno Press, 1972.

Mizener, Arthur. *The Far Side of Paradise.* 1951; rpt. Boston: Houghton Mifflin, 1965.

Moser, Tilmann. *Years of Apprenticeship on the Couch.* New York: Urizen Books, 1977.

Nabokov, Vladimir. *Bend Sinister.* 1947; rpt. New York: McGraw-Hill, 1974.

———. *Pnin.* New York: Doubleday, 1957.

———. *Pale Fire.* New York: Putnam, 1962.

———. *Ada or Ardor: A Family Chronicle.* New York: McGraw-Hill, 1969.

———. *The Annotated Lolita,* ed., with Preface, Introduction, and Notes by Alfred Appel, Jr. New York: McGraw-Hill, 1970.

———. *The Portable Nabokov,* 3rd ed., ed. Page Stegner. New York: Viking, 1973.

————. *Strong Opinions.* New York: McGraw-Hill, 1973.

————. *Lectures on Literature,* ed. Fredson Bowers. New York: Harcourt Brace Jovanovich, 1980.

O'Neill, William. *Everyone Was Brave.* Chicago: Quadrangle Books, 1971.

Peter, John. "A New Interpretation of *The Waste Land.*" *Essays in Criticism,* 2 (July 1952), pp. 242–266.

Pfister, Oscar. *The Psychoanalytic Method,* trans. Charles Rockwell Payne. New York: Moffat, Yard and Company, 1917.

Pickering, George. *Creative Malady.* 1974; rpt. New York: Delta, 1976.

Piper, Henry Dan. *F. Scott Fitzgerald: A Critical Portrait.* New York: Holt, Rinehart and Winston, 1965.

Plath, Sylvia. *The Bell Jar.* 1963; rpt. New York: Harper and Row, 1971.

————. *Letters Home,* ed. Aurelia Schober Plath. New York: Harper and Row, 1975.

————. *The Collected Poems,* ed. Ted Hughes. New York: Harper and Row, 1981.

————. *The Journals of Sylvia Plath,* ed. Frances McCullough. New York: Dial Press, 1982.

Rein, David M. *S. Weir Mitchell as a Psychiatric Novelist.* New York: International Universities Press, 1952.

Rieff, Philip. *The Triumph of the Therapeutic.* New York: Harper and Row, 1966.

Roazen, Paul. *Freud and His Followers.* New York: New York University Press, 1985.

Robertiello, Richard C. " 'Acting Out' or Working Through?' " *Acting Out: Theoretical and Clinical Aspects,* eds. Lawrence Edwin Abt and Stuart L. Weissman. New York: Grune and Stratton, 1965, pp. 40–45.

Robitscher, Jonas. *The Powers of Psychiatry.* Boston: Houghton Mifflin, 1980.

Rogow, Arnold A. *The Psychiatrists.* New York: Putnam, 1970.

Roth, Philip. *Letting Go.* New York: Random House, 1962.

————. *Portnoy's Complaint.* New York: Random House, 1969.

————. *The Breast.* New York: Holt, Rinehart and Winston, 1972.

————. *My Life as a Man.* New York: Holt, Rinehart and Winston, 1974.

————. *The Professor of Desire.* New York: Farrar, Straus and Giroux, 1977.

————. *Reading Myself and Others.* New York: Farrar, Straus and Giroux, 1977.

Roth, Phyllis A. "Toward the Man Behind the Mystification." *Nabokov's*

Fifth Arc, eds. J. E. Rivers and Charles Nicol. Austin: University of Texas Press, 1982, pp. 43–59.

Rubenstein, Roberta. "Doris Lessing's *The Golden Notebook:* The Meaning of Its Shape." *American Imago,* 32 (Spring 1975), pp. 40–58.

———. *The Novelistic Vision of Doris Lessing.* Urbana: University of Illinois Press, 1979.

Rubin, Stephen E. "Conversations with the Author of 'I Never Promised You a Rose Garden.' " *The Psychoanalytic Review,* 59 (1972), pp. 201–215.

Russell, Bertrand. *The Autobiography of Bertrand Russell: 1914–1944.* Boston: Little Brown, 1968.

Savage, D. S. "The Significance of F. Scott Fitzgerald." *F. Scott Fitzgerald: A Collection of Critical Essays,* ed. Arthur Mizener. Englewood Cliffs, New Jersey: Prentice-Hall, 1963, pp. 146–156.

Schreiber, Flora Rheta. *Sybil.* New York: Warner Books, 1976.

Schur, Max. *Freud: Living and Dying.* New York: International Universities Press, 1972.

Schwartz, Murray, and Christopher Bollas. "The Absence at the Center: Sylvia Plath and Suicide." *Sylvia Plath: New Views on the Poetry,* ed. Gary Lane. Baltimore: Johns Hopkins University Press, 1979, pp. 179–202.

Searles, H. "The Effort to Drive the Other Person Crazy—An Element in the Aetiology and Psychotherapy of Schizophrenia." *Collected Papers on Schizophrenia and Related Subjects.* New York: International Universities Press, 1965, pp. 254–283.

Shaffer, Peter. *Equus.* New York: Avon, 1974.

Shechner, Mark. "Philip Roth." *Partisan Review,* 41 (1974), pp. 410–427.

Sievers, W. David. *Freud on Broadway.* New York: Cooper Square Publishers, 1970.

Sinclair, Andrew. *The Better Half: The Emancipation of the American Woman.* New York: Harper and Row, 1965.

Singer, Melvin. "The Experience of Emptiness in Narcissistic and Borderline States," Parts I and II. *The International Review of Psychoanalysis,* 4, Part 4 (1977), pp. 460–479.

Spacks, Patricia Meyer. *The Female Imagination.* New York: Avon, 1976.

Spender, Stephen. *T. S. Eliot.* New York: Viking, 1975.

Stanton, Robert. " 'Daddy's Girl': Symbol and Theme in 'Tender Is the Night.' " *Modern Fiction Studies,* 4 (Summer 1958), pp. 136–142.

Stegner, Page. *Escape Into Aesthetics.* New York: Dial Press, 1966.

Steiner, Nancy Hunter. *A Closer Look at Ariel*. New York: Popular Library, 1973.

Sternberg-Perrakis, Phyllis. "*The Golden Notebook:* Separation and Symbiosis." *American Imago,* 38 (Winter 1981), pp. 407–428.

Thomas, D. M. *The White Hotel*. New York: Viking, 1981.

Trilling, Lionel. "Freud and Literature." *The Liberal Imagination*. Garden City: Anchor Books, 1953, pp. 32–54.

———. *The Opposing Self*. New York: Viking, 1968.

Trosman, Harry. "T. S. Eliot and *The Waste Land:* Psychopathological Antecedents and Transformations." *Archives of General Psychiatry,* 30 (May 1974), pp. 709–717.

———. "After *The Waste Land:* Psychological Factors in the Religious Conversion of T. S. Eliot." *International Review of Psychoanalysis,* 4 (1977), pp. 295–304.

Turnbull, Andrew. *Scott Fitzgerald*. New York: Scribner's, 1962.

Unger, Leonard. "T. S. Eliot's Images of Awareness." *T. S. Eliot: The Man and His Work,* ed. Allen Tate. London: Chatto and Windus, 1967, pp. 203–213.

Vlastos, Marion. "Doris Lessing and R. D. Laing: Psychopolitics and Prophecy." *PMLA,* 91 (March 1976), pp. 245–257.

Waelder, Robert. "The Principle of Multiple Function." *Psychoanalytic Quarterly,* 5 (1936), pp. 45–62.

Whiteside, George. "T. S. Eliot: The Psychobiographical Approach." *The Southern Review* (University of Adelaide, Australia), 6 (March 1973), pp. 3–26.

Wilson, Edmund. *The Wound and the Bow*. 1941; rpt. New York: Oxford University Press, 1965.

Winnicott, D. W. "Hate in the Counter-Transference." *International Journal of Psycho-Analysis,* 30 (1949), Part 2, pp. 69–74.

———. *Playing and Reality*. London: Tavistock Publications, 1971.

Wolfe, Kary K., and Gary K. Wolfe. "Metaphors of Madness: Popular Psychological Narratives." *Journal of Popular Culture,* 9 (Spring 1976), pp. 895–907.

Wolff, Cynthia. *A Feast of Words: The Triumph of Edith Wharton*. Oxford: Oxford University Press, 1977.

Wolf-Man. *The Wolf-Man*. With *The Case of the Wolf-Man* by Sigmund Freud and *A Supplement* by Ruth Mack Brunswick. Edited, with Notes, an Introduction, and Chapters by Muriel Gardiner. New York: Basic Books, 1971.

Woolf, Leonard. *Downhill All the Way: An Autobiography of the Years 1919–1939.* New York: Harcourt, Brace and World, 1967.

Woolf, Virginia. *Mrs. Dalloway.* 1925; rpt. London: Chatto and Windus, 1968.

———. *The Letters of Virginia Woolf.* Vol. IV: *1929–1931,* eds. Nigel Nicolson and Joanne Trautmann. New York: Harcourt Brace Jovanovich, 1978.

Wortis, Joseph. *Fragments of an Analysis with Freud.* New York: McGraw-Hill, 1975.

INDEX